Angular for Enterprise Applications

Third Edition

Build scalable Angular apps using the minimalist Router-first architecture

Doguhan Uluca

BIRMINGHAM—MUMBAI

"Angular" and the Angular Logo are trademarks of the Google LLC

Angular for Enterprise Applications

Third Edition

Copyright © 2024 Packt Publishing

All rights reserved. No part of this book may be reproduced, stored in a retrieval system, or transmitted in any form or by any means, without the prior written permission of the publisher, except in the case of brief quotations embedded in critical articles or reviews.

Every effort has been made in the preparation of this book to ensure the accuracy of the information presented. However, the information contained in this book is sold without warranty, either express or implied. Neither the author nor Packt Publishing or its dealers and distributors, will be held liable for any damages caused or alleged to have been caused directly or indirectly by this book.

Packt Publishing has endeavored to provide trademark information about all of the companies and products mentioned in this book by the appropriate use of capitals. However, Packt Publishing cannot guarantee the accuracy of this information.

Senior Publishing Product Manager: Suman Sen

Acquisition Editor – Peer Reviews: Gaurav Gavas

Project Editor: Amisha Vathare

Content Development Editor: Shazeen Iqbal

Copy Editor: Safis Editing

Technical Editor: Anjitha Murali

Proofreader: Safis Editing

Indexer: Subalakshmi Govindhan

Presentation Designer: Ajay Patule

Developer Relations Marketing Executive: Priyadarshini Sharma

First published: May 2018

Second edition: May 2020

Third edition: January 2024

Production reference: 2300124

Published by Packt Publishing Ltd.

Grosvenor House

11 St Paul's Square

Birmingham

B3 1RB, UK.

ISBN 978-1-80512-712-3

`www.packt.com`

Contributors

About the author

Doguhan Uluca is a Principal Fellow at Excella in Washington DC, leading strategic GenAI initiatives and delivering critical systems. He is an industry-recognized expert in usability, mobility, performance, scalability, cybersecurity, and architecture. Doguhan is the author of the best-selling *Angular for Enterprise Applications* books, a speaker at 30+ conferences, and an Angular GDE Alumni. Doguhan has delivered solutions for Silicon Valley startups, Fortune 50 companies, and the U.S. Federal Government. He enjoys building Lego, playing Go, and traveling.

Never say never. This edition is a testament to that. Many thanks to my family, Chanda and Ada, for their continued support and sacrifice, which allows me to spend many sleepless nights putting unreasonable amounts of time into untangling the complicated mess that web development is. Thanks also to my colleagues at Excella and the Angular community for their continued support.

About the reviewer

Jurgen Van de Moere is a Front-end architect based in Belgium. He worked as a Web developer and System engineer for large companies across Europe until 2012, when, driven by his passion for Web technologies, Jurgen decided to specialize in JavaScript and Angular. Since then, he has helped leading businesses to build secure, maintainable, testable, and scalable Angular applications. In his mission to share his knowledge with others, Jurgen serves as a private advisor and mentor to world-renowned global businesses and developers. Jurgen is actively involved in growing the Belgian Angular community as co-organizer of NG-BE, Belgium's first-ever Angular conference. In 2016, he was awarded through the Google GDE program for being the first Google Developer Expert in Belgium for Web technologies.

Join our community on Discord

Join our community's Discord space for discussions with the authors and other readers:

`https://packt.link/AngularEnterpise3e`

Table of Contents

Chapter 4: Creating a Router-First Line-of-Business App 145

Chapter 9: Recipes – Master/Detail, Data Tables, and NgRx 409

Preface

Welcome to the wonderful world of Angular enterprise development! Standalone projects, signals, and the control flow syntax have injected fresh blood into the framework. At the time that this book is published, Angular 17.1 has been released with features to bring Signals-based components closer to reality, keeping the Angular ecosystem as vibrant as ever. If this trajectory holds, by Angular 20, the framework will be easier than ever to use and will make it possible to create reliable and high-performance applications of any size. This new edition of the book refocuses the content on enterprise architecture and continues the journey toward mastering sophisticated and scalable Angular solutions ready for complex business needs.

Much like the previous edition, this book has been meticulously designed to equip you with indispensable knowledge and pragmatic examples so you can architect, build, and deliver robust Angular applications. The emphasis remains on adopting an efficient and minimalist approach – maximizing the capabilities of Angular itself and eschewing unnecessary dependencies. This results in streamlined code that is simpler to maintain as Angular continues its rapid pace of progress.

The fundamental concepts you will learn from this book remain evergreen, even as tools and techniques continue to evolve. Router-first architecture, Angular components, the reactive programming model, the powerful routing system, and intuitive template syntax have stood the test of time. And they will provide you with a solid foundation as frameworks change and new versions emerge.

This edition includes extensively expanded coverage of key topics like change detection, state management, decoupled components, modular design, router orchestration, and integration with backend systems. You'll also learn crucial real-world skills for enterprise development, like user authentication, data validation, optimization best practices, and CI/CD pipelines.

This definitive guide shares hard-won lessons on building web systems ready for the demands of any business. Over the years, the code and the content have been reviewed and improved by leading experts in the industry, and this edition is no different. Learn from the collective experience of these experts with actionable recipes, insider tips, and sample apps that showcase professional techniques.

Visit the companion site at `https://AngularForEnterprise.com` to join the community and stay current.

Who this book is for

This book is for experienced developers. If you're new to Angular, start with the excellent tutorials at `https://angular.dev/tutorials` to become familiar with the basics and return to this book. As an Angular developer, you will deepen your understanding of the framework and be exposed to the entire gamut of designing and deploying an Angular application to production. You will learn about Angular patterns that are easy to understand and teach others. As a freelancer, you will pick up effective tools and technologies to deliver your Angular app securely, confidently, and reliably. As an enterprise developer, you will learn patterns and practices to write Angular applications with a scalable architecture and leverage popular enterprise tools.

What this book covers

Chapter 1, Angular's Architecture and Concepts, introduces Angular as a mature platform for building sophisticated, high-performance web applications using TypeScript, RxJS, and NgRx. It introduces key concepts like reactive programming, the Flux pattern, standalone components, fine-grained reactivity with Signals, and the importance of keeping Angular updated.

Chapter 2, Forms, Observables, Signals, and Subjects, covers creating search functionality, using forms, enabling interaction between components, avoiding memory leaks, comparing imperative and reactive programming, chaining API calls, using signals for better performance, and building a small weather application to demonstrate basic Angular concepts.

Chapter 3, Architecting an Enterprise App, covers best practices and considerations for succeeding as a technical lead or architect on an enterprise Angular project, including ingredients for running a successful project, why Angular suits enterprise needs, performance optimization tools and techniques like the 80-20 rule and Router-first architecture, and agile planning with Kanban boards.

Chapter 4, Creating a Router-First Line-of-Business App, covers using the Angular CLI to generate project scaffolding and components, implementing branding and icons, debugging routers with DevTools, and the core tenets of router-first architecture – defining roles early, lazy loading, walking skeleton navigation, designing around data entities, completing high-level UX design, achieving stateless and decoupled components, differentiating controls and components, and maximizing code reuse with TypeScript/ECMAScript.

Chapter 5, Designing Authentication and Authorization, covers implementing token-based authentication with JWTs using TypeScript for safe data handling, building extendable services with OOP principles like inheritance and abstract classes, the fundamentals of caching and HTTP interceptors to preserve login state, and an in-memory authentication service for testing. The key topics are building secure authentication and authorization services and applying SOLID principles to make them extensible.

Chapter 6, Implementing Role-Based Navigation, covers designing conditional navigation experiences, creating reusable UI services for alerts, using route guards to control access, emphasizing server-side security, dynamically providing different auth providers based on environment, and implementing authentication with Firebase.

Chapter 7, Working with REST and GraphQL APIs, covers full-stack architecture using the MEAN stack – building a Node.js server with TypeScript, containerization with Docker, infrastructure as code with Docker Compose, CI/CD verification, designing REST APIs with OpenAPI and GraphQL with Apollo, implementing JWT authentication and RBAC middleware in Express, and building custom authentication providers in Angular using HttpClient and Apollo. The key topics are full-stack development, API design, RBAC, and end-to-end authentication.

Chapter 8, Recipes – Reusability, Forms, and Caching, covers building reusable forms, directives and user controls in Angular, including multi-step responsive forms, removing boilerplate code through inheritance and abstraction, dynamic form elements like date pickers, typeahead, and form arrays, interactive controls with input masking and custom components, seamless integration via `ControlValueAccessor`, and scaling form complexity linearly by extracting sections – as well as layout techniques like grid lists. The key topics are reusable, dynamic, and interactive form building blocks.

Chapter 9, Recipes – Master/Detail, Data Tables, and NgRx, completes coverage of major Angular application design considerations using router-first architecture and recipes to implement a line-of-business application, including editing users, resolving route data, reusing components, building master/detail views and data tables, implementing state management with NgRx or SignalStore, comparing state management options like NgRx Data, ComponentStore, Signals, Akita, and Elf, adding preload animations and global spinners, and previewing Angular's signal-based future by refactoring an application to use SignalStore.

Chapter 10, Releasing to Production with CI/CD, covers implementing continuous integration/continuous delivery pipelines, emphasizing automated testing to enable rapid delivery in enterprises, configuring CI with CircleCI, enforcing quality gates with trunk-based development using GitHub flow, deploying to Vercel and Firebase, infrastructure as code techniques with Docker and NPM scripts, containerization and deployment to Google Cloud Run, gated CI workflows, CircleCI orchestration with workflows and orbs, code coverage metrics, and automated deployments to enable continuous delivery – allowing the rapid iteration and sharing of app builds.

Appendix A, Setting Up Your Development Environment, wraps things up with setting up efficient Angular development environments using CLI tools for automation and consistency across Windows and macOS, creating an initial Angular project, optimizing VS Code configuration, implementing automated linting and fixing for coding standard enforcement and error catching, documenting team norms through scripts, and how standardized environments and coding styles boost team productivity and troubleshooting.

To get the most out of this book

- Set up your system for web development following the scripts covered in *Appendix A, Setting Up Your Development Environment*.
- If you're new to Angular, complete the tutorials at `https://angular.dev/tutorials`.
- Follow the *Technical requirements* section at the beginning of each chapter and information boxes within sections.
- Check the latest code examples on GitHub at `https://github.com/duluca`.
- Sign up for the companion site to complete the self-assessment at `https://angularforenterprise.com`.
- For beginners, developers new to Angular, or inexperienced developers:
    1. Follow the book in the published order, coding your solution alongside the content in each chapter.
    2. It helps to be familiar with full-stack web development but is not a prerequisite.

Download the example code files

You can get the latest version of the example code files on GitHub. Four projects directly support the content in this book:

1. Web Development Environment Setup Scripts at `https://github.com/duluca/web-dev-environment-setup`
2. Local Weather App at `https://github.com/duluca/local-weather-app`

3. LemonMart at `https://github.com/duluca/lemon-mart`
4. LemonMart Server at `https://github.com/duluca/lemon-mart-server`

In each chapter, you can find specific instructions to access chapter-specific versions of code examples referred to as stages. When demonstrating continuous integration and deployment configuration, Git branches and GitHub pull requests are utilized to demonstrate specific configuration elements.

Note that the code on GitHub may differ from the book's content as Angular evolves.

Download the color images

We also provide a PDF file with color images of the screenshots/diagrams used in this book. You can download it here: `https://packt.link/gbp/9781805127123`.

Conventions used

There are a number of text conventions used throughout this book.

`CodeInText`: Indicates code words in text, database table names, folder names, filenames, file extensions, pathnames, dummy URLs, user input, and `X` handles. For example, "Mount the downloaded `WebStorm-10*.dmg` disk image file as another disk in your system."

A block of code is set as follows:

```
{
  "name": "local-weather-app",
  "version": "0.0.0",
  "license": "MIT",
  ...
}
```

When we wish to draw your attention to a particular part of a code block, the relevant lines or items are set in bold:

```
  "scripts": {
    "ng": "ng",
    "start": "ng serve",
    "build": "ng build",
    "test": "ng test",
    "lint": "ng lint",
```

```
    "e2e": "ng e2e"
  },
```

Any cross-platform or macOS-specific command-line input or output is written as follows:

```
$ brew tap caskroom/cask
```

Windows-specific command-line input or output is written as follows:

```
PS> Set-ExecutionPolicy AllSigned; iex ((New-Object System.Net.WebClient).
DownloadString('https://chocolatey.org/install.ps1'))
```

Bold: Indicates a new term, an important word, or words that you see on the screen. For instance words in menus or dialog boxes also appear in the text like this. For example: "Select **System info** from the **Administration** panel."

Warnings or important notes appear like this.

Tips and tricks appear like this.

Get in touch

Feedback from our readers is always welcome.

General feedback: Email `feedback@packtpub.com` and mention the book's title in the subject of your message. If you have questions about any aspect of this book, please email us at `questions@packtpub.com`.

Errata: Although we have taken every care to ensure the accuracy of our content, mistakes do happen. If you have found a mistake in this book, we would be grateful if you reported this to us. Please visit `http://www.packtpub.com/submit-errata`, click **Submit Errata**, and fill in the form.

Piracy: If you come across any illegal copies of our works in any form on the internet, we would be grateful if you would provide us with the location address or website name. Please contact us at `copyright@packtpub.com` with a link to the material.

If you are interested in becoming an author: If there is a topic that you have expertise in and you are interested in either writing or contributing to a book, please visit `http://authors.packtpub.com`.

Share your thoughts

Once you've read *Angular for Enterprise Applications, Third Edition*, we'd love to hear your thoughts! Scan the QR code below to go straight to the Amazon review page for this book and share your feedback.

https://packt.link/r/1805127128

Your review is important to us and the tech community and will help us make sure we're delivering excellent quality content.

Download a free PDF copy of this book

Thanks for purchasing this book!

Do you like to read on the go but are unable to carry your print books everywhere?

Is your eBook purchase not compatible with the device of your choice?

Don't worry, now with every Packt book you get a DRM-free PDF version of that book at no cost.

Read anywhere, any place, on any device. Search, copy, and paste code from your favorite technical books directly into your application.

The perks don't stop there, you can get exclusive access to discounts, newsletters, and great free content in your inbox daily

Follow these simple steps to get the benefits:

1. Scan the QR code or visit the link below

`https://packt.link/free-ebook/9781805127123`

2. Submit your proof of purchase
3. That's it! We'll send your free PDF and other benefits to your email directly

1

Angular's Architecture and Concepts

Angular is a popular **Single-Page Application** (**SPA**) framework for building web applications. It is often preferred in enterprise application development because it is an opinionated, batteries-included framework that supports type-checking with TypeScript and concepts like **Dependency Injection** (**DI**) that allow for engineering scalable solutions by large teams. In contrast, React is a flexible and unopinionated library rather than a complete framework, requiring developers to pick their flavor from the community to build fully featured applications.

React is undoubtedly the more popular choice of the two. The numbers don't lie. React's easier learning curve and deceptively small and simple starting point have attracted the attention of many developers. The many "Angular vs React" articles you have undoubtedly encountered online add to the confusion. These articles are usually too shallow, often contain misleading information about Angular, and lack insights into the very bright future of Angular.

This chapter aims to give you a deeper understanding of why Angular exists, the variety of patterns and paradigms you can leverage to solve complex problems, and, later in the book, the pitfalls to avoid as you scale your solution. It's important to take your time to read through this material because every journey begins with a choice. The real story of your choice today can only be written several years into a project when it's too late and expensive to switch technologies.

This chapter covers the following topics:

- Two Angulars
- A brief history of web frameworks

- Angular and the philosophies behind it
- Component architecture
- Reactive programming
- Modular architecture
- Standalone architecture
- Angular Router
- State management
- React.js architecture
- The future of Angular

Chapter 2, Forms, Observables, Signals, and Subjects, covers Angular fundamental concepts and building blocks. *Chapter 3, Architecting an Enterprise App*, covers technical, architectural, and tooling concerns for delivering large applications. With *Chapter 4, Creating a Router-First Line-of-Business App*, we dive into creating scalable Angular applications ready for the enterprise.

Each chapter introduces new concepts and progressively builds on best practices while covering optimal working methods with popular open-source tools. Along the way, tips and information boxes provide additional background and history, numbered steps, and bullet points that describe actions you need to take.

The code samples provided in this book have been developed using Angular 17. Since the second edition, significant changes occurred in the JavaScript and Angular ecosystems. The transition to Angular's Ivy engine meant some third-party tools stopped working. ESLint has superseded TSLint. Karma and Jasmine have become outdated and superseded by Jest or the more modern Vitest. Significant headway was made in replacing `commonjs` modules with **ES modules (ESM)**. The totality of these changes meant that much of the second edition's supporting tools were beyond repair. As a lesson learned, the example projects now utilize minimal tooling to allow for the best possible DevEx with the least possible amount of npm packages installed. The core samples of the book, which intentionally avoided third-party libraries, were initially written for Angular 5 and have survived the test of time. This book adopts the Angular Evergreen motto and encourages incremental, proactive, and timely upgrades of your dependencies to maintain the health of your project and your team.

This book is supported by the companion site `https://AngularForEnterprise.com`. Visit the site for the latest news and updates.

The world of JavaScript, TypeScript, and Angular is constantly changing. To maintain consistency for my readers, I published a collection of open-source projects that support the content of the book:

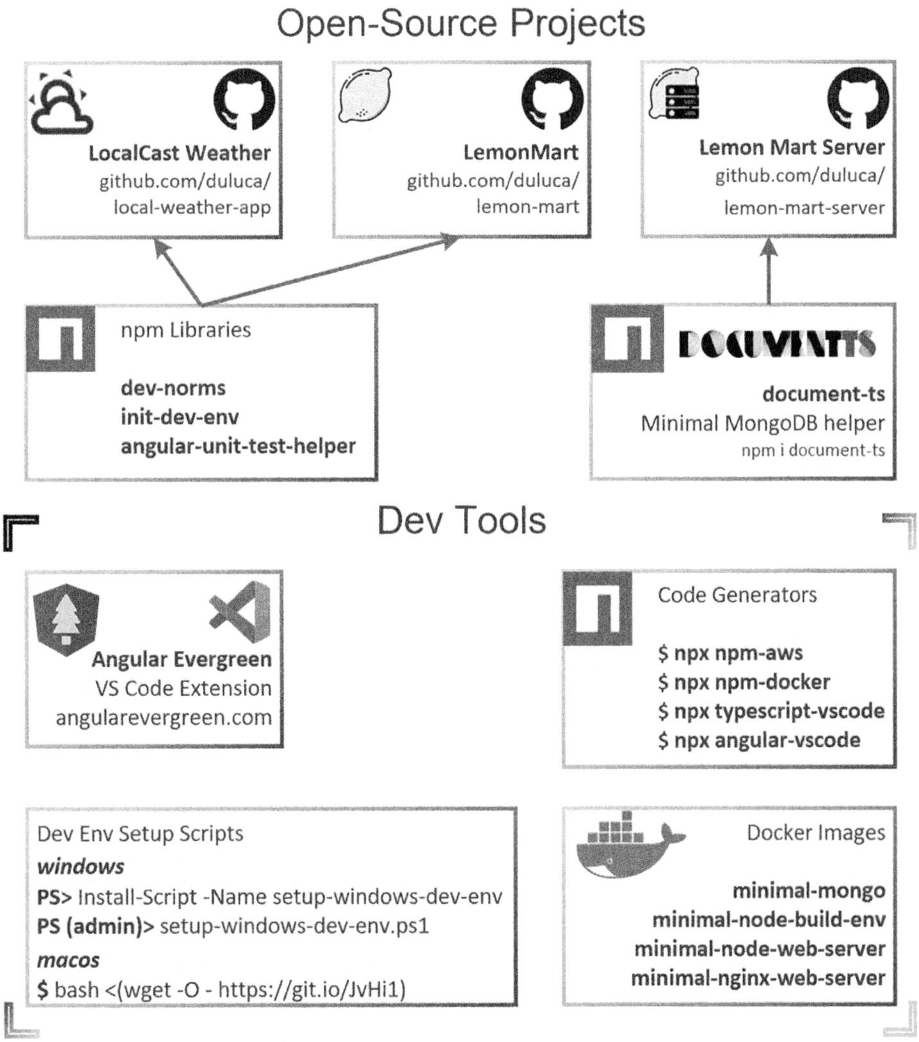

Open-Source Projects

LocalCast Weather
github.com/duluca/
local-weather-app

LemonMart
github.com/duluca/
lemon-mart

Lemon Mart Server
github.com/duluca/
lemon-mart-server

npm Libraries
dev-norms
init-dev-env
angular-unit-test-helper

DOCUMENTTS
document-ts
Minimal MongoDB helper
npm i document-ts

Dev Tools

Angular Evergreen
VS Code Extension
angularevergreen.com

Code Generators
$ npx npm-aws
$ npx npm-docker
$ npx typescript-vscode
$ npx angular-vscode

Dev Env Setup Scripts
windows
PS> Install-Script -Name setup-windows-dev-env
PS (admin)> setup-windows-dev-env.ps1
macos
$ bash <(wget -O - https://git.io/JvHi1)

Docker Images
minimal-mongo
minimal-node-build-env
minimal-node-web-server
minimal-nginx-web-server

Figure 1.1: Code developed in support of this book

The diagram above shows you the moving parts that make up the technical content supporting this book. Each component is detailed in the coming chapters. The code samples contain chapter-by-chapter snapshots and the final state of the code. The most up-to-date versions of the sample code for the book are on GitHub at the repositories linked below:

- For *Chapters 2* and *9*, LocalCast Weather: `https://github.com/duluca/local-weather-app`
- For *Chapters 4* to *10*, Lemon Mart: `https://github.com/duluca/lemon-mart`
- For *Chapter 5*, Lemon Mart Server: `https://github.com/duluca/lemon-mart-server`

You may read more about updating Angular in the supplemental reading, *Keeping Angular and Tools Evergreen*, available at `https://angularforenterprise.com/evergreen`.

Now that you're oriented with the book's structure and supporting content, and before we dive into a prolonged history of the web, let's first disambiguate the two major architectures of Angular and the underlying themes that motivated a dramatic rewrite of the framework in 2016.

Two Angulars

In its original incarnation, Angular.js, aka 1.x, pioneered the SPA era, a technique that tricks the browser into thinking that a single `index.html` houses an interactive application containing many pages. Angular.js also popularized the concept of two-way binding in web development, which automatically updates the view to match the state of the ViewModel. To implement such a feature, Angular.js used **Change Detection** to keep track of **Document Object Model (DOM)** elements of the browser and the ViewModel state of the application.

Change Detection depends on a sophisticated rendering loop to detect user interactions and other events to determine if the application needs to react to changes. Whenever a rendering loop is involved, like in games, performance can be measured as a frame rate expressed in **Frames per Second (FPS)**. A slow change detection process results in a low FPS count, translating into a choppy **User Experience (UX)**. With the demand for more interactive and complicated web applications, it became clear that the internal architecture of Angular.js couldn't be improved to maintain a consistent FPS output. However, UX and performance are only one side of the experience story. As an application grows more complicated better tooling is needed to support a great **Developer Experience (DevEx)** – sometimes called **DevX** or **DX** – which is key to developer wellbeing.

The Angular 2 rewrite, now simply referred to as Angular, aimed to solve both sides of the problem. Before frameworks and libraries like React, Angular, and Vue, we suffered from unmanaged complexity and JavaScript-framework-of-the-week syndrome. These frameworks succeeded with promises to fix all problems, bring about universally reusable web components, and make it easier to learn, develop, and scale web applications- at least for a while, some being better than others during different periods. The same problems that plagued early SPA are returning as the demand for ever more complicated web experiences increases, and the tooling to resolve these problems grows ever complex. To master Angular or any other modern framework, it is critical to learn about the past, present, and future of web development. The adolescent history of the web has taught us a couple of essential lessons. First, change is inevitable, and second, the developer's happiness is a precious commodity that can make or break entire companies.

As you can see, Angular's development has been deeply impacted by performance, UX, and DevEx concerns. But this wasn't a unique problem that only impacted Angular. Let's roll back the clock further and look at the last quarter century or so of web development history so that you can contextualize modern frameworks like Angular, React, and Vue.

A brief history of web frameworks

It is essential to understand why we use frameworks such as Angular, React, or Vue in the first place to get an appreciation of the value they bring. As the web evolves, you may find that, in some cases, the framework is no longer necessary and should be discarded, and in others, critical to your business and must be retained. Web frameworks rose as JavaScript became more popular and capable in the browser. In 2004, the **Asynchronous JavaScript and XML (AJAX)** technique became very popular in creating websites that did not have to rely on full-page refreshes to create dynamic experiences, utilizing standardized web technologies like HTML, JavaScript/ECMAScript, and CSS. Browser vendors are supposed to implement these technologies as defined by the **World Wide Web Consortium (W3C)**.

Internet Explorer (IE) was the browser that most internet users relied on at the time. Microsoft used its market dominance to push proprietary technologies and APIs to secure IE's edge as the go-to browser. Things started to get interesting when Mozilla's Firefox challenged IE's dominance, followed by Google's Chrome browser. As both browsers successfully gained significant market share, the web development landscape became a mess. New browser versions appeared at breakneck speed. Competing corporate and technical interests led to the diverging implementation of web standards.

This fracturing created an unsustainable environment for developers to deliver consistent experiences on the web. Differing qualities, versions, and names of implementations of various standards created an enormous challenge: successfully writing code that could manipulate the DOM of a browser consistently. Even the slightest difference in the APIs and capabilities of a browser would be enough to break a website.

The jQuery era

In 2006, jQuery was developed to smooth out the differences between APIs and browser capabilities. So instead of repeatedly writing code to check browser versions, you could use jQuery, and you were good to go. It hid away all the complexities of vendor-specific implementations and gracefully filled the gaps when there were missing features. For almost a decade, jQuery became the web development framework. It was unimaginable to write an interactive website without using jQuery.

However, to create vibrant user experiences, jQuery alone was not enough. Native web applications ran all their code in the browser, which required fast computers to run the dynamically interpreted JavaScript and render web pages using complicated object graphs. In the 2000s, many users ran outdated browsers on relatively slow computers, so the user experience wasn't great.

Combined with AJAX, jQuery enabled any web developer to create interactive and dynamic websites that could run on any browser without running expensive server hardware and software. To have a solid understanding of the architectural nuances of code that runs on the client and server side, consider a traditional three-tier software architecture. Each tier is described in three primary layers, as shown in the following diagram:

Figure 1.2: Three-tiered software architecture

The presentation layer contains **User Interface (UI)** related code. This is primarily code that runs on the client, referred to as a **thick client**. However, the presentation logic can instead reside on the server. In these cases, the client becomes a **thin client**. The business layer contains business logic and normally resides on the server side. An undisciplined implementation can result in business logic spreading across all three layers. This means a bug or a change in the logic needs to be implemented in many locations. In reality, no individual can locate every occurrence of this logic and can only partially repair code. This, of course, results in the creation of more exotic bugs. The persistence layer contains code related to data storage.

To write easy-to-maintain and bug-free code, our overall design goal is to aim for low coupling and high cohesion between the components of our architecture. Low coupling means that pieces of code across these layers shouldn't depend on each other and should be independently replaceable. High cohesion means that pieces of code related to each other, like code regarding a particular domain of business logic, should remain together. For example, when building an app to manage a restaurant, the code for the reservation system should be together and not spread across other systems like inventory tracking or user management.

With jQuery and AJAX, writing thick clients for the web became possible, making it easier than ever to write unmaintainable code. Modern web apps have way more moving parts than a basic three-tiered application. The diagram that follows shows additional layers that fit around the presentation, business, and persistence layers:

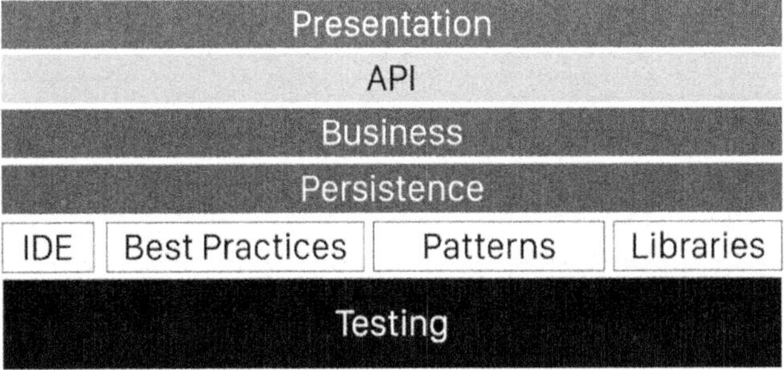

Figure 1.3: Modern Web Architecture

You can observe the essential components of modern web development in the expanded architecture diagram, which includes an API layer that usually transforms and transfers data between the presentation and business layers. Beyond code within the operating environment, the tools and best practices layer defines and enforces patterns used to develop the software. Finally, the testing layer defines a barrage of automated tests to ensure the correctness of code, which is crucial in today's iterative and fast-moving development cycles.

While there was a big appetite to democratize web development with thick clients primarily consuming client-side computing resources, the tooling wasn't ready to enforce proper architectural practices and deliver maintainable software. This meant businesses kept investing in server-side rendering technologies.

The server-side MVC era

In the late 2000s, many businesses still relied on server-side rendered web pages. The server dynamically created all the HTML, CSS, and data needed to render a page. The browser acted as a glorified viewer that would display the result. The following is a diagram that shows an example architectural overview of a server-side rendered web application in the ASP.NET MVC stack:

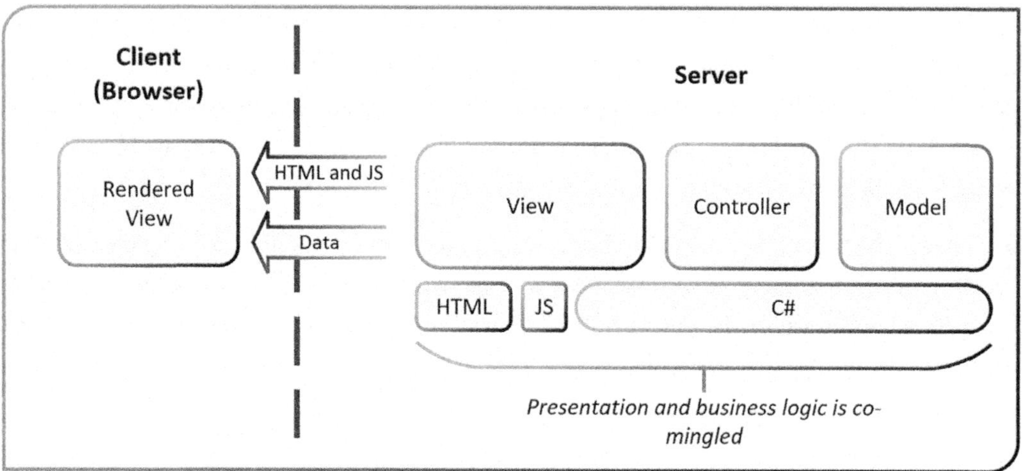

Figure 1.4: Server-side rendered MVC architecture

Model-View-Controller (**MVC**) is a typical pattern of code that has data manipulation logic in models, business logic in controllers, and presentation logic in views. In the case of ASP.NET MVC, the controller and model are coded using C#, and views are created using a templated version of HTML, JavaScript, and C#. The result is that the browser receives HTML, JavaScript, and needed data, and through jQuery and AJAX magic, web pages look to be interactive. Server-side rendering and MVC patterns are still popular and in use today. There are justified niche uses, such as `Facebook.com`. Facebook serves billions of devices that range from the very slow to the very fast. Without server-side rendering, it would be impossible for Facebook to guarantee consistent UX across its user base.

The combination of server-side rendering and MVC is an intricate pattern to execute; there are a lot of opportunities for presentation and business logic to become co-mingled. To ensure the low coupling of components, every member of the engineering team must be very experienced. Teams with a high concentration of senior developers are hard to come by, which would be an understatement.

Further complicating matters is that C# (or any other server-side language) cannot run natively in the browser. So developers who work on server-side rendered applications must be equally skilled at using frontend and backend technologies. It is easy for inexperienced developers to unintentionally co-mingle presentation and business logic in such implementations. When this happens, the inevitable UI modernization of an otherwise well-functioning system becomes impossible. In other words, to replace the sink in your kitchen with a new one, you must renovate your entire kitchen. Due to insufficient architecture, organizations spend millions of dollars writing and rewriting the same applications every decade.

Rich client era

In the 2000s, it was possible to build rich web applications decoupled from their server APIs using Java Applets, Flash, or Silverlight. However, these technologies relied on browser plugins that needed a separate installation. Most often, these plugins were outdated, created critical security vulnerabilities, and consumed too much power on mobile computers. Following the iPhone revolution in 2008, it was clear such plugins wouldn't run on mobile phones, despite the best attempts by the Android OS. Besides, Apple CEO Steve Jobs' disdain for such inelegant solutions marked the beginning of the end for the support of such technologies in the browser.

In the early 2010s, frameworks like Backbone and AngularJS started showing up, demonstrating how to build rich web applications with a native feel and speed and do so in a seemingly cost-effective way. The following diagram shows a **Model-View-ViewModel (MVVM)** client with a **Representational State Transfer (REST)** API. When we decouple the client from the server via an API, we can architecturally enforce the implementation of presentation and business logic separately. Theoretically, this RESTful web services pattern would allow us to replace the kitchen sink as often as possible without remodeling the entire kitchen.

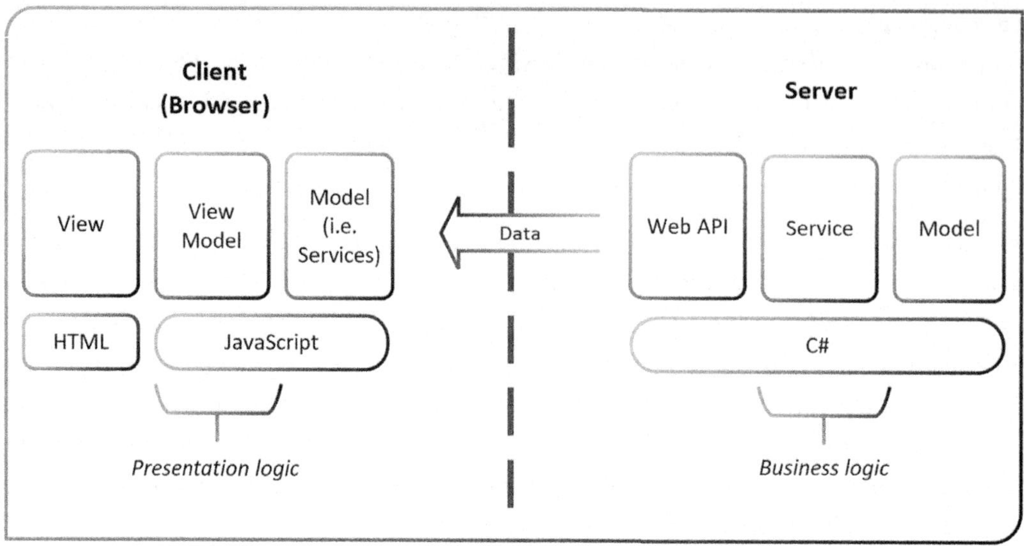

Figure 1.5: Rich-client decoupled MVVM architecture

The MVVM architecture above shows a near doubling of boxes compared to the server-side MVC architecture. Does this mean we need to write twice as much code? Yes and no. Yes, we need to write more code to maintain a disciplined architecture; however, over time, we'll write a lot less code because of the overall maintainability of the solution. The architecture surrounding the presentation logic indeed becomes a lot more complicated. The client and server must implement their presentation/API, business, and persistence layers.

Unfortunately, many early development efforts leveraging frameworks like Backbone and AngularJS collapsed under their weight because they failed to implement the client-side architecture properly.

These early development efforts also suffered from ill-designed RESTful Web APIs. Most APIs didn't version their URIs, making it very difficult to introduce new functionality while supporting existing clients. Further, APIs often returned complicated data models exposing their internal relational data models to web apps. This design flaw creates a tight coupling between seemingly unrelated components/views written in HTML and models created in SQL. If you don't implement additional layers of code to translate or map the structure of data, then you create an unintentional and uncontrolled coupling between layers. Over time, dealing with such coupling becomes very expensive very quickly, in most cases necessitating significant rewrites.

Today, we use the API layer to flatten the data model before sending it to the client to avoid such problems. Newer technologies like GraphQL go further by exposing a well-defined data model and letting the consumer query for the exact data it needs. Using GraphQL, the number of HTTP requests and the amount of data transferred over the wire is optimal without the developers having to create many specialized APIs.

Backbone and AngularJS proved that creating web applications that run natively in the browser was viable. All SPA frameworks at the time relied on jQuery for DOM manipulation. Meanwhile, web standards continued to evolve, and evergreen browsers supporting new standards became commonplace. However, change is constant, and the evolution of web technologies made it unsustainable to gracefully evolve this first generation of SPA frameworks, as I hinted in the *Two Angulars* section.

The next generation of web frameworks needed to solve many problems; they needed to enforce good architecture, be designed to evolve with web standards and be stable and scalable to enterprise needs without collapsing. Also, these new frameworks needed to gain acceptance from developers, who were burned out with too many rapid changes in the ecosystem. Remember, unhappy developers do not create successful businesses. Achieving these goals required a clean break from the past, so Angular and React emerged as platforms to address the problems of the past in different ways. As you'll discover in the following sections, Angular offers the best tools and architecture for building scalable enterprise-grade applications.

Angular and the philosophies behind it

Angular is an open-source project maintained by Google and a community of developers. The new Angular platform vastly differs from the legacy framework you may have used. In collaboration with Microsoft, Google made TypeScript the default language for Angular. TypeScript is a superset of JavaScript that enables developers to target legacy browsers, such as Internet Explorer 11, while allowing them to write modern JavaScript code that works in evergreen browsers such as Chrome, Firefox, and Edge. The legacy version of Angular in the 1.x range, called AngularJS, was a monolithic JavaScript SPA framework. The modern version, Angular 2+, is a platform capable of targeting browsers, hybrid-mobile frameworks, desktop applications, and server-side rendered views.

In the prior generation, upgrading to new versions of AngularJS was risky and costly because even minor updates introduced new coding patterns and experimental features. Each update introduced deprecations or refactored API surfaces, requiring rewriting of large portions of code. Also, updates were delivered in uncertain intervals, making it impossible for a team to plan resources to upgrade to a new version. The release methodology eventually led to an unpredictable, ever-evolving framework with seemingly no guiding hand to carry code bases forward. If you used AngularJS, you were likely stuck on a particular version because the specific architecture of your code base made it very difficult to move to a new version. In 2018, the Angular team released the last major update to AngularJS with version 1.7. This release marked the beginning of the end for the legacy framework, with end-of-life coming in January 2022.

Deterministic releases

Angular improves upon AngularJS in every way imaginable. The platform follows **semver**, as defined at `https://semver.org/`, where minor version increments denote new feature additions and potential deprecation notices for the following major version, but no breaking changes. Furthermore, the Angular team at Google has committed to a deterministic release schedule with major versions released every 6 months. After this 6-month development window, starting with Angular 4, all major releases receive LTS with bug fixes and security patches for an additional 12 months. From release to end-of-life, each major version receives updates for 18 months. Refer to the following chart for the tentative release and support schedule for Angular:

Version	Status	Released	Active Ends	LTS Ends
^14.0.0	LTS	2022-06-02	2022-11-18	2023-11-18
^15.0.0	LTS	2022-11-18	2023-05-03	2024-05-18
^16.0.0	LTS	2023-05-03	2023-11-03	2024-11-18
^17.0.0	Active	2023-11-06	2024-05-08	2025-05-15

Figure 1.6: Actively supported versions

What does this mean for you? You can be confident that your Angular code is supported and backward compatible for approximately 24 months, even if you make no changes to it. For example, if you wrote an Angular app in version 17 in November 2023, and you didn't use any deprecated functionality, your code will be runtime compatible with Angular 18 and supported through May 2025. To upgrade your Angular 17 code to Angular 19, you must ensure that you're not using any deprecated APIs that receive a deprecation notice in Angular 18.

In practice, most deprecations are minor and are straightforward to refactor. Unless you work with low-level APIs for highly specialized user experiences, the time and effort it takes to update your code base should be minimal. However, this is a promise made by Google and not a contract. The Angular team has a significant incentive to ensure backward compatibility because Google runs around 1,000+ Angular apps with a single version of Angular active at any one time throughout the organization. So, by the time you read this, all of Google's 1,000+ apps will be running on the latest version of Angular.

First-class upgrades

You may think Google has infinite resources to update thousands of apps regularly. Like any organization, Google, too, has limited resources. It would be too expensive to assign a dedicated team to maintain every app. So the Angular team must ensure compatibility through automated tests and make it as painless as possible to move through major releases in the future. In Angular 6 `ng update` was introduced, making the update process a first-class experience.

The Angular team continually improves its release process with automated CLI tools to make upgrading deprecated functionality a mostly automated, reasonable endeavor. Air France and KLM demonstrated this strategy's benefits, reducing their upgrade times from 30 days in Angular 2 to 1 day in Angular 7.

A predictable and well-supported upgrade process is excellent news for developers and organizations. Instead of being perpetually stuck on a legacy version of Angular, you can plan and allocate the necessary resources to keep moving your application to the future without costly rewrites. As I wrote in a 2017 blog post, *The Best New Feature of Angular 4*, at `https://bit.ly/NgBestFeature`, the message is clear:

> **For developers and managers:** *Angular is here to stay, so you should be investing your time, attention, and money in learning it – even if you're currently in love with some other framework.*
>
> **For decision makers (CIOs, CTOs, and so on):** *Plan to begin your transition to Angular in the next 6 months. It'll be an investment you'll be able to explain to business-minded people, and your investment will pay dividends for many years to come, long after the initial LTS window expires, with graceful upgrade paths to Angular vNext and beyond.*

So why do Google (Angular) and Microsoft (TypeScript and Visual Studio Code) give away such technologies for free? There are multiple reasons:

- A sophisticated framework that makes it easy to develop web apps demonstrates technical prowess, which retains and attracts developer talent.
- An open-source framework enables the proving and debugging of new ideas and tools with millions of developers at scale.
- Allowing developers to create great web experiences drives more business for Google and Microsoft.

I don't see any nefarious intent here and welcome open, mature, and high-quality tools that, if necessary, I can tinker with and bend to my own will. Not having to pay for a support contract for a proprietary piece of tech is a welcome bonus.

Beware - looking for Angular help on the web may be tricky. You'll need to disambiguate between AngularJS or Angular, which may be referred to as Angular2, but also be aware that some advice given about versions 13 or below may not apply to 14+ because of the rendering engine change to Ivy. I always recommend reading the official documentation when learning. Documentation for Angular is at `https://angular.dev`. This should not be confused with `angularjs.org`, which is about the legacy AngularJS framework or the retired `angular.io` site.

For the latest updates on the upcoming Angular releases, view the official release schedule at `https://angular.dev/reference/releases`.

Maintainability

Your time is valuable, and your happiness is paramount, so you must carefully choose the technologies to invest your time in. With this in mind, we must answer why Angular is the tool you should learn over React, Vue, or others. Angular is a great framework to start learning. The framework and the tooling help you get off the ground quickly and continue being successful, with a vibrant community and high-quality UI libraries you can use to deliver exceptional web applications. React and Vue are great libraries with their strengths and weaknesses. Every tool has its place and purpose.

In some cases, React is the right choice for a project, while Vue is the right one in others. Becoming somewhat proficient in other web frameworks can only help further your understanding of Angular and make you a better developer overall. SPAs such as Backbone and AngularJS grabbed my full attention in 2012 when I realized the importance of decoupling frontend and backend concerns. Server-side rendered templates are nearly impossible to maintain and are the root cause of many expensive rewrites of software systems. If you care about creating maintainable software, you must abide by the prime directive: keep the business logic behind the API decoupled from the presentation logic implemented in the UI.

Angular neatly fits the Pareto principle or the 80-20 rule. It has become a mature and evolving platform, allowing you to achieve 80% of tasks with 20% of the effort. As mentioned in the previous section, every major release is supported for 18 months, creating a continuum of learning, staying up to date, and deprecating old features. From the perspective of a full-stack developer, this continuum is invaluable since your skills and training will remain relevant and fresh for many years to come.

The philosophy behind Angular is to err on the side of configuration over convention. Although convention-based frameworks may seem elegant from the outside, they make it difficult for newcomers to pick up the framework. Configuration-based frameworks aim to expose their inner workings through explicit configuration and hooks, where you can attach your custom behavior to the framework. In essence, where AngularJS had tons of magic, which can be confusing, unpredictable, and challenging to debug, Angular tries to be non-magical.

Configuration over convention results in verbose coding. Verbosity is a good thing. Terse code is the enemy of maintainability, only benefiting the original author. As Andy Hunt and David Thomas put it in *The Pragmatic Programmer*:

> *Remember that you (and others after you) will be reading the code many hundreds of times, but only writing it a few times.*

Further, Andy Hunt's *Law of Design* dictates:

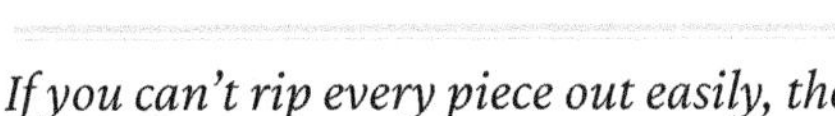

> *If you can't rip every piece out easily, then the design sucks.*

Verbose, decoupled, cohesive, and encapsulated code is the key to future-proofing your code. Through its various mechanisms, Angular enables the proper execution of these concepts. It eliminates many custom conventions invented in AngularJS, such as `ng-click`, and introduces a more natural language that builds on the existing HTML elements and properties. As a result, `ng-click` becomes `(click)`, extending HTML rather than replacing it.

Next, we'll review Angular's evergreen mindset and the reactive programming paradigm, the latest extensions of Angular's initial philosophy.

Angular Evergreen

When you're learning Angular, you're not learning one specific version of Angular but a platform that is continually evolving. Since the first drafts, I designed this book to deemphasize the specific version of Angular you're using. The Angular team champions this idea. Over the years, I have had many conversations with the Angular team and thought leaders within the community and listened to many presentations. As a result, you can depend on Angular as a mature web development platform. Angular frequently receives updates with great attention to backward compatibility. Furthermore, any code made incompatible by a new version is brought forward with help from automated tools or explicit guidance on updating your code by locating the **Angular Update Guide** on `https://angular.dev/update`, so you're never left guessing or scouring the internet for answers. The Angular team is committed to ensuring you – the developer – have the best web development experience possible.

To bring this idea front and center with developers, several colleagues and I have developed and published a Visual Studio Code extension called Angular Evergreen, as shown in the following image:

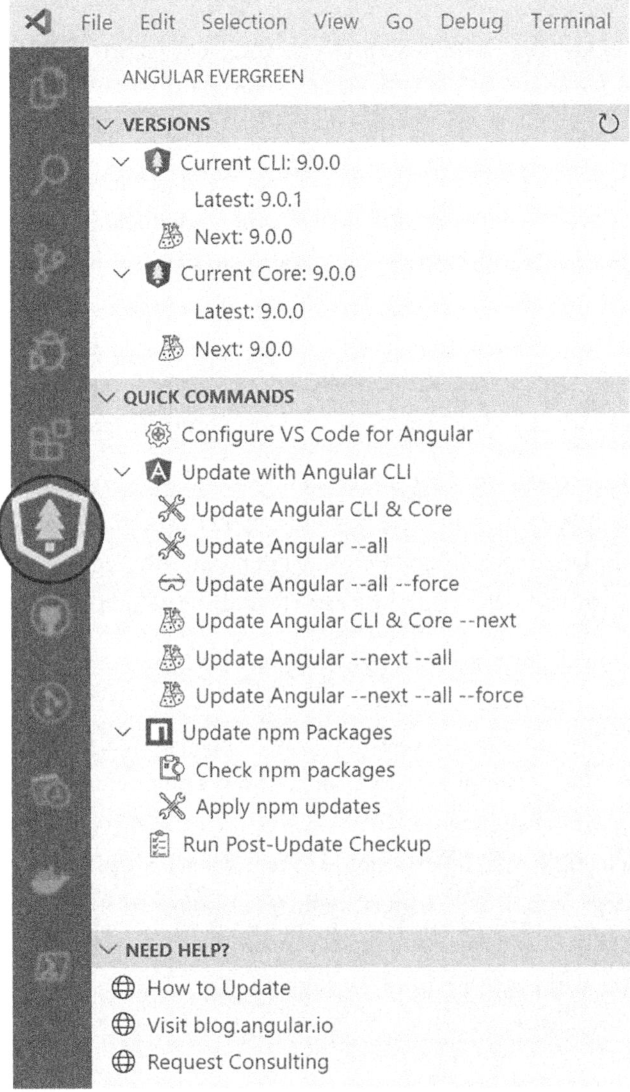

Figure 1.7: Angular Evergreen VS Code extension

This extension detects your current version of Angular and compares it to the latest and next releases of Angular. Releases labeled next are meant for early adopters and testing your code's compatibility with an upcoming version of Angular. Do not use next-labeled releases for production deployments.

Find more information, feature requests, and bug reports on the Angular Evergreen extension at `https://AngularEvergreen.com`.

One of the critical components of Angular that allows the platform to remain evergreen is TypeScript. TypeScript allows new features to be implemented efficiently while supporting older browsers, so your code can reach the widest audience possible.

TypeScript

Angular is coded using TypeScript. Anders Hejlsberg of Microsoft created TypeScript to address several major issues with applying JavaScript at a large enterprise scale.

Anders Hejlsberg is the creator of Turbo Pascal and C# and Delphi's chief architect. Anders designed C# to be a developer-friendly language built upon the familiar syntax of C and C++. As a result, C# became the language behind Microsoft's popular .NET Framework. TypeScript shares a similar pedigree with Turbo Pascal and C# and their ideals, which made them a great success.

JavaScript is a dynamically interpreted language where the browser parses and understands the code you write at runtime. Statically typed languages like Java or C# have an additional compilation step where the compiler can catch programming and logic errors during compile time. Detecting and fixing bugs at compile time versus runtime is much cheaper. TypeScript brings the benefits of statically typed languages to JavaScript by introducing types and generics. However, TypeScript is not a compiler in the traditional sense. It is a transpiler. A compiler builds code into machine language with C/C++ or **Intermediary Language** (**IL**) with Java or C#. A transpiler, however, transforms the code from one dialect to another. So, when TypeScript code is built, compiled, or transpiled, the result is pure JavaScript.

JavaScript's official name is ECMAScript. The language's feature set and syntax are maintained by the ECMA Technical Committee 39, or TC39 for short.

Transpilation has another significant benefit. The same tooling that converts TypeScript to JavaScript can be used to rewrite JavaScript with a new syntax to an older version that older browsers can parse and execute. Between 1999 and 2009, the JavaScript language didn't see any new features. ECMAScript abandoned version 4 due to various technical and political reasons. Browser vendors have struggled to implement new JavaScript features within their browsers, starting with the introduction of ES5 and then ES2015 (also known as ES6).

As a result, user adoption of these new features has remained low. However, these new features meant developers could write code more productively. This created a gap known as the JavaScript Feature Gap, as demonstrated by the graphic that follows:

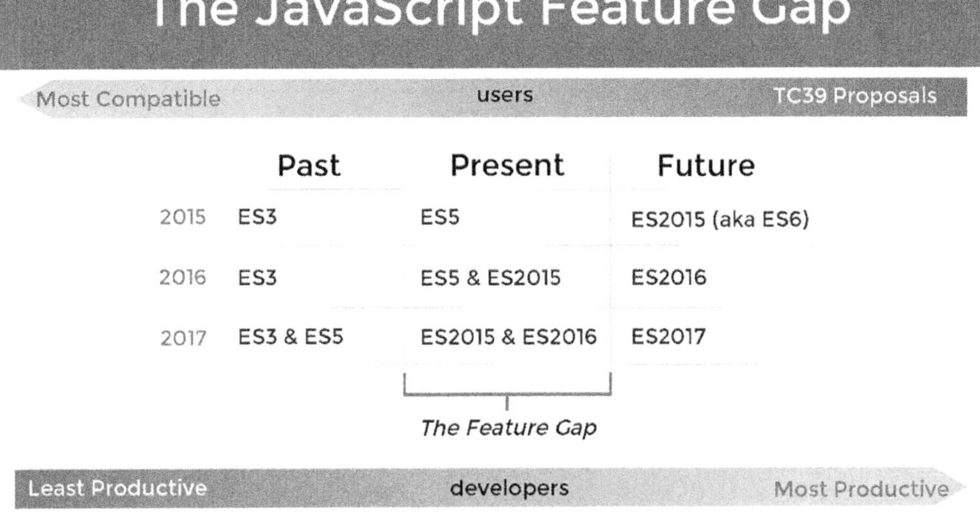

Figure 1.8: The JavaScript Feature Gap

The JavaScript Feature Gap is sliding, as TC39 has committed to updating JavaScript every year. As a result, TypeScript represents JavaScript's past, present, and future. You can use future features of JavaScript today and still be able to target browsers of the past to maximize the audience you can reach. In 2023, this gap is smaller than ever, with ES2022 being a mature language with wide support from every major browser.

Now, let's go over Angular's underlying architecture.

Component architecture

Angular follows the MV* pattern, a hybrid of the MVC and MVVM patterns. Previously, we went over the MVC pattern. At a high level, the architecture of both patterns is relatively similar, as shown in the diagram that follows:

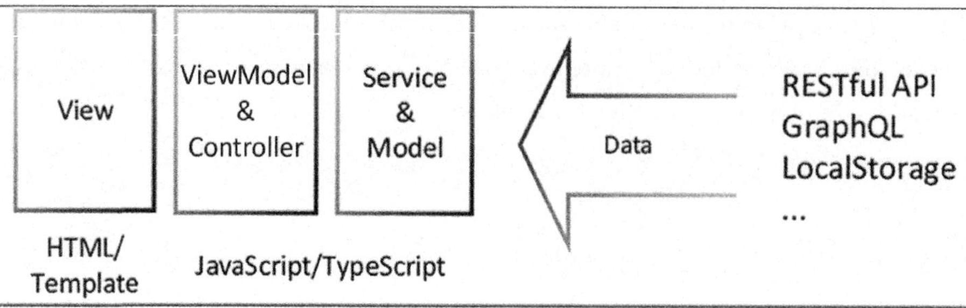

Figure 1.9: MV architecture*

The new concept here is the ViewModel, which represents the glue code that connects your view to your model or service. In Angular, this glue is known as binding. Whereas MVC frameworks like Backbone or React must call a `render` method to process their HTML templates, in Angular, this process is seamless and transparent for the developer. Binding is what differentiates an MVC application from an MVVM one.

The most basic unit of an Angular app is a component. A component combines a JavaScript class, written in TypeScript, and an Angular template, written in HTML, CSS, and TypeScript, as one element. The class and the template fit together like a jigsaw puzzle through bindings so that they can communicate with each other, as shown in the diagram that follows:

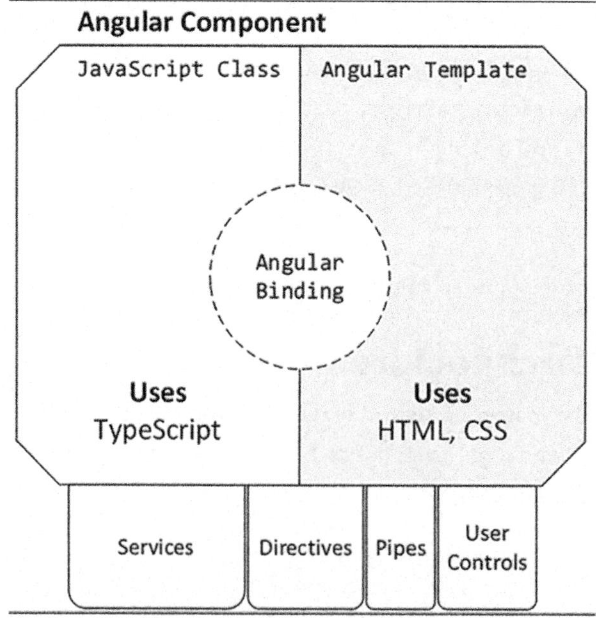

Figure 1.10: Anatomy of a component

Classes are an **Object-Oriented Programming** (**OOP**) construct. If you invest the time to dig deeper into the OOP paradigm, you will vastly improve your understanding of how Angular works. The OOP paradigm allows for the **Dependency Injection** (**DI**) of dependent services in your components, so you can make HTTP calls or trigger a toast message to be displayed to the user without pulling that logic into your component or duplicating your code. DI makes it very easy for developers to use many interdependent services without worrying about the order of the instantiation, initialization, or destruction of such objects from memory.

Angular templates allow similar code reuse via directives, pipes, user controls, and other components. These are pieces of code that encapsulate highly interactive end-user code. This kind of interactivity code is often complicated and convoluted and must be kept isolated from business logic or presentation logic to keep your code maintainable.

Angular 17 introduces a new **control flow syntax** (in preview), which replaces directives like `*ngIf` with `@if`, `*ngFor` with `@for`, and `*ngSwitch` with `@switch` and introduces `@empty`, `@defer`, contextual variables, and conditional statements. The new syntax makes templates easier to read and avoids importing legacy directives to every component in a standalone project. This book will exclusively use the control flow syntax.

You can run `npx ng generate @angular/core:control-flow` to convert your existing template to the new syntax.

Angular apps can be created in two different ways:

- An NgModule project
- A standalone project

As of Angular 17, the default way is to bootstrap your app as a standalone project. This approach has many benefits, as further explained in *The Angular Router* section below. There is a lot of new terminology to learn, but modules as a concept aren't going away. It's just that they're no longer required.

Whether your app starts with `bootstrapApplication` or `bootstrapModule`, at the root level of your application, Angular components, services, directives, pipes, and user controls are provided to the `bootstrapApplication` function or organized under modules. The root level configuration renders your first component, injects any services, and prepares any dependencies it may require. In a standalone app, you can lazily load individual components.

You may also introduce **feature modules** to lazy load groups of services and components. All these features help the initial app load up very quickly, improving First Contentful Paint times because the framework doesn't have to download and load all web application components in the browser simultaneously. For instance, sending code for the admin dashboard to a user without admin privileges is useless.

Being able to create standalone components allows us to ditch contrived modules. Previously, you were forced to place shared components in a shared module, leading to inefficiencies in reducing app size because developers wouldn't necessarily want to create a module per shared component. For example, the LocalCast Weather app is a simple app that doesn't benefit from the concept of a module, but the LemonMart app naturally reflects a modular architecture by implementing separate business functions in different modules. More on this later in the chapter in the *Modular architecture* section.

Standalone components shouldn't be confused with Angular elements, an implementation of the web standard, custom elements, also known as Web Components. Implementing components in this manner would require the Angular framework to be reduced to only a few KB in size, as opposed to the current framework of around 150 KB. If this is successful, you will be able to use an Angular component you develop in any web application. Exciting stuff but also a tall order. You can read more about Angular elements at `https://angular.dev/guide/elements`.

Angular heavily uses the RxJS library, which introduces reactive development patterns to Angular instead of more traditional imperative development patterns.

Reactive programming

Angular supports multiple styles of programming. The plurality of coding styles within Angular is one of the reasons it is approachable to programmers with varying backgrounds. Whether you come from an object-oriented programming background or are a staunch believer in functional programming, you can build viable apps using Angular. In *Chapter 2, Forms, Observables, Signals, and Subjects*, you'll begin leveraging reactive programming concepts in building the LocalCast Weather app.

As a programmer, you are most likely used to imperative programming. Imperative programming is when you, as the programmer, write sequential code describing everything that must be done in the order that you've defined them and the state of your application, depending on just the right variables to be set to function correctly. You write loops, conditionals, and call functions; you fire off events and expect them to be handled. Imperative and sequential logic is how you're used to coding.

Reactive programming is a subset of functional programming. In functional programming, you can't rely on variables you've set previously. Every function you write must stand on its own, receive its own set of inputs, and return a result without being influenced by the state of an outer function or class. Functional programming supports **Test Driven Development** (**TDD**) very well because every function is a unit that can be tested in isolation. As such, every function you write becomes composable. So you can mix, match, and combine any function you write with any other and construct a series of calls that yield the result you expect.

Reactive programming adds a twist to functional programming. You no longer deal with pure logic but an asynchronous data stream that you transform and mold into any shape you need with a composable set of functions. So when you subscribe to an event in a reactive stream, you're shifting your coding paradigm from reactive programming to imperative programming.

Later in the book, when implementing the LocalCast Weather app, you'll leverage `subscribe` in action in the `CurrentWeatherComponent` and `CitySearchComponent`.

Consider the following example, aptly put by Mike Pearson in his presentation *Thinking Reactively: Most Difficult*, of providing instructions to get hot water from the faucet to help understand the differences between imperative and reactive programming:

Instructions to get hot water from the faucet

Imperative

0 Initial state: Water is off

1 Grab a hose

2 Spray water into the heater

3 Turn on the faucet for hot water

4 Send a text to the utility company to get gas

5 Wait for hot water

6 Undo the previous five steps to restore the initial state

Reactive

0 Initial state: Water is off

1 Turn on the faucet for hot water

2 Turn off the faucet to restore the initial state

Figure 1.11: Imperative vs Reactive methodology

As you can see, with imperative programming, you must define every step of the code execution. There are six steps in total. Every step depends on the previous step, which means you must consider the state of the environment to ensure a successful operation. In such an environment, it is easy to forget a step and very difficult to test the correctness of every individual step. In functional reactive programming, you work with asynchronous data streams resulting in a stateless workflow that is easy to compose with other actions. There are two steps in total, but *step 2* doesn't require any new logic. It simply disconnects the code in *step 1*.

RxJS is the library that allows you to implement your code in the reactive paradigm.

Angular 16 introduced signals, in a developer preview, as a new paradigm to enable fine-grained reactivity within Angular. In *Chapter 2, Forms, Observables, Signals, and Subjects*, you will implement signals in your Angular application. Refer to the *Future of Angular* section later in the chapter for more information.

RxJS

RxJS stands for **Reactive Extensions**, a modular library that enables reactive programming. It is an asynchronous programming paradigm that allows data stream manipulation through transformation, filtering, and control functions. You can think of reactive programming as an evolution of event-based programming.

Reactive data streams

In event-driven programming, you would define an event handler and attach it to an event source. In more concrete terms, if you had a **Save** button, which exposes an `onClick` event, you would implement a `confirmSave` function that, when triggered, would show a popup to ask the user '**Are you sure?**'. Look at the following diagram for a visualization of this process:

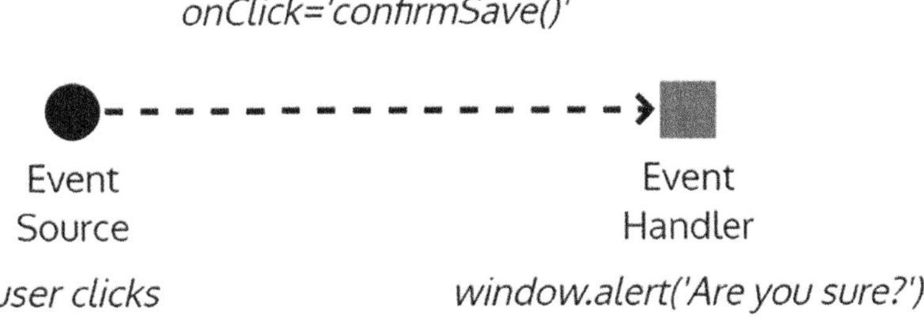

Figure 1.12: Event-driven implementation

In short, you would have an event firing once per user action. If the user clicks on the **Save** button many times, this pattern will gladly render as many popups as there are clicks, which doesn't make much sense.

The **publish-subscribe (pub/sub)** pattern is a different type of event-driven programming. In this case, we can write multiple handlers to all simultaneously act on a given event's result. Let's say that your app just received some updated data. The publisher goes through its list of subscribers and passes the updated data to each.

Refer to the following diagram on how the updated data event triggers multiple functions:

- An `updateCache` function updates your local cache with new data
- A `fetchDetails` function retrieves further details about the data from the server

- A `showToastMessage` function informs the user that the app just received new data

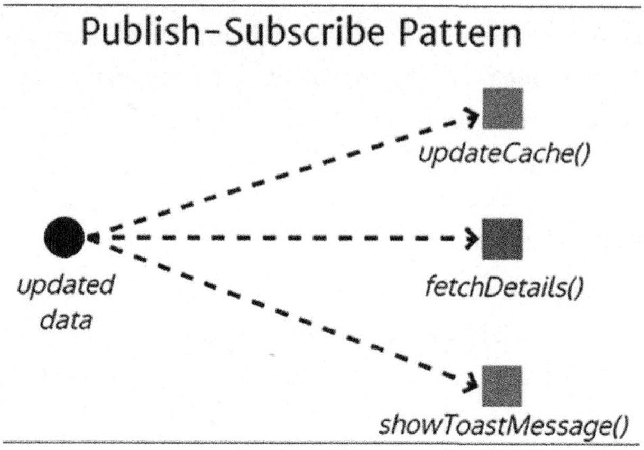

Figure 1.13: Pub/sub pattern implementation

All these events can happen asynchronously; however, the `fetchDetails` and `showToastMessage` functions will receive more data than they need, and it can get convoluted to try to compose these events in different ways to modify application behavior.

In reactive programming, everything is treated as a stream. A stream will contain events that happen over time, which can contain some or no data. The following diagram visualizes a scenario where your app is listening for mouse clicks from the user. Uncontrolled streams of user clicks are meaningless. You exert some control over this stream by applying the `throttle` function, so you only get updates every 250 **milliseconds (ms)**. If you subscribe to this new event stream, every 250 ms, you will receive a list of click events. You may try to extract some data from each click event, but in this case, you're only interested in the number of click events that happened. Using the `map` function, we can shape the raw event data into the sum of all clicks.

Further down the stream, we may only be interested in listening for events with two or more clicks, so we can use the `filter` function to act only on what is essentially a double-click event. Every time our filter event fires, it means that the user intended to double-click, and you can act on that information by popping up an alert.

The true power of streams comes from the fact that you can choose to act on the event at any time as it passes through various control, transformation, and filter functions. You can choose to display click data on an HTML list using `@for` and Angular's `async` pipe so that the user can monitor the types of click data being captured every 250 ms.

Reactive Streams

Event Source
mouse clicks
throttle(250ms)
map(list.length)
filter(x >= 2)
<li *ngFor="let i in list | async">
window.alert('Are you sure?')

Figure 1.14: A reactive data stream implementation

Now let's consider some more advanced Angular architectural patterns.

Modular architecture

As mentioned earlier in the *Component architecture section*, if you create an `NgModule` project, Angular components, services, and dependencies are organized into modules. Angular apps are bootstrapped via their root module, as shown in the diagram that follows:

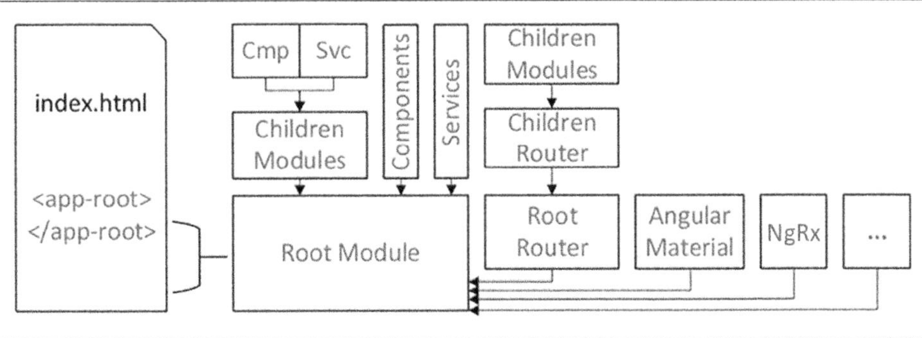

Figure 1.15: Angular Bootstrap process showing major architectural elements

The root module can import other modules, declare components, and provide services. As your application grows, you must create sub-modules containing their components and services. Organizing your application in this manner allows you to implement lazy loading, allowing you to control which parts of your application get delivered to the browser and when. As you add more features to your application, you import modules from other libraries, like Angular Material or NgRx. You implement the router to enable rich navigational experiences between your components, allowing your routing configuration to orchestrate the creation of components.

Chapter 4, Creating a Router-First Line-of-Business App, introduces router-first architecture, where I encourage you to start developing your application by creating all your routes ahead of time.

In Angular, services are provided as singletons to a module by default. You'll quickly get used to this behavior. However, you must remember that if you provide the same service across multiple modules, each module has its own instance of the provided service. In the case of an authentication service, where we wish to have only one instance across our entire application, you must be careful to provide that instance of the authentication service only at the root module level. Any service, component, or module provided at the root level of your application becomes available in the feature module.

Standalone architecture

If you create a standalone project, your dependencies will be provided at the root level `bootstrapApplication` function. First-party and third-party libraries are updated to expose provider functions instead of modules. These provider functions are inherently tree-shakable, meaning the framework can remove them from the final package if unused. The provider functions can be customized using "with" functions, where a function named `withFeature()` can enable a certain feature.

In standalone projects and while using standalone components in general, we must explicitly import the features they use that are not included in the providers. This means pipes, directives (including fundamental directives like `*ngIf` -- unless you're using `@if`, of course), and child components must be provided. This can feel more verbose and restrictive than an NgModule project, but the long-term benefits outweigh the short-term pain. The better information we can provide to the framework about our projects, the better the framework can optimize our code and improve performance.

You can migrate existing NgModule projects to a standalone project using the following command:

```
$ npx ng g @angular/core:standalone
```

Beware - this is not a foolproof or entirely automated process. Read about it more at `https://angular.dev/reference/migrations/standalone`.

The router is the next most powerful technology you must master in Angular.

Angular Router

The Angular Router, shipped in the `@angular/router` package, is a central and critical part of building SPAs that act and behave like regular websites that are easy to navigate, using browser controls or the zoom or micro zoom controls.

The Angular Router has advanced features such as lazy loading, router outlets, auxiliary routes, smart active link tracking, and the ability to be expressed as an `href`, which enables a highly flexible Router-first app architecture leveraging stateless data-driven components, using RxJS `BehaviorSubject` or a `signal`.

A class (a component or a service in Angular) is stateless if it doesn't rely on instance variables in executing any of its behavior (via functions or property getters/setters). A class is data-driven when it's used to manage access to data. A stateless data-driven component can hold references to data objects and allow access to them (including mutations via functions) but would not store any bookkeeping or state information in a variable.

Large teams can work against a single code base, with each team responsible for a module's development, without stepping on each other's toes while enabling easy continuous integration. With its billions of lines of code, Google works against a single code base for a very good reason: integration after the fact is very expensive.

Small teams can remix their UI layouts on the fly to quickly respond to changes without having to rearchitect their code. It is easy to underestimate the time wasted due to late-game changes in layout or navigation. Such changes are easier for larger teams to absorb but costly for small teams.

Consider the following diagram; first off, depending on the bootstrap configuration, the app will either be a standalone or `NgModule` project. Regardless, you'll define a `rootRouter` at the root of your application; components `a`, `master`, and `detail`; services; pipes; directives; and other modules will be provided. All these components will be parsed and eagerly loaded by the browser when a user first navigates to your application.

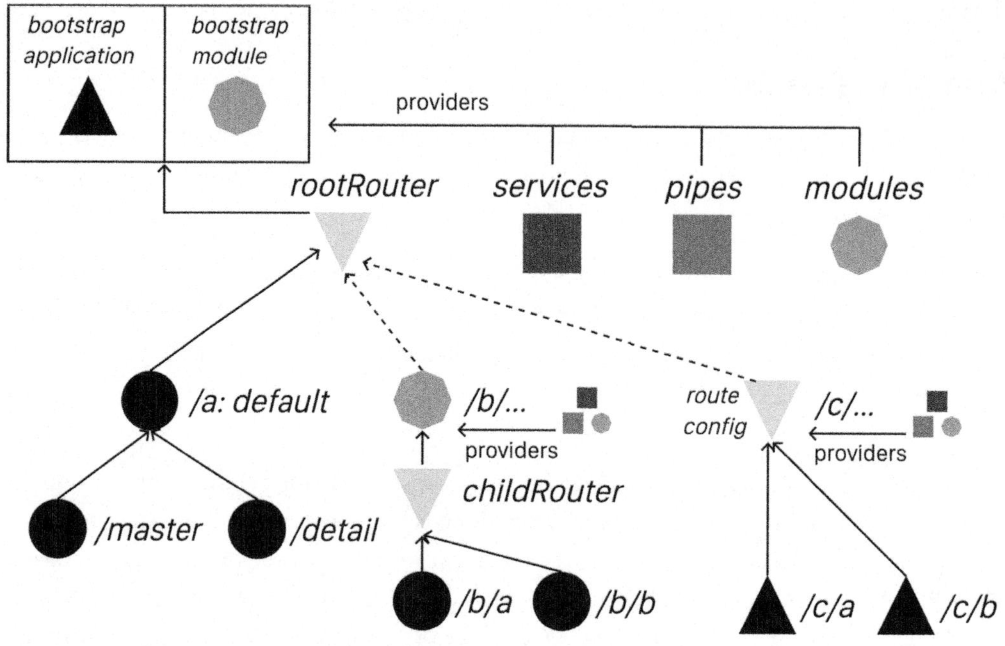

Figure 1.16: Angular architecture

If you were to implement a lazily loaded route, `/b`, you would need to create a feature module named `b`, which would have its `childRouter`; components `/b/a` and `/b/b`; services; pipes; directives; and other modules provided for it. During transpilation, Angular will package these components into a separate file or bundle, and this bundle will only be downloaded, parsed, and loaded if the user ever navigates to a path under `/b`.

In a standalone project, you can lazy load other standalone components represented by the triangles. You can organize components in a route configuration file. The `/c/a` and `/c/b` components will have access to providers at the root level. You may provide an **environment injector** for a specific component in the route config file. Practically speaking, this is only useful if you want to provide a service only ever used by that component or one with a specific scope, e.g., a state that's only used by that component. In contrast to a `NgModule` app, you will have to declare the modules you're using in each component granularly. However, unlike an `NgModule` app, root-level providers not used by any component are tree-shakable. The combination of these two properties results in a small app bundle, and given each module can be individually lazy loaded, the size of each bundle will be smaller as well, leading to better overall performance.

Let's investigate lazy loading in more detail.

Lazy loading

The dashed line connecting `/b/...` to `rootRouter` demonstrates how lazy loading works. Lazy loading allows developers to achieve a sub-second First Meaningful Paint quickly. By deferring the loading of additional modules, we can keep the bundle size delivered to the browser to a minimum. The size of a module negatively impacts download and loading speeds because the more a browser has to do, the longer it takes for a user to see the app's first screen. By defining lazily loaded modules, each module is packaged as separate files, which can be downloaded and loaded individually and on demand.

The Angular Router provides smart active link tracking, which results in a superior developer and user experience, making it very easy to implement highlighting features to indicate to the user the current tab or portion of the currently active app. Auxiliary routes maximize components' reuse and help easily pull off complicated state transitions. With auxiliary routes, you can render multiple master and detail views using only a single outer template. You can also control how the route is displayed to the user in the browser's URL bar and compose routes using `routerLink` in the template and `Router.navigate` in the component class, driving complicated scenarios.

In *Chapter 4, Creating a Router-First Line-of-Business App*, I cover implementing router basics, and advanced recipes are covered in *Chapter 8, Recipes – Reusability, Forms, and Caching*.

Beyond routing, state management is another crucial concept to master if you want to build sophisticated Angular applications.

State management

An `EcmaScript` class backs every component and service in Angular. When instantiated, a class becomes an object in memory. As you work with an object, if you store values in object properties, you're introducing state to your Angular application. If unmanaged, the state becomes a significant liability to the success and maintainability of your application.

I'm a fan of stateless design both in the backend and frontend. From my perspective, state is evil, and you should pay careful attention to not introduce state into your code. Earlier, we discussed how services in Angular are singletons by default. This is a terrible opportunity to introduce state to your application. You must avoid storing information in your services. In *Chapter 4, Creating a Router-First Line-of-Business App*, I introduce you to `readonly BehaviorSubject`, which acts as a data anchor for your application. In this case, we store these anchors in services to share them across components to synchronize data. The data anchor is a reference to the data instead of a copy. The service doesn't store any metadata or do any bookkeeping.

In Angular components, the class is a ViewModel acting as the glue code between your code and the template. Components are relatively short-lived compared to services, and it is okay to use object properties in this context.

However, beyond design, there are specific use cases for introducing robust mechanisms to maintain complicated data models in the state of your application. **Progressive web applications (PWA)** and mobile applications are cases where connectivity is not guaranteed. In these cases, being able to save and resume the entire state of your application is a must to provide a great UX for your end user.

The NgRx library for Angular leverages the Flux pattern to enable sophisticated state management for your applications. In *Chapter 2, Forms, Observables, Signals, and Subjects,* and *Chapter 9, Recipes – Master/Detail, Data Tables, and NgRx,* I provide alternative implementations for various features using NgRx to demonstrate the differences in implementation between more lightweight methods.

The Flux pattern

Flux is the application architecture created by Facebook to assist in building client-side web applications. The Flux pattern defines a series of components that manage a store that stores the state of your application, via dispatchers that trigger/handle actions and view functions that read values from the store. Using the Flux pattern, you keep the state of your application in a store where access to the store is only possible through well-defined and decoupled functions, resulting in architecture that scales well because, in isolation, decoupled functions are easy to reason with and write automated unit tests for.

Consider the diagram that follows to understand the flow of information between these components:

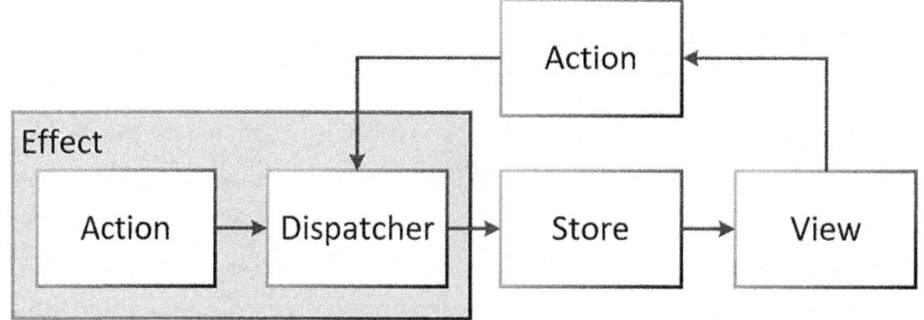

Figure 1.17: NgRx data flow

NgRx implements the Flux pattern in Angular using RxJS.

NgRx

The NgRx library brings Redux-like (a popular React.js library) reactive state management to Angular based on RxJS. State management with NgRx allows developers to write atomic, self-contained, and composable pieces of code, creating actions, reducers, and selectors. This kind of reactive programming allows side effects in state changes to be isolated and feels right at home with the general coding patterns of React.js. NgRx creates an abstraction layer over already complex and sophisticated tooling like RxJS.

There are excellent reasons to use NgRx, such as if you deal with 3+ input streams in your application. In such a scenario, the overhead of dealing with so many events makes it worthwhile to introduce a new coding paradigm to your project. However, most applications only have two input streams: REST APIs and user input. NgRx may make sense for offline-first **Progressive Web Apps (PWAs)**, where you may have to persist and restore complicated state information (or niche enterprise apps with similar needs).

Here's an architectural overview of NgRx:

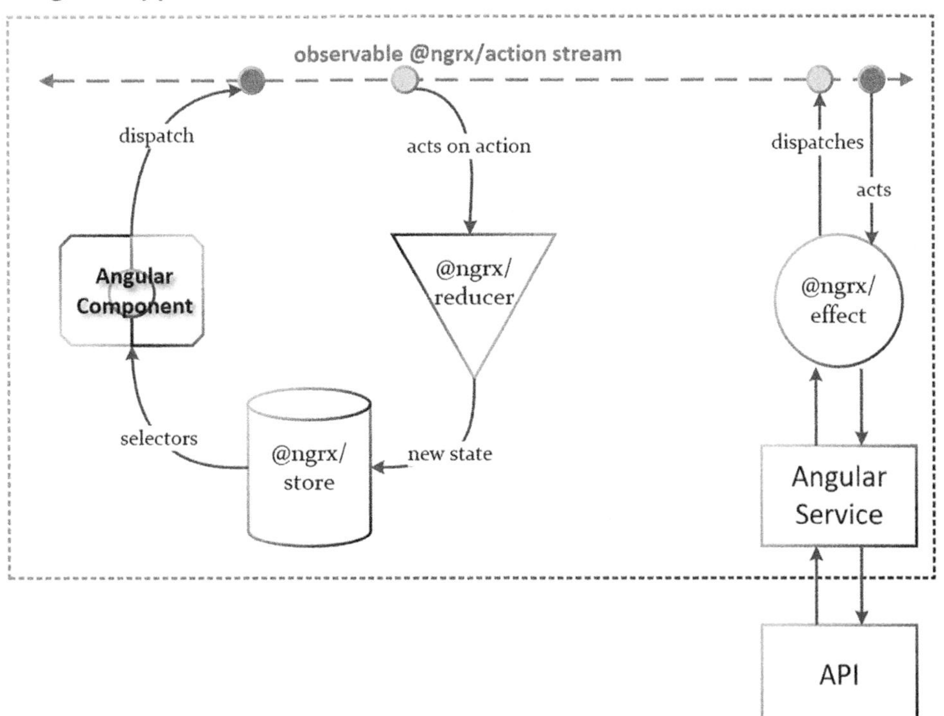

Figure 1.18: NgRx architectural overview

Consider the very top of the diagram as an observable action stream, where actions can be dispatched and acted upon as denoted by the circles. Effects and components can dispatch an action. Reducers and effects can act upon these actions to either store values in the store or trigger an interaction with the server. Selectors are leveraged by components to read values from the store.

Given my positive attitude toward minimal tooling and a lack of definite necessity for NgRx beyond the niche audiences previously mentioned, I do not recommend NgRx as a default choice. `RxJS/BehaviorSubject` are powerful and capable enough to unlock sophisticated and scalable patterns to help you build great Angular applications, as is demonstrated in the chapters that lead up to *Chapter 9, Recipes – Master/Detail, Data Tables, and NgRx.*

You can read more about NgRx at `https://ngrx.io`.

NgRx component store

The NgRx component store, with the package name `@ngrx/component-store`, is a library that aims to simplify state management by targeting local/component states. It is an alternative to a reactive push-based subject-in-a-service approach. For scenarios where the state of a component is only changed by the component itself or a small collection of components, you can improve the testability, complexity, and performance of your code by using this library.

In contrast to global-state solutions like NgRx, the NgRx component store, with its limited scope, can automatically clear itself when its associated view is detached from the component tree. Unlike a singleton service, you can have multiple instances of a component store, enabling distinct states for different components. Additionally, the conceptual model for the component store is straightforward. One only needs to grasp the select, updater, and effect concepts, all operating within a confined scope. Hence, for those crafting a standalone Angular app or seeking component-specific storage, the NgRx component store provides a sustainable and easily testable approach.

You can find out more about the NgRx component store at `https://ngrx.io/guide/component-store`.

React.js architecture

In contrast to Angular, React.js implements the Flux pattern hollistically. Following is a router-centric view of a React application, where components/containers and providers are represented in a strict tree-like manner.

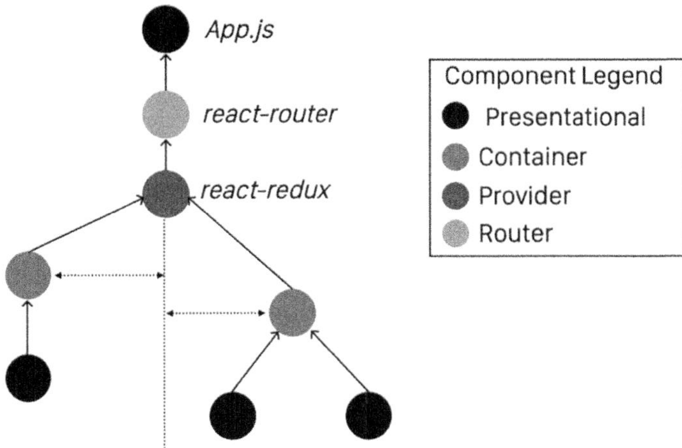

Figure 1.19: React.js architectural overview

In the initial releases of React, one had to laboriously pass values up/down the inheritance tree of every component for even the most basic functionality to work. Later, `react-redux` was introduced, so each component can read/write values directly to the store without traversing the tree.

This basic overview should give you a sense of the significant architectural differences between Angular and React. However, keep in mind that just like Angular, React's community, patterns, and practices are continually evolving and getting better over time.

If you dig simplicity, check out Vue. It. Is. Simple. In a good way: `https://vuejs.org`.

You can learn more about React at `https://reactjs.org`.

Future of Angular

One of the biggest benefits of Angular is that you can count on major releases every 6 months. However, with a regular cadence comes the pressure to release meaningful and splashy updates with every major release. We can probably blame Google for creating this pressure. If you're not constantly producing, you're out. This has an unfortunate side effect of new features being released in preview or an unfinished state. While an argument can be made that releasing upcoming features in preview allows for feedback to be collected from the developer community, no guarantees are made that performance regressions will not be introduced.

If your team is not consuming every bit of Angular news coming out regularly, you may miss these nuances and roll out code into production that negatively impacts your business, potentially impacting revenue. For example, some users have noticed performance regressions in Angular 16, and the Angular team knew about this and fixed it in Angular 17, but this posture puts businesses who've taken up the new version at risk.

The ambitious Angular Elements feature best exemplifies another aspect of this. Circa Angular 9, a big deal was made when announcing web component support for Angular. The promise was that you could create universally reusable components using your favorite framework. The team highlighted the great challenge of shipping a pared-down version of Angular along with the component – reducing the framework size from 150 KB to only a few KB. Instead of focusing on finalizing this feature, and despite making great incremental process, the team has found the task too daunting. So the team has moved on to different ideas to tackle this problem. But even those new ideas are being rushed and rolled out in a preview state, e.g., Angular signals adding to the pile of unfinished work in production software. In Angular 17, signals are partially out of preview and have the potential to transform how Angular apps are built in the future with the implementation of signal-based components. Signals do not easily leak memory compared to RxJS's leaky subscription concept. Signals can also work with async/await calls, avoiding many unnatural uses of reactive coding with RxJS. The stable delivery of all these features is probably due in Angular 19.

Find out up-to-date information about upcoming and in-preview features at `https://angular.dev/roadmap`.

A large Angular application suffers from crippling performance issues just like Angular.js did, except the goalposts around the definition of *large* have moved significantly. The major trouble here is that it's impossible to resolve these performance issues, at least not without significant engineering investment that leaves you digging under the hood of the Angular rendering engine.

Further, in 2023, by leveraging ES2022 features, it is possible to build reactive and interactive web applications using pure JavaScript. Angular signals expose these ES2022 features to enable fine-grained reactivity by replacing Zone.js with native JavaScript. This means that only the parts of the DOM that need to get updated are updated, significantly reducing render times. This is a topic I further explore in *Chapter 3, Architecting an Enterprise App*. Combining these changes results in a more optimized change detection cycle, resulting in smoother FPS.

Every release of Angular seeks to improve **Time-to-Interactive** (**TTI**) for modern browsers. In the past, this meant improving bundle sizes, introducing lazy loading of modules, and now individual components. Angular now supports **Server-side Rendering** (**SSR**) with non-destructive hydration. This means that a server can compute the DOM of a view and transfer it to the client, and the client can update the DOM displayed to the user without completely replacing it.

Angular is also moving away from Jasmine to Jest. Jasmine has always been a great unit-testing framework. However, making it work in a web application context always requires a lot of configuration and additional tools like Karma to execute the tests and get coverage reports. Jest includes all these features. The support is currently experimental, and it's unclear whether Vitest will be a better option than Jest. Angular is moving away from webpack to esbuild, which is about 40x faster than webpack. Once again, it is only available as a (developer) preview.

As you can see, some of the most exciting things happening in Angular are in preview features. The ground truth is that teams are heads down, working on delivering features for their projects and trying their best to keep up with all the latest changes. It's tough enough to keep updating dependencies continually; big changes in the mental model of the framework, combined with performance issues, risk losing the confidence of developers and businesses alike. Trust is hard to build and easy to lose.

The reality is the Angular team is doing great work, and the framework is making the necessary changes to evolve and meet ever-growing expectations. It bears repeating Google mandates that the 2,000+ Angular projects they have must all be on the same version of Angular. This means that every new update to Angular is well-tested, and there are no backward compatibility surprises.

Angular remains an exciting, agile, and capable framework. My motivation is to inform you of where the land mines are. I hope you are as excited as I am about the state of modern web development and the future possibilities it unlocks. Buckle up your seatbelt, Dorothy, 'cause Kansas is going bye-bye.

Summary

In summary, web technologies have evolved to a point where it is possible to create rich, fast, and native web applications that can run well on the vast majority of desktop and mobile browsers deployed today. Angular has become a mature and stable platform, applying lessons learned from the past. It enables sophisticated development methodologies that enable developers to create maintainable, interactive, and fast applications using technologies like TypeScript, RxJS, and NgRx-enabled patterns from object-oriented programming, reactive programming, the Flux pattern, and standalone components, along with the NgRx component store.

Angular is meant to be consumed in an evergreen manner, so it is a great idea always to keep your Angular up to date. Visit `https://AngularForEnterprise.com` for the latest updates and news.

Angular is engineered to be reactive through and through; therefore, you must adjust your programming style to fit this pattern. With signals, Angular even gains fine-grained reactivity. However, presentation layer reactivity is not the same as reactive programming. When signal-based components arrive circa Angular 19, Angular will no longer require reactive programming to achieve a reactive presentation layer. In *Chapter 9, Recipes – Master/Detail, Data Tables, and NgRx*, I provide an example of a nearly observable and subscription-free application using signals and NgRx SignalStore to show what's possible with Angular 17. Until then, the official documentation should be your bible, found at `https://angular.dev`.

In the next chapter, we will review the LocalCast Weather app as a standalone app; you will learn about capturing user input with reactive forms, keeping components decoupled, enabling data exchange between them using `BehaviorSubject` and how the NgRx component store and Angular signals differ from these concepts. In the following chapters, you will learn about advanced architectural patterns to create scalable applications and how your Angular frontend works within the context of a full-stack TypeScript application using minimal MEAN. The book wraps up by introducing you to DevOps and continuous integration techniques to publish your apps.

Further reading

- *Design Patterns: Elements of Reusable Object-Oriented Software*, Erich Gamma, Richard Helm, Ralph Johnson, John Vlissides, 1994, Addison Wesley, ISBN 0-201-63361-2.
- *Human JavaScript*, Henrik Joreteg, 2013, `http://read.humanjavascript.com`.
- *What's new in TypeScript x MS Build 2017*, Anders Hejlsberg, 2017, `https://www.youtube.com/watch?v=0sMZJ02rs2c`.
- *The Pragmatic Programmer, 20th Anniversary Edition*, David Thomas and Andrew Hunt, 2019, Addison Wesley, ISBN 978-0135957059.
- *Thinking Reactively: Most Difficult*, Mike Pearson, 2019, `https://www.youtube.com/watch?v=-4cwkHNguXE`.
- *Data Composition with RxJS, Deborah Kurata*, 2019, `https://www.youtube.com/watch?v=Z76QlSpYcck`.
- *Flux Pattern In-Depth Overview*, Facebook, 2019, `https://facebook.github.io/flux/docs/in-depth-overview`.
- *Developer experience: What is it and why should you care?*, GitHub, 2023, `https://github.blog/2023-06-08-developer-experience-what-is-it-and-why-should-you-care`.

- *Standalone Components*, Google, 2023, `https://angular.dev/reference/migrations/standalone`.
- *Built-in control flow*, Google, 2023, `https://angular.dev/guide/templates/control-flow`.

Questions

Answer the following questions as best as possible to ensure you've understood the key concepts from this chapter without googling anything. Do you know if you got all the answers right? Visit `https://angularforenterprise.com/self-assessment` for more:

1. What is the difference between a standalone and an NgModule project?
2. What is the concept behind Angular Evergreen?
3. Using the double-click example for reactive streams, implement the following steps using RxJS: listen to click events from an HTML target with the `fromEvent` function. Determine whether the mouse was double-clicked within a 250 ms timeframe using the `throttleTime`, `asyncScheduler`, `buffer`, and `filter` operators. If a double-click is detected, display an alert in the browser. Hint: use `https://stackblitz.com` or implement your code and use `https://rxjs.dev/` for help.
4. What is NgRx, and what role does it play in an Angular application?
5. What is the difference between a module, a component, and a service in Angular?

Join our community on Discord

Join our community's Discord space for discussions with the authors and other readers:

`https://packt.link/AngularEnterpise3e`

2

Forms, Observables, Signals, and Subjects

In this chapter, we'll work on a simple weather app, **LocalCast Weather**, using Angular and a third-party web API from `OpenWeatherMap.org`. The source code for this project is provided on GitHub at `https://github.com/duluca/local-weather-app`, including various stages of development in the `projects` folder.

If you've never used Angular before and need an introduction to Angular essentials, I recommend checking out *What is Angular?* on Angular.dev at `https://angular.dev/overview` and going through the *Learn Angular Tutorial* at `https://angular.dev/tutorials/learn-angular`.

Feeling brave? Just type the following into your terminal:

```
$ npm create @angular
```

LocalCast Weather is a simple app that demonstrates the essential elements that make up an Angular application, such as components, standalone components, modules, providers, pipes, services, RxJS, unit testing, e2e using Cypress, environment variables, Angular Material, and **Continuous Integration** and **Continuous Delivery** (**CI/CD**) pipelines leveraging CircleCI.

I've created a Kanban board for this project on GitHub. You can access it at the following link to get more context about the project:

`https://github.com/users/duluca/projects/1`.

A Kanban board is a great way to document your plans for building an app. I touch on the importance of building a roadmap and creating information radiators for the status of your project in *Chapter 3, Architecting an Enterprise App*.

An information radiator is a physical or virtual display that is easily visible or accessible, conveying key information about a project or process. It typically includes metrics, progress charts, or status indicators and is designed to provide at-a-glance awareness without requiring the viewer to seek out information. The goal of an information radiator is to promote transparency, facilitate communication among team members, and enable stakeholders to get updates without interrupting the team's workflow.

As a bonus, I created a rudimentary wiki page on my repository at `https://github.com/duluca/local-weather-app/wiki`. Note that you can't upload images to `README.md` or wiki pages. To get around this limitation, you can create a new issue, upload an image in a comment, and copy and paste the URL for it to embed images in `README.md` or wiki pages. In the sample wiki, I followed this technique to embed the wireframe design into the page.

The source code for the sample projects in the book is divided into **stages** to capture snapshots of various states of development. In this chapter, we pick up the app development from `stage5` and evolve it into `stage6`. In `stage5`, the app is polished, but it can only pull weather information for one city, which is hardcoded into the app. As a result, it is not a very useful app.

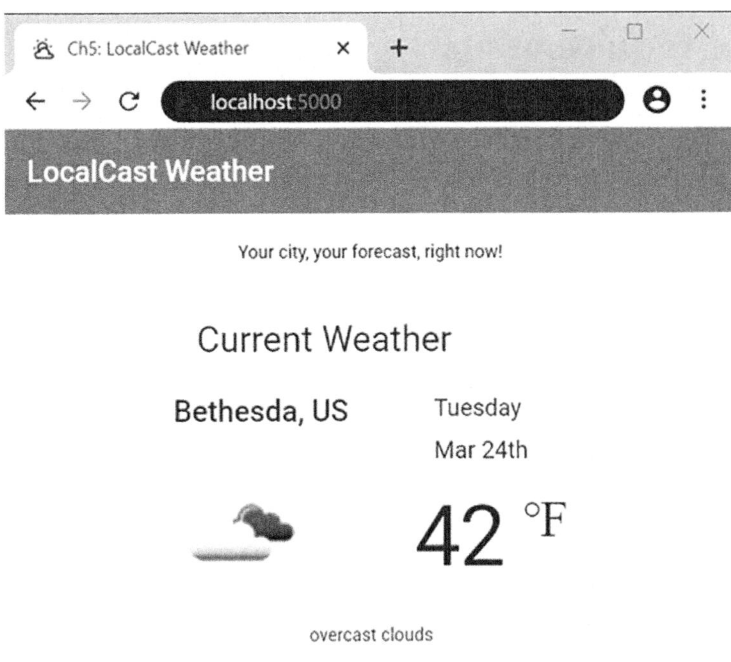

Figure 2.1: The LocalCast Weather app as in projects/stage5

You will inherit an existing project that is not interactive yet. To build an interactive app, we need to be able to handle user input. Enabling user input in your application opens possibilities for creating great user experiences.

We will cover the following main topics in this chapter:

- Great UX should drive implementation
- Reactive forms versus template-driven forms
- Component interaction with observables and RxJS/BehaviorSubject
- Managing subscriptions and memory leaks
- Coding in the reactive paradigm
- Chaining API calls
- Using Angular Signals
- Generating apps with ChatGPT

Technical requirements

The most up-to-date versions of the sample code for the book are on GitHub at the repository linked shortly. The repository contains the final and completed state of the code. You can verify your progress at the end of this chapter by looking for the end-of-chapter snapshot of code under the `projects` folder.

For *Chapter 2*:

1. Clone the `https://github.com/duluca/local-weather-app` repo.
2. Execute `npm install` on the root folder to install dependencies.
3. The beginning state of the project is reflected at:

```
projects/stage5
```

4. The end state of the project is reflected at:

```
projects/stage6
```

5. Add the stage name to any `ng` command to act only on that stage:

```
npx ng build stage6
```

Note that the `dist/stage6` folder at the root of the repository will contain the compiled result.

Beware that the source code provided in the book and the version on GitHub are likely to be different. The ecosystem around these projects is ever evolving. Between changes to how the Angular CLI generates new code, bug fixes, new versions of libraries, and side-by-side implementations of multiple techniques, there's a lot of variation impossible to account for. If you find errors or have questions, please create an issue or submit a pull request on GitHub.

By the end of the chapter, you should be comfortable leveraging observables and signals to build apps that provide a great UX. As a bonus, I'll touch on how you can leverage **Generative AI (GenAI)** tools like ChatGPT (`https://chat.openai.com/`) to build quick prototypes. But first, let's get back to UX because no matter how much you run, crawl, or scale the city walls, if you nail the UX, your app will be loved; but if you miss the mark, your app will be a dime a dozen.

Great UX should drive implementation

Creating an easy-to-use and rich **User Experience** (**UX**) should be your main goal. You shouldn't pick a design just because it's easiest to implement. However, often, you'll find a great UX that is simple to implement in the front end of your app but a lot more difficult on the back end. Consider google.com's landing page:

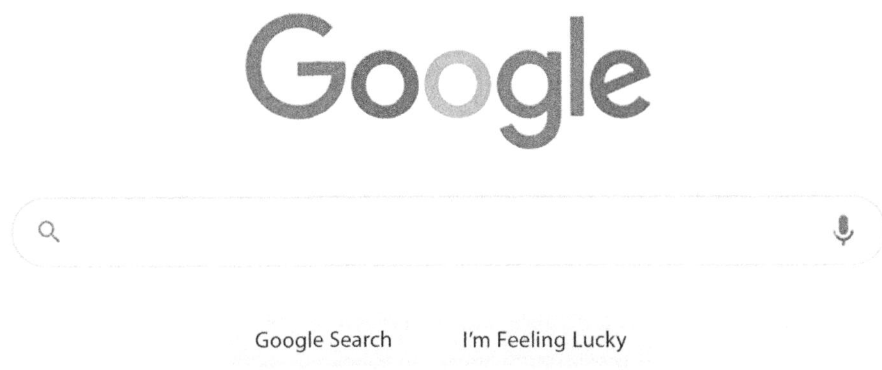

Figure 2.2: Google's landing page

In this context, Google Search is just a simple input field with two buttons. Easy to build, *right?* That simple input field unlocks some of the world's most sophisticated and advanced software technologies backed by a global infrastructure of custom-built data centers and **Artificial Intelligence** (**AI**). It is a deceptively simple and insanely powerful way to interact with users. You can augment user input by leveraging modern web APIs like `GeoLocation` and add critical context to derive new meaning from user input. So, when the user types in `Paris`, you don't have to guess whether they mean Paris, France, or Paris, Texas, or whether you should show the current temperature in Celsius or Fahrenheit. With `LocalStorage`, you can cache user credentials and remember user preferences to enable dark mode in your app.

In this book, we won't be implementing an AI-driven super app, but we will enable users to search for their cities using a city name or postal code (often called *zip codes* in the US). Once you realize how complicated it can get to implement something as seemingly simple as a search by postal code, you may gain a new appreciation for well-designed web apps.

To accomplish the UX goal, we need to build a UI centered around an input field. To do this, we need to leverage Angular forms with validation messages to create engaging search experiences with *search-as-you-type* functionality.

Behind the scenes, `RxJS/BehaviorSubject` or `signals` enables us to build decoupled components that can communicate with one another, and a reactive data stream allows us to merge data from multiple web APIs without increasing the complexity of our app. In addition, you will be introduced to Angular Signals and see how it differs from RxJS.

Next, let's see how to implement an input field using forms. Forms are the primary mechanism that we need to capture user input. In Angular, there are two kinds of forms: **reactive** and **template-driven**. We need to cover both techniques so that you're familiar with how forms work in Angular.

Reactive versus template-driven forms

Now, we'll implement the search bar on the home screen of the application. The next user story states **Display forecast information for current location**, which may be taken to imply an inherent GeoLocation functionality. However, as you may note, GeoLocation is a separate task. The challenge is that with native platform features such as GeoLocation, you are never guaranteed to receive the actual location information. This may be due to signal loss issues on mobile devices, or the user may simply refuse to give permission to share their location information.

First and foremost, we must deliver a good baseline UX and implement value-added functionality such as GeoLocation only afterward. In `stage5`, the status of the project is represented on the Kanban board, as captured in the following snapshot:

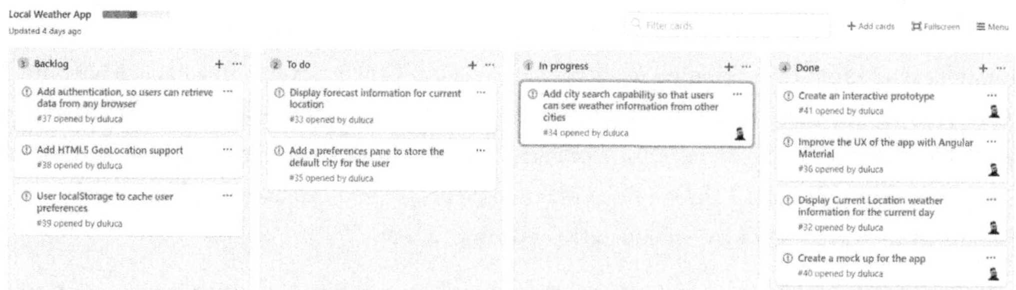

Figure 2.3: GitHub project Kanban board

We'll implement the **Add city search capability** card (which captures a user story), as shown in the **In progress** column. As part of this story, we are going to implement a search-as-you-type functionality while providing feedback to the user if the service is unable to retrieve the expected data.

Initially, it may be intuitive to implement a type-search mechanism; however, `OpenWeatherMap` APIs don't provide such an endpoint. Instead, they provide bulk data downloads, which are costly and are in the multiples-of-megabytes range.

We will need to implement our application server to expose such an endpoint so that our app can effectively query while using minimal data.

The free endpoints for `OpenWeatherMap` do pose an interesting challenge, where a two-digit country code may accompany either a city name or zip code for the most accurate results. This is an excellent opportunity to implement a feedback mechanism for the user if more than one result is returned for a given query.

We want every iteration of the app to be a potentially releasable increment and avoid doing too much at any given time.

Before you begin working on a story, it is a good idea to break it into technical tasks. The following is the task breakdown for this story:

1. Add an Angular form control so that we can capture user input events.
2. Use an Angular Material input as documented at `https://material.angular.io/components/input` to improve the UX of the input field.
3. Create the search bar as a separate component to enforce the separation of concerns and a decoupled component architecture.
4. Extend the existing endpoint to accept a zip code and make the country code optional in `weather.service.ts` to make it more intuitive for end users to interact with our app.
5. Throttle requests so that we don't query the API with every keystroke but at an interval where users still get immediate feedback without clicking a separate button.

Let's tackle these tasks over the following few sections.

Adding Angular reactive forms

You may wonder why we're adding Angular forms since we've got just a single input field, not a form with multiple inputs. As a general rule of thumb, any time you add an input field, it should be wrapped in a `<form>` tag. The `Forms` module contains `FormControl` that enables you to write the backing code behind the input field to respond to user inputs and provide the appropriate data or the validation or message in response.

There are two types of forms in Angular:

- **Template-driven forms**: These forms are like what you may be familiar with in the case of AngularJS, where the form logic is mainly inside the HTML template. I'm not a fan of this approach because it is harder to test these behaviors, and fat HTML templates become challenging to maintain quickly.

- **Reactive forms:** The behavior of reactive forms is driven by TypeScript code in the controller. This means that your validation logic can be unit tested and, better yet, reused across your application. Reactive forms are the core technology that, in the future, will enable the Angular Material team to write automated tools that can autogenerate an input form based on a TypeScript interface.

Read more about reactive forms at `https://angular.dev/guide/forms/reactive-forms`.

In Angular, dependencies are encapsulated in modules provided by the framework. User-created modules are no longer mandatory, and our code sample is configured as a standalone app. For the component we define in the next section, you must import `FormsModule` and `ReactiveFormsModule` to be able to use these features in your template.

In a pure reactive form implementation, you only need `ReactiveFormsModule`. Note that `FormsModule` supports template-driven forms and other scenarios where you may only want to declare `FormControl` without `FormGroup`. This is how we implement the input field for this app. `FormGroup` is defined in the next section.

Note that reactive forms allow you to code in the reactive paradigm, which is a net positive when using observables. Next, let's add a city search component to our app.

Adding and verifying components

We will be creating a `citySearch` component using Angular Material form and input modules:

1. Create the new `citySearch` component:

```
$ npx ng g c citySearch
```

2. Import the form dependencies from the previous section and Material dependencies, `MatFormFieldModule` and `MatInputModule`:

```
src/app/city-search/city-search.component.ts
import { FormsModule, ReactiveFormsModule } from '@angular/forms'
import { MatButtonModule } from '@angular/material/button'
import { MatFormFieldModule } from '@angular/material/form-field'
import { MatIconModule } from '@angular/material/icon'
import { MatInputModule } from '@angular/material/input'
```

```
...
@Component({
  ...
  standalone: true,
  imports: [
    FormsModule,
    ReactiveFormsModule,
    MatFormFieldModule,
    MatInputModule,
  ],
})
export class CitySearchComponent
...
```

We're adding `MatFormFieldModule` because each input field should be wrapped in a `<mat-form-field>` tag to get the most out of the Angular Material functionality.

At a high level, `<form>` encapsulates numerous default behaviors for keyboard, screen-reader, and browser extension users; `<mat-form-field>` enables easy two-way data binding, a technique that should be used in moderation, and also allows graceful label, validation, and error message displays.

3. Create a basic template, replacing the existing content:

src/app/city-search/city-search.component.html

```
<form>
  <mat-form-field appearance="outline">
    <mat-label>City Name or Postal Code</mat-label>
    <mat-icon matPrefix>search</mat-icon>
    <input matInput aria-label="City or Zip" [formControl]="search">
  </mat-form-field>
</form>
```

4. Declare a property named `search` and instantiate it as an instance of `FormControl`:

src/app/city-search/city-search.component.ts

```
import { FormControl } from '@angular/forms'
...
export class CitySearchComponent implements
```

```
  OnInit {

  search = new FormControl()
  ...
```

Reactive forms have three levels of control:

- `FormControl` is the most basic element with a one-to-one relationship with an input field.
- `FormArray` represents repetitive input fields that represent a collection of objects.
- `FormGroup` registers individual `FormControl` or `FormArray` objects as you add more input fields to a form.

Finally, the `FormBuilder` object is used to orchestrate and maintain the actions of a `FormGroup` object more easily. `FormBuilder` and `FormGroup` are first used in *Chapter 6, Implementing Role-Based Navigation*, and all controls, including `FormArray`, are covered in depth in *Chapter 8, Recipes – Reusability, Forms, and Caching*.

5. In `app.component.ts`, import `CitySearchComponent`, then add `<app-city-search>` as a new `div` in between the row that contains the tagline of the app and the row that contains `mat-card`:

```
src/app/app.component.ts
template: `
  ...
    </div>
    <div fxLayoutAlign="center">
      <app-city-search></app-city-search>
    </div>
    <div fxLayout="row">
  ...
`,
  standalone: true,
  imports: [
    FlexModule,
    CitySearchComponent,
    ...
  ],
})
export class AppComponent {
```

6. Launch your app from your terminal:

```
$ npm start
```

7. Test the integration of components by checking out the app in the browser, as shown:

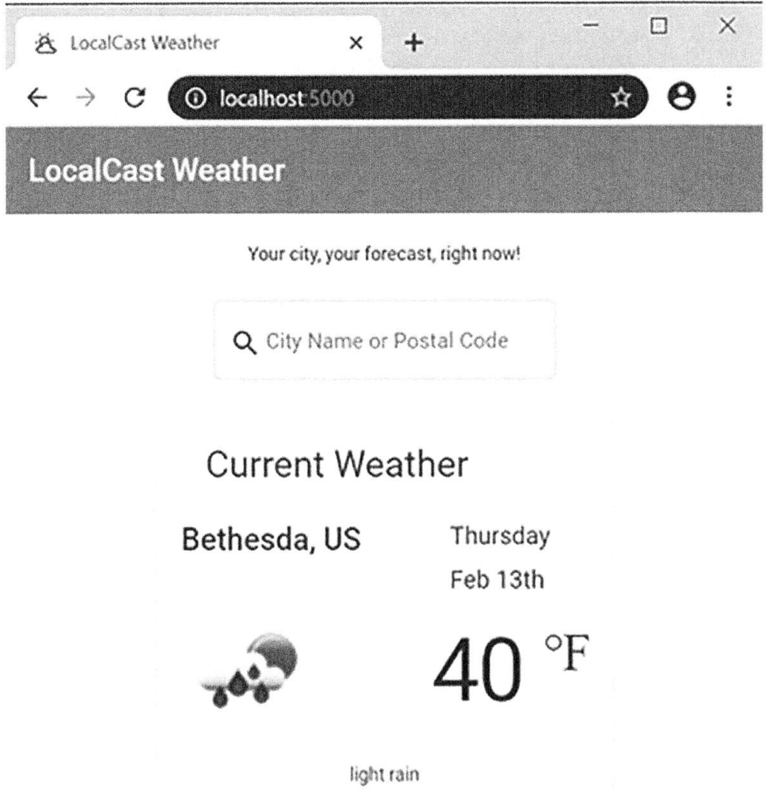

Figure 2.4: The LocalCast Weather app with a search field

If no errors occur, we can start adding the `FormControl` elements and wire them up to a search endpoint.

Adding a search option to the weather service

So far, we have been passing parameters to get the weather for a city using its name and country code. By allowing users to enter zip codes, we must make our service more flexible in accepting both types of inputs.

OpenWeatherMap's API accepts URI parameters, so we can refactor the existing `getCurrentWeather` function using a TypeScript **union type** and a **type guard**.

That means we can supply different parameters while preserving type checking:

1. Refactor the `getCurrentWeather` function in `weather.service.ts` to handle both `zip` and `city` inputs:

   src/app/weather/weather.service.ts
   ```
   getCurrentWeather(
     search: string | number,
     country?: string
   ): Observable<ICurrentWeather> {
     let uriParams = new HttpParams()
     if (typeof search === 'string') {
       uriParams = uriParams.set('q',
         country ? `${search},${country}` : search
       )
     } else {
       uriParams = uriParams.set('zip', 'search')
     }

     uriParams = uriParams.set('appid', environment.appId)
     return this.httpClient
       .get<ICurrentWeatherData>(
         `${environment.baseUrl}api.openweathermap.org/data/2.5/
           weather`,
         { params: uriParams }
       )
     .pipe(map(
       data => this.transformToICurrentWeather(data)))
   }
   ```

   We renamed the `city` parameter to `search` since it can be a city name or a zip code. We then allowed its type to be either a `string` or a `number`, and depending on what the type is at runtime, we will either use `q` or `zip`. We also made `country` optional and only append it to the query if it exists.

   `getCurrentWeather` now has business logic embedded into it and is thus a good target for unit testing. Following the single responsibility principle from the SOLID principles, we will refactor the HTTP call to its own function, `getCurrentWeatherHelper`.

If you're unfamiliar with SOLID principles, I cover them in the Agile engineering best practices section of *Chapter 3, Architecting an Enterprise App*. If you want to read more about it now, see the Wikipedia entry here: `https://en.wikipedia.org/wiki/SOLID`.

2. Refactor the HTTP call into `getCurrentWeatherHelper`.

   In the next sample, note the use of a backtick character, `` ` ``, instead of a single-quote character, `'`, which leverages the template literals' functionality that allows embedded expressions in JavaScript:

   src/app/weather/weather.service.ts

```
  getCurrentWeather(
    search: string | number,
    country?: string
  ): Observable<ICurrentWeather> {
    let uriParams = new HttpParams()
    if (typeof search === 'string') {
      uriParams = uriParams.set('q',
        country ? `${search},${country}` : search
      )
    } else {
      uriParams = uriParams.set('zip', 'search')
    }

    return this.getCurrentWeatherHelper(uriParams)
  }
  private getCurrentWeatherHelper(uriParams: HttpParams):
    Observable<ICurrentWeather> {
    uriParams = uriParams.set('appid', environment.appId)
    return this.httpClient
      .get<ICurrentWeatherData>(
        `${environment.baseUrl}api.openweathermap.org/data/2.5/
          weather`,
        { params: uriParams }
      )
      .pipe(map(
```

```
      data => this.transformToICurrentWeather(data)))
  }
```

As a positive side effect, `getCurrentWeatherHelper` adheres to the open/closed principle from SOLID. After all, it is open to extension by our ability to change the function's behavior by supplying different `uriParams` and is closed to modification because it won't have to be changed frequently.

To demonstrate the latter point, let's implement a new function to get the current weather by latitude and longitude.

3. Implement `getCurrentWeatherByCoords`:

src/app/weather/weather.service.ts

```
getCurrentWeatherByCoords(coords: Coordinates):
Observable<ICurrentWeather> {
  const uriParams = new HttpParams()
      .set('lat', coords.latitude.toString())
      .set('lon', coords.longitude.toString())
  return this.getCurrentWeatherHelper(uriParams)
}
```

As you can see, the functionality of `getCurrentWeatherHelper` is extensible without modifying its code.

4. Ensure that you update `IWeatherService` with the changes made earlier:

src/app/weather/weather.service.ts

```
export interface IWeatherService {
  getCurrentWeather(
    search: string | number, country?: string
  ): Observable<ICurrentWeather>
  getCurrentWeatherByCoords(coords: Coordinates):
Observable<ICurrentWeather>
}
```

As a result of adhering to the SOLID design principles, we make it easier to robustly unit test flow-control logic and ultimately write code that is more resilient to bugs and cheaper to maintain.

Implementing a search

Now, let's connect the new service method to the input field:

1. Update `citySearch` to inject `weatherService` and subscribe to input changes:

```
src/app/city-search/city-search.component.ts
import { WeatherService } from '../weather/weather.service'
...
export class CitySearchComponent implements OnInit {
  search = new FormControl()

  constructor(private weatherService: WeatherService) {}
  ...
  ngOnInit(): void {
    this.search.valueChanges.subscribe()
  }
```

We are treating all input as `string` at this point. The user input can be a city and zip code, city and country code, or a zip code and country code, separated by a comma. While a city or zip code is required, a country code is optional. We can use the `String.split` function to parse any potential comma-separated input and then trim any whitespace out from the beginning and the end of the string with `String.trim`. We then ensure that we trim all parts of the string by iterating over them with `Array.map`.

We then deal with the optional parameter with the ternary operator `?:`, only passing in a value if it exists, otherwise leaving it undefined.

2. Implement the search handler:

```
src/app/city-search/city-search.component.ts
this.search.valueChanges
  .subscribe(
    (searchValue: string) => {
    if (searchValue) {
      const userInput = searchValue.split(',').map(s => s.trim())
      this.weatherService.getCurrentWeather(
        userInput[0],
        userInput.length > 1 ? userInput[1] : undefined
      ).subscribe(data => (console.log(data)))
  }
})
```

3. Add a hint for the user under the input field, informing them about the optional country functionality:

```
src/app/city-search/city-search.component.html
...
  <mat-form-field appearance="outline">
    ...
    <mat-hint>Specify country code like 'Paris, US'</mat-hint>
  </mat-form-field>
...
```

At this point, the subscribe handler will call the server and log its output to the console.

Observe how this works using Chrome DevTools. Note how often the `search` function is run and that we are not handling service errors.

Limiting user inputs with throttle/debounce

We currently submit a request to the server with every keystroke. This is not desirable behavior because it can lead to a bad user experience and drain battery life, resulting in wasted network requests and performance issues both on the client and server side. Users make typos; they can change their minds about what they are inputting, and rarely do the first few characters of information input result in useful results.

We can still listen to every keystroke, but we don't have to react to every stroke. By leveraging `throttle/debounce`, we can limit the number of events generated to a predetermined interval and maintain the type-as-you-search functionality.

Note that `throttle` and `debounce` are not functional equivalents, and their behavior will differ from framework to framework. In addition to throttling, we expect to capture the last input that the user has typed. In the `lodash` framework, the `throttle` function fulfills this requirement, whereas, in `RxJS`, `debounce` fulfills it.

It is easy to inject throttling into the observable stream using `RxJS/debounceTime`. Implement `debounceTime` with `pipe`:

```
src/app/city-search/city-search.component.ts
```

```
import { debounceTime } from 'rxjs/operators'
  this.search.valueChanges
    .pipe(debounceTime(1000))
    .subscribe(...)
```

`debounceTime` will, at a maximum, run a search every second, but also run another search after the user has stopped typing. In comparison, `RxJS/throttleTime` will only run a search every second, on the second, and will not necessarily capture the last few characters the user may have input.

RxJS also has the `throttle` and `debounce` functions, which you can use to implement custom logic to limit input that is not necessarily time-based.

Since this is a time- and event-driven functionality, breakpoint debugging is not feasible. You may monitor the network calls within the **Chrome Dev Tools | Network** tab, but to get a more real-time feel for how often your search handler is being invoked, add a `console.log` statement.

It is not a good practice to check in code with active `console.log` statements. These debug statements make it difficult to read the actual code, which creates a high cost of maintainability. Even if debug statements are commented out, do not check them.

Input validation and error messages

`FormControl` is highly customizable. It allows you to set a default initial value, add validators, or listen to changes on `blur`, `change`, and `submit` events, as follows:

```
example
new FormControl('Bethesda', { updateOn: 'submit' })
```

We won't be initializing `FormControl` with a value, but we need to implement a validator to disallow single-character inputs:

1. Import `Validators` from `@angular/forms`:

   ```
   src/app/city-search/city-search.component.ts
   import { FormControl, Validators } from '@angular/forms'
   ```

2. Modify `FormControl` to add a minimum length validator:

   ```
   src/app/city-search/city-search.component.ts
   search = new FormControl('', [Validators.minLength(2)])
   ```

3. Modify the template to show a validation error message below the hint text:

```
src/app/city-search/city-search.component.html
...
<form style="margin-bottom: 32px">
  <mat-form-field appearance="outline">
    ...
    @if (search.invalid) {
      <mat-error>
        Type more than one character to search
      </mat-error>
    }
  </mat-form-field>
</form>
...
```

Note the addition of some extra margin to make room for lengthy error messages.

If you are handling different kinds of errors, the `hasError` syntax in the template can get repetitive. You may want to implement a more scalable solution that can be customized through code, as shown:

```
example
@if (search.invalid) {
  <mat-error>
    {{getErrorMessage()}}
  </mat-error>
}
getErrorMessage() {
  return this.search.hasError('minLength') ?
    'Type more than one character to search' : '';
}
```

4. Modify the `search` function to not execute a search with invalid input, replacing the condition in the existing `if` statement:

```
src/app/city-search/city-search.component.ts
```

```
this.search.valueChanges
  .pipe(debounceTime(1000))
  .subscribe((search Value: string) => {
    if (!this.search.invalid) {
      ...
```

Instead of doing a simple check to see whether `searchValue` is defined and not an empty string, we can tap into the validation engine for a more robust check by calling `this.search.invalid`.

For now, we're done with implementing `search` functionality. Next, let's go over a what-if scenario to see how a template-driven form implementation would appear.

Template-driven forms with two-way binding

The alternative to reactive forms is template-driven forms. If you're familiar with `ng-model` from AngularJS, you'll find that the new `ngModel` directive is an API-compatible replacement for it.

Behind the scenes, `ngModel` implements `FormControl` that automatically attaches itself to `FormGroup`. `ngModel` can be used at the `<form>` level or the individual `<input>` level. You can read more about `ngModel` at `https://angular.dev/api/forms/NgModel`.

In the `stage6` example code of the LocalCast Weather app repository on GitHub, I have included a template-driven component in `app.component.ts` named `<app-city-search-tpldriven>` rendered under `<div class="example">`. You can experiment with this component to see what the alternate template implementation looks like:

`projects/stage6/src/app/city-search-tpldriven/city-search-tpldriven.component.html`

```
...
  <input matInput aria-label="City or Zip"
    [(ngModel)]="model.search"
    (ngModelChange)="doSearch($event)" minlength="2"
    name="search" #search="ngModel">
...
  @if(search.invalid) {
    <mat-error>
      Type more than one character to search
    </mat-error>
```

```
    }
  ...
```

Note the `[()]` "box of bananas" two-way binding syntax in use with `ngModel`.

The differences in the components are implemented as follows:

projects/stage6/src/app/city-search-tpldriven/city-search-tpldriven.component.ts

```
import { WeatherService } from '../weather/weather.service'
export class CitySearchTpldrivenComponent {
  model = {
    search: '',
  }
  constructor(private weatherService: WeatherService) {}

  doSearch(searchValue) {
    const userInput = searchValue.split(',').map(s => s.trim())
    this.weatherService
      .getCurrentWeather(userInput[0], userInput.length > 1 ?
        userInput[1] : undefined
      )
      .subscribe(data => console.log(data))
  }
}
```

As you can see, most of the logic is implemented in the template; as such, you are required to maintain an active mental model of the template and the controller. Any changes to event handlers and validation logic require you to switch back and forth between the two files.

Furthermore, we have lost input limiting and the ability to prevent service calls when the input is invalid. It is still possible to implement these features, but they require convoluted solutions and do not neatly fit into the new Angular syntax and concepts.

Overall, I do not recommend the use of template-driven forms. There may be a few instances where it may be very convenient to use the box-of-bananas syntax. However, this sets a bad precedent for other team members to replicate the same pattern around the application.

Component interaction with BehaviorSubject

To update the current weather information, we need the `citySearch` component to interact with the `currentWeather` component. There are four main techniques to enable component interaction in Angular:

- Global events
- Parent components listening for information bubbling up from children components
- Sibling, parent, or children components within a module that works off of similar data streams
- Parent components passing information to children components

Let's explore them in detail in the following sections.

Global events

This technique has been leveraged since the early days of programming in general. In JavaScript, you may have achieved this with global function delegates or jQuery's event system. In AngularJS, you may have created a service and stored variables within it.

In Angular, you can still create a root-level service, store values in it, use Angular's `EventEmitter` class, which is meant for directives, or use `RxJS/Subscription` to create a fancy messaging bus for yourself.

As a pattern, global events are open to rampant abuse, and rather than helping to maintain a decoupled application architecture, they lead to a global state over time. A global state or a localized state at the controller level, where functions read and write to variables in any given class, is enemy number one of writing maintainable and unit-testable software.

Ultimately, if you're storing all your application data or routing all events in one service to enable component interaction, you're merely inventing a better mousetrap. A single service will grow large and complex over time. This leads to unforeseen bugs, side effects from unintentional mutations of unrelated data, continuously increasing memory usage because data from previous views can't be discarded, and low cohesion due to data stored from unrelated components of the application. Overusing a service is an anti-pattern that should be avoided at all costs. In a later section, you will find that, essentially, we will still be using services to enable component interaction; however, I want to point out that there's a fine line that exists between a flexible architecture that enables decoupling and the global or centralized decoupling approach that does not scale well.

Child-parent relationships with event emitters

Your child component should be completely unaware of its parent. This is key to creating reusable components.

We can implement the communication between `CitySearchComponent` and the `CurrentWeatherComponent`, leveraging `AppComponent` as a parent element and letting the `AppComponent` controller orchestrate the data.

Commit your code now! In the next two sections, you will be making code changes that you will need to discard.

Let's see how this implementation will look:

1. `CitySearchComponent` exposes `EventEmitter` through an `@Output` property:

```
src/app/city-search/city-search.component.ts
import { Component, OnInit, Output, EventEmitter } from '@angular/
core'
export class CitySearchComponent implements OnInit {
  @Output() searchEvent = new EventEmitter<string>()
  ...
  this.search.valueChanges
    .pipe(debounceTime(1000))
    .subscribe((search Value: string) => {
      if (!this.search.invalid) {
        this.searchEvent.emit(searchValue)
      }
    })
  ...
}
```

2. `AppComponent` consumes that and calls `weatherService`, setting the `currentWeather` variable:

```
src/app/app.component.ts
import { WeatherService } from './weather/weather.service'
import { ICurrentWeather } from './interfaces'
...
```

```
template: `
  ...
    <app-city-search (searchEvent)="doSearch($event)">
    </app-city-search>
  ...
`,
export class AppComponent {
  currentWeather: ICurrentWeather
  constructor(private weatherService: WeatherService) { }
  doSearch(searchValue) {
    const userInput = searchValue.split(',').map(
      s => s.trim())
    this.weatherService
      .getCurrentWeather(
        userInput[0], userInput.length > 1 ?
        userInput[1] : undefined
    )
    .subscribe(data => this.currentWeather = data)
  }
}
```

Note that we are binding to `searchEvent` with the parenthesis syntax. The `$event` variable automatically captures the output from the event and passes it into the `doSearch` method.

We successfully bubbled the information up to the parent component, but we must also be able to pass it down to `CurrentWeatherComponent`.

Parent-child relationships with input binding

By definition, the parent component will know what child components it is working with. Since the `currentWeather` property is bound to the `current` property on `CurrentWeatherComponent`, the results are passed down for display. This is achieved by creating an `@Input` property:

src/app/current-weather/current-weather.component.ts

```
import { Component, Input } from '@angular/core'
...
export class CurrentWeatherComponent {
  @Input() current: ICurrentWeather
```

```
  ...
}
```

Note that the `ngOnInit` function of `CurrentWeatherComponent` is now superfluous and can be removed.

You can then update `AppComponent` to bind the data to the current weather:

```
src/app/app.component.ts
template: `
  ...
  <app-current-weather [current]="currentWeather">
  </app-current-weather>
  ...
`
```

At this point, your code should work! Try searching for a city. If `CurrentWeatherComponent` updates, then success!

The event emitter to input binding approach is appropriate in cases where you are creating well-coupled components or user controls, and the child is not consuming any external data. A good demonstrator for this might be by adding forecast information to `CurrentWeatherComponent` as shown:

Figure 2.5: Weather forecast wireframe

Each day of the week can be implemented as a component that is repeated using `@for`, and it will be perfectly reasonable for `CurrentWeatherComponent` to retrieve and bind this information to its child component:

```
example
@for (dailyForecast of forecastArray; track dailyForecast) {
  <app-mini-forecast [forecast]="dailyForecast">
  </app-mini-forecast>
}
```

In general, if you're working with data-driven components, the parent-child or child-parent communication pattern results in an inflexible architecture, making it difficult to reuse or rearrange your components. A good example of tight coupling is when we imported `WeatherService` in `app.component.ts`. Note that `AppComponent` should have no idea about `WeatherService`; its only job is to lay out several components. Given ever-changing business requirements and design, this is an important lesson to remember.

Discard changes from the two sections before moving on. We will instead be implementing an alternate solution.

Next, we cover a better way for two components to interact with each other without introducing additional coupling with subjects.

Sibling interactions with subjects

The main reason for components to interact is to send or receive updates to data either provided by the user or received from the server. In Angular, your services expose `RxJS/Observable` endpoints, which are data streams that your components can subscribe to. `RxJS/Observer` complements `RxJS/Observable` as a consumer of events emitted by `Observable`. `RxJS/Subject` brings the two functionalities together in an easy-to-work-with package.

You can essentially describe a stream that belongs to a particular set of data, such as the current weather data that is being displayed, with subjects:

```
example
import { Subject } from 'rxjs'
...
export class WeatherService implements IWeatherService {
  currentWeather$: Subject<ICurrentWeather>
  ...
}
```

`currentWeather$` is still a data stream and does not simply represent one data point. You can subscribe to changes to `currentWeather$` data using `subscribe`, or you can publish changes to it using `next` as follows:

```
example
currentWeather$.subscribe(data => (this.current = data))
  currentWeather$.next(newData)
```

Note the naming convention for the `currentWeather$` property, which is postfixed with `$`. This is the naming convention for observable properties.

The default behavior of `Subject` is very much like generic pub/sub mechanisms, such as jQuery events. However, in an asynchronous world where components are loaded or unloaded in unpredictable ways, using the default `Subject` is not very useful.

There are three advanced variants of subjects:

- `ReplaySubject` remembers and caches data points that occurred within the data stream so that a subscriber can replay old events at any given time.
- `BehaviorSubject` remembers only the last data point while listening for new data points.
- `AsyncSubject` is for one-time-only events that are not expected to reoccur.

`ReplaySubject` can have severe memory and performance implications on your application, so it should be used carefully. In the case of `CurrentWeatherComponent`, we are only interested in displaying the latest weather data received, but through user input or other events, we are open to receiving new data to keep `CurrentWeatherComponent` up to date. `BehaviorSubject` would be the appropriate mechanism to meet these needs:

1. Add `currentWeather$` as a read-only property to `IWeatherService`:

   src/app/weather/weather.service.ts

   ```
   import { BehaviorSubject, Observable } from 'rxjs'
   export interface IWeatherService {
     readonly currentWeather$: BehaviorSubject<ICurrentWeather>
     ...
   }
   ```

   `currentWeather$` is declared as read-only because its `BehaviorSubject` should not be reassigned. It's our data anchor or a reference, not a copy of the data itself. Any updates to the value should be sent by calling the `next` function on the property.

2. Define `BehaviorSubject` in `WeatherService` and set a default value:

src/app/weather/weather.service.ts

```
...
export class WeatherService implements IWeatherService {
  readonly currentWeather$ =
    new BehaviorSubject<ICurrentWeather>({
    city: '--',
    country: '--',
    date: Date.now(),
    image: '',
    temperature: 0,
    description: '',
  })
...
}
```

3. Add a new function named `updateCurrentWeather`, which will trigger `getCurrentWeather` and update the value of `currentWeather$`:

src/app/weather/weather.service.ts

```
...
updateCurrentWeather(search: string | number,
  country?: string): void {
  this.getCurrentWeather(search, country)
    .subscribe(weather =>
      this.currentWeather$.next(weather)
    )
}
...
```

4. Update `IWeatherService` with the new function so that it appears as follows:

src/app/weather/weather.service.ts

```
...
export interface IWeatherService {
  readonly currentWeather$: BehaviorSubject<ICurrentWeather>
  getCurrentWeather(city: string | number, country?: string):
    Observable<ICurrentWeather>
  getCurrentWeatherByCoords(coords: Coordinates):
    Observable<ICurrentWeather>
    updateCurrentWeather(
      search: string | number, country?: string
    ): void
}
```

5. Update `CurrentWeatherComponent` to subscribe to the new `BehaviorSubject`:

src/app/current-weather/current-weather.component.ts

```
...
  ngOnInit() {
    this.weatherService.currentWeather$
      .subscribe(data => (this.current = data))
  }
...
```

6. In `CitySearchComponent`, update the `getCurrentWeather` function call to utilize the new `updateCurrentWeather` function:

src/app/city-search/city-search.component.ts

```
...
  this.weatherService.updateCurrentWeather(
    userInput[0],
    userInput.length > 1 ? userInput[1] : undefined
  )
...
```

7. Test your app in the browser; it should appear as follows:

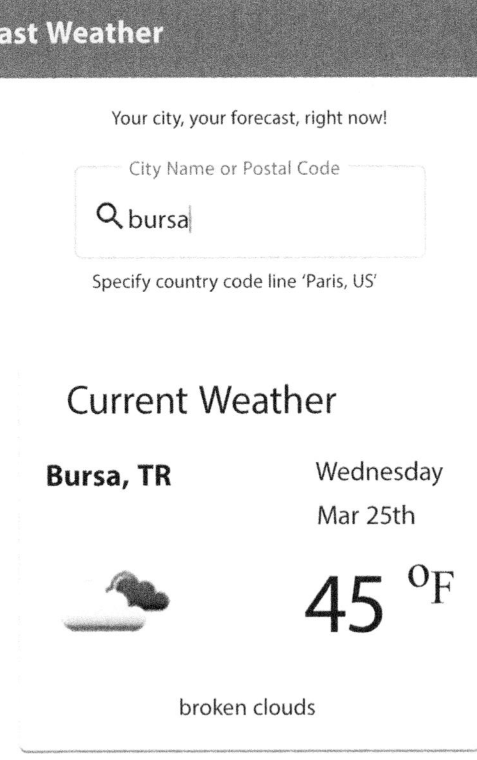

Figure 2.6: Weather information for Bursa, Turkey

When you type in a new city, the component should update to include the current weather information for that city. We can move the **Add city search capability...** task to the **Done** column, as shown on our Kanban board:

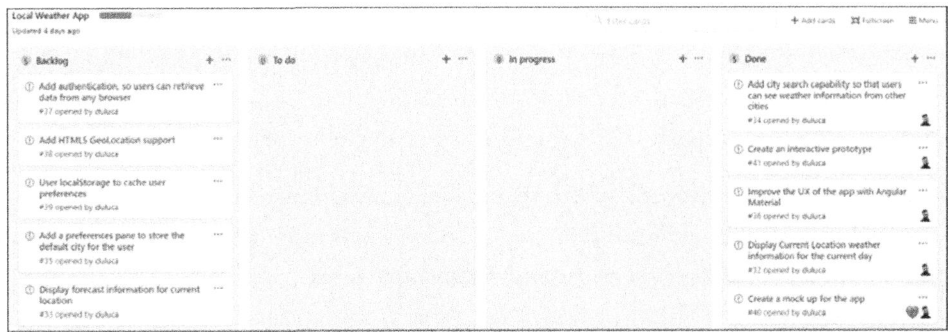

Figure 2.7: GitHub project Kanban board status

We have a functional app. However, we have introduced a memory leak in the way we handled the subscription to `currentWeather$`. In the next section, we'll review how memory leaks can happen and avoid them altogether by using `first` and `takeUntilDestroyed` operations.

Managing subscriptions

Subscriptions are a convenient way to read a value from a data stream for your application logic. If unmanaged, they can create memory leaks in your application. A leaky application will consume ever-increasing amounts of RAM, eventually leading the browser tab to become unresponsive, leading to a negative perception of your app and, even worse, potential data loss, which can frustrate end users.

The source of a memory leak may not be obvious. In `CurrentWeatherComponent`, we inject `WeatherSevice` to access the value of `BehaviorSubject`, `currentWeather$`. If we mismanage subscriptions,`currentWeather$`, we can end up with leaks in the component or the service.

Lifecycle of services

By default, Angular services are **shared instance services** or singletons automatically registered to a **root provider**. This means that, once created in memory, they're kept alive as long as the app or feature module they're a part of remains in memory. See the following example of a shared instance service:

```
@Injectable({
  providedIn: 'root'
})
export class WeatherService implements IWeatherService
...
```

From a practical perspective, this will mean that most services in your application will live in the memory for the application's lifetime. However, the lifetime of a component may be much shorter, or there could be multiple instances of the same component created repeatedly.

Additionally, there are use cases where a component needs its own instance or a copy of the service (e.g., caching values input into a form or displaying weather for different cities simultaneously). To create **multiple instance services,** see the example below:

```
@Injectable()
export class WeatherService implements IWeatherService
...
```

You would then provide the service with a **component provider**:

```
@Component({
  selector: 'app-current-weather',
  standalone: true,
  providers: [WeatherService]
})
export class CurrentWeatherComponent {
...
```

In this case, the service would be destroyed when the component is destroyed. But this is not protection against memory leaks. If we don't manage the interactions between long-lived and short-lived objects carefully, we can end up with dangling references between objects, leading to memory leaks.

Exposé of a memory leak

When we subscribe to `currentWeather$`, we attach an event handler to it so that `CurrentWeatherComponent` can react to value changes pushed to `BehaviorSubject`. This presents a problem when the component needs to be destroyed.

In managed languages such as JavaScript, memory is managed by the garbage collector, or GC for short, as opposed to having to allocate and deallocate memory by hand in unmanaged languages such as C or C++. At a very high level, the GC periodically scans the stack for objects not referenced by other objects.

If an object is found to be dereferenced, then the space it takes up in the stack can be freed up. However, if an unused object still has a reference to another object that is still in use, it can't be garbage collected. The GC is not magical and can't read our minds. When an object is unused and can't be deallocated, the memory taken up by the object can never be used for another purpose so long as your application is running. This is considered a memory leak.

My colleague, Brendon Caulkins, provides a helpful analogy:

> *Imagine the memory space of the browser as a parking lot; every time we assign a value or create a subscription, we park a car in that lot. If we happen to abandon a car, we still leave the parking spot occupied; no one else can use it. If all the applications in the browser do this, or we do it repeatedly, you can imagine how quickly the parking lot gets full, and we never get to run our application.*

Next, let's see how we can ensure we don't abandon our car in the parking lot.

Unsubscribing from a subscription

Subscriptions or event handlers create references to other objects, such as from a short-lived component to a long-lived service. Granted, in our case, `CurrentWeatherComponent` is also a singleton, but that could change if we added more features to the app, navigating from page to page or displaying weather from multiple cities at once. If we don't unsubscribe from `currentWeather$`, then any instance of `CurrentWeatherComponent` would be stuck in memory. We subscribe in `ngOnInit`, so we must unsubscribe in `ngOnDestroy`. `ngOnDestroy` is called when Angular determines that the framework no longer uses the component.

Let's see an example of how you can unsubscribe from a subscription in the sample code in the following:

```
example
import { ..., OnDestroy } from '@angular/core'
import { ..., Subscription } from 'rxjs'
export class CurrentWeatherComponent implements OnInit, OnDestroy {
  currentWeatherSubscription: Subscription
  ...
  ngOnInit() {
    this.currentWeatherSubscription =
      this.weatherService.currentWeather$
        .subscribe((data) => (this.current = data))
  }
  ngOnDestroy(): void {
    this.currentWeatherSubscription.unsubscribe()
  }
...
```

First, we need to implement the `OnDestroy` interface for the component. Then, we update `ngOnInit` to store a reference to the subscription in a property named `currentWeatherSubscription`. Finally, in `ngOnDestroy`, we can call the `unsubscribe` method.

Should our component get destroyed, it will no longer result in a memory leak. However, if we have multiple subscriptions in a component, this leads to tedious amounts of coding.

Note that in `CitySearchComponent`, we subscribe to the `valueChanges` event of a `FormControl` object. We don't need to manage the subscription to this event because `FormControl` is a child object of our component. When the parent component is dereferenced from all objects, all its children can be safely collected by the GC.

Subscribing to values in data streams itself can be considered an anti-pattern because you switch your programming model from reactive to imperative. But of course, we must subscribe at least once to activate the data stream. In the next section, we will cover how you ensure you don't leak memory when subscribing.

Subscribe with first or takeUntilDestroyed

By default, an observable stream doesn't end. Given how engrained RxJS is within every Angular operation, this is rarely the desired outcome. There are two common strategies that we can apply at the time of subscribing to a resource so we can ensure that streams will complete predictably and won't lead to memory leaks.

The first strategy is, well, the first method. Observe the `updateCurrentWeather` method in `WeatherService`:

src/app/weather/weather.service.ts

```
import { map, switchMap, first } from 'rxjs/operators'

export class WeatherService implements IWeatherService{
  ...
    updateCurrentWeather(searchText: string, country?: string): void {
      this.getCurrentWeather(searchText, country)
        .pipe(first())
        .subscribe((weather) => this.currentWeather$.next(weather))
    }
  ...
```

In the example above, we intend to get the current weather and display it – and do this only once per request. By piping in a `first()` call into the observable stream, we instruct RxJS to complete the stream after it receives one result. This way, when a resource that utilizes this stream is being GC'd, the relevant RxJS objects will not cause a leak.

The second strategy is takeUntilDestroyed. The first() strategy doesn't make sense with components that will update multiple times, that will update multiple times. For example CurrentWeatherComponent can update after the user enters new search text, so we want to receive updates as long as the component exists. See the following example:

src/app/current-weather/current-weather.component.ts

```
import { takeUntilDestroyed } from '@angular/core/rxjs-interop'

export class CurrentWeatherComponent implements OnInit {
  private destroyRef = inject(DestroyRef);
  ...
  ngOnInit(): void {
    this.weatherService
      .getCurrentWeather('Bethesda', 'US')
      .pipe(takeUntilDestroyed(this.destroyRef))
      .subscribe((data) => (this.current = data))
  }
  ...
```

takeUntilDestroyed can only be used within an injector context, i.e., a constructor. When using it in lifecycle hook calls, like ngOnInit, we must inject DestroyRef and pass it into the function. It automatically registers itself, so when the component is destroyed, it completes the stream. This way, the component can receive messages while it's needed, but with no risk of leaking memory.

By applying these alongside the subscribe method, we don't have to rely on difficult-to-trace unsubscribe methods, and we can easily verify their implementation with a quick search of the word subscribe.

The best part is no part at all. Next, let's see how we can consume an observable component without subscribing to it all.

Coding in the reactive paradigm

As covered in *Chapter 1, Angular's Architecture and Concepts*, we should only subscribe to an observable stream to activate it. If we treat a subscribe function as an event handler, we implement our code imperatively.

Seeing anything other than an empty subscribe() call in your code base should be considered a red flag because it deviates from the reactive paradigm.

In reactive programming, when you subscribe to an event in a reactive stream, you shift your coding paradigm from reactive programming to imperative programming. There are two places in our application where we subscribe, one in `CurrentWeatherComponent`, and the other in `CitySearchComponent`.

Let's start by fixing `CurrentWeatherComponent` so we don't mix paradigms.

Binding to an observable with an async pipe

Angular has been designed to be an asynchronous framework from the ground up. You can get the most out of Angular by staying in the reactive paradigm. It can feel unnatural to do so at first, but Angular provides all the tools you need to reflect the current state of your application to the user without having to shift to imperative programming.

You may leverage the `async` pipe in your templates to reflect the current value of an observable. Let's update `CurrentWeatherComponent` to use the `async` pipe:

1. Start by replacing `current: ICurrentWeather` with an observable property:

   ```
   current$: Observable<ICurrentWeather>
   ```

2. In the constructor, assign `weatherService.currentWeather$` to `current$`:

   ```
   src/app/current-weather/current-weather.component.ts
   import { Observable } from 'rxjs'
   export class CurrentWeatherComponent {
     current$: Observable<ICurrentWeather>
     constructor(private weatherService: WeatherService) {
       this.current$ = this.weatherService.currentWeather$
     }
     ...
   ```

3. Remove all code related to `SubSink`, `ngOnInit`, and `ngOnDestroy`.
4. Update the template to so you can bind to `current$`:

   ```
   src/app/current-weather/current-weather.component.html
   @if (current$ | async; as current) {
     <div> ... </div>
   }
   ```

The async pipe automatically subscribes to the current value of current$ and makes it available to the template to be used imperatively as the current variable. The beauty of this approach is that the async pipe implicitly manages the subscription, so you don't have to worry about unsubscribing.

5. Remove the @else { <div>no data</div> } block, which is no longer needed because BehaviorSubject is always initialized.

So far, the reactive paradigm has allowed us to streamline and clean up our code.

The async pipe allows you to display a loading message with simple if-else logic. To display a message while your observable is resolved, see the following technique:

```
example
@if (current$ | async; as current) {
  <div>{{current}}</div>
} @else {
  <div>Loading…</div>
}
```

Next, let's further improve our code.

Tapping into an observable stream

The CitySearchComponent implements a callback within a subscribe statement when firing the search function. This leads to an imperative style of coding and mindset. The danger with switching programming paradigms is that you can introduce unintentional side effects to your code base by making it easier to store state or create bugs.

Let's refactor CitySearchComponent to be in the reactive functional programming style, as shown in the following example:

```
src/app/city-search/city-search.component.ts
import { debounceTime, filter, tap } from 'rxjs/operators'
import { takeUntilDestroyed } from '@angular/core/rxjs-interop'

export class CitySearchComponent {
  search = new FormControl('',
    [Validators.required, Validators.minLength(2)])
  constructor(private weatherService: WeatherService) {
```

```
      this.search.valueChanges
        .pipe(
          takeUntilDestroyed(),
          filter(() => this.search.valid),
          debounceTime(1000),
          tap((searchValue: string) => this.doSearch(searchValue))
          takeUntilDestroyed()
        ).subscribe()
  }
  doSearch(searchValue: string) {
    const userInput = searchValue.split(',').map(s => s.trim())
    const searchText = userInput[0]
    const country = userInput.length > 1 ? userInput[1] : undefined
    this.weatherService.updateCurrentWeather(searchText, country)
  }
  }
```

In the preceding code, we removed the `OnInit` implementation and implemented our filtering logic reactively. The `tap` operator will only get triggered if `this.search` is valid.

`constructor` should only be used when working with properties and events local to the class context. In this case, search is initialized when defined, and `valueChanges` can only be triggered by a user interacting with the component. So, it's okay to set up the subscribe logic in it.

However, if you're referencing any properties within the template, `@Input` variables, or registering an external service call, you must use `ngOnInit`. Otherwise, you will run into render errors or unpredictable behavior. This is because template properties, including `@Input` variables, won't be accessible until `ngOnInit` is called. Further, external service calls may return a response before the component is initialized, leading to change detection errors.

Simply put, 99% of the time you should use `ngOnInit`.

In addition, `doSearch` is called in a functional context, making it very difficult to reference any other class property within the function. This reduces the chances of the state of the class impacting the outcome of our function. As a result, `doSearch` is a composable and unit-testable function, whereas in the previous implementation, it would have been very challenging to unit test `ngOnInit` in a straightforward manner.

Note that `subscribe()` must be called on `valueChanges` to activate the observable data stream. Otherwise, no event will fire.

The fact that we didn't need to implement `ngOnInit` reflects the truly asynchronous nature of our code, which is independent of the lifecycle or state of the application. However, you should stick with `ngOnInit` as a general best practice.

With our refactoring complete, the app should function the same as before but with less boilerplate code. Now, let's look into enhancing our app to handle postal codes from any country.

Chaining API calls

Currently, our app can only handle 5-digit numerical postal or zip codes from the US. A postal code such as `22201` is easy to differentiate from a city name with a simplistic conditional such as `typeof search === 'string'`. However, postal codes can vary widely from country to country, the UK being a great example, with postal codes such as `EC2R 6AB`. Even if we had a perfect understanding of how postal codes are formatted for every country, we still couldn't ensure that the user didn't fat-finger a slightly incorrect postal code. Today's sophisticated users expect web applications to be resilient toward such mistakes. However, as web developers, we can't be expected to code up a universal postal code validation service by hand. Instead, we need to leverage an external service before we send our request to OpenWeatherMap APIs. Let's explore how we can chain back-to-back API calls that rely on each other.

After the first edition of this book was published, I received some passionate reader feedback on their disappointment that the sample app could only support US zip codes. I've implemented this feature because it demonstrates how simple requests can introduce unplanned complexity to your apps. As a bonus, the app now works worldwide.

Let's add a new item, **Support international zip codes**, to the backlog and move it to **In progress**:

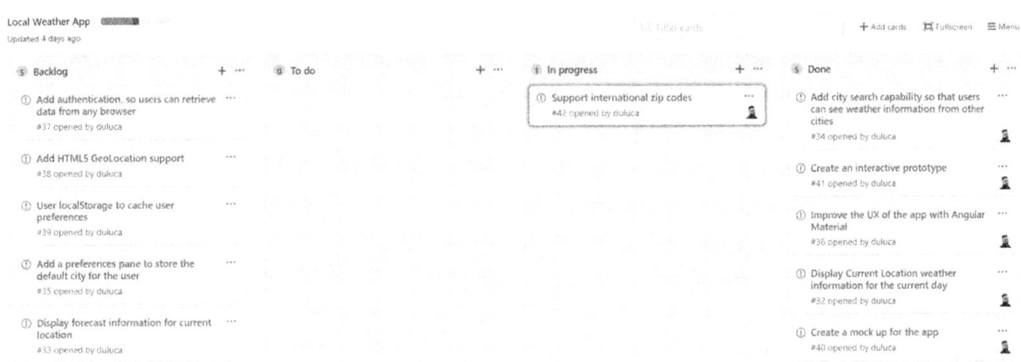

Figure 2.8: Adding an international zip codes story

Implementing a postal code service

To properly understand whether the user inputs a valid postal code versus the name of a city, we must rely on a third-party API call provided by `geonames.org`. Let's see how we can inject a secondary API call into the search logic of our app.

You need to sign up for a free account on `geonames.org`. Afterward, store username as a new parameter in `environment.ts` and `environment.prod.ts`.

You may experiment with the postal code API interactively at `https://www.geonames.org/postal-codes`.

We need to implement a service that adheres to the following interface:

```
interface IPostalCodeService {
  resolvePostalCode(postalCode: string): Observable<IPostalCode>
}
```

Declaring an interface for your service is a useful practice when you're initially designing your app. You and your team members can focus on providing the right interaction model without being bogged down by implementation details. Once your interface is defined, you can quickly stub out functionality and have a walking skeleton version of your app in place. Stubbed-out functions help validate design choices and encourage early integration between components. Once in place, team members will no longer need to guess whether they are coding in the right spot. You should always export your interface, so you can use the type information for writing unit tests, creating test doubles or fakes.

Interfaces are key to practicing **Test-Driven Development** (**TDD**).

Now implement `PostalCodeService` as shown below:

You may generate the service by executing `npx ng generate service postalCode --project=local-weather-app --no-flat`.

src/app/postal-code/postal-code.service.ts

```
import { HttpClient, HttpParams } from '@angular/common/http'
import { Injectable } from '@angular/core'
import { Observable } from 'rxjs'
import { defaultIfEmpty, flatMap } from 'rxjs/operators'
import { environment } from '../../environments/environment'
export interface IPostalCode {
  countryCode: string
  postalCode: string
  placeName: string
  lng: number
  lat: number
}
export interface IPostalCodeData {
  postalCodes: [IPostalCode]
}
export interface IPostalCodeService {
  resolvePostalCode(postalCode: string): Observable<IPostalCode>
}
```

```
@Injectable({
  providedIn: 'root',
})
export class PostalCodeService implements IPostalCodeService {
  constructor(private httpClient: HttpClient) {}
  resolvePostalCode(postalCode: string): Observable<IPostalCode> {
    const uriParams = new HttpParams()
      .set('maxRows', '1')
      .set('username', environment.username)
      .set('postalcode', postalCode)
    return this.httpClient
      .get<IPostalCodeData>(
        `${environment.baseUrl}${environment.geonamesApi}.geonames.org/
          postalCodeSearchJSON`,
      { params: uriParams }
    )
    .pipe(
      flatMap(data => data.postalCodes),
      defaultIfEmpty(null)
    )
  }
}
```

Note the new environment variable, `environment.geonamesApi`. In `environment.ts`, set this value to `api` and, in `environment.prod.ts`, to `secure`, so calls over HTTPS work correctly to avoid the mixed-content error, as covered in *Chapter 10, Releasing to Production Using CI/CD.*

In the preceding code segment, we implement a `resolvePostalCode` function that calls an API, which is configured to receive the first viable result the API returns. The results are then flattened and piped out to the subscriber. With `defaultIfEmpty`, we ensure that a null value will be provided if we don't receive a result from the API. If the call is successful, we will get back all the information defined in `IpostalCode`, making it possible to leverage `getCurrentWeatherByCoords` using coordinates.

Observable sequencing with switchMap

Let's update the weather service so that it can call the `postalCode` service to determine whether the user input was a valid postal code:

1. Start by updating the interface so we only deal with a string:

   src/app/weather/weather.service.ts

   ```
   ...
   export interface IWeatherService {
   ...
     getCurrentWeather(search: string, country?: string):
       Observable<ICurrentWeather>
     updateCurrentWeather(search: string, country?: string)
   }
   ```

2. Inject `PostalCodeService` to the weather service as a private property:

   src/app/weather/weather.service.ts

   ```
   import {
     PostalCodeService
   } from '../postal-code/postal-code.service'
   ...
   constructor(
     private httpClient: HttpClient,
     private postalCodeService: PostalCodeService
   ) {}
   ```

3. Update the method signature for `updateCurrentWeather`.
4. Update `getCurrentWeather` to try and resolve `searchText` as a postal code:

   src/app/weather/weather.service.ts

   ```
   import { map, switchMap } from 'rxjs/operators'
   ...
   getCurrentWeather(
     searchText: string,
     country?: string
   ): Observable<ICurrentWeather> {
     return this.postalCodeService.
   ```

```
      resolvePostalCode(searchText)
      .pipe(
        switchMap((postalCode) => {
          if (postalCode) {
            return this.getCurrentWeatherByCoords({
              latitude: postalCode.lat,
              longitude: postalCode.lng,
            } as Coordinates)
          } else {
            const uriParams = new HttpParams().set(
              'q',
              country ? `${searchText},${country}` : searchText
            )
            return this.getCurrentWeatherHelper(uriParams)
          }
        })
      )
  }
```

If you run into TypeScript issues when passing the latitude and longitude into `getCurrentWeatherByCoords`, you may have to cast the object using the `as` operator. So, your code would look like this:

```
return this.getCurrentWeatherByCoords({
  latitude: postalCode.lat,
  longitude: postalCode.lng,
} as Coordinates)
```

In the preceding code segment, our first call is to the `postalCode` service. We then react to postal codes posted on the data stream using `switchMap`. Inside `switchMap`, we can observe whether `postalCode` is null and make the appropriate follow-up call to either get the current weather by coordinates or by city name.

Now, LocalCast Weather should work with global postal codes, as shown in the following screenshot:

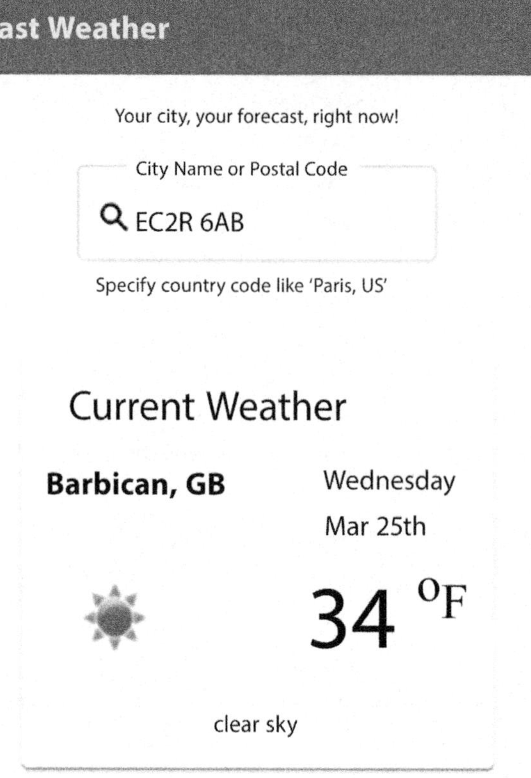

Figure 2.9: LocalCast Weather with global postal codes

We are done with implementing international zip code support. Move it to the **Done** column on your Kanban board:

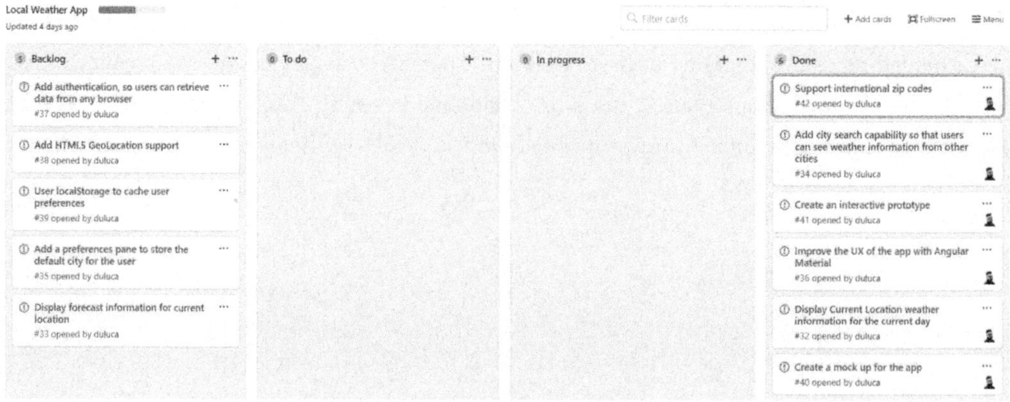

Figure 2.10: International zip code support done

As we complete our implementation of LocalCast Weather, there's still room for improvement. Initially, the app looks broken when it first loads because of the dashes and empty fields shown. There are at least two different ways to handle this. The first is to hide the entire component at the `AppComponent` level if there's no data to display. For this to work, we must inject `WeatherService` into `AppComponent`, ultimately leading to a less flexible solution. Another way is to enhance `CurrentWeatherComponent` so that it is better able to handle missing data.

You improve the app further by implementing geolocation to get the weather for the user's current location upon launching the app. You can also leverage `window.localStorage` to store the city that was last displayed or the last location retrieved from `window.geolocation` upon initial launch.

We are done with the LocalCast Weather app until *Chapter 9*, *Recipes – Master/Detail, Data Tables, and NgRx*, where I demonstrate how a state store like NgRx compares to using `RxJS/BehaviorSubject`.

Using Angular Signals

A signal is a reactivity primitive that keeps track of its value changing over time. Angular Signals implements this primitive to granularly sync the application state with the DOM. By focusing on granular changes in state and only the relevant DOM nodes, the number and severity of change detection operations are significantly reduced. As covered in *Chapter 1*, *Angular's Architecture and Concepts*, change detection is one of the most expensive operations that the Angular framework performs. As an app grows in complexity, change detection operations may be forced to traverse or update larger parts of the DOM tree. As the number of interactive elements increases in your app, change detection events occur more frequently. App complexity combined with the frequency of events can introduce significant performance issues, resulting in slow or choppy rendering of the app. Usually, there's no quick fix for a problem like this. So, it is critical to understand how signals work and implement them in your app to avoid costly performance issues.

As of this publication, Angular Signals is in preview. This means that the functionality and performance characteristics of the feature set can and likely will change. Refer to the following guide for the latest information: `https://angular.dev/guide/signals`.

Angular Signals provides a few simple functions to interact with it:

- `signal`: A wrapper around a value. It works like a value getter or setter in a class and is conceptually similar to how `BehaviorSubject` works:

```
const mySignal = signal('Hello')
console.log(mySignal()) // outputs: Hello (only once)
mySignal.set('Goodbye') // updates the value. Update and mutate
methods have subtle differences in setting a new value.
// To display the new value, you must call console.log again.
```

- `computed`: A computed signal. It utilizes one or more signals to modify the outcome:

```
const someSignal = computed(() => `${mySignal()}, World`)
console.log(someSignal()) // outputs: Hello, World. If needed, it
lazily updates when mySignal is set to a new value.
```

- `effect`: An event that triggers when a signal changes:

```
effect(() => {
  console.log(`A robot says: ${someSignal}`)
})
// console.log will be called any time mySignal changes.
```

Signals are a new foundational concept, and they change how we think about observables, binding data, and syncing state between components. They are performant, surgical in their nature, and best of all, they're memory safe. No subscriptions to worry about here.

Let's start by covering a simple example of using signals.

Implementing dark mode

For our app to be considered cool by techies, we must implement a dark mode for it. Let's use signals to implement this feature and go a step further by remembering the user's selection in `localStorage`:

src/app/app.component.ts

```
const darkClassName = 'dark-theme'

@Component({
  selector: 'app-root',
  standalone: true,
  imports: [...],
  template: `
    <mat-toolbar color="primary">
      <span data-testid="title">LocalCast Weather</span>
      <div fxFlex></div>
```

```
      <mat-icon>brightness_5</mat-icon>
      <mat-slide-toggle
        color="warn"
        data-testid="darkmode-toggle"
        [checked]="toggleState()"
        (change)="toggleState.set($event.checked)"></mat-slide-toggle>
      <mat-icon>bedtime</mat-icon>
    </mat-toolbar>
    <div fxLayoutAlign="center">
      <div class="mat-caption vertical-margin">
        Your city, your forecast, right now!
      </div>
    </div>
    <div fxLayoutAlign="center">
      <app-city-search></app-city-search>
    </div>
    <div fxLayout="row">
      <div fxFlex></div>
      <mat-card appearance="outlined" fxFlex="300px">
        <mat-card-header>
          <mat-card-title>
            <div class="mat-headline-5">Current Weather</div>
          </mat-card-title>
        </mat-card-header>
        <mat-card-content>
          <app-current-weather></app-current-weather>
        </mat-card-content>
      </mat-card>
      <div fxFlex></div>
    </div>
  `,
})
export class AppComponent {
  readonly toggleState = signal(localStorage.getItem(darkClassName) ===
'true')

  constructor() {
    effect(() => {
```

```
      localStorage.setItem(darkClassName, this.toggleState().toString())
      document.documentElement.classList.toggle(
        darkClassName, this.toggleState()
      )
    })
  }
}
```

If this were production code, I would not use this terse line of code:

```
document.documentElement.classList.toggle(darkClassName,
this. toggleState())
```

Here, I wanted to keep the lines of code to a minimum, and the toggle function provided by the DOM API contains the logic needed to make this work correctly. The line should be refactored to adhere to the single responsibility principle.

Observe the `readonly` property named `toggleState`. This is our signal. It holds a Boolean value. We can initialize it by reading a value from `localStorage`; if it doesn't exist, it will default to `false`.

In the toolbar, we define mat-slide-toggle and assign its [`checked`] state to `toggleState()`. This binds the value of the signal to the component. By assigning `(change)="toggleState.set($event.checked)"`, we ensure that when the user flips the toggle, its value will be written back to the signal.

Finally, we implement the `effect` method to react to the changes in the value of the signal. In the constructor, we can define the behavior we want within the `effect` function. First, we update `localStorage` with the current value of `toggleState`, and second, we set the `dark-theme` class on the DOM to toggle the dark mode state.

We leverage Angular Material's built-in dark theme functionality to define a dark theme and attach it to a CSS class named `dark-theme`. Refer to `styles.scss` to see how this is configured.

We could've implemented this functionality at least a half-dozen different ways, but signals do offer a very economical way of doing it.

We can build on these concepts and replace the uses of `BehaviorSubject` and `[(ngModel)]` throughout our application. Doing so greatly simplifies how our Angular app works, while also reducing package size and complexity.

Replacing BehaviorSubject with signals

Now, let's see what it looks like to use signals instead of `BehaviorSubject`. Implementing a signal means we must change the end-to-end pipeline of how a value is retrieved and displayed. A signal is a synchronous pipeline, whereas RxJS is asynchronous.

You may wonder, isn't asynchronous better than synchronous? Yes, but not when the synchronous code can run in a non-blocking manner. Asynchronous is expensive, and due to the fundamental technologies that are being leveraged under the hood, signals are way cheaper and faster. This is due to great features that are now built into JavaScript. See `https://www.arrow-js.com` by Justin Schroeder as an example of this. Certain kinds and sizes of projects no longer need full-fat frameworks like Angular, React, or Vue.

We will need to update `WeatherService`, `CitySearchComponent`, and `CurrentWeatherComponent`:

1. First replace `currentWeather$` with `currentWeatherSignal` in `WeatherService`:

   ```
   src/app/weather/weather.service.ts
   import { signal } from '@angular/core'

   export class WeatherService implements IWeatherService{
     ...
     readonly currentWeatherSignal = signal(defaultWeather)
     ...
   ```

2. Implement a new `getCurrentWeatherAsPromise` function to convert the observable to a `Promise` and a new `updateCurrentWeatherSignal` function to await the result of the call and assign the result to the signal:

   ```
   src/app/weather/weather.service.ts

   import { ..., firstValueFrom } from 'rxjs'

     getCurrentWeatherAsPromise(
       searchText: string,
       country?: string
     ): Promise<ICurrentWeather> {
   ```

```
    return firstValueFrom(
      this.getCurrentWeather(searchText, country)
    )
  }

  async updateCurrentWeatherSignal(searchText: string,
    country?: string): Promise<void> {
    this.currentWeatherSignal.set(
      await this.getCurrentWeatherAsPromise(
        searchText, country
      )
    )
  }
```

Note that we use `firstValueFrom` to make sure the stream completes as intended.

3. Next, replace the `current$` property with `currentSignal` in `CurrentWeatherComponent`:

src/app/current-weather/current-weather.component.ts

```
export class CurrentWeatherComponent {
  readonly currentSignal: WritableSignal<ICurrentWeather>

  constructor(private weatherService: WeatherService) {
    this.currentSignal = this.weatherService.currentWeatherSignal
...
```

4. Update the template to use the signal:

src/app/current-weather/current-weather.component.html

```
@if (currentSignal(); as current) {
  ...
}
```

5. Finally, update `CitySearchComponent` to trigger the new service call:

src/app/city-search/city-search.component.ts

```
export class CitySearchComponent {
  ...
  this.weatherService.updateCurrentWeatherSignal(
    searchText, country
  )
  ...
```

We have transformed our app to use a signal to communicate between components. A signal is less sophisticated than `BehaviorSubject`, but most of the time, the extra capabilities aren't used. Signals are memory safe, lightweight, and allow novel applications by leveraging computed signals, like the RxJS merge technique discussed earlier in this chapter.

Ultimately, RxJS and signals are complementary technologies. For example, we wouldn't consider replacing the debounce logic in the search input away from RxJS. Angular also ships with `toSignal` and `fromSignal` interoperability functions; however, I would caution against mixing paradigms. To get the full benefit of signals, always prefer an end-to-end refactor, as this section covers.

With so many options, paradigms, techniques, and gotchas, you may be wondering if you can just generate this code using AI. I did just that for you. Read on.

Generating apps with ChatGPT

Let's see what result we get if we ask ChatGPT to generate a weather app. In August 2023, I asked ChatGPT to generate a weather app using GPT-4 with the `CodeInterpreter` plugin. I gave it the following prompt:

> *Write an Angular app that displays real-time weather data from openweathermap.org APIs, using Angular Material, with a user input that accepts city name, country, or postal code as input.*

After making a few minor corrections, this is the result I got:

Figure 2.11: ChatGPT weather app – August 2023

ChatGPT created a very simple and straightforward app for me, with a weather-display component using two-way binding for the input field. The service call was correctly implemented in a dedicated weather service triggered by the **Fetch Weather** button. To achieve similar results to the `LocalCast` app we built, we would have to provide a prompt with far more technical details. Non-technical people won't know to ask for specific implementation details, and developers may simply find it easier to iteratively develop their solution. Nevertheless, the results are impressive.

Four months later, I questioned my premise from the paragraph above.

What if developers were okay with providing one or two more prompts?

In December 2023, I provided the same prompt from above to ChatGPT using GPT-4 without using any plugins, and after it generated the code, I provided an additional prompt:

> *Can you rewrite weather.component.html and style it in a way that looks like a professional design on desktop and mobile devices alike?*

And boom, I got a result that looked a lot better!

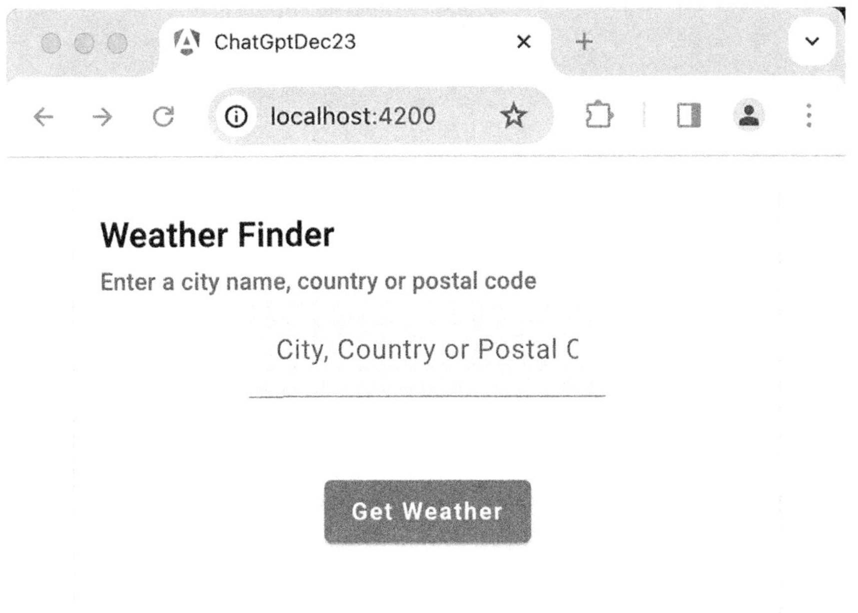

Figure 2.12: ChatGPT Weather app initial version – December 2023

Still, this output doesn't look like my design. Of course, ChatGPT has no idea what my design is, and it's too cumbersome to meticulously describe it in writing. Then I remembered I had a hand-drawn mockup of the weather app I created for the 1st edition in 2018.

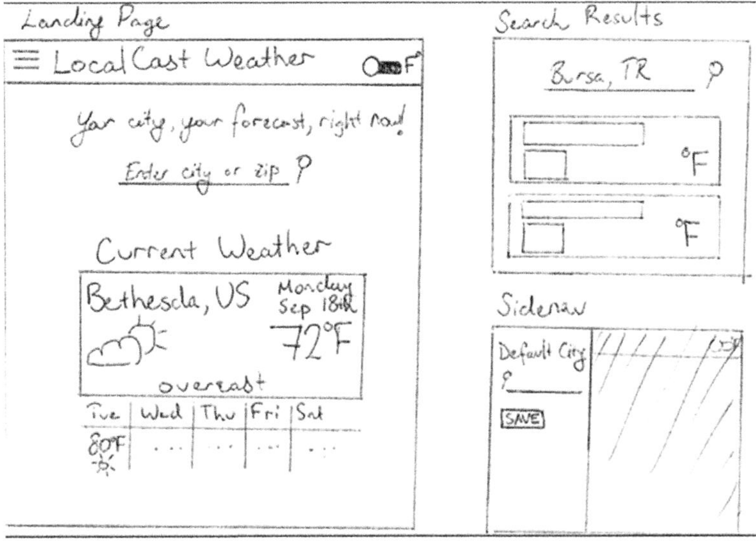

Figure 2.13: Hand-drawn wireframe for LocalCast

Yes, I did use a ruler!

In August 2023, ChatGPT couldn't see, but since then, it has gained computer vision. I uploaded the mockup as is and said, "Redesign the UI to follow this mockup." Remember that my mockup has three screens and difficult-to-read handwriting in it.

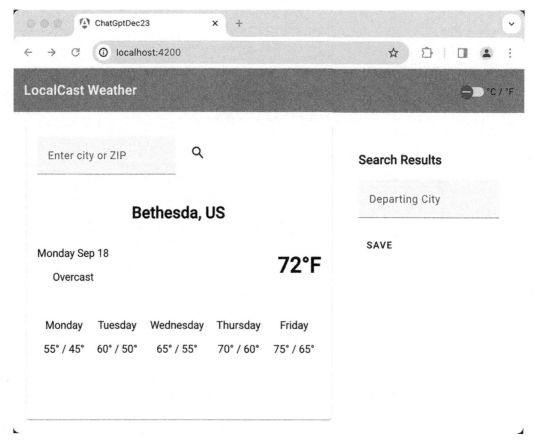

Figure 2.14: ChatGPT weather app second version – December 2023

I'm shocked that it picked up on `SideNav` and incorporated it using proper Material components and `FlexLayout` media queries to make it responsive – never mind the misinterpretation of my handwriting.

I updated the generated UI code to make it interactive and included it as a project named `chat-get-dec23` in the repo. Here's the result:

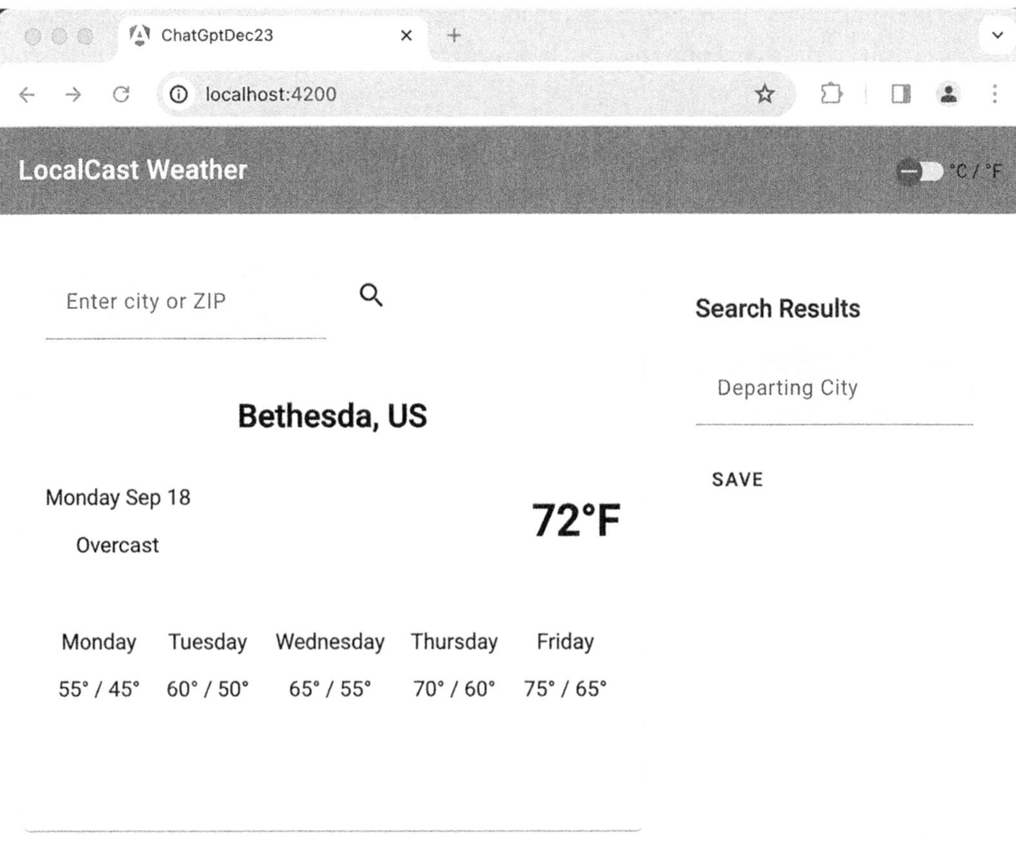

Figure 2.15: ChatGPT weather app final version – December 2023

This is beyond impressive. By the time the next edition of this book is published, this chapter may be only a few pages long and filled with tips, highlighting the crucial need to use a ruler when drawing your mockups.

Summary

In this chapter, you learned how to create search-as-you-type functionality using `MatInput`, validators, reactive forms, and data-stream-driven handlers. You became aware of two-way binding and template-driven forms. You also learned about different strategies to enable inter-component interactions and data sharing. You dove into understanding how memory leaks can be created and the importance of managing your subscriptions.

You can now differentiate between imperative and reactive programming paradigms and understand the importance of sticking with reactive programming where possible. Finally, you learned how to implement sophisticated functionality by chaining multiple API calls together. You learned about the signal primitive and how you can use it to build simpler and more performant applications.

LocalCast Weather is a straightforward application that we used to cover the basic concepts of Angular. As you saw, Angular is great for building such small and dynamic applications while delivering a minimal amount of framework code to the end user. You should consider leveraging Angular for quick and dirty projects, which is always great practice for building larger applications. You also learned you can use GenAI tools like ChatGPT to give yourself a quick start when beginning a new project.

In the next chapter, we will dive into considerations around architecting a web application in an enterprise app and learn where all the monsters are hidden. We will go over how you can build a **Line-of-Business (LOB)** application using a router-first approach to designing and architecting scalable Angular applications with first-class authentication and authorization, user experience, and numerous recipes that cover a vast majority of requirements that you may find in LOB applications.

Exercises

After completing the **Support international zip codes** feature, did we switch coding paradigms here? Is our implementation above imperative, reactive, or a combination of both? If our implementation is not entirely reactive, how would you implement this function reactively? I'll leave this as an exercise for the reader.

Don't forget to execute `npm test`, `npm run e2e`, and `npm run test:a11y` before moving on. It is left as an exercise for the reader to fix the unit and end-to-end tests.

Visit GitHub to see the unit tests I implemented for this chapter at `https://github.com/duluca/local-weather-app/tree/master/projects/stage6`.

Questions

Answer the following questions as best as possible to ensure you've understood the key concepts from this chapter without googling anything. Do you know if you got all the answers right? Visit `https://angularforenterprise.com/self-assessment` for more:

1. What is the async pipe?

2. Explain how reactive and imperative programming is different and which technique we should prefer.
3. What is the benefit of `BehaviorSubject`, and what is it used for?
4. What are memory leaks and why should they be avoided?
5. What is the best method for managing subscriptions?
6. How are Angular signals different than RxJS streams?
7. What are ways you can use Angular Signals to simplify your application?

3

Architecting an Enterprise App

In *Chapter 2, Forms, Observables, Signals, and Subjects*, we used the LocalCast Weather app to demonstrate various features of Angular to learn as well as experiment with and inform us if these features are suitable for more complex enterprise applications. Building enterprise applications is as much about the people building them as it is the technology used to build them. An over-eager approach to consuming and rolling out unproven tech is guaranteed to create the **sinkhole effect** in your project. If you're unfamiliar with sinkholes, they are a natural phenomenon that occurs due to the dissolution of underlying ground material. At some point, usually suddenly, the ground collapses to devastating effect, revealing a giant hole in the ground.

In this book, I've done my best only to include tried and true, mature, and well-supported technologies and practices. LocalCast Weather includes all the cutting-edge features of Angular, like a root-level standalone project with standalone components, signals, and control flow syntax. With standalone components, we shed the concept of shared modules, helping resolve circular dependency issues and unnecessary bloat due to overstuffed shared modules. However, frustrations exist. Standalone projects require libraries to support providers instead of modules; when a provider is missing, applying a library to a project with feature modules becomes tedious guesswork.

Control flow syntax, in preview, produces easier-to-read templates and removes the need to import structural directives, which reduces boilerplate. Meanwhile, Angular Signals, in partial preview, won't bring major value until signal-based components are rolled out. Regardless, Angular Signals draws from new JavaScript primitives, covered later, in the *Minimalist JavaScript solutions* section, you should know and learn to use outside of Angular. Before diving into specifics, let's consider the bigger picture.

The most common type of app built in an enterprise is a **Line-of-Business (LOB)** application. LOB apps are the bread and butter of the software development world. As Wikipedia defines it, LOB is a general term that refers to a product or a set of related products that serve a particular customer transaction or business need. LOB apps present an excellent opportunity to demonstrate various features and functionality without getting into the contorted or specialized scenarios that large enterprise applications usually need to address.

The Pareto principle, also known as the 80-20 rule, states that we can accomplish 80% of our goals with 20% of the overall effort. We will apply the 80-20 rule to the design and architecture of our LOB app. Given the common use cases LOB apps cover, they are perfect for the 80-20 learning experience. With only 20% of the effort, you can learn about 80% of what you need to deliver high-quality experiences to your users.

LOB apps have a curious property to them. If you build a semi-useful app, its demand grows uncontrollably, and you quickly become the victim of your success. It's challenging to balance the architectural needs of a project; you want to avoid potentially devastating under-engineering and, on the flip side, avoid costly over-engineering for an app that will never need it.

In this chapter, I'm going to introduce you to ingredients that will allow you to be successful in your enterprise, things you should consider as an architect, various tools you should consider when building a performant app, how to design a large app using router-first architecture, and the 80-20 design solution to address the challenges of delivering a modern web application incrementally and iteratively.

As you read in *Chapter 1, Angular's Architecture and Concepts*, software architecture doesn't stay static. It's essential to experiment with new ideas by using coding katas, proof-of-concept apps, and reference projects to practice getting better at creating more flexible architectures.

In this and the remaining chapters of the book, we'll set up a new application with rich features that can meet the demands of an LOB application with scalable architecture and engineering best practices that will help you start small and be able to grow your solution quickly if there's demand. We will follow the **Router-First Architecture**, a design pattern relying on reusable components to create a grocery store LOB application named **LemonMart**. We'll discuss designing around major data entities and the importance of completing high-level mock-ups for your application before implementing various conditional navigation elements, which may change significantly during the design phase.

In this chapter, you will learn about the following:

- Succeeding as a technical lead or architect
- Ingredients for succeeding in your enterprise
- Kanban planning using GitHub projects
- Tools for building high-performance apps
- Applying the 80-20 solution to software development
- Learning how to build router-first apps

Let's start by covering non-technical aspects of a project that you must have a grasp of, so you can set up your team for success.

Succeeding as a technical lead or architect

I will be using the terms **technical lead** and **architect** interchangeably. Depending on the size of your organization, this may be two separate roles or one. But no matter which specific role you fulfill, in these roles, it is up to you to ensure the success of your project and, most importantly, the well-being of your team members.

Understand the business impact

Your first task should be to understand the business impact of your project. Some questions to ask are:

- How critical is the success of this project to the business?
- What are the consequences of failure?
- What does it mean to fail?
- Which features will deliver the most value?
- What are the parameters you must operate under?
- What's negotiable and what's not?

The answers you get to these questions will vary how your project should operate significantly. If the survival or reputation of the business is at stake, you must amplify the aspects of the project that'll ensure the business survives or its reputation isn't tarnished. If a certain feature set will bring the most value, then focus all attention on getting performant and high-quality UX in that section and simplify the rest for the initial release. If certain personnel or technology is being dictated, weigh that against other factors. Expend all your energy and capital ensuring that the technology picked by your **Chief Technology Officer** (**CTO**) is a good fit for a project that will be a sink or swim moment for the company. Don't fight unnecessary battles.

Set parameters of success

As a general principle, it's advisable to leverage the strengths and passions of your team members. This is critical if resources or time is tight. People will work harder to invest in your project if they're also investing their time in a technology that they're passionate about. But don't do this at the cost of failure – going back to my point on over-eager use of new tech at the beginning of the chapter.

It is important to establish clear parameters for success for your team. This will only be possible if you *yourself* have a clear understanding of the business impact. You and your team members are on a journey. You're all walking on a path. Falling off the path means peril, either for individual team members or the project's success. It is up to you to vary how wide or narrow this path is. If you leave it too narrow, your team members will suffocate and be frustrated due to the lack of freedom or intense scrutiny. On the contrary, if you leave it too wide, you'll have more experimentation than any real work to do. You must set guard rails on the path at just the right amount to match the team and project needs.

Elastic leadership

Your leadership style can't be static. It must be *elastic*. All teams and projects have a lifecycle. They can go through periods of survival, learning, or self-organizing. Depending on deadlines or outside factors, teams can be forced from one state to another.

Check out Roy Osherove's excellent content on elastic leadership at `https://www.elasticleadership.com`.

Understand what state your team is in and vary your leadership style accordingly. Survival mode requires a dictator- or protector-style leader, where you're heavily involved with all team activities and are directing individual tasks and actions. Your goal should be to move teams in this state to learning mode. This is where you become a coach, where you are not as involved in daily activities but instead focus on what team members should learn and how they should grow. The next step up would be a team in *self-organizing* mode. These teams are resilient, they grow on their own, and they can take general direction and strategy and execute them. At this point, you need to be a facilitator or a servant leader. If you dictate to a mature team, you'll quickly lose that team.

Google's **DevOps Research and Assessment** (**DORA**) program contains 30 capabilities across technical, process, and cultural topics that your team and organization can master to become a high-performing team. The research program has been running since 2014, considering input from 33,000 professionals from various industries and governments. Learn more about the program at `https://dora.dev`.

If you don't understand these concepts, you're likely to put your team members in situations where they'll burn out, working overtime and with low morale, which could also impact family life and cause stress and high turnover. In that case, you may need to look in the mirror, with so many people standing there. All factors lead to a vicious cycle that is not good for running a healthy organization. As the saying goes, it's not a sprint but a marathon. It's as much about the journey as reaching the end goal. Don't fail your team.

Ingredients of a successful project

You understand the business impact of your project and you have a team eager to start; now what? You must have a plan, of course. As the German field marshal Moltke the Elder put it (or at least the modern paraphrase of it), *"No plan survives first contact with the enemy."*

Half a century later, Winston Churchill and Dwight D. Eisenhower added, *"Plans are of little importance [or are worthless], but planning is essential [or indispensable]."*

Agile software development

Over the past decade, Agile software management has taken over the world, replacing waterfall project execution with Scrum and Gantt charts with Kanban boards and iterative and incremental delivery every two weeks instead of multi-year development cycles with long lead times and expensive **Quality Assurance** (**QA**) and support cycles. Statistics show that Agile projects have a higher success rate than waterfall projects. This intuitively makes sense because iterative and incremental delivery ensures success happens as soon as possible.

The Agile Manifesto, located at `http://agilemanifesto.org`, published in 2001, highlights the key ingredients for becoming Agile:

> *Individuals and interactions over processes and tools*
>
> *Working software over comprehensive documentation*
>
> *Customer collaboration over contract negotiation*
>
> *Responding to change over following a plan*

Most individuals are introduced to Agile when they join a Scrum team, and because of this most people conflate Agile and Scrum. Scrum is a management framework. Concepts like sprints, planning meetings, retrospectives, and other optional elements like user stories and story points have nothing to do with Agile. It is possible to execute Scrum and abuse every Agile value possible.

At the *deliver:Agile 2018* conference in Austin, Texas, I listened to a talk by Ron Jeffries (a signatory of the 2001 Agile Manifesto) and Chet Hendrickson (a guy with an incredible sense of humor who rightly picked on me for having all sorts of JavaScript stickers on the lid of my MacBook) about Agile development. They focused on the "working software" component of the Agile Manifesto to drive home an important point. No amount of process, management oversight, or meetings will result in software delivery. As I aptly put it in my 2018 talk titled, Ship It or It Never Happened:

> *"It's not up to them [the managers]*
>
> *it's up to us [the developers]."*

It's not about creating pretty diagrams with endless iterations over imaginary architecture. It's not about delivering story points, checking boxes, and moving cards from one column to another. In short, don't be a process monkey. Focus on delivering working code.

Agile engineering best practices

The best way to accomplish this is by delivering and adhering to Agile engineering best practices:

1. **Test-Driven Development (TDD)**: Writing tests before writing actual code to ensure code meets requirements.
2. **Continuous Integration (CI)**: Running automated builds and tests on code commits frequently to catch issues early.

3. **Continuous Delivery (CD)**: Ensure every product iteration is in a releasable state.
4. **Pair programming**: Team members learn from each other as they work on tasks together.
5. **Refactoring**: Continuously improve the codebase as part of daily work.
6. **Simple and evolutionary design**: Designs should be as simple as possible to achieve current requirements without over-engineering and be flexible or open-ended enough that they can evolve over time.
7. **Behavior-Driven Development (BDD)**: Use tests based on the expected behavior of software, backed with concrete examples, in a syntax like Gherkin (`Given`, `When`, `Then` format) so technical and non-technical people can collaborate.
8. **Frequent releases**: Deliver software in small batches frequently.
9. **High cohesion and low coupling**: Modules or components focus on a single task, while these modules or components have minimal dependencies on each other.
10. Adhere to SOLID principles:

    a. **Single responsibility principle**: A function or class should only be responsible for one task.

    b. **Open/closed principle**: Code should be open for extension (i.e., extensible) but closed for modification (i.e., extensible without having to rewrite the algorithm).

    c. **Liskov substitution principle**: Inheriting from a super/base class shouldn't result in unexpected behavior.

    d. **Interface segregation principle**: Expose the most minimal interface required.

    e. **Dependency inversion principle**: Modules/components should depend on abstractions instead of concrete implementations.

11. **DRY principle**: Don't repeat yourself. Applying DRY helps make code easier to maintain. If you need to change something, you only have to change it in one place instead of many places. However, taking DRY too far can sometimes overcomplicate code, so use judgment to find the right balance. The principle is about sensibly reducing duplication, not eliminating it entirely.

Engineering excellence and craftsmanship

Adhering to these principles requires engineering excellence and a craftsmanship mindset. People on your team need to care about their work, be proud of the code they write, and be satisfied with the results they produce.

Translating requirements and designs to working code is not easy. Doing it iteratively and incrementally requires a deep understanding of technology, tools, and business requirements. However, being able to write code simultaneously without over-engineering it while also keeping it flexible is not only possible, but it should also be the goal of every engineer.

Oh, and pick a component library and stick to it, but also avoid vendor lock-in. Good luck!

Angular in an enterprise

Angular is not appropriate for use on every project. However, Angular is preferred in an enterprise because of the advanced concepts supported by the framework, such as **Dependency Injection** (**DI**), native TypeScript support, a modular architecture, robust packaging, testing, accessibility tools, and a commitment to release new versions regularly. The amalgamation of these tools helps applications scale beyond small apps to truly large-scale applications with 1,000+ views.

For **Content Management System** (**CMS**) style use cases and simple applications, you should consider using Analog. Analog is a meta-framework for building apps and websites with Angular: `https://analogjs.org`. Analog comes pre-configured with **Server-Side Rendering** (**SSR**), **Static Site Generation** (**SSG**), Vite (`https://vitejs.dev`) tooling, and convention-based routing and API routes for a no-frills, all-excitement development experience.

In fact, `https://AngularForEnterprise.com` was created using Analog.

Diverse coding paradigm support

Angular allows for different styles of programming. You can choose between imperative and reactive coding, leverage OOP concepts or completely ignore them, have inline and compact single-file components, or use up to four files to contain the same code. This variety is a strength when supporting a diverse population of developers, but it can also be a weakness by allowing multiple implementation styles within the same project. It is important to control this by establishing team norms around which programming style and paradigm to use. Linting and code-style tools like ESLint can help keep the code's appearance uniform but are ineffective at detecting or preventing paradigm shifts in code.

Community support

Angular has a great and engaged community filled with brilliant, respectful, and positive individuals who collaborate to build tools around Angular and evangelize it across the tech community. Google also supports Angular with the Google Developer Expert program, which I've been lucky to have been a part of, where the Angular team meets with active community members, gives them early access, listens to their feedback, and encourages collaboration. This means that when your enterprise needs support, there's a trustworthy community of individuals out there that you can tap into for advice.

As discussed in the introduction and *Future of Angular* sections of *Chapter 1, Angular's Architecture and Concepts*, as the size of a web application grows, performance issues begin cropping up in rendering the application, the tooling struggles to support the number of contributors to the project, and the architecture becomes inadequate in handling the complexity and variety of requirements. More on architecture when we discuss the 80-20 solution and router-first architecture later in the chapter.

You can find and contribute to a community-curated list of tools for building enterprise applications using Angular at `https://angularforenterprise.com/enterprise-tools`.

Next, let's dive into tools that can support building high-performance apps with good UX and DevEx.

Tools and techniques for high-performance apps

In this section, we will cover topics related to building high-performance apps. While some of these tools are specific to Angular, the general sentiment and advice apply to all web applications. This means that a complicated and large application should still be able to:

- Hit a smooth 60 FPS rendering target
- Respond to user clicks within 340 ms
- Provide fast feedback loops to developers
- Run builds and automated tests as quickly as possible

Let's first talk about runtime performance.

Runtime performance

Bad performance has real consequences for a business. In 2008, it was reported that a latency increase of 100 ms reduced Amazon's sales by 1%. In 2006, Google observed that an additional 0.5 seconds in generating a search page led to a 20% decrease in traffic. These are astounding numbers at Amazon and Google's scales, where milliseconds translate to millions of dollars. This may mean thousands or hundreds of thousands of dollars at your organization's scale. Considering performance trends over time, these smaller numbers can still multiply to millions.

The browser is a complicated runtime environment, and the frameworks we use to develop web applications obfuscate the runtime in exchange for rich features and easier-to-maintain code. This obfuscation introduces performance issues specific to framework code on top of native browser-related optimization requirements. And in 2024, the frameworks we use have become incredibly complicated.

Let's understand what kind of indicators we can use to understand the runtime performance of a web application:

- **First Contentful Paint (FCP)**: Measures the time from page start to the first visual content displayed
- **Time to Interactive (TTI)**: Measures a page's load responsiveness and helps identify where a page looks interactive but isn't
- **Latency**: The delay between a user's action and its response
- **Frame drops**: Occurrences when frames can't be generated fast enough to render a UI smoothly

We can use the profiling tools in our browser's DevTools to discover these issues. Below is an annotated example of a **flame chart** (often referred to as a flame graph) created by Michael Hladky, which highlights the various stages of the bootstrap process of an Angular app:

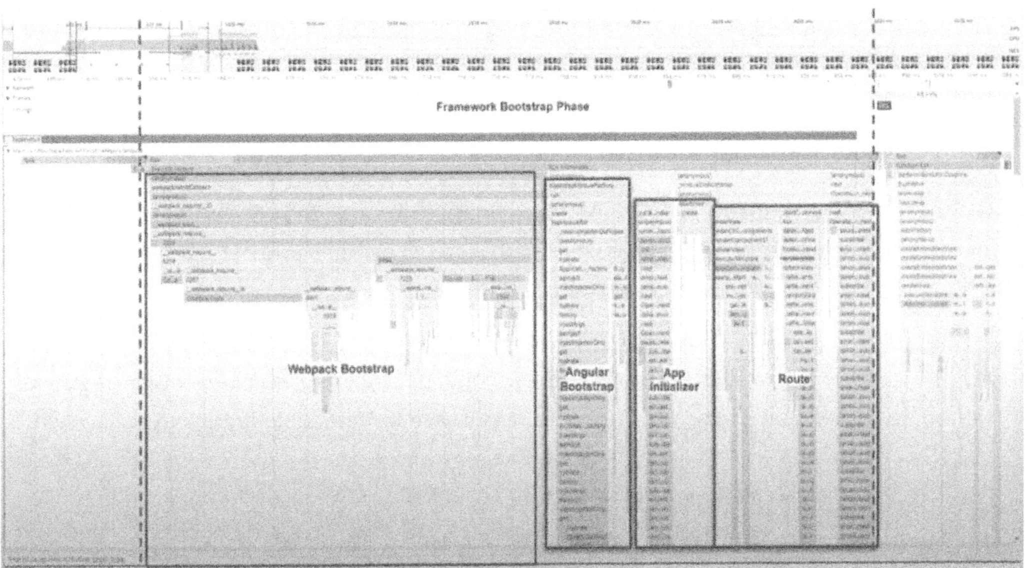

Figure 3.1: Flame chart of Angular Bootstrap phase. Credit Michael Hladky

The x axis of the chart shows times, and the y-axis shows the stack of function calls. A wide bar indicates a function taking a long time to execute or being called frequently. A tall stack includes a deep chain of function calls. You may use these visual clues to zoom into the chart and investigate performance issues.

If you're unfamiliar with using Chrome's profiling features, please refer to `https://developer.chrome.com/docs/devtools/performance/reference`.

Root cause of performance bottlenecks

What's slowing us down? During the bootstrap process of an application or when loading a new page, several things happen:

1. **Downloading JavaScript**: This includes application, framework, and third-party library code. The larger the size, the slower it is.
2. **Executing JavaScript**: Code needs to be unzipped and loaded into memory, then parsed by the JavaScript engine for just-in-time execution; DOM elements and framework hooks need to be scaffolded.

3. **Hydrating app code**: The framework must compute the application's state (visual and data), connect event listeners to the DOM, and render.
4. **Change detection**: The framework must traverse the component tree to determine if the UI should be updated due to a state change.

Executing these steps sequentially, presuming your application or API code is free of major issues, is the main root cause of performance issues with large web applications. In the current state of SPA frameworks, these issues are inescapable and/or very expensive to overcome.

An example of an inescapable issue would be rendering too many interactive components on the screen. A very expensive solution to this might be to patch every single component with custom code to circumvent the normal lifecycle of the framework and coerce it to behave in a way that could only benefit the application you're building.

Minimalist JavaScript solutions

ECMAScript 2022, widely supported by all major browsers, has built-in fundamentals that allow us to build performant and reactive web applications from scratch. For only 1-2 kb of "framework" code, we can vastly improve the DevEx and create modern and fast websites.

ArrowJS

At the Frontrunners 2023 conference in Washington DC, I attended a talk by Justin Schroeder about his frontend library named ArrowJS, Reactivity without the framework. More information can be found at `https://www.arrow-js.com`. In his talk, Justin covered the fundamentals that made his library possible:

- **WeakMap**: A WeakMap is a collection of key-value pairs where the keys are objects with arbitrary values. The keys are weakly referenced, meaning they can be garbage collected if no other references exist. Normally the map itself would count as a reference and thus remain in memory.
- **Proxy**: A proxy is an object that wraps another object or function and allows you to intercept and define custom behavior for fundamental operations. They are like middleware for your objects. Signals use a proxy under the covers. They are also useful in form validation.
- **Set**: A set is a collection of values where each value must be unique, meaning the same value cannot appear more than once. They are useful for tracking dependencies.

- **Tagged** template literals: These allow parsing template literals with a function, enabling custom string interpolation and processing. They are like middleware for strings. They are useful for parsing templated HTML code as a function.

When all these concepts are put together, observe how you can replicate a to-do list app in ArrowJS:

```
import { html, reactive } from '@arrow-js/core'

const data = reactive({
  items: [
    { id: 17, task: 'Check email' },
    { id: 21, task: 'Get groceries' },
    { id: 44, task: 'Make dinner' },
  ]
})

function addItem(e) {
  e.preventDefault()
  const input = document.getElementById('new-item')
  data.items.push({
    id: Math.random(),
    task: input.value,
  })
  input.value = ''
}

html`
<ul>
  ${() => data.items.map(
      item => html`<li>${item.task}</li>`.key(item.id)
    )}
</ul>

<form @submit="${addItem}">
  <input type="text" id="new-item">
  <button>Add</button>
</form>`
```

This code doesn't require any compilation or further processing. The next solution, however, leverages similar technologies under the covers but also tackles all the big problems.

Qwik.js

The father of Angular, Miško Hevery, along with industry veteran Adam Bradley (jQuery Mobile, Ionic, Stencil.js) and whizbang coder Manu Almeida, created Qwik.js as a response to address the fundamental issues baked into popular SPA frameworks like Angular, React, and Vue. You can check out this framework at `https://qwik.builder.io`.

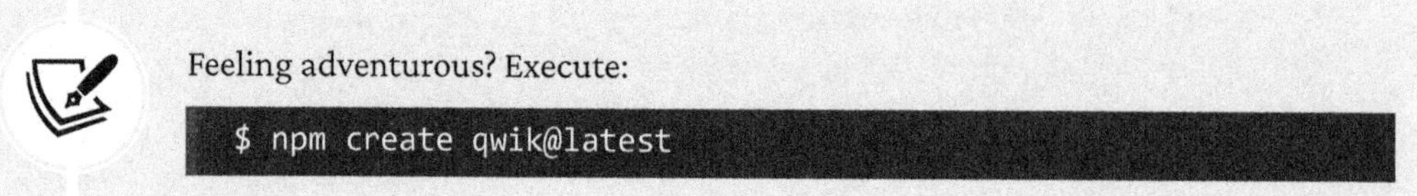

Feeling adventurous? Execute:

```
$ npm create qwik@latest
```

Qwik.js was built from the ground up to enforce a reactive coding paradigm, leveraging the signal primitive and resumability as a built-in feature to ensure that apps of any size or scale always do a full-page load under 1 second and perform 5-10x faster overall. All with a library that is ~1 kb in size.

Qwik ships "batteries included" with rich user controls, a Vite dev server, testing with Vitest and Playwright, extendable styling, and server-side rendering, and it doesn't require hydration. To understand the difference between hydration and resumability, see the following graphic:

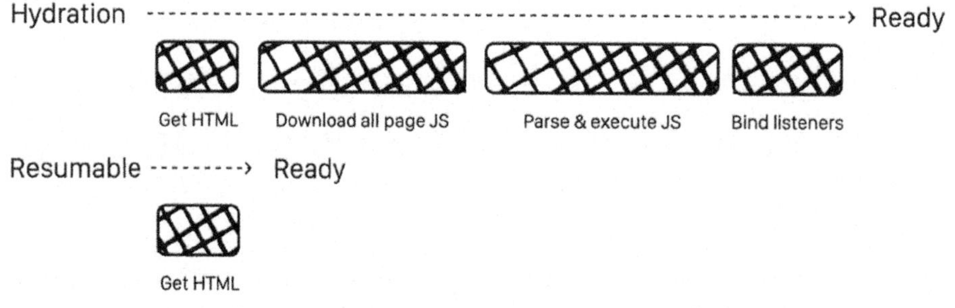

Figure 3.2: Hydration vs resumability. Adapted from Miško Hevery

At the top, you can see the hydration steps to load a traditional SPA. Each individual box takes longer the more your application grows. However, a resumable app is downloaded as a ready-to-render HTML payload, with its state embedded, bringing the complexity from O(∞) down to O(1).

If you find O(∞) intimidating, don't worry. It's meant to be a joke.

After the initial load, Qwik pre-fetches only the required amount of JavaScript to enable interactivity. This can mean downloading individual functions at a time. Qwik is also aggressive about lazily executing code. So, only the elements that the user interacts with come alive, keeping performance concerns in check. Naturally, there are some smart pre-fetching algorithms working in the background to make this a seamless experience.

If you would like to learn more about Qwik, check out my talk on YouTube at `https://www.youtube.com/watch?v=QDqp_qTa4Ww&t=40s` and the slides at `https://slides.com/doguhanuluca/intro-to-qwik`.

Next, let's see what tools we can use to address these issues in Angular.

Angular performance solutions

There are two categories of issues at play, one regarding the initial load of the application and the second ensuring smooth rendering by keeping change detection in check.

Let's start with **Server-Side Rendering (SSR)**.

Server-side rendering and hydration

Angular server-side rendering enables rendering the SPA, an otherwise client-side technology with code executing in the browser on a server. The server can pre-bake the initial state of a view as simple HTML and JavaScript that the browser doesn't have to spend a lot of time interpreting. As a result, the downloaded content renders very quickly, solving delays caused by downloading and executing large amounts of JavaScript. This is especially critical in mobile or outdated devices with limited processing and bandwidth. The server can perform this task consistently regardless of user hardware.

Another benefit of SSR is to facilitate web crawlers to enable **Search Engine Optimization (SEO)** on your website.

While the user is gawking at your landing page – since it is largely static at this point, they can only look, but not touch – Angular uses **web workers** to load the rest of the application.

The most logical way to incorporate SSR into your project is at the very beginning, so you can tackle and test for configuration issues incrementally.

To create a new project with SSR, execute:

```
$ npm create @angular -- --ssr
```

or

```
$ npx @angular/cli new app_name --ssr
```

Woke up in a good mood? Try adding SSR to your existing project:

```
$ npx ng add @angular/ssr
```

After all the assets are loaded, and your SPA is ready to be fully interactive, the app must transition from a static state to a dynamic one. This transition can be jarring. As we learned when covering Qwik, hydration is essential to seamlessly transition from a static to a dynamic state.

If you're using `FlexLayout`, use `FlexLayoutServerModule` to enable the framework in an SSR configuration. More details can be found at `https://github.com/angular/flex-layout/wiki/Using-SSR-with-Flex-Layout`.

Enter stage left **client hydration**. You can enable client hydration by using its provider in your `AppComponent`:

```
import {provideClientHydration} from '@angular/platform-browser';
// ...

@NgModule({
  // ...
  providers: [ provideClientHydration() ],  // add this line
  bootstrap: [ AppComponent ]
})
export class AppModule {
  // ...
}
```

With client hydration, your SPA can reuse already rendered server-side DOM structures, application state, downloaded data, and other processes for a smooth transition.

You can read more about using Angular SSR at https://angular.dev/guide/ssr and Angular hydration at https://angular.dev/guide/hydration.

App shell

An app shell is like SSR conceptually, but instead of the server rendering your page, you can pre-render a route or a page at build time. This way, you can craft a static landing experience on the landing page or when lazy loading a large feature module and then have Angular transition to an interactive state when ready.

Pre-rendering is conceptually and mechanically easier to handle. However, you may have to simplify certain aspects of your landing pages for them to work with prerendering.

Are you about to miss your project delivery deadline but still need a solution for loading issues? Try adding an app shell:

```
$ npx ng generate app-shell
```

As the saying goes, try it, but your mileage may vary. Learn more about app shell at https://angular.dev/ecosystem/service-workers/app-shell.

App shells are also useful in offline apps. Next, let's see how service workers can help with performance.

Service workers

You can also leverage service workers to make your web application feel like a native application. Service workers enable **Progressive Web Application** (**PWA**) features, like offline support, push notifications, and background data syncing for web applications.

Running these tasks in a background thread frees up the main thread to perform tasks related to rendering and user interactivity. This is low-hanging fruit to improve the performance of your application. Read more about service workers at https://angular.dev/ecosystem/service-workers.

You know you want to do it. Add PWA support today:

```
$ npx ng add @angular/pwa -project <project-name>
```

The technical reviewer of this book, Jurgen Van de Moere, also recommends Workbox by Google, a set of production-ready service worker libraries and tools regularly used in enterprises for complex scenarios.

Read more about Workbox at `https://developer.chrome.com/docs/workbox`.

Alas, it is finally time to peel to the core of the onion, change detection.

RxAngular

Michael Hladky and co. created RxAngular to overcome performance issues with large Angular applications. RxAngular "offers a comprehensive toolset for handling fully reactive Angular applications, focusing mainly on runtime performance and template rendering."

The following diagram details the lifecycle of an Angular change detection event:

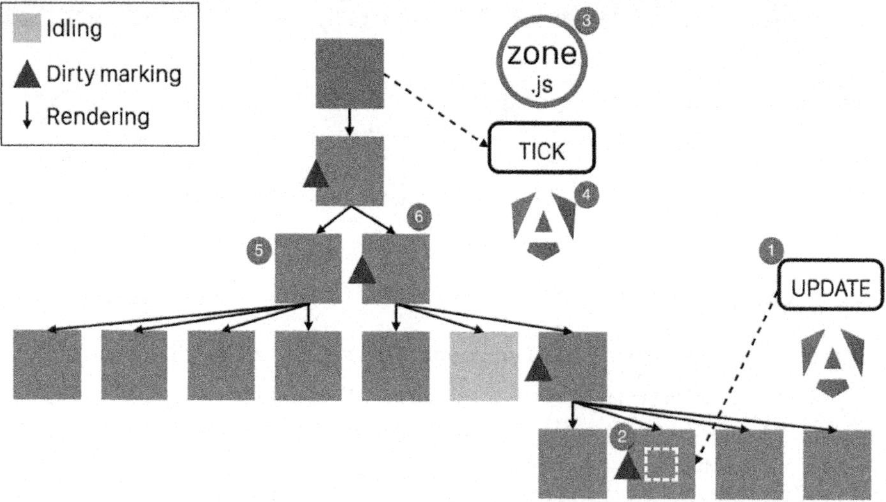

Figure 3.3: Default change detection in Angular. Adapted from Michael Hladky

Allow me to go over it step by step:

1. First, user interaction triggers an event.
2. Angular then marks the element for a dirty check.

3. Zone.js is utilized to transition between the Angular app state and DOM.
4. The Angular engine "ticks," triggering the execution of pending tasks.
5. The change detection algorithm avoids branches that are not dirty.
6. The algorithm identifies the topmost level component that must be re-rendered to react to the event triggered in *step 1.*

Angular's default change detection process is a computationally expensive process that can force the re-rendering of larger-than-necessary portions of the application. Angular also offers an `OnPush` change detection strategy.

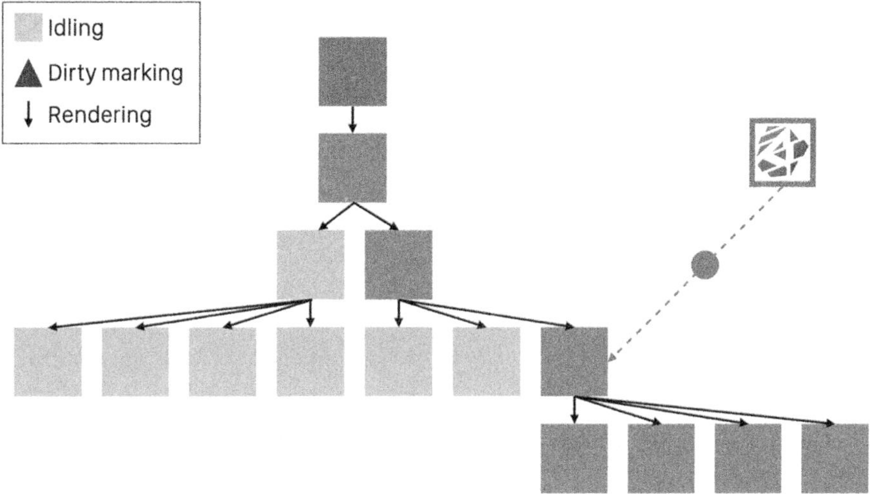

Figure 3.4: OnPush change detection in Angular. Adapted from Michael Hladky

`OnPush` disables automatic change detection until manually reactivated. We can use this strategy only to activate component sub-trees that the user interacts with, limiting the amount and scope of change detection Angular must perform. You can read more about this at `https://angular.dev/best-practices/skipping-subtrees`.

Finally, using RxAngular's directives and pipes, like `RxLet`, `RxFor`, and `RxIf`, we can trick the Angular engine to only detect changes when observables tied to these directives change.

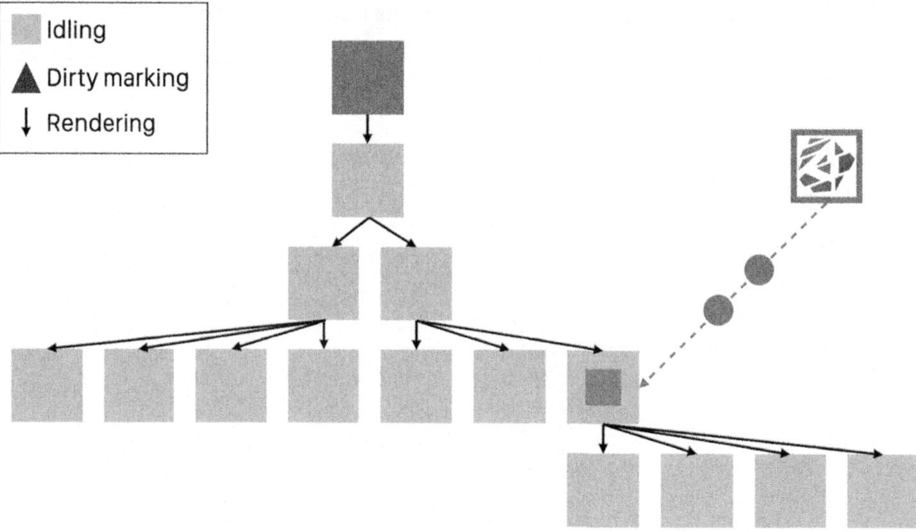

Figure 3.5: Change detection using RxAngular's directives. Adapted from Michael Hladky

As shown in the figure above, we can ensure only the element that needs to change is updated without going through an expensive change detection process. If you already have a large Angular application where a rewrite is not an option, RxAngular may be your only option to resolve performance issues.

Dive deeper into Angular performance at scale with Michael's talk at Angular DC: `https://www.youtube.com/watch?v=HTU4WYWGTIk`.

Learn more about RxAngular at `https://www.rx-angular.io`.

Angular Signals

Angular Signals can deliver the same kind of fine-grained change detection as shown in *Figure 3.5* in the *RxAngular* section. As you can imagine, this can potentially solve Angular's most egregious performance and scaling issues. However, as of Angular 17, signals are still in partial preview, and signal-based components are expected to be delivered and become stable around Angular 19. When this happens, we'll still need to rewrite significant portions of our applications to take advantage of the performance benefits.

A pure signals-based application won't require heavy RxJS use to enable reactivity. I predict its use will be rare, as most service and API calls can be converted into async/await-enabled promise-based calls. This would be revolutionary in making Angular very easy to learn.

In the *Rewriting Angular Apps with NgRx/SignalStore* section of *Chapter 9, Recipes – Master/Detail, Data Tables, and NgRx*, I demonstrate how far you can go with signals with Angular 17.

Next, let's talk about build issues that large applications can create.

Build performance

Like runtime performance issues, the codebase size can play a major role in the quality of DevEx. When more code is present in a project, building the code and running tests on it becomes slower. This lengthens the developer feedback cycle. A slow feedback cycle results in a slow development process with more bugs and fewer quality features delivered.

While minimalist solutions like ArrowJS or Qwik.js handle this by requiring none to minimalist state-of-the-art tooling, existing SPA frameworks can't do this easily, given a large install base and complicated requirements. But this doesn't mean there aren't great solutions.

The tools described in the following sections can speed up your development process and improve DevEx.

Nx

Nx is a next-generation build system with first-class monorepo support and powerful integrations. Nx allows you to break up your application code into libraries and utilize build caching only to re-build portions of the app that need it. So, a small change doesn't have to trigger a full build, but instead a short 30-second build and only re-running tests that are impacted. The great thing about this is that the cache can be shared remotely across servers and dev machines.

Nx also offers an opinionated architecture, which is welcome for very large teams and enterprises. Nx also automates dependency updates, a critical and time-consuming maintenance task for all modern web projects.

You can create a new Nx application by running:

```
$ npx create-nx-workspace@latest
```

Or you can migrate your existing apps to Nx by running:

```
$ npx nx@latest init
```

You can learn more about Nx at `https://nx.dev/`.

esbuild

esbuild is an extremely fast bundler for the web. It runs 40x faster than webpack 5, which Angular currently relies on to pack up the SPA, contributing significantly to slow build times.

As of Angular 17, the esbuild-based **ES Module** (**ESM**) build system is the default builder. You can read more about it at `https://angular.dev/tools/cli/esbuild`.

The webpack-based legacy build system is still considered stable and fully supported.

To migrate to the new build system, follow the instructions at `https://angular.dev/tools/cli/esbuild#using-the-browser-esbuild-builder`.

The new esbuild-based build system also enables next-generation frontend tooling with Vite. Learn more about Vite at `https://vitejs.dev/`.

You can learn more about esbuild at `https://esbuild.github.io/`.

Test automation

The Karma and Jasmine tools are showing their age. Karma was never built with headless unit tests in mind. The original **end-to-end (e2e)** testing tool for Angular, Protractor, has already been deprecated and replaced by Cypress. This is covered in depth in *Chapter 4, Creating a Router-First Line-of-Business App*. Cypress is great to work with and a great replacement for Protractor.

Let's go over a few alternatives to Karma and Jasmine for faster unit testing:

- Jest, `https://jestjs.io`, is a near drop-in replacement for Jasmine with a built-in test runner. I've had a great experience leveraging Jest with my CLI tools; however, Jest was never built with supporting ES modules. This results in significant compatibility issues when using CommonJS modules and ES modules together, which is often the case in any existing application. The issues were so opaque and significant I had to abandon an effort to upgrade the sample code for the book to Jest.

As of the time of publication, Angular supports Jest in preview. However, I don't recommend that you use it.

- Vitest, `https://vitest.dev/`, powered by Vite, is a blazing-fast unit test framework and represents an acceptable future state. However, to seamlessly leverage Vitest, you should also use the esbuild-based build configuration that also comes with Vite.
- Cypress, `https://www.cypress.io/`, is generally known for its e2e testing capabilities. However, you can also write component tests with Cypress. Once you configure Cypress for an Angular project, any time you generate a new component, a new Cypress component test file will also be added. Cypress's black-box approach to component testing makes it easier to write new tests, but they can't be referred to as unit tests.

Once (and if) all the half-dozen or more in-preview pieces of tech graduate to Angular production status, the heavy-hitting SPA framework will be ready for the future. In the meantime, don't discount alternatives like Qwik.js for extremely performance-sensitive applications.

Now that you know where the monsters are hiding, you're ready to tackle the execution of your project. But wait, don't start coding just yet. Having a plan in place is indispensable.

Planning using Kanban and GitHub projects

Having a roadmap before getting on the road is critical in reaching your destination. Similarly, building a rough plan of action before you start coding is crucial in ensuring project success. Building a plan early on enables your colleagues or clients to be aware of what you're planning to accomplish. However, any initial plan is guaranteed to change over time.

Agile software development aims to account for changing priorities and features over time. Kanban and Scrum are the two most popular methodologies that you can use to manage your project. Each methodology has a concept of a backlog and lists that capture planned, in progress, and completed work. A backlog, which contains a prioritized list of tasks, establishes a shared understanding of what needs to be worked on next. Lists that capture the status of each task act as information radiators, where stakeholders can get updates without interrupting your workflow. Whether you're building an app for yourself or someone else, keeping a live backlog and tracking the progress of tasks pays dividends and keeps the focus on the goal you're trying to achieve.

You can leverage a GitHub project to act as a Kanban board. In an enterprise, you can use ticketing systems or tools to keep a backlog, implement the Scrum methodology, and display Kanban boards. In GitHub, issues represent your backlog. You can leverage the built-in **Projects** tab to define a scope of work representing a release or a sprint to establish a Kanban board. A GitHub project directly integrates with your GitHub repository's issues and keeps track of the status of issues via labels. This way, you can keep using the tool of your choice to interact with your repository and still effortlessly radiate information.

An **information radiator** is a dynamic tool used in agile project management and software development to display critical project information in a highly visible area. Designed to promote transparency and facilitate passive communication, it ensures that team members are continuously and effortlessly informed about key aspects of the project, such as progress, goals, deadlines, and potential issues. Typically placed in a common workspace, an information radiator might take the form of a large whiteboard or digital display, showing easy-to-understand visuals like charts, graphs, or Kanban boards. Its primary function is to keep the information current and relevant, providing a real-time snapshot of the project's status. By doing so, it enhances collaboration, helps in identifying bottlenecks quickly, and allows for prompt decision-making. The information radiator, therefore, serves as both a focal point for team interaction and a catalyst for a more engaged and informed team dynamic.

In the next section, you will set up a project to achieve this goal.

Setting up a GitHub project

Let's set up a GitHub project:

1. Navigate to your GitHub repository in your browser.
2. Switch over to the **Projects** tab.

3. Select **New project**.

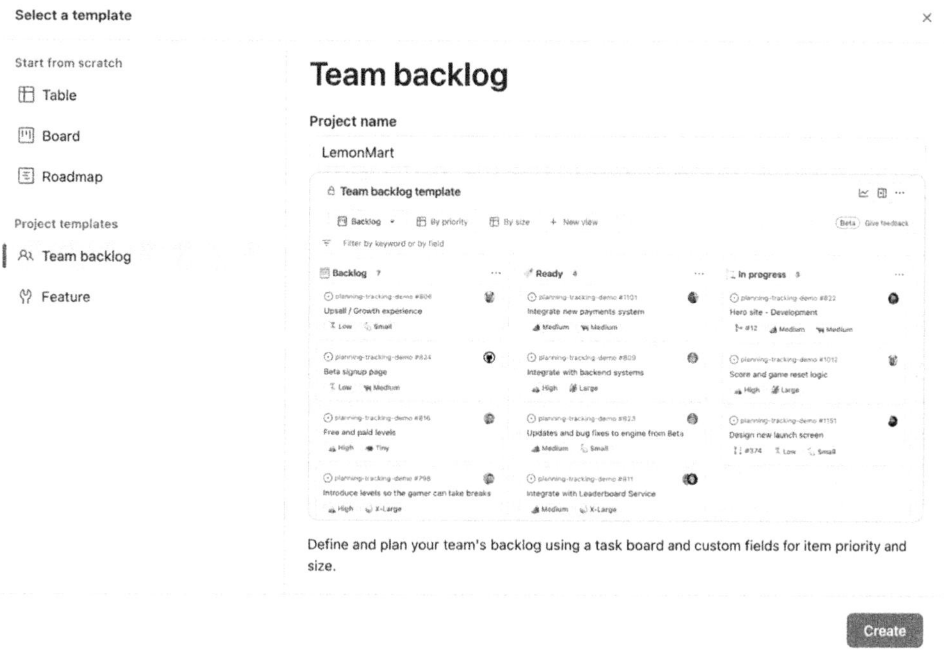

Figure 3.6: Creating a new project in GitHub

4. Provide a name in the **Project name** box.
5. Select the project template named **Team backlog**.
6. Click on **Create**.

We just created a Kanban board, a lightweight methodology to organize your work you might choose over other methodologies like Scrum. Observe your Kanban board, which should appear as follows:

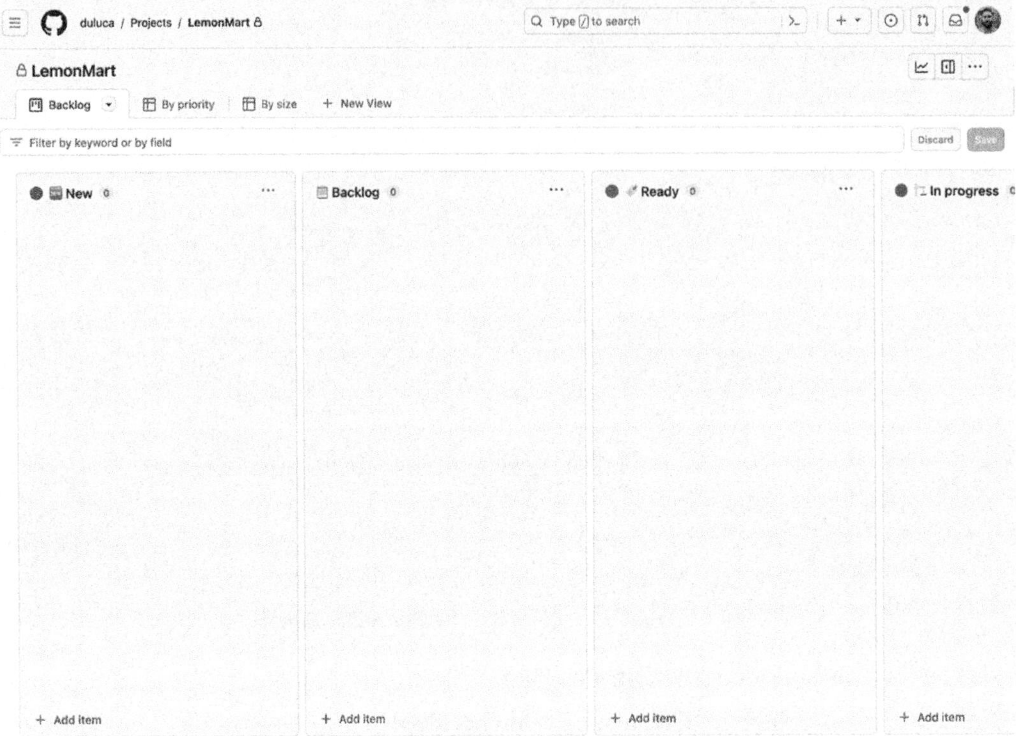

Figure 3.7: The Kanban board for your project

The default configuration of the board includes the following columns:

- **New**: Should be used for adding new issues
- **Backlog**: A prioritized list of tasks to work on
- **Ready**: Tasks that meet the definition of ready and can be immediately worked on
- **In progress**: Tasks that are in progress; using the triple-dot menu, you can set an item limit, enforcing a **Work-in-Progress** (**WIP**) limit
- **In review**: Work that's under code review, QA testing, and **Product Owner** (**PO**) approval
- **Done**: Work that meets the definition of done

The Definition of Ready defines *"criteria to know when a Backlog item is refined enough to start working on it"* and the Definition of Done defines *"criteria to know when a Backlog item is completed."* It is critical to define these criteria as part of team norms. To learn more about running successful Kanban projects, check out this article by my colleague Nicole Spence-Goon: `https://www.excella.com/insights/successful-agile-project-with-transient-teams`.

If you have existing GitHub issues or pull requests in your repository, you can add them to your project individually or in bulk using the **+ Add item** button. You can also combine issues from different repositories.

Customizing the Kanban board

Your board is configured as a Kanban board with all the necessary columns out of the box. By default, issues created and **Pull Requests (PRs)** opened in your project will be automatically added to the board.

You can do this by opening the **Workflows** screen from the triple-dot menu marked as **1** in the following screenshot:

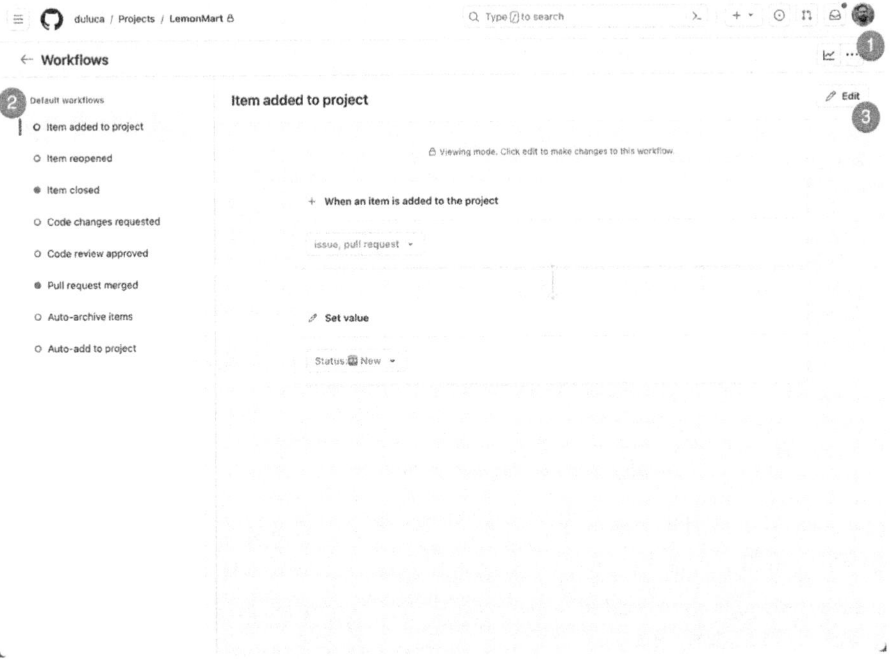

Figure 3.8: Kanban board workflows

Number **2** shows a list of the default workflows listed. You can select one and use the **Edit** button, marked with **3**, to change the automated behavior.

GitHub projects also have a concept of milestones. You can create milestones and assign them to issues or PRs to set up a sprint or a release and track percentage completion or other stats via the **Insights** screen, accessed next to the triple-dot menu, marked with number **1**.

You may also add a roadmap using the on **+ New View** button to get a different view. The most powerful feature of GitHub projects is the integration with developer workflows. See the following PR:

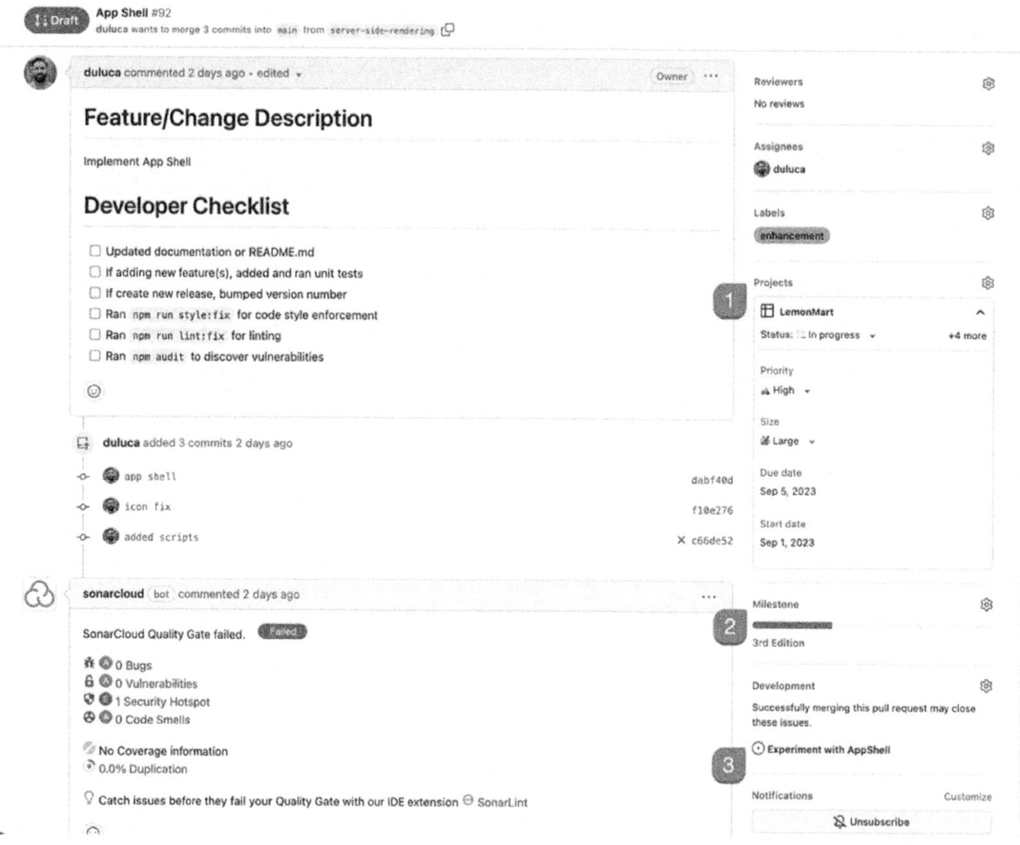

Figure 3.9: Pull request with project integration

Number **1** shows that the PR is in the **In progress** column of the **LemonMart** project. Developers get glanceable information and the ability to manipulate project files within the PR. At number **2**, we can see the PR is assigned to the **3rd Edition** milestone, where we can see a progress bar showing percentage completion. And finally, number **3** shows one or more issues that this PR can resolve.

Creating a prioritized backlog for your app

Get together with your team and create a backlog of issues to keep track of your progress as you implement the design of your application. When creating issues, you should focus on delivering functional iterations that bring some value to the user.

Refrain from creating purely technical tasks. The technical hurdles you must clear to achieve those results are of no interest to your users or clients. Bug tickets are okay because they impact your users. However, technical tasks become part of the functional problem you're trying to solve, so address them within that context. This way, you'll always be ready to translate the work being done into value being delivered when approached by business leaders at your organization.

As you add items to the backlog, be sure to prioritize them. The first items to be worked on go to the top and descend in order of importance. New items go into the **New** column and are only added to the backlog in a grooming session so their necessity and priority can be properly assessed. With a prioritized backlog, you have your roadmap in hand, and your team is ready to start work.

Ultimately, GitHub projects provide an easy-to-use GUI so that non-technical people can easily interact with GitHub issues. By allowing non-technical people to participate in the development process on GitHub, you unlock the benefits of GitHub becoming the single source of information for your entire project. Questions, answers, and discussions about features and issues are tracked as part of GitHub issues instead of being lost in emails. You can also store wiki-type documentation on GitHub. So, by centralizing all project-related information, data, conversations, and artifacts on GitHub, you are greatly simplifying the potentially complicated interaction of multiple systems that require continued maintenance at a high cost. GitHub has a very reasonable cost for private repositories and on-premises enterprise installations. If you're sticking with open source, as we are in this chapter, all these tools are free.

With a roadmap in place, let's investigate the philosophy of how to prioritize work and execute the design and architecture of our apps.

The 80-20 solution

Whether we develop apps at home, for passion projects, or at the office, for work, we must remain mindful of our purpose: to deliver value. If we don't deliver value with our passion projects, we won't feel fulfilled or happy. If we fail to deliver value at work, we may not get paid.

Delivering a modern web application is difficult. There are numerous challenges that we need to overcome to be successful:

- Deliver iteratively and incrementally
- Be scalable
- Serve dozens of screens and input types
- Be usable
- Be accessible
- Manage a team
- Groom a prioritized backlog
- Ensure acceptance criteria are clear, concise, and concrete

If you've ever led a project or tried to implement and deliver a project on your own, you'll have realized that there's never enough time and resources to cover the wide variety of stakeholder, team, and technical needs on any given project. Remember that the Pareto principle, also known as the 80-20 rule, implies that we can accomplish 80% of our goals with 20% of the overall effort.

If we apply the 80-20 rule to our work, we can maximize our output, quality, and happiness. Line-of-business applications are the bread and butter of our industry. Applying the 80-20 rule, we can surmise that most of us will earn most of our income by delivering such applications. Therefore, we should keep our engineering overhead to a minimum and reduce the delivery risk of our project. By limiting experimentation in production code, we create a predictable environment for our team members and only introduce changes that we had a chance to vet in proof-of-concept or small apps.

Our 80-20 strategy, combined with discipline, can help us deliver the same project at the same time with more features and better quality. By treating your career as a marathon and not a series of sprints, you can find yourself in a position to deliver high-quality solutions, project after project, without feeling burned out.

Understanding line-of-business apps

According to Wikipedia, line-of-business applications are a *"set of critical computer applications perceived as vital to running an enterprise."* LOB apps are what most developers end up developing, even though we may think we develop small apps or large enterprise apps. Consider the following illustration, which demonstrates the kinds of apps we might develop, placed on an axis relative to their size and scope:

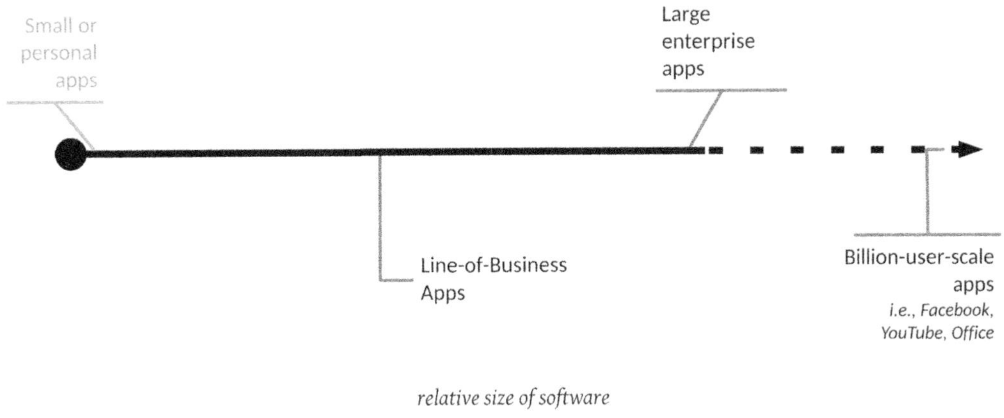

Figure 3.10: Relative size and scope of four kinds of apps

From my perspective, we think about four kinds of apps when we begin developing software:

- Small apps
- LOB apps
- Large enterprise apps
- Billion-user-scale apps

Billion-user-scale apps are completely niche implementations that rarely have needs that align with most apps out there. For this reason, we must classify these apps as outliers.

Small apps start small. Architecturally, they're likely to be initially under-engineered. As you add features and team members to work on a small app, at some point, you're going to run into trouble. As your team size and feature set grow, or the overall complexity of the app increases, the architectural needs of the application grow exponentially.

Once you cross the inflection point of the complexity your architecture can bear, you're left with a costly reengineering effort to get back on track. See the following graph illustrating this idea:

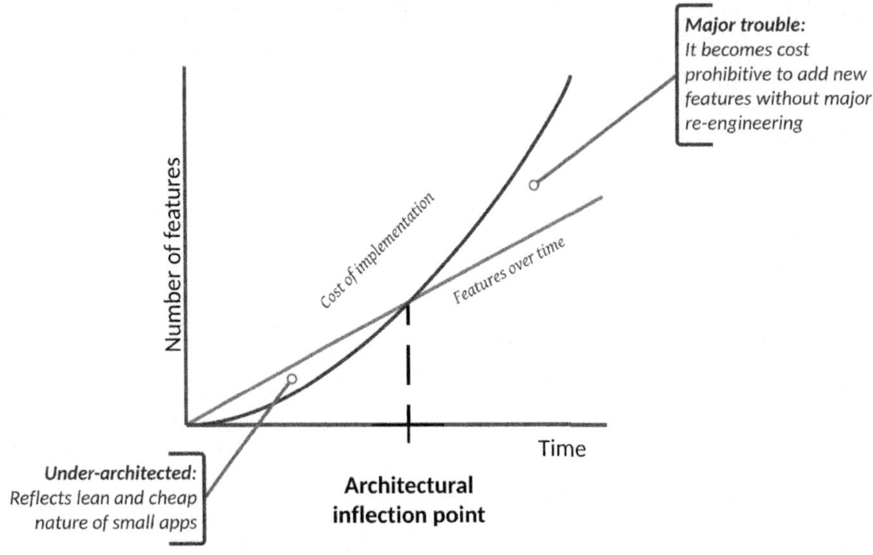

Figure 3.11: Architectural journey of a small app

The area under the feature line represents under-engineering, which introduces risk to your project. The area above the feature line shows the required engineering overhead to support the features needed. In comparison, large enterprise apps start with a massive over-engineering effort, as shown in the following diagram:

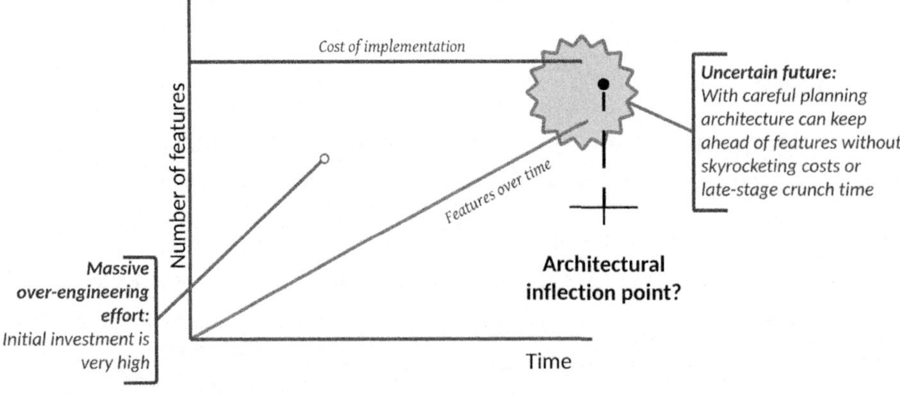

Figure 3.12: Architectural journey of a large enterprise app

As time goes on and the system's overall complexity increases, large enterprise apps can also face a similar inflection point, where the original architecture can become inadequate. With careful planning and management, you can avoid trouble and protect the significant initial investment made. Such large enterprise apps require hundreds of developers, with multiple levels of managers and architects, to execute successfully. Like billion-user-scale apps, these apps can also have niche architectural needs. In between the small apps and the large enterprise apps that we develop lie LOB apps.

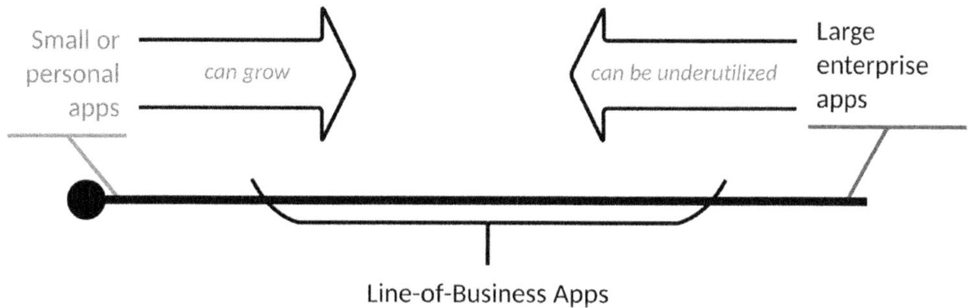

Figure 3.13: Dynamic nature of software evolution

As shown in the preceding diagram, small apps can grow and morph into LOB apps, and large enterprise apps can become under-utilized as users ignore the features they never need but keep the app to serve a singular purpose as a LOB app. In either case, despite our best efforts, we ultimately deliver an inefficient solution for the problem we're solving. None of us have a crystal ball to see the future, and planning and engineering can only do so much for us in an unpredictable business setting; we need to rely on the 80-20 rule to come up with an architecture that is flexible to change, but adequate to meet most business requirements.

Router-first architecture, covered in a later section, aims to maintain optimal architectural overhead so that costly re-engineering or late-stage crunch can be avoided in the rush to deliver all required features. Let's see how.

I coined the term router-first architecture in 2018 with the first edition of this book. Since then, I've spoken about it at a dozen conferences and executed it on multi-million dollar projects successfully. Here's my first presentation at the Angular DC meet-up in June 2018: `https://www.youtube.com/watch?v=XKuFNiV-TWg`.

Disciplined and balanced approach

We covered the *what* of software development, but we must also consider the *why*, *when*, *where*, and *who* before we can get to the *how*. We usually under-engineer our projects when we develop apps for learning or passion projects. If your passion project somehow becomes an overnight success, it becomes costly to maintain or keep adding features to your app. In this case, you will have to bear the ongoing maintenance cost or face a rewrite of your application.

When we develop apps for work, we tend to be more conservative and will likely over-engineer our solution. However, if you only code for work, you will likely experiment with production-bound code. It is dangerous to experiment in a codebase with other team members. You may be introducing a new pattern without your team understanding the consequences of your choices. You're also less likely to know the mid-to-long-term risks or benefits of the technologies you introduce.

Reckless experimentation can also have a severe negative impact on your team members. In a team of senior and experienced software engineers, you can likely get away with experimenting in a moving car. However, we will likely have team members of varying backgrounds and learning styles on our teams. Some of us have computer science degrees, some of us are lone wolves, and some of us depend a bit too much on Stack Overflow. Some of us work at companies that are great at supporting professional growth, but some of us work at places that won't give us a day to learn something new. So, when experimenting, we must consider our environment; otherwise, we can cause our colleagues to work overtime or feel helpless and frustrated.

With a disciplined and balanced approach, we can reduce the number of bugs delivered, avoid costly rework, and work with a group of people moving in the same direction. We also need the right architecture, tools, and patterns/practices to deliver successfully. In summary, our approach must consider the following:

- The size of our app
- The reason we are developing the app
- The skill level of developers
- Iterative and incremental delivery
- The constant forward flow of features
- Cloud architecture, operational costs, and cybersecurity

Ideally, we need to maintain optimal engineering overhead. Our architecture should support our short-term needs while being extensible, so we can pivot in different directions if our mid- or long-term needs change without having to rewrite large swathes of code. Consider the following diagram, in contrast to the ones about small and large enterprise apps in the previous section:

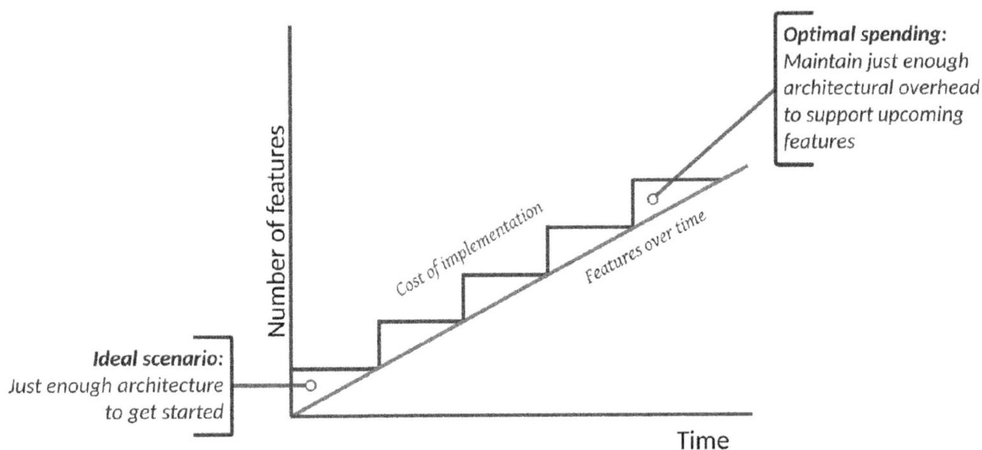

Figure 3.14: Ideal architectural journey of an LOB app

Router-first architecture aims to help you find the balance between your codebase's engineering overhead, feature delivery, and flexibility. However, you are responsible for managing the discipline side of things.

Shu Ha Ri is a concept that can help bring discipline to your work. It is a way of thinking that instructs you first to master the basics without worrying about the underlying theory, then master the theory, and finally be able to adapt what you mastered to your needs. However, if you skip steps 1 or 2, you will find yourself adapting the wrong thing incorrectly.

Having covered the *what, why, when, where,* and *who,* let's jump into the *how* in the next section.

Router-first architecture

Router-first architecture is a way to:

- **Enforce** high-level thinking
- **Ensure** consensus on features *before* you start coding
- **Plan** for your codebase/team to grow
- **Introduce** little engineering overhead

There are seven steps to implementing the router-first architecture:

1. Develop a roadmap and scope (*Chapter 4*).
2. Design with lazy loading in mind (*Chapter 4*).
3. Implement a walking-skeleton navigation experience (*Chapter 4*).
4. Achieve a stateless, data-driven design (*Chapters 4-5*).
5. Enforce a decoupled component architecture (*Chapters 6-9*).
6. Differentiate between user controls and components (*Chapter 8*).
7. Maximize code reuse with TypeScript and ES features (*Chapters 5-9*).

As noted previously, each step will be covered in more detail in this and coming chapters. Before we go over these steps at a high level, let's first cover feature modules in Angular, which are important fundamental technical concepts.

Feature modules

In *Chapter 1, Angular's Architecture and Concepts*, we covered Angular's architecture at a high level and introduced the concepts of lazy loading and routing. Feature modules are a key component in implementing lazy loading. There are two kinds of modules: the root module and the feature module. Modules are implemented by the class `NgModule`. `NgModule` contains all the necessary metadata to render components and inject services. Before the introduction of standalone components, a component without a module couldn't do much. But now, a standalone component can import its dependent modules, components, and providers without needing a module.

An Angular application is defined by `NgModule` that sits at the root of the application. This is called the root module. Starting with Angular 17, standalone projects are enabled by default. So, instead of a root module, an `AppConfig` object is created, which fulfills a similar role to the root module during the bootstrap process. The root module renders what appears in the `<app-root>` element in your `index.html` file. Locate the root module, which is interchangeable with `AppConfig`, in the following diagram:

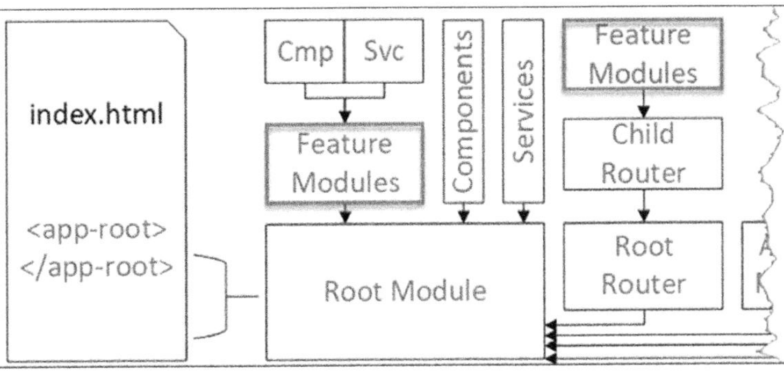

Figure 3.15: Major architectural components of Angular

`NgModule` can contain many other `NgModules`. An Angular app can only have one root module or none. This means `NgModule` you implement is a feature module. In the preceding diagram, you can see that you can organize a group of components (**Cmp**) and services (**Svc**) into feature modules. Grouping functionality into modules allows us to organize our code into chunks, which can be separated from the initial bundle of our application.

This idea of root and feature modules represents a parent/child relationship, which is a concept that extends to other functionality and frameworks. For example, note that the preceding diagram injects a root router into the root module. A root router can have child routes. Child routes can be configured to load feature modules. Similarly, NgRx has root and feature module-level stores to organize the state data of your application.

Any mention of a sub-module, child module, or feature module in this book refers to the same thing: a module that is not the root module.

Feature modules and child routes allow for a separation of concerns between major components of your application. Two teams can work on two different modules without interfering with each other. This separation means that any dependency required by a feature module must be explicitly added to the imports, declarations, or providers of that module. In the case of standalone components, these imports and providers must be added to every single component. This can seem repetitive and annoying, but it is a necessary evil.

As explained in *Chapter 2, Forms, Observables, Signals, and Subjects*, services, by default, are singletons – one instance per module. However, you can remove the `providedIn: 'root'` property from the `@Injectable` annotation and use the service within different injection contexts. You can provide copies of a service at the feature module or component level. When doing this, be aware that if you provide the same service in multiple contexts within the same inheritance chain, e.g., in the root and a feature module or a component, you will end up having multiple instances of that service that could be injected, which breaks the expectations of the dependency injection system.

As you can appreciate, modules introduce a complicated and often unnecessary abstraction layer in most scenarios. This is the main reason Angular now generates standalone projects by default.

Now, let's review the seven steps of router-first architecture at a high level.

Developing a roadmap and scope

Developing a roadmap and establishing the scope of your project early on is critical to getting the high-level architecture right. Creating a backlog, wireframes, mock-ups, and interactive prototypes will help you define the map before getting on the road and capture the vision concretely. It is important to remember to use tools only when necessary. Don't start with Photoshop when a piece of paper and a pencil will do. If stakeholders and team members understand what is being developed, it will be possible to deliver your solution iteratively and incrementally. However, don't fall into the perfection trap. Save the tweaking and furniture rearranging until after the fundamentals are in place and agreed upon.

Document every artifact you create. *Chapter 4, Creating a Router-First Line-Of-Business App*, we cover how to leverage GitHub wikis to store your artifacts.

Later in this chapter, we will go over how to develop a roadmap and a technique to define your scope, building on the roadmap-building techniques covered in the *Planning using Kanban and GitHub projects* section.

Designing with lazy loading in mind

Your first paint matters a lot! According to Google Analytics data from the Angular team in 2018, 53% of mobile users abandoned a website when load times exceeded 3 seconds. During the same period, most websites were consumed on mobile devices – around 70% in the US and 90% in China. UI libraries and static assets can add significant size to your application. Since most content is consumed on mobile, it's very important to defer the loading of non-critical assets.

We defer the loading of assets by divvying up the parts of our Angular application into feature modules. This way, Angular can load only the assets necessary to render the current screen and dynamically download further resources as needed. You can start thinking about ways to divide your application into feature modules by defining the various user roles your application may use. User roles normally indicate a user's job function, such as a manager or data-entry specialist. In technical terms, they can be thought of as a group of actions a particular user role can execute. After all, a data-entry specialist won't ever see most of the screens a manager can, so why deliver those assets to those users and slow down their experience?

A more definitive strategy to divide your application would be by business function. You can think of each job function as a sub-module of your application. Following the principle of low coupling and high cohesion, you would want to group related functionality into modules that can be lazily loaded. This way, as users execute a task within a business function, they're not interrupted by delays. However, as the user switches from one business function to another, we can load the new module, and a slight delay would be acceptable.

You can set a preloading strategy to eagerly load all modules in the background as the user interacts with your app. This would eliminate any transition delay.

For more information, see `https://angular.dev/guide/ngmodules/lazy-loading#preloading`.

Lazy loading is critical in creating a scalable application architecture, allowing you to deliver high-quality and efficient products. Lazy loading is a low-hanging fruit we will tackle as a baseline design goal. It can be costly to implement lazy loading after the fact.

It is also possible to lazy load individual standalone components. Standalone components do not require all the bootstrapping that an Angular application requires.

You can read more about these components in detail at `https://angular.io/guide/standalone-components#lazy-loading-a-standalone-component`.

Later in this chapter, you will learn how to implement lazy loading using feature modules.

Implementing a walking skeleton

Configuring lazy loading can be tricky, so it is essential to nail down a walking-skeleton navigation experience early on. Implementing a clickable version of your app will help you gather feedback from users early on. That way, you'll be able to work out fundamental workflow and integration issues quickly. Additionally, you'll be able to establish a concrete representation of the scope of your current development effort. Developers and stakeholders alike will be able to visualize better how the product will look.

A walking skeleton also sets the stage for multiple teams to work together. Multiple people can start developing different feature modules or components simultaneously without worrying about how the puzzle pieces will come together later. By the end of this chapter, you will have completed implementing the walking skeleton of the sample app LemonMart.

Achieve a stateless, data-driven design

As highlighted in *Chapter 5, Designing Authentication and Authorization*, stateless design in full-stack architecture is critical to implementing a maintainable application. As covered in *Chapter 1, Angular's Architecture and Concepts*, and later in *Chapter 9, Recipes – Master/Detail, Data Tables, and NgRx*, the flux pattern and NgRx make it possible to achieve an immutable state for your application. However, the flux pattern is likely to be overkill for most applications. NgRx itself leverages a lot of the core technologies present in RxJS.

We will use RxJS and the reactive programming paradigm to implement a minimal, stateless, and data-driven pattern for our application. Identifying major data entities, such as invoices or people, that your users will work with will help you avoid over-engineering your application. Designing around major data entities will inform API design early on and help define the `BehaviorSubject` data anchors you will use to achieve a stateless, data-driven design. That design will, in turn, ensure a decoupled component architecture, as detailed in *Chapter 2, Forms, Observables, Signals, and Subjects*.

By defining observable data anchors, you can ensure that data across various components will be kept in sync. We can implement immutable data streams by writing functional reactive code, leveraging RxJS features, and not storing state in components.

We will cover how to design the data models for your application in *Chapter 5, Designing Authentication and Authorization*, and will continue using these models in the following chapters.

Enforce a decoupled component architecture

As discussed in *Chapter 1, Angular's Architecture and Concepts*, decoupling components of your architecture is critical in ensuring a maintainable codebase. You can decouple components in Angular by leveraging `@Input` and `@Output` bindings and router orchestration.

Bindings will help you maintain a simple hierarchy of components and avoid using dynamic templates in situations where static designs are more effective, such as creating multi-page forms.

Router outlets and auxiliary paths allow you to compose your view using the router. Resolvers can help load data by consuming router parameters. Auth guards can help control access to various modules and components. Using router links, you can dynamically customize elements that a user will see in an immutable and predictable way, like the way we designed and developed data anchors in the previous step.

If you ensure every component is responsible for loading its data, then you can compose components via URLs. However, overusing the router can become an anti-pattern. If a parent component logically owns a child component, then the effort to decouple them will be wasted.

In *Chapter 2, Forms, Observables, Signals, and Subjects*, you learned how to enable component interactions using `BehaviorSubject` and `Signals`. In *Chapter 8, Recipes – Reusability, Forms, and Caching*, you will learn how to implement `@Input` and `@Output` bindings, and in the upcoming chapters, you will learn how to implement router features.

Differentiate between user controls and components

Another important idea is differentiating user controls from components. A user control is like a custom date input or star rater. It is often highly interactive and dynamic code that is highly coupled, convoluted, and complicated. Such controls may utilize rarely used Angular APIs, like `NgZone`, `Renderer2`, `ViewContainerRef`, or `DynamicComponentLoaders`. These highly specialized and specific APIs are out of the scope of this book.

A component is more like a form with fields, which may contain simple date inputs or a star rater. Because forms encapsulate business functionality, their code must be easily read and understood. Your code should stick to Angular fundamentals so it is stable and easy to maintain, like most of the code in this book.

By differentiating between user controls and components, you can make better decisions when deciding what kind of reusable code you want to make. Creating reusable code is costly. If you create the right reusable code, you can save time and resources. If you create the wrong reusable code, then you can waste a lot of time and resources.

Wireframing allows you to identify reusable elements early on. User controls will help keep user interaction code separate from business logic. Well-crafted component reuse will enable you to encapsulate domain-specific behavior and share it later.

It's important to identify self-contained user controls that encapsulate unique behaviors you wish to create for your app. User controls will likely be created as directives or components with data-binding properties and tightly coupled controller logic and templates.

Conversely, components leverage router lifecycle events to parse parameters and perform CRUD operations on data. Identifying these component reuses early on will create more flexible components that can be reused in multiple contexts (as orchestrated by the router), maximizing code reuse.

We will cover creating reusable components and user controls in *Chapter 8, Recipes – Reusability, Forms, and Caching*.

Maximize code reuse with TypeScript and ES

It's essential to remember the underlying features of the language you work with before considering the features offered by Angular, RxJS, and all the libraries you use. There are decades of software engineering fundamentals that you can leverage to write readable and maintainable code.

First and foremost is the DRY principle, which stands for don't repeat yourself. So, don't copy-paste code. Don't just change a variable or two. Proactively refactor your code to make your functions stateless and reusable. In a few words: don't repeat yourself, don't repeat yourself, and don't repeat yourself.

Leverage object-oriented design. Move behavior to classes; if the `person` class has a `fullName` property, don't re-implement the logic of assembling a full name in a dozen different places. Implement it once in the `person` class.

This means you will need to become familiar with hydration, essentially injecting a JSON object into a newly instantiated class and serialization using `toJSON`. It is important not to abuse OOP. You should remain stateless and functional by avoiding storing state in class parameters.

You can unleash the power of object-oriented design by leveraging generics, inheritance, and abstract classes. We will go over concrete examples of these techniques later in the book.

TypeScript introduces the concept of interfaces to JavaScript. Interfaces are a concept mostly reserved for statically typed languages. An interface represents an abstract notion of what an object can do without specifying implementation details. Furthermore, an interface can be used to document the shape of data. For example, you can write a partial interface of a third-party API to document the fields you're interested in consuming. When other developers read your code, they understand the structure of the data they're consuming without having to read the documentation on another website.

Interfaces also allow you to morph the shape of your data in a well-defined manner. So, you can write a transform function to transform the shape of external data into internal data. TypeScript will catch any errors you may make. Taking this concept further, you can also use interfaces to flatten data. If the data you receive has a multi-entity relational structure, you can flatten the relationship to decouple the data design from your UI code.

Don't overly flatten your data. Arrays and simple shapes for common objects are okay, such as a `name` object (with `first`, `middle`, `last`, `prefix`, and `suffix` properties) or commonly used domain-specific objects.

You should also avoid using string literals in your code. Writing business logic where you compare `'apples' !== 'Oranges'` results in unmaintainable code. You should leverage `enums` in TypeScript, so your code isn't subject to the spelling mistakes of coders or changing business requirements. So, `'oranges' === Fruit.Oranges`.

Beyond TypeScript and ECMAScript, Angular also offers helpful functions to reuse logic. Angular validators, pipes, route resolvers, and route guards allow you to share code across components and templates.

Summary

This chapter taught you what it takes to succeed as a technical lead or an architect. You learned about the ingredients of running a successful project. We went over why Angular is a great fit for an enterprise. Then we dove into various tools and features to consider for building a high-performance solution. You learned how to create a Kanban board and became familiar with the 80-20 rule and the router-first architecture method to tackle complicated projects.

In the next chapter, you will be creating a far more complicated **LOB** application, using a router-first approach to designing and architecting scalable Angular applications with first-class authentication and authorization, user experience, and numerous recipes that cover a vast majority of requirements that you may find in LOB applications.

Further reading

- Analog, the full-stack Angular meta-framework: `https://analogjs.org/`
- Manifesto for Agile Software Development: `https://agilemanifesto.org`
- DevOps Research and Assessment (DORA) research program: `https://dora.dev/`
- DORA capability catalog: `https://dora.dev/devops-capabilities`
- What is Scrum and how to get started, Atlassian, 2023: `https://www.atlassian.com/agile/scrum`
- How to Have a Successful Agile Project with Transient Teams, Nicole Spence-Goon, December 14, 2021: `https://www.excella.com/insights/successful-agile-project-with-transient-teams`
- *Ha, Not Ready to Ri: The Shu Ha Ri Approach to Agile Development*, Brian Sjoberg and Ken Furlong, July 29, 2015: `https://www.excella.com/insights/ha-not-ready-to-ri-the-shu-ha-ri-approach-to-agile-development`
- *Nx: Smart, Fast Extensible Build System:* `https://nx.dev`
- *RxAngular: Performance & DX:* `https://www.rx-angular.io`
- Webpack module bundler: `https://webpack.js.org/`

Questions

Answer the following questions as best as possible to ensure you've understood the key concepts from this chapter without googling anything. Do you know if you got all the answers right? Visit `https://angularforenterprise.com/self-assessment` for more:

1. What three things should you do to succeed as a technical lead or architect?
2. What are the ingredients of a successful project?
3. Why should you use Angular in your enterprise?
4. What are the most important considerations for building Angular apps for your enterprise?
5. What causes performance issues in web applications?
6. How can we solve performance issues in large web applications?
7. What is an LOB app?
8. What is the Pareto principle?
9. What are the main goals of the router-first architecture?

Join our community on Discord

Join our community's Discord space for discussions with the authors and other readers:

`https://packt.link/AngularEnterpise3e`

4

Creating a Router-First Line-of-Business App

As you read in *Chapter 3, Architecting an Enterprise App*, **Line-of-Business** (**LOB**) applications are the bread and butter of the software development world.

In this and the remaining chapters of the book, we'll set up a new application with rich features that can meet the demands of an LOB application with scalable architecture and engineering best practices that will help you start small and be able to grow your solution quickly if there's demand. We will follow the router-first design pattern, relying on reusable components to create a grocery store LOB application named LemonMart. We'll discuss designing around major data entities and the importance of completing high-level mock-ups for your application before implementing various conditional navigation elements, which may change significantly during the design phase.

The source code for this project is provided on GitHub at `https://github.com/duluca/lemon-mart`, including various stages of development in the `Projects` folder. The project is supported by unit tests using Jasmine and E2E tests using Cypress, environment variables, Angular Material, and a **Continuous Integration and Continuous Delivery** (**CI/CD**) pipeline leveraging CircleCI. You can find more information on CI/CD in *Chapter 10, Releasing to Production with CI/CD*.

LemonMart is a separate Angular repo. For enterprise or full-stack development, you may ask, why is it not configured as a monorepo? In *Chapter 5, Designing Authentication and Authorization*, we cover how to create a monorepo using Git's submodule feature. For a more opinionated and ergonomic approach to working on large Angular applications, I urge you to consider Nx. Its smart build system alone can save hours of build time. Check it out at `https://nx.dev`. However, a deep dive of this tool is outside the scope of this book.

Feeling adventurous? Run the following command to create your Nx workspace:

```
$ npx create-nx-workspace
```

In this chapter, we're going to cover the following topics:

- Creating LemonMart
- Generating router-enabled modules
- Branding, customization, and Material icons
- Feature modules with lazy loading
- Creating the walking skeleton
- Common testing module
- Designing around major data entities
- High-level UX design

In *Chapters 5* to *9*, we will evolve LemonMart to demonstrate the aforementioned concepts.

Technical requirements

The most up-to-date versions of the sample code for the book are on GitHub at the following linked repository. The repository contains the final and completed state of the code. You can verify your progress at the end of this chapter by looking for the end-of-chapter snapshot of code under the `projects` folder.

For *Chapter 4*:

1. Clone the repo: `https://github.com/duluca/lemon-mart`.
2. Execute `npm install` on the root folder to install dependencies.
3. The end state of the project is reflected at:

   ```
   projects/stage7
   ```

4. Add the stage name to any `ng` command to act only on that stage:

   ```
   npx ng build stage7
   ```

Note that the `dist/stage7` folder at the root of the repository will contain the compiled result.

Beware that the source code provided in the book and the version on GitHub are likely to be different. The ecosystem around these projects is ever-evolving. Between changes to how the Angular CLI generates new code, bug fixes, new versions of libraries, or side-by-side implementations of multiple techniques, there's a lot of variation that's impossible to account for. If you find errors or have questions, please create an issue, or submit a pull request on GitHub.

Read more about updating Angular in the supplemental guide *Keeping Angular and Tools Evergreen* at `https://angularforenterprise.com/evergreen`.

Next, let's start by creating LemonMart™, a fully featured LOB app you can use as a template to kickstart your next professional project. LemonMart is a robust and realistic project that can support feature growth and different backend implementations, and it comes with a complete and configurable authentication and authorization solution out of the box.

Since its introduction in 2018, LemonMart has served over 257,000 lemons to more than 32,500 developers. Zesty!

You can always clone the finished project from GitHub, `https://www.github.com/duluca/lemon-mart`, whenever needed. Let's jump right into it.

Creating LemonMart

LemonMart will be a mid-sized line-of-business application with over 90 code files. We will start our journey by creating a new Angular app, with routing and Angular Material configured.

It is presumed that you have installed all the requisite software mentioned in *Appendix A, Setting Up Your Development Environment*. If you have not, execute the following commands for your OS to configure your environment.

On Windows PowerShell, execute:

```
PS> Install-Script -Name setup-windows-dev-env
PS> setup-windows-dev-env.ps1
```

On macOS Terminal, execute:

```
$> bash <(wget -O - https://git.io/JvHi1)
```

For more information, refer to `https://github.com/duluca/web-dev-environment-setup`.

Creating a router-first app

We will create LemonMart as a standalone project, which means a root module is not required to bootstrap the application, and all components created within the application will be configured as a standalone component. We will implement a modular architecture using lazy-loaded feature modules and selectively use lazy-loaded standalone components for components shared across feature modules. With the router-first approach, we want to enable routing early on in our application:

1. You can create the new application, with routing already configured, by executing this command:

```
$ npm create @angular
(Enter project name)
(select SCSS)
(respond no to SSR)
```

2. A new `app.routes.ts` file has been created for us:

   src/app/app.routes.ts

   ```
   import { Routes } from '@angular/router'

   export const routes: Routes = []
   ```

   We will be defining `routes` inside the routes array.

3. Observe that the `routes` are provided in `app.config.ts`, as shown:

   src/app/app.config.ts

   ```
   import { ApplicationConfig } from '@angular/core';
   import { provideRouter } from '@angular/router';

   import { routes } from './app.routes';

   export const appConfig: ApplicationConfig = {
     providers: [provideRouter(routes) ]
   };
   ```

4. Ultimately, `ApplicationConfig` is consumed by `bootstrapApplication` in `main.ts`, which kicks off the application bootstrap process:

   src/main.ts

   ```
   import { bootstrapApplication } from '@angular/platform-browser';
   import { appConfig } from './app/app.config';
   import { AppComponent } from './app/app.component';

   bootstrapApplication(AppComponent, appConfig)
     .catch((err) => console.error(err));
   ```

5. Execute your project by running `npm start`.

Configuring Angular and VS Code

Apply the following configuration steps to your project using `mrm`, a command-line tool to help keep configuration files in projects in sync:

The following scripts do not require you to use VS Code. If you wish to use another IDE like WebStorm, the `npm` scripts that are configured will run equally well.

You can read more about `mrm` at `https://mrm.js.org/docs/getting-started`.

1. Apply the Angular VS Code configuration:

```
npx mrm angular-vscode
```

2. Apply the `npm` scripts for the Docker configuration:

```
npx mrm npm-docker
```

3. Implement an `npm` script to build your application in production mode named `build:prod`:

```
"scripts": {
  ...,
  "build:prod": "ng build --configuration production",
}
```

By default, Angular will build your code in production mode. However, this behavior can be changed in `angular.json`. For this reason, I prefer to explicitly request a production build for code that's intended to be shipped, to avoid mistakes.

These settings are continually tweaked to adapt to the ever-evolving landscape of extensions, plug-ins, Angular, and VS Code. Alternatively, you can use the Angular Evergreen extension for VS Code to run the configuration commands with one click.

Note that if the preceding configuration scripts fail to execute, the following `npm` scripts will also fail. In this case, you have two options: revert your changes and ignore these scripts, or manually implement these scripts as covered in earlier chapters (or as demonstrated on GitHub).

4. Execute `npm run style:fix`.
5. Execute `npm run lint:fix`.
6. Execute `npm start`.

Refer to *Appendix A, Setting Up Your Development Environment*, for further configuration details.

For more information on the `mrm` tasks, refer to:

- `https://github.com/expertly-simple/mrm-task-angular-vscode`
- `https://github.com/expertly-simple/mrm-task-npm-docker`
- `https://github.com/expertly-simple/mrm-task-npm-aws`

Configuring Angular Material and styles

Several years ago, it was a necessary practice to apply a reset or normalize CSS stylesheet to themed projects to account for discrepancies in how browsers handled layout or spacing. However, current browsers are more faithful to the CSS specification, so a legacy reset stylesheet can be overkill. Below, I implement `styles.scss` with reset parameters like `body { margin: 0 }` and `html, body { height: 100% }`.

If you want to check out a modern version of a normalize stylesheet, I recommend `https://github.com/sindresorhus/modern-normalize`. It's easy to set up and works seamlessly when imported in `styles.scss`.

We will also need to set up Angular Material and configure a theme to use:

1. Install Angular Material:

```
$ npx ng add @angular/material
(select Custom, No to global typography, Yes to browser animations)
$ npm i @ngbracket/ngx-layout
```

Note that since this is a standalone project, we will need to import the required Material modules and `FlexModule` on each individual component that requires it. When the `@ngbracket/ngx-layout` package implements a root-level provider, adding `FlexModule` manually won't be needed anymore.

2. Append common CSS to `styles.scss` as shown in the following code:

`src/styles.scss`

```
...
html, body { height: 100%; }
body { margin: 0; font-family: Roboto, 'Helvetica Neue',
  sans-serif; }

.top-pad { margin-top: 16px; }
.h-pad { margin: 0 16px; }
.v-pad { margin: 16px 0; }
.left-pad { margin-left: 8px; }
.flex-spacer { flex: 1 1 auto; }
```

3. Update your application's title in `index.html`.

We will apply custom branding to the app later in this chapter. Next, let's start designing our line-of-business application.

Designing LemonMart

It is important to build a rudimentary roadmap to follow, from the database to the frontend, while also avoiding over-engineering. This initial design phase is critical to the long-term health and success of your project, where any existing silos between teams must be broken down and an overall technical vision must be well understood by all members of the team. This is easier said than done, and there are volumes of books written on the topic.

In engineering, there's no right answer to a problem, so it is important to remember that no person can ever have all the answers or a crystal-clear vision. It is important that technical and non-technical leaders create a safe space with opportunities for open discussion and experimentation as part of the culture. The humility and empathy that come along with being able to court such uncertainty as a team is as important as any single team member's technical capability. Every team member must be comfortable leaving their egos at the door because our collective goal will be to grow and evolve an application to ever-changing requirements during the development cycle. You will know that you have succeeded if individual parts of the software you created are easily replaceable by anyone.

So, let's start by developing a roadmap and identifying the scope of our application. For this, we will be defining user roles and then building a site map to create a vision of how our app might work.

Identifying user roles

The first step of our design will be to think about who is using the application and why.

We envision four user states, or roles, for LemonMart:

- **Authenticated**: any authenticated user would have access to their profile
- **Cashier**, whose sole role is to check out customers
- **Clerk**, whose sole role is to perform inventory-related functions
- **Manager**, who can perform all actions a cashier and a clerk can perform but also has access to administrative functions

With this in mind, we can start to create a high-level design for our app.

Identifying high-level modules with a site map

Develop a high-level site map of your application, as shown in the following image:

Landing/Login Page

Manager

Inventory

Point of Sale (POS)

User Profile

Figure 4.1: Landing pages for users

I used MockFlow.com's SiteMap tool to create the site map shown: `https://sitemap.mockflow.com`.

Upon first examination, three high-level modules emerge as lazy-loading candidates:

- **Point of Sale (POS)**
- **Inventory**
- **Manager**

The cashier will only have access to the **POS** module and component. The clerk will only have access to the **Inventory** module, which will include additional screens for the **Stock Entry**, **Products**, and **Categories** management components:

Figure 4.2: Inventory pages

Finally, the **Manager** will be able to access all three modules with the **Manager** module, including user management and receipt lookup components:

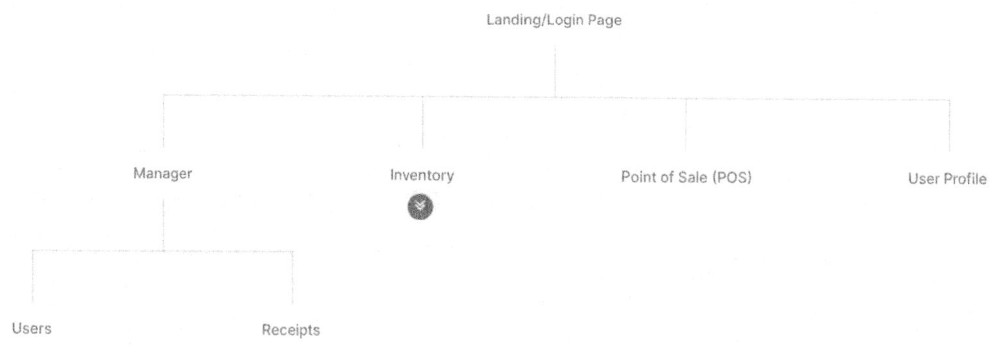

Figure 4.3: Manager pages

There will be great benefits from enabling lazy loading for all three modules; since Cashiers and Clerks will never use components belonging to other user roles, there's no reason to send those bytes down to their devices. As the **Manager** module gains more advanced reporting features or new roles are added to the application, the **POS** module will be unaffected by the bandwidth and memory impact of an otherwise growing application.

This means fewer support calls and consistent performance on the same hardware for much longer.

Generating router-enabled modules

Now that we have our high-level components defined as **Manager**, **Inventory**, and **POS**, we can define them as modules. These modules will be different from the ones you've created for routing and Angular Material. We can create the user profile as a component on the app module; however, note that the user profile will only ever be used for already-authenticated users, so it makes sense to define a fourth module only meant for authenticated users in general. This way, you will ensure that your app's first payload remains as minimal as possible. In addition, we will create a `home` component to contain the landing experience for our app so that we can keep implementation details out of `app.component`:

1. Generate `manager`, `inventory`, `pos`, and `user` feature modules by specifying their names and routing capabilities:

```
$ npx ng g m manager --routing
$ npx ng g m inventory --routing
$ npx ng g m pos --routing
$ npx ng g m user --routing
```

Note the abbreviated command structure, where `ng generate module manager` becomes `ng g m manager`, and similarly, `--module` becomes `-m`.

2. Verify that you don't have CLI errors.

Note that using `npx` on Windows may throw an error such as `Path must be a string. Received undefined`. This error doesn't seem to affect the successful operation of the command, which is why it is critical always to inspect what the CLI tool generates.

3. Verify that the folder and the files are created:

```
/src/app
│   app.component.scss
│   app.component.html
│   app.component.spec.ts
│   app.component.ts
│   app.config.ts
```

```
|   app.routes.ts
├──inventory
|      inventory-routing.module.ts
|      inventory.module.ts
├──manager
|      manager-routing.module.ts
|      manager.module.ts
├──pos
|      pos-routing.module.ts
|      pos.module.ts
└──user
|      user-routing.module.ts
|      user.module.ts
```

Let's examine how `ManagerModule` has been configured. Remember that a feature module is decorated by the `@NgModule` annotation. In Angular apps configured with a root `NgModule`, you'll notice that it implements the `bootstrap` property, whereas a feature module does not implement this. See the generated code below:

src/app/manager/manager.module.ts

```
import { NgModule } from '@angular/core'
import { CommonModule } from '@angular/common'
import { ManagerRoutingModule } from './manager-routing.module'
@NgModule({
  imports: [CommonModule, ManagerRoutingModule],
  declarations: [],
})
export class ManagerModule {}
```

Since we specified the `--routing` option, a `routing` module has been created and imported into `ManagerModule`:

src/app/manager/manager-routing.module.ts

```
import { NgModule } from '@angular/core'
import { Routes, RouterModule } from '@angular/router'
const routes: Routes = []
@NgModule({
  imports: [RouterModule.forChild(routes)],
```

```
  exports: [RouterModule],
})
export class ManagerRoutingModule {}
```

Note that `RouterModule` is being configured using `forChild`, as opposed to the optional `forRoot` method, either configured in an `AppRouting` module or a router provider in `ApplicationConfig`. By specifying the context, we allow the router to understand the proper relationship between routes defined in different module contexts. For example, all child routes defined in `ManagerRoutingModule` will be prepended by the route segment `/manager`.

Be sure to execute `style` and `lint fix` commands before moving on:

```
$ npm run style:fix && npm run lint:fix
```

Now, let's design how the landing page for LemonMart will look and work.

Designing the home route

Consider the following mock-up as the landing experience for LemonMart:

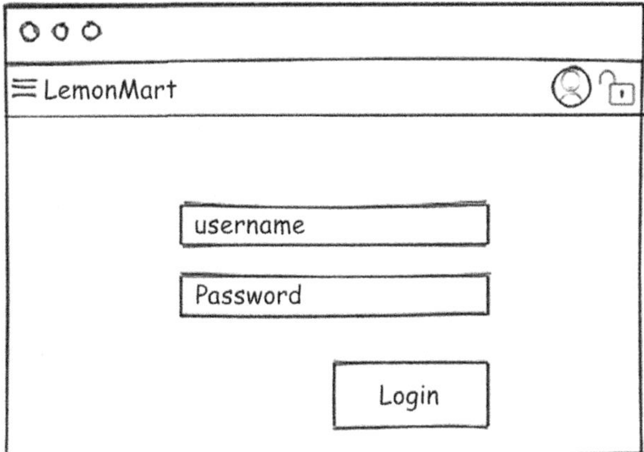

Figure 4.4: LemonMart landing experience

Unlike the LocalCast Weather app, we don't want a lot of layout markup in `AppComponent`. The `AppComponent` is the root element of your entire application; therefore, it should only contain elements that will persistently appear throughout your application. In the following annotated mock-up, the toolbar marked as **1** will be persistent throughout the app.

The area marked as **2** will house the `home` component, which itself will contain a login user control marked as **3**:

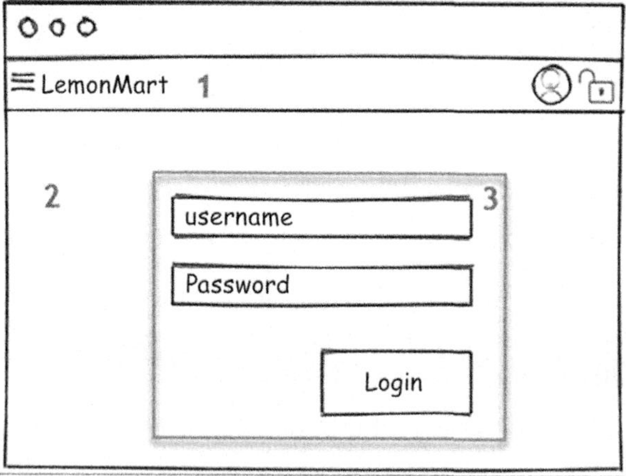

Figure 4.5: LemonMart layout structure

It's best practice to create your default or landing component as a separate element in Angular. This helps reduce the amount of code that must be loaded and logically executed on every page, but it also results in a more flexible architecture when utilizing the router.

Generate the `home` component with an inline template and styles:

```
$ npx ng g c home --inline-template --inline-style
```

> Note that a component with an inline template and a style is also called a **Single File Component** or an **SFC**.

Now, you are ready to configure the router.

Setting up default routes

Let's get started with setting up a simple route for LemonMart. We need to set up the `/` route (also known as the empty route) and the `/home` route to display the `HomeComponent`. We also need a wildcard route to capture all undefined routes and display a `PageNotFoundComponent`, which must also be created:

src/app/app.routes.ts

```
...
```

```
import { HomeComponent } from './home/home.component'
import {
  PageNotFoundComponent
} from './page-not-found/page-not-found.component'

const routes: Routes = [
  { path: '', redirectTo: 'home', pathMatch: 'full' },
  { path: 'home', component: HomeComponent },
  { path: '**', component: PageNotFoundComponent },
]
...
```

Let's put together the route configuration above step by step:

1. Define a path for `'home'` and direct the router to render `HomeComponent` by setting the `component` property.
2. Set the default path of the application `''` to be redirected to `'/home'`. By setting the `pathMatch` property, we always ensure that this specific instance of the home route will be rendered as the landing experience; otherwise, in its default prefix setting, `pathMatch` considers an empty path to be a prefix of all routes, resulting in an endless redirect loop.
3. Create a `pageNotFound` component with an inline template.
4. Configure a wildcard route for `PageNotFoundComponent` as the last entry.

By configuring the wildcard route as the last entry, we handle any route that is not matched gracefully by redirecting it to `PageNotFoundComponent`. The wildcard path must be the last property in the array; otherwise, routes defined after will not be considered.

RouterLink

When a user lands on the `PageNotFoundComponent`, we would like them to be able to get back to the `HomeComponent` using the `routerLink` directive:

On `PageNotFoundComponent`, replace the inline template to link back to home using `routerLink`:

```
src/app/page-not-found/page-not-found.component.ts
...
  template: `
    <p>
      This page doesn't exist. Go back to
```

```
    <a routerLink="/home">home</a>.
  </p>
`,
...
```

This navigation can also be done via an `<a href>` tag implementation; however, in more dynamic and complicated navigation scenarios, you will lose features such as automatic active link tracking or dynamic link generation.

The Angular bootstrap process will ensure that `AppComponent` is inside the `<app-root>` element in `index.html`. However, we must manually define where we would like `HomeComponent` to render to finalize the router configuration.

Router outlet

`AppComponent` is considered a root element for the root router defined in `app-routes.ts`, which allows us to define outlets within this root element to dynamically load any content we wish using the `<router-outlet>` element:

1. Configure `AppComponent` to use inline templates and styles, deleting any existing content in the `html` and `scss` file.
2. Add the toolbar for your application.
3. Add the name of your application as a button link so that it takes the user to the home page when clicked on.
4. Import `RouterLink`, `RouterOutlet`, and `MatToolbarModule` in the component.
5. Add `<router-outlet>` for the content to render:

```
src/app/app.component.ts
...
template: `
  <mat-toolbar color="primary">
    <a mat-button routerLink="/home"><h1>LemonMart</h1></a>
  </mat-toolbar>
  <router-outlet></router-outlet>
`,
```

Now, the contents of `home` will render inside `<router-outlet>`.

Branding, customization, and Material icons

To construct an attractive and intuitive toolbar, we must introduce some iconography and branding to the app so that the users can easily navigate through the app with the help of familiar icons.

Branding

In terms of branding, you should ensure that your web app has a custom color palette and integrates with desktop and mobile browser features to bring forward your app's name and iconography.

Color palette

Pick a color palette using the **Material Color** tool, located at `https://m2.material.io/design/color/the-color-system.html#tools-for-picking-colors`. For LemonMart, I picked the following values:

1. **Primary Color**- `#2E7D32`:

   ```
   $lemon-mart-primary: mat.define-palette(mat.$green-palette, 800);
   ```

2. **Secondary Color**- `#C6FF00`:

   ```
   $lemon-mart-accent: mat.define-palette(mat.$lime-palette, A400);
   ```

   You may either implement your theme in `styles.scss` or create a separate theme file. A separate file is useful if you intend to further customize individual components.

3. Add a file named `lemonmart-theme.scss`
4. Move theme-related CSS from `styles.scss` over to the new file. Theme-related content will be above the following line:

   styles.scss
   ```
   ...
   /* You can add global styles to this file and also import other
   style files */
   ...
   ```

5. Update `styles.scss` to include the new theme in the first line of the file:

   styles.scss
   ```
   @use 'lemonmart-theme';
   ...
   ```

6. Configure your custom theme with the chosen color palette.

You can also grab LemonMart-related assets from GitHub at https://github.com/duluca/lemon-mart.

For the LocalCast Weather app, we replaced the `favicon.ico` file to brand our app in the browser. While this would've been enough 10 years ago, today's devices vary wildly, and each platform can leverage optimized assets better to represent your web app within its operating system. Next, let's implement a more robust favicon.

Implementing a browser manifest and icons

You must ensure the browser shows the correct title text and icon in a **Browser** tab. Further, a manifest file should be created that implements specific icons for various mobile operating systems so that if a user pins your website, a desirable icon is displayed similarly to other app icons on the phone. This will ensure that if a user favorites or pins your web app on their mobile device's home screen, they'll get a native-looking app icon:

1. Create or obtain an SVG version of your website's logo from a designer or a site like https://www.flaticon.com.
2. In this case, I will be using the likeness of the Eureka lemon:

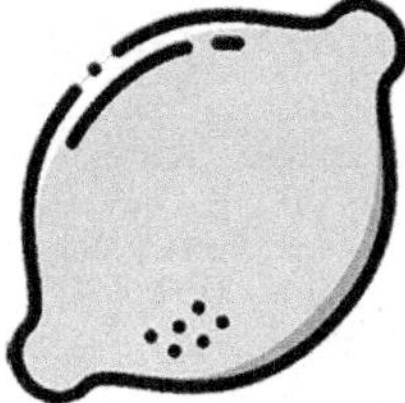

Figure 4.6: LemonMart's signature logo

When using images you find online, pay attention to applicable copyrights. In this case, I have purchased a license to be able to publish this lemon logo, but you may grab your own copy at the following URL, given that you provide the required attribution to the author of the image: https://www.flaticon.com/free-icon/lemon_605070.

3. Generate the `favicon.ico` and manifest files using a tool such as https://realfavicongenerator.net.

4. Adjust settings for iOS, Android, Windows, and macOS Safari to your liking.
5. In the generator, be sure to set a version number, as favicons can be notorious for caching; a random version number will ensure that users always get the latest version.
6. Download and extract the generated `favicons.zip` file into your `src` folder.
7. Edit the `angular.json` file to include the new assets in your app:

```
angular.json
"apps": [
  {
  ...
    "assets": [
      "src/assets",
      "src/favicon.ico",
      "src/android-chrome-192x192.png",
      "src/favicon-16x16.png",
      "src/mstile-310x150.png",
      "src/android-chrome-512x512.png",
      "src/favicon-32x32.png",
      "src/mstile-310x310.png",
      "src/apple-touch-icon.png",
      "src/manifest.json",
      "src/mstile-70x70.png",
      "src/browserconfig.xml",
      "src/mstile-144x144.png",
      "src/safari-pinned-tab.svg",
      "src/mstile-150x150.png"
    ]
```

8. Insert the generated code in the `<head>` section of `index.html`:

```
src/index.html
<link rel="apple-touch-icon" sizes="180x180"
  href="/apple-touch- icon.png?v=rMlKOnvxlK">
<link rel="icon" type="image/png" sizes="32x32"
  href="/favicon-32x32.png?v=rMlKOnvxlK">
<link rel="icon" type="image/png" sizes="16x16"
  href="/favicon-16x16.png?v=rMlKOnvxlK">
<link rel="manifest" href="/manifest.json?v=rMlKOnvxlK">
```

```
<link rel="mask-icon"
  href="/safari-pinned-tab.svg?v=rMlKOnvxlK" color="#b3ad2d">
<link rel="shortcut icon" href="/favicon.ico?v=rMlKOnvxlK">
<meta name="theme-color" content="#ffffff">
```

Place the generated code between the favicon declaration and the CSS style imports. The order does matter. Browsers load data top-down. You want your application's icon to be parsed before the user must wait for CSS files to be downloaded.

9. Ensure that your new favicon displays correctly.

Once your basic branding work has been completed, consider whether you'd like to establish a more unique look and feel with theming.

Custom themes

You may further customize Material's look and feel to achieve a unique experience for your app by leveraging tools listed at `https://m2.material.io/resources` and some other tools that I have discovered, which are listed as follows:

- Material Design Theme Palette Generator will generate the necessary code to define your custom color palette to create truly unique themes at `http://mcg.mbitson.com`
- Color Blender helps with finding midway points between two colors, which is useful when defining in-between colors for the color swatches, located at `https://meyerweb.com/eric/tools/color-blend`

In 2021, Google announced **Material 3**, aka Material You, a dynamic theming system that adapts to user preferences around OS-level color use. In 2023, Angular Material is still based on Material 2. The Angular team transitioned to new **Material Design Components for Web** (**MDC**) style components in Angular 15 and will deprecate the old styles with Angular 17. The MDC-style components support adjustable density and are more dynamic as a result. After this milestone, the Angular team plans to tackle the implementation of Material You.

You can follow this thread for updates: `https://github.com/angular/components/issues/22738`.

There is a wealth of information at `https://material.io` on the in-depth philosophy behind the Material design, with great sections on things like the color system, `https://material.io/design/color/the-color-system.html`, which dives deep into selecting the right color palette for your brand and other topics, such as creating a dark theme for your app.

It is very important to distinguish your brand from other apps or your competitors. Creating a high-quality custom theme will be a time-consuming process; however, the benefits of creating a great first impression with your users are considerable.

Next, we will show you how to add custom icons to your Angular apps.

Custom icons

Now, let's add your custom branding to your Angular app. You will need the svg icon you used to create your favicon:

1. Place the image under `src/assets/img/icons`, named `lemon.svg`.
2. In `app.config.ts`, add `provideHttpClient()` as a provider so that the `.svg` file can be requested over HTTP.
3. Update `AppComponent` to register the new .svg file as an icon:

```
src/app/app.component.ts
import { MatIconRegistry } from '@angular/material/icon'
import { DomSanitizer } from '@angular/platform-browser'
...
export class AppComponent {
  constructor(
    iconRegistry: MatIconRegistry,
    sanitizer: DomSanitizer
  ) {
    iconRegistry.addSvgIcon(
      'lemon',
      sanitizer.bypassSecurityTrustResourceUrl(
        'assets/img/icons/lemon.svg'
      )
    )
  }
}
```

Beware that adding an svg icon from a URL resource doesn't work in a **Server-Side Rendering (SSR)** configuration. Instead, you can add your svg icon as a const string in a TypeScript file import and register it as shown below:

```
import { LEMON_ICON } from './svg.icons'iconRegistry.

addSvgIconLiteral('lemon', sanitizer.
bypassSecurityTrustHtml(LEMON_ICON))
```

4. Import MatIconModule.
5. Following the pattern in the documentation for MatToolbar, found at https://material.angular.io/components/toolbar, add the icon to the toolbar:

```
src/app/app.component.ts
template: `
  <mat-toolbar color="primary">
    <mat-icon svgIcon="lemon"></mat-icon>
    <a mat-button routerLink="/home"><h1>LemonMart</h1></a>
  </mat-toolbar>
  <router-outlet></router-outlet>
`,
```

Now, let's add the remaining icons for the menu, user profile, and logout.

Material icons

Angular Material works out of the box with the Material Design icon font, automatically imported into your app as a web font in index.html. It is possible to self-host the font; however, if you go down that path, you don't get the benefit if the user's browser has already cached the font from when they visited another website, which could save the speed and latency of downloading a 42-56 KB file in the process. The complete list of icons can be found at https://fonts.google.com/icons.

Now let's update the toolbar with some icons and set up the home page with a minimal template for a fake login button:

1. Ensure that the Material icons <link> tag has been added to index.html:

```
src/index.html
<head>
  ...
```

```
  <link href="https://fonts.googleapis.com icon?family=Material+Icons"
    rel="stylesheet">
</head>
```

Instructions on self-hosting can be found under the **Self Hosting** section at `http://google.github.io/material-design-icons/#getting-icons`.

Once configured, working with Material icons is easy.

2. On `AppComponent`, update the toolbar to place a **Menu** button to the left of the title.
3. Add the `fxFlex` directive so that the remaining icons are right-aligned.
4. Import `FlexModule` and `MatButtonModule`.
5. Add user profile and logout icons:

src/app/app.component.ts

```
template: `
  <mat-toolbar color="primary">
    <button mat-icon-button>
      <mat-icon>menu</mat-icon>
    </button>
    <mat-icon svgIcon="lemon"></mat-icon>
    <a mat-button routerLink="/home"><h1>LemonMart</h1></a>
    <span class="flex-spacer"></span>
    <button mat-icon-button>
      <mat-icon>account_circle</mat-icon>
    </button>
    <button mat-icon-button>
      <mat-icon>lock_open</mat-icon>
    </button>
  </mat-toolbar>
  <router-outlet></router-outlet>
`,
```

6. On `HomeComponent`, add a minimal template for a login experience, replacing any existing content. Don't forget to import `FlexModule` and `MatButtonModule`:

src/app/home/home.component.ts

```
  styles: [`
```

```
    div[fxLayout] {margin-top: 32px;}
  `],
  template: `
    <div fxLayout="column" fxLayoutAlign="center center">
      <span class="mat-display-2">Hello, Limoncu!</span>
      <button mat-raised-button color="primary">Login</button>
    </div>
  `
```

Your app should look similar to this screenshot:

Figure 4.7: LemonMart with minimal login

There's still some work to be done in terms of implementing and showing/hiding the menu, profile, and logout icons, given the user's authentication status. We will cover this functionality in *Chapter 7, Working with REST and GraphQL APIs*.

To debug the router, get a visualization of your routes, and tightly integrate Angular with Chrome debugging features, use Angular DevTools, available from Chrome Web Store (also compatible with Microsoft Edge) or Firefox add-ons at `https://angular.dev/tools/devtools`.

Now that you've set up basic routing for your app, we can move on to setting up lazily loaded modules with subcomponents. If you're unfamiliar with troubleshooting and debugging Angular, please refer to `https://angular.dev/tools/devtools` before moving forward.

Feature modules with lazy loading

There are two ways resources are loaded: eagerly or lazily. When the browser loads up `index.html` for your app, it starts processing it from top to bottom. First, the `<head>` element is processed, then `<body>`. For example, the CSS resources we defined in `<head>` of our app will be downloaded before our app is rendered because our Angular app is defined as `<script>` in `<body>` of the HTML file.

When you use the `ng build` command, Angular leverages the webpack module bundler to combine all the JavaScript, HTML, and CSS into minified and optimized JavaScript bundles.

If you don't leverage lazy loading in Angular, the entire contents of your app will be eagerly loaded. The user won't see the first screen of your app until all screens are downloaded and loaded.

Lazy loading allows the Angular build process, working in tandem with webpack, to separate your web application into different JavaScript files called chunks. We can enable this chunking by separating out portions of the application into feature modules. Feature modules and their dependencies can be bundled into separate chunks. Remember that the root module and its dependencies will always be in the first downloaded chunk. So, by chunking our application's JavaScript bundle size, we keep the size of the initial chunk at a minimum. With a minimal first chunk, no matter how big your application grows, the time to First Meaningful Paint remains constant. Otherwise, your app would take longer and longer to download and render as you add more features and functionality to it. Lazy loading is critical to achieving a scalable application architecture.

Consider the following graphic to determine which routes are eagerly loaded and which ones are lazily loaded:

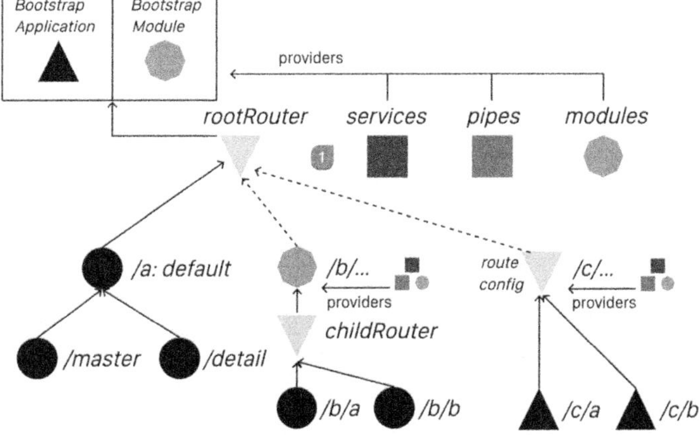

Figure 4.8: Angular router eager vs lazy loading

The black triangles are standalone components, and the black circles are components that depend on a module. `rootRouter` defines three routes: `a`, `b`, and `c`. `/master` and `/detail` represent named router outlets, which are covered in *Chapter 9, Recipes – Master/Detail, Data Tables, and NgRx*. Route `a` is the default route for the app. Routes `a` and `c` are connected to `rootRouter` with a solid line, whereas route `b` is connected using a dashed line. In this context, route `b` is configured as a lazy-loaded route. This means route `b` will dynamically load a feature module, `BModule`, containing `childRouter`. `childRouter` can define any number of components, even reusing route names that were reused elsewhere. In this case, `b` defines two additional routes: `/b/a` and `/b/b`.

Consider the example router definition for `rootRouter`:

rootRouter example

```
const routes: Routes = [
  { path: '', redirectTo: '/a', pathMatch: 'full' },
  {
    path: 'a',
    component: AComponent,
    children: [
      { path: '', component: MasterComponent, outlet: 'master' },
      { path: '', component: DetailComponent, outlet: 'detail' },
    ],
  },
  {
    path: 'b',
    loadChildren:
      () => import('./b/b.module')
        .then((module) => module.BModule),
    canLoad: [AuthGuard],
  },
  { path: 'c', loadChildren: () => import('./c/routes').then(mod => mod.C_
ROUTES)},},
  { path: '**', component: PageNotFoundComponent },
]
```

Note that the definitions for routes `/b/a`, `/b/b`, `/c/a`, and `/c/b` do not exist in `rootRouter`. See the example router definition for `childRouter`:

```
/b childRouter example
const routes: Routes = [
  { path: '', redirectTo: '/b/a', pathMatch: 'full' },
  { path: 'a', component: BAComponent },
  { path: 'b', component: BBComponent },
]
```

```
/c route config example
const routes: Routes = [
  { path: '', redirectTo: '/c/a', pathMatch: 'full' },
  { path: 'a', component: CAComponent },
  { path: 'b', component: CBComponent },
]
```

As you can see, the routes defined in `childRouter` are independent of the ones defined in `rootRouter`. Child routes exist in a hierarchy, where `/b` is the parent path. To navigate to `BAComponent`, you must use the path `/b/a`, and to navigate to `CAComponent`, you use `/c/a`.

Given this example configuration, every component defined in `rootRouter` and their dependencies would be in the first chunk of our app and thus eagerly loaded. The first chunk would include the components `A`, `Master`, `Detail`, and `PageNotFound`. The second chunk would contain the components `BA` and `BB`. This second chunk would not be downloaded or loaded until the user navigated to a path starting with `/b`; thus, it's lazily loaded. In a standalone configuration, this chunking can be granular at the component level.

I cover lazy loading standalone components in *Chapter 8, Recipes – Reusability, Forms, and Caching,* when we add shared components used across different modules.

You can read about it more in detail at `https://angular.io/guide/standalone-components#lazy-loading-a-standalone-component`.

We will now go over how to set up a feature module with components and routes. We will also use Angular DevTools to observe the effects of our various router configurations.

Configuring feature modules with components and routes

The manager module needs a landing page, as shown in this mock-up:

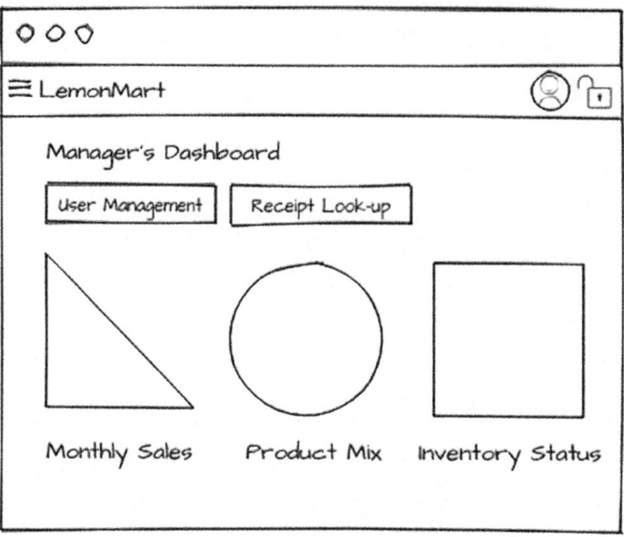

Figure 4.9: Manager's dashboard

Let's start by creating the home screen for `ManagerModule`:

1. Create the `ManagerHome` component:

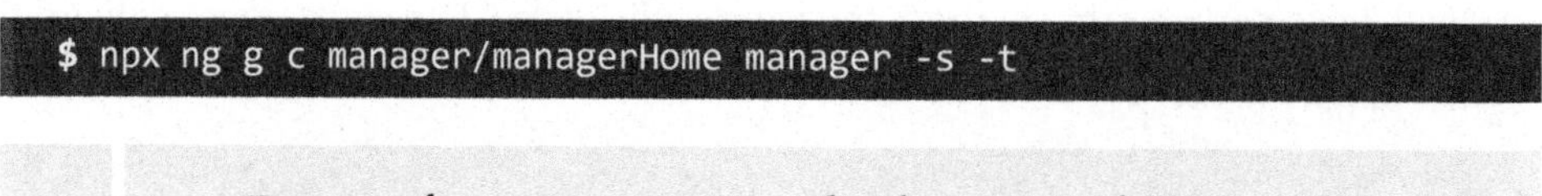

```
$ npx ng g c manager/managerHome manager -s -t
```

> To create the new component under the `manager` folder, we must prefix `manager/` before the component name. Since this is another landing page, it is unlikely to be complicated enough to require separate HTML and CSS files. You can use `--inline-style` (alias `-s`) and/or `--inline-template` (alias `-t`) to avoid creating additional files.

2. Verify that your folder structure looks as follows:

```
/src
├──app
| |
| ├──manager
| | | manager-routing.module.ts
| | | manager.module.ts
```

```
| | |
| | └──manager-home
| | | | manager-home.component.spec.ts
| | | | manager-home.component.ts
```

3. Configure the `ManagerHome` component's route in `manager-routing.module.ts`, similar to how we configured the `Home component` in `app.route.ts`:

   src/app/manager/manager-routing.module.ts

   ```
   import {
     ManagerHomeComponent
   } from './manager-home/manager-home.component'
   const routes: Routes = [
     { path: '', redirectTo: 'home', pathMatch: 'full' },
     { path: 'home', component: ManagerHomeComponent },
   ]
   ```

Note that `http://localhost:4200/manager` doesn't resolve to a component yet, because our Angular app isn't aware that `ManagerModule` exists. Eager-loading modules in a standalone project simply don't make sense; we will only consider the lazy loading of a feature module.

Next, let's implement lazy loading for `ManagerModule`, so Angular can navigate to it.

Lazy loading

Lazy loading code may seem like black magic (aka misunderstood) code. To load routes from a different module, we know we can't simply import them; otherwise, they will be eagerly loaded. The answer lies in configuring a route using the `loadChildren` attribute with an inline `import` statement informing the router how to load a feature module in `app.routes.ts`:

1. In `app.routes.ts`, implement or update the `'manager'` path with the `loadChildren` attribute:

   src/app/app.routes.ts

   ```
   import { Routes } from '@angular/router'
   import { HomeComponent } from './home/home.component'
   import { PageNotFoundComponent } from './page-not-found/page-not-
   found.component'

     const routes: Routes = [
       ...
   ```

```
      {
        path: 'manager',
        loadChildren:
          () => import('./manager/manager.module')
            . then(m=> m.ManagerModule),
      },
      ...
    ]
  ...
```

Lazy loading is achieved via a clever trick that avoids using an `import` statement at the file level. A function delegate is set to the `loadChildren` property, which contains an inline `import` statement defining the location of the feature module file, such as `./manager/manager.module`, allowing us to refer to `ManagerModule` in a type-safe manner without fully loading it. The inline `import` statement can be interpreted during the build process to create a separate JavaScript chunk that can be downloaded only when needed. `ManagerModule` is self-sufficient as a feature module; it manages all its child dependencies and routes.

2. Update the `manager-routing.module.ts` routes, considering that `manager` is now their root route:

src/app/manager/manager-routing.module.ts

```
const routes: Routes = [
  { path: '', redirectTo: 'home', pathMatch: 'full' },
  { path: 'home', component: ManagerHomeComponent },
]
```

We can now update the route for `ManagerHomeComponent` to a more meaningful `'home'` path. This path won't clash with the one found in `app.routes.ts` because, in this context, `'home'` resolves to `'manager/home'` and, similarly, where `path` is empty, the URL will look like `http://localhost:4200/manager`.

3. Restart your `ng serve` or `npm start` command, so Angular can chunk the app properly.
4. Navigate to `http://localhost:4200/manager`.
5. Confirm that lazy loading is working by observing the CLI output contains a new **Lazy Chunk Files** section:

```
Lazy Chunk Files               | Names          |  Raw Size |
src_app_manager_module_ts.js| manager-module | 358.75 kB |
```

We have successfully set up a feature module with lazy loading. Next, let's implement the walking skeleton for LemonMart.

Creating the walking skeleton

Using the site map we created for LemonMart earlier in the chapter, we need to create the walking skeleton navigation experience for the app. To create this experience, we must create some buttons to link all modules and components together. We will go at this module by module.

Before we start, update the `Login` button on `HomeComponent` to navigate to the `'manager'` path using the `routerLink` attribute and rename the button:

src/app/home/home.component.ts

```
...
<button mat-raised-button color="primary" routerLink="/manager">
  Login as Manager
</button>
...
```

Now, we can navigate to the `ManagerHome` component by clicking on the **Login** button.

The manager module

Since we already enabled lazy loading for `ManagerModule`, let's go ahead and complete the rest of the navigational elements for it.

In the current setup, `ManagerHomeComponent` renders in `<router-outlet>` defined in `AppComponent's` template, so when the user navigates from `HomeComponent` to `ManagerHomeComponent`, the toolbar implemented in `AppComponent` remains in place. See the following mock-up for **Manager's Dashboard**:

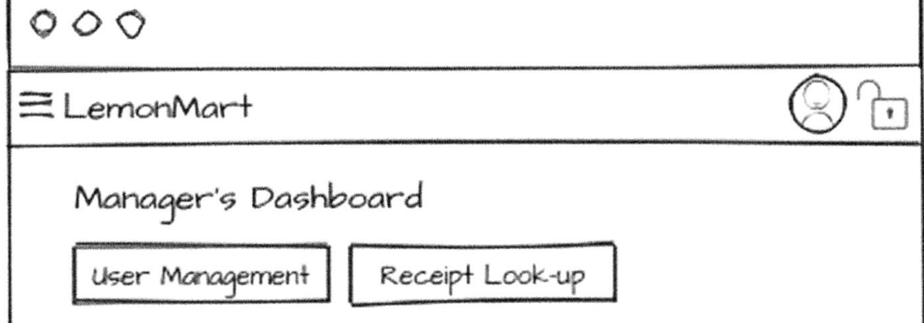

Figure 4.10: App-wide and feature module toolbars

The app-wide toolbar remains in place no matter where we navigate to. Imagine that we can implement a similar toolbar for the feature module that persists throughout `ManagerModule`. So, the navigational **User Management** and **Receipt Look-up** buttons would always be visible. This allows us to create a consistent UX for navigating subpages across modules.

To implement a secondary toolbar, we need to replicate the parent-child relationship between `AppComponent` and `HomeComponent`, where the parent implements the toolbar and `<router-outlet>` so that child elements can be rendered in there:

1. Start by creating the base `manager` component:

```
$ npx ng g c manager/manager --flat -s -t
```

The `--flat` option skips directory creation and places the component directly under the `manager` folder, just like `AppComponent` residing directly under the app folder.

2. In `ManagerComponent`, implement a navigational toolbar with `activeLink` tracking:

src/app/manager/manager.component.ts

```
styles: `
  div[fxLayout] {
    margin-top: 32px;
  }
  .active-link {
    font-weight: bold;
    border-bottom: 2px solid #005005;
  }
`,
  template: `
    <mat-toolbar color="accent" fxLayoutGap="8px">
      <a mat-button routerLink="home" routerLinkActive="active-link">
        Manager's Dashboard
      </a>
      <a mat-button routerLink="users" routerLinkActive="active-link">
        User Management
      </a>
      <a mat-button routerLink="receipts"
        routerLinkActive="active- link">
        Receipt Lookup
```

```
      </a>
    </mat-toolbar>
    <router-outlet></router-outlet>
  `,
```

In a standalone project, every new component is created as a standalone component. This means that every component must import its own dependencies. Don't forget to granularly import every feature used in the template.

3. Create components for the subpages:

```
$ npx ng g c manager/userManagement
$ npx ng g c manager/receiptLookup
```

4. Create the parent-children routing. We know that we need the following routes to be able to navigate to our subpages, as follows:

```
example
{ path: '', redirectTo: 'home', pathMatch: 'full' },
{ path: 'home', component: ManagerHomeComponent },
{ path: 'users', component: UserManagementComponent },
{ path: 'receipts', component: ReceiptLookupComponent },
```

To target `<router-outlet>` defined in `ManagerComponent`, we need to create a parent route first and then specify routes for the subpages:

```
src/app/manager/manager-routing.module.ts
...
import { NgModule } from '@angular/core'
import { RouterModule, Routes } from '@angular/router'

import {
  ManagerHomeComponent
} from './manager-home/manager-home.component'
import {
  ManagerComponent
} from './manager.component'
import {
  ReceiptLookupComponent
} from './receipt-lookup/receipt-lookup.component'
```

```
import {
  UserManagementComponent
} from './user-management/user-management.component'
const routes: Routes = [
  {
    path: '',
    component: ManagerComponent,
    children: [
      { path: '', redirectTo: 'home', pathMatch: 'full' },
      { path: 'home', component: ManagerHomeComponent },
      { path: 'users', component: UserManagementComponent },
      { path: 'receipts', component: ReceiptLookupComponent },
    ],
  },
]
```

You should now be able to navigate through the app. When you click on the **Login as Manager** button, you will be taken to the page shown here. The clickable targets are highlighted:

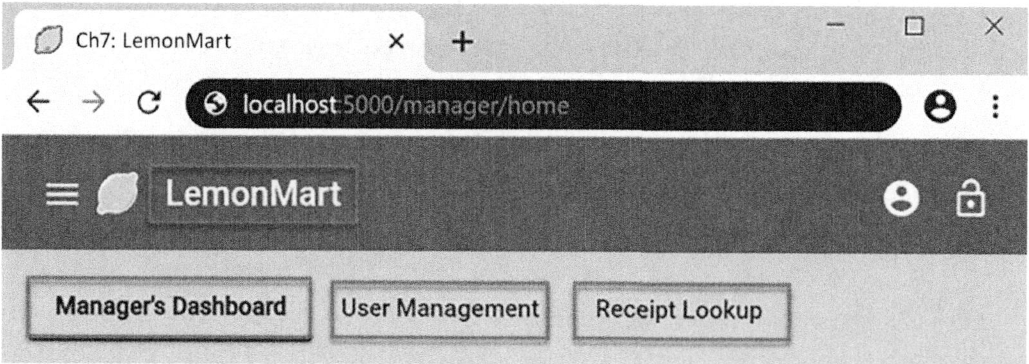

Figure 4.11: Manager's Dashboard with all router links highlighted

If you click on **LemonMart**, you will be taken to the home page. If you click on **Manager's Dashboard**, **User Management**, or **Receipt Lookup**, you will be navigated to the corresponding subpage, while the active link will be bold and underlined on the toolbar.

User module

Upon login, users can access their profiles and view a list of actions they can access in the LemonMart app through a side navigation menu. In *Chapter 6, Implementing Role-Based Navigation*, when we implement authentication and authorization, we will be receiving the role of the user from the server. Based on the user's role, we can automatically navigate or limit the options users can see. We will implement these components in this module so that they will only be loaded once a user is logged in. To complete the walking skeleton, we will ignore authentication-related concerns:

1. Create the necessary components:

   ```
   $ npx ng g c user/profile
   $ npx ng g c user/logout -t -s
   $ npx ng g c user/navigationMenu -t -s
   ```

2. Implement routing.

   Start with implementing the lazy loading in `app.routes.ts`:

   ```
   src/app/app.routes.ts
   ...
   {
     path: 'user',
     loadChildren:
       () => import('./user/user.module')
         .then(m => m.UserModule),
   },
   ```

   As explained earlier, ensure that the `PageNotFoundComponent` route is always the last route in `app.routes.ts` – because it has a wildcard matcher, it will overwrite routes defined after it.

   Now implement the child routes in `user-routing.module.ts`:

   ```
   src/app/user/user-routing.module.ts
   ...
   ```

```
const routes: Routes = [
  { path: 'profile', component: ProfileComponent },
  { path: 'logout', component: LogoutComponent },
]
```

We are implementing routing for `NavigationMenuComponent` because it'll be directly used as an HTML element. In addition, since `UserModule` doesn't have a landing page, there's no default path defined.

3. In `AppComponent`, wire up the `user` and `logout` icons:

```
src/app/app.component.ts
...
<mat-toolbar>
  ...
  <button
    mat-mini-fab routerLink="/user/profile"
    matTooltip="Profile" aria-label="User Profile"
  >
    <mat-icon>account_circle</mat-icon>
  </button>
  <button
     mat-mini-fab routerLink="/user/logout"
     matTooltip="Logout" aria-label="Logout"
  >
    <mat-icon>lock_open</mat-icon>
  </button>
</mat-toolbar>
```

Icon buttons can be cryptic, so it's a good idea to add tooltips. For tooltips to work, switch from the `mat-icon-button` directive to the `mat-mini-fab` directive and ensure you import `MatTooltipModule` as required. In addition, ensure that you add `aria-label` for icon-only buttons so that users with disabilities relying on screen readers can still navigate your web application.

4. Ensure that the app works.

You'll note that the two buttons are too close to each other, as follows:

Figure 4.12: Toolbar with icons

5. You can fix the icon layout issue by adding `fxLayoutGap="8px"` to `<mat-toolbar>`; however, now the lemon logo is too far apart from the app name, as shown:

Figure 4.13: Toolbar with padded icons

6. The logo layout issue can be fixed by merging the icon and the button:

src/app/app.component.ts

```
...
<mat-toolbar>
  ...
  <a mat-icon-button routerLink="/home">
    <mat-icon svgIcon="lemon"></mat-icon>
    LemonMart
  </a>
  ...
</mat-toolbar>
```

As shown in the following screenshot, the grouping fixes the layout issue:

Figure 4.14: Toolbar with grouped and padded elements

7. Another alternative is to wrap the text around `<span>`; however, in that case, you need to add some padding to maintain the look:

```
<span class="left-pad" data-testid="title">LemonMart</span>
```

This is more desirable from a UX perspective; now, users can return to the home page by clicking on the lemon.

POS and inventory modules

Our walking skeleton presumes the role of the manager. To be able to access all the components we are about to create, we need to enable the manager to be able to access the POS and inventory modules.

Update ManagerComponent with two new buttons:

```
src/app/manager/manager.component.ts
<mat-toolbar color="accent" fxLayoutGap="8px">
  ...
  <span class="flex-spacer"></span>
  <button
    mat-mini-fab routerLink="/inventory"
    matTooltip="Inventory" aria-label="Inventory"
  >
    <mat-icon>list</mat-icon>
  </button>
  <button
    mat-mini-fab routerLink="/pos"
    matTooltip="POS" aria-label="POS"
  >
    <mat-icon>shopping_cart</mat-icon>
  </button>
</mat-toolbar>
```

Note that these router links will navigate us out of the realm of `ManagerModule`, so it is normal for the manager-specific secondary toolbar to disappear.

Now, it'll be up to you to implement the last two remaining modules. For the two new modules, I provide high-level steps and refer you to a previous module on which you can model the new one. If you get stuck, refer to the `projects/stage7` folder on the GitHub project at `https://github.com/duluca/lemon-mart`.

PosModule

`PosModule` is very similar to `UserModule`, except that `PosModule` was a default path. `PosComponent` will be the default component. This has the potential to be a complicated component with some subcomponents, so don't use inline templates or styles:

1. Create `PosComponent`.
2. Register `PosComponent` as the default path.
3. Configure lazy loading for `PosModule`.
4. Ensure that the app works.

Now let's implement `InventoryModule`.

InventoryModule

`InventoryModule` is very similar to `ManagerModule`, as shown:

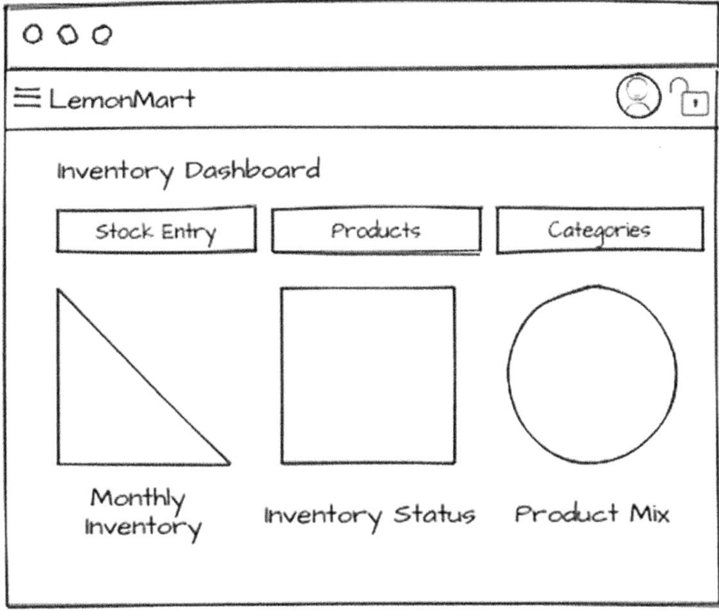

Figure 4.15: Inventory Dashboard mock-up

1. Create a base `Inventory` component.
2. Register `MaterialModule`.
3. Create **Inventory Home**, **Stock Entry**, **Products**, and **Categories** components.
4. Configure parent-children routes in `inventory-routing.module.ts`.
5. Configure lazy loading for `InventoryModule`.
6. Implement a secondary toolbar for internal `InventoryModule` navigation in `InventoryComponent`.

7. Ensure that the app works, as shown:

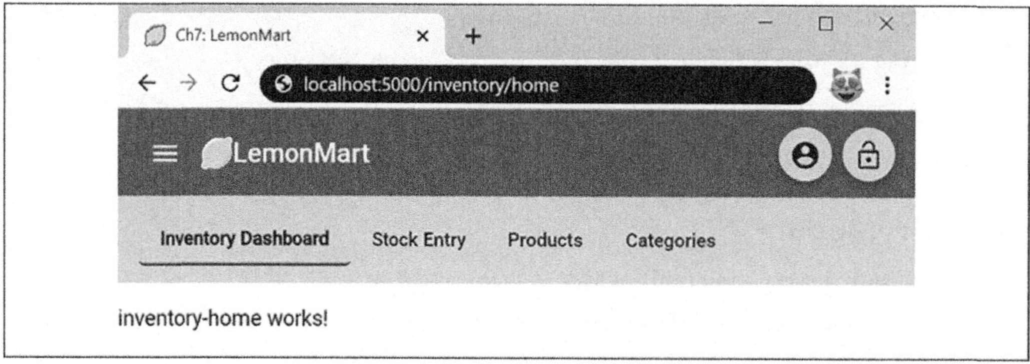

Figure 4.16: LemonMart Inventory Dashboard

Now that the walking skeleton of the app is completed, it is important to inspect the CLI output to ensure that all expected modules or components are being lazy loaded.

Be sure to resolve any testing errors before moving on. Ensure that `npm test` and `npm run e2e` execute without errors.

Common testing module

Now that we have a lot of modules to deal with, it becomes tedious to configure the imports and providers for each `spec` file individually. For this purpose, create a common testing module to contain a generic configuration that you can reuse across the board.

First, start by creating a new `.ts` file:

1. Create `common/common.testing.ts`.
2. Populate it with common testing providers, fakes, and modules.

   I have provided a `commonTestingModules` array:

   src/app/common/common.testing.ts

   ```
   import {
     HttpClientTestingModule
   } from '@angular/common/http/testing'
   import { ReactiveFormsModule } from '@angular/forms'
   import {
   ```

```
  NoopAnimationsModule
} from '@angular/platform-browser/animations'
import { RouterTestingModule } from '@angular/router/testing'
import {
  MatIconTestingModule
} from '@angular/material/icon/testing'

export const commonTestingProviders = [
  // Intentionally left blank! Used in later chapters.
]

export const commonTestingModules = [
  ReactiveFormsModule,
  NoopAnimationsModule,
  HttpClientTestingModule,
  RouterTestingModule,
  MatIconTestingModule,
] as unknown[]
```

Now let's see a sample use of this shared configuration file:

src/app/app.component.spec.ts

```
...
describe('AppComponent', () => {
  beforeEach(waitForAsync(() => {
    TestBed.configureTestingModule({
      imports: [...commonTestingModules, AppComponent],
      providers: [],
    }).compileComponents()
  }))
...
```

While `commonTestingModules` is convenient, as your application grows, it'll start slowing down test runs by importing unnecessary modules. Standalone components go a long way to mitigate this issue since they bring their own imports with them. Be mindful not to overload this convenience module.

Stop! Did you ensure all your unit tests are passing? To ensure your tests are always passing, implement a CI pipeline in CircleCI, as demonstrated in *Chapter 10, Releasing to Production with CI/CD.*

With your tests up and running, the walking skeleton for LemonMart is completed. Now, let's look ahead and start thinking about what kinds of data entities we might be working with.

Designing around major data entities

The fourth step in router-first architecture is achieving a stateless, data-driven design. To achieve this, it helps a lot to organize your APIs around major data components. This will roughly match how you consume data in various components in your Angular application. We will start off by defining our major data components by creating a rough data **Entity Relationship Diagram** (**ERD**). In *Chapter 5, Designing Authentication and Authorization*, we will review the design and implementation of an API for the user data entity using Swagger.io and Express.js for REST and Apollo for GraphQL.

Defining entities

Let's start by looking at what kind of entities you would like to store and how these entities might relate to one another.

Here's a sample design for LemonMart, created using `draw.io`:

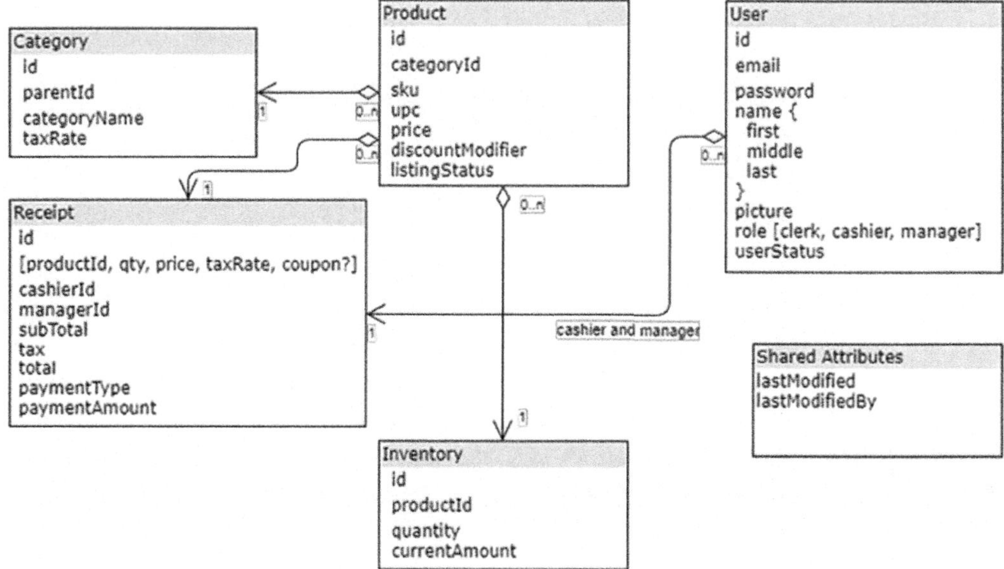

Figure 4.17: ERD for LemonMart

Currently, whether your entities are stored in a SQL or NoSQL database is inconsequential. My suggestion is to stick to what you know, but if you're starting from scratch, a NoSQL database like MongoDB will offer the most flexibility as your implementation and requirements evolve.

Generally, you will need CRUD APIs for each entity. Considering these data elements, we can also imagine user interfaces around these CRUD APIs. Let's do that next.

High-level UX design

Mock-ups are important in determining what kind of components and user controls we will need throughout the app. Any user control or component that will be used across components must be defined at the root level, and others must be scoped with their own modules.

Earlier in this chapter, we identified the sub modules and designed landing pages for them to complete the walking skeleton. Now that we have defined the major data components, we can complete mock-ups for the rest of the app. When designing screens at a high level, keep several things in mind:

- Can a user complete common tasks required for their role with as little navigation as possible?
- Can users readily access all information and functionality of the app through visible elements on the screen?
- Can a user search for the data they need easily?
- Once a user finds a record of interest, can they drill down into detailed records or view related records with ease?
- Is that pop-up alert necessary? You know users won't read it, right?

Remember that there's no one right way to design any UX, which is why when designing screens, you should always keep modularity and reusability in mind.

Creating an artifacts wiki

As mentioned earlier in the chapter, it is important to document every artifact you create. Wikis offer a way to create living documentation that can be collaboratively updated or edited. While Slack, Teams, email, and whiteboards offer good collaboration opportunities, their ephemeral nature leaves much to be desired.

So, as you generate various design artifacts, such as mock-ups or design decisions, take care to post them on a wiki reachable by all team members:

1. On GitHub, switch over to the **Wiki** tab.

   You may check out my sample wiki at `https://github.com/duluca/lemon-mart/wiki`, as shown:

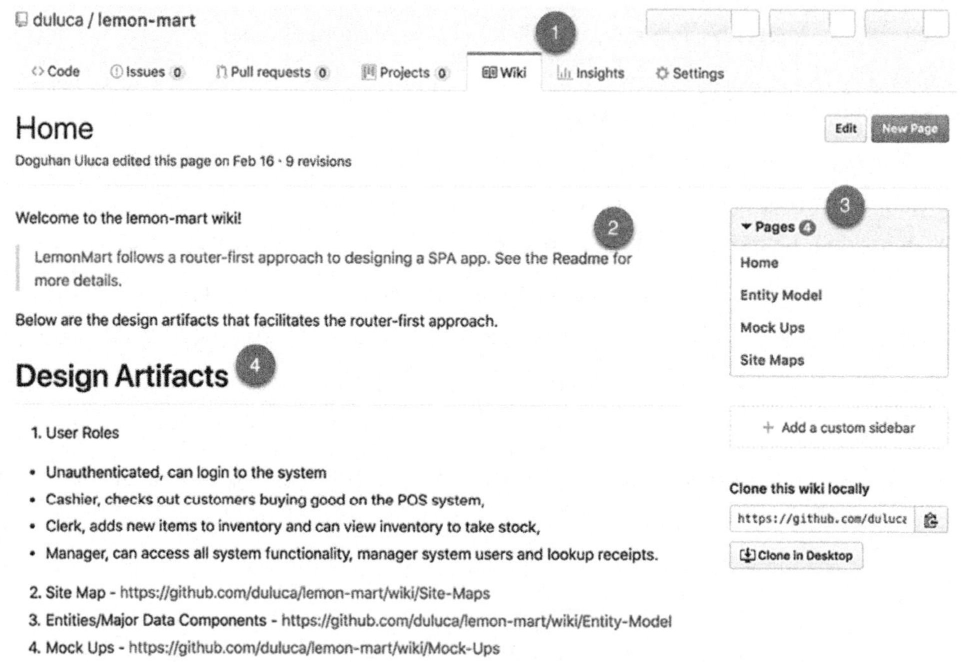

Figure 4.18: GitHub.com LemonMart wiki

2. When creating a wiki page, ensure that you cross-link between any other documentation available, such as **Readme**.
3. Note that GitHub shows subpages on the wiki under **Pages**.
4. However, an additional summary is helpful, such as the **Design Artifacts** section, since some people may miss the navigational element on the right.
5. As you complete mock-ups, post them on the wiki.

You can see a summary view of the wiki here:

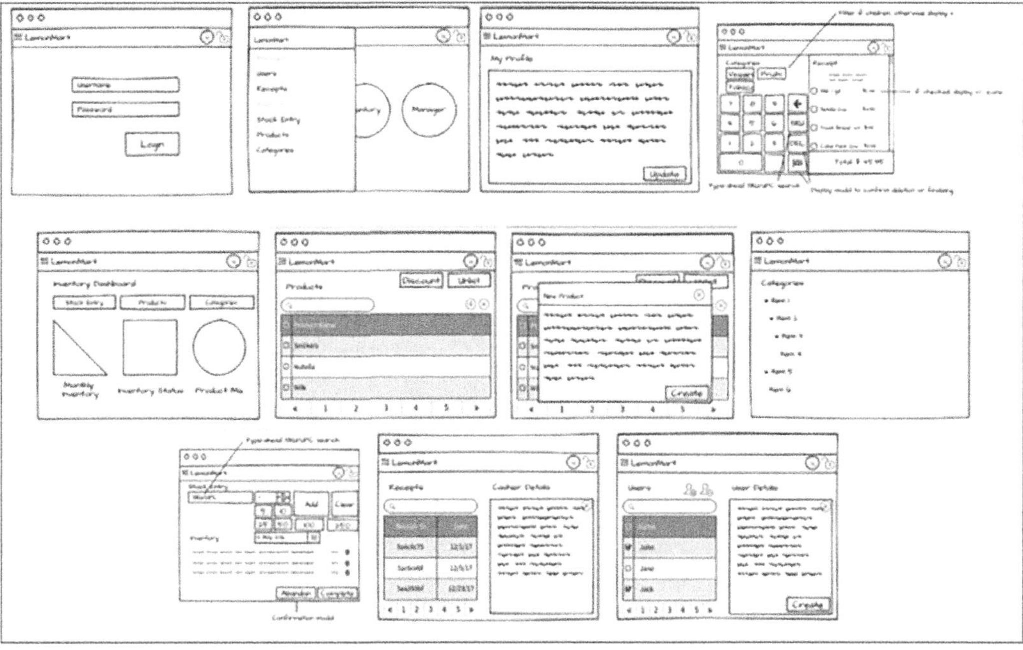

Figure 4.19: Summary view of LemonMart mock-ups

Now that your artifacts are in a centralized place, it is accessible to all team members. They can add, edit, update, or groom the content. This way, your wiki becomes useful, living documentation of the information that your team needs, as opposed to a piece of documentation you feel like you're being forced to create. Raise your hand if you've ever found yourself in that situation!

Next, integrate your mock-ups into your app, so you can collect early feedback from your stakeholders and test out the flow of your application.

Leveraging mock-ups in your app

Place the mock-ups in the walking skeleton app so that testers can better envision the functionality that is yet to be developed. See an example of this idea in action here:

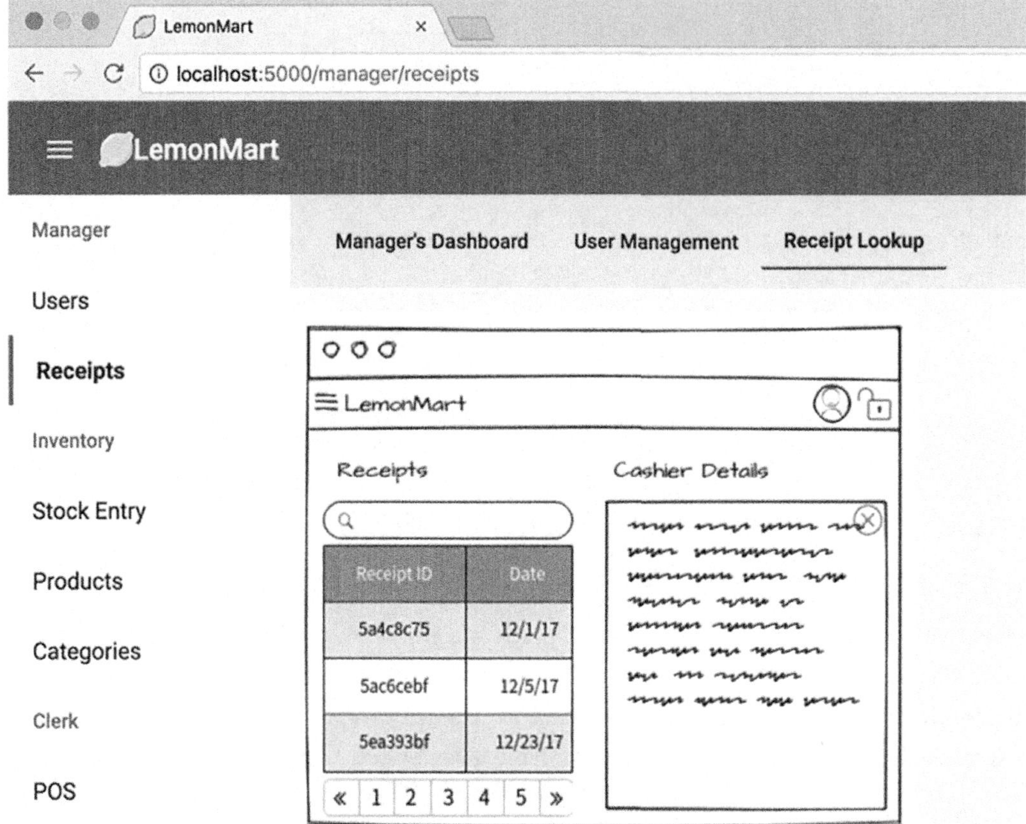

Figure 4.20: Using mock-ups in the UI to verify the flow of the app

This will also be helpful when designing and implementing your authentication and authorization workflow. With the mock-ups completed, we need to implement a backend in *Chapter 5, Designing Authentication and Authorization*, before we can continue the implementation of LemonMart's authentication and authorization workflow in *Chapter 6, Implementing Role-Based Navigation*.

Summary

In this chapter, you mastered effectively using the Angular CLI to create major Angular components and scaffolding. You created the branding of your app, leveraging custom and built-in Material iconography.

You learned how to debug complicated router configurations with Angular DevTools. Finally, you began building router-first apps, defining user roles early on, designing with lazy loading in mind, and nailing down a walking-skeleton navigation experience early on. We went over designing around major data entities. We also covered the importance of completing and documenting the high-level UX design of our entire app so that we can properly design a great conditional navigation experience.

To recap, to pull off a router-first implementation, you need to do this:

1. Develop a roadmap and scope.
2. Design with lazy loading in mind.
3. Implement a walking-skeleton navigation experience.
4. Achieve a stateless, data-driven design.
5. Enforce a decoupled component architecture.
6. Differentiate between user controls and components.
7. Maximize code reuse with TypeScript and ES6.

In this chapter, you executed steps 1-3; in the following chapters, you will execute steps 4-7. In *Chapter 5, Designing Authentication and Authorization,* you will see a concrete full-stack implementation using the minimal MEAN stack. In *Chapter 6, Implementing Role-Based Navigation,* and *Chapter 7, Working with REST and GraphQL APIs,* we will tap into OOP design and inheritance and abstraction, along with a deep dive into security considerations and designing a conditional navigation experience. *Chapter 8, Recipes – Reusability, Forms, and Caching,* and *Chapter 9, Recipes – Master/Detail, Data Tables, and NgRx,* will tie everything together by sticking to a decoupled component architecture, smartly choosing between creating user controls and components, and maximizing code reuse with various TypeScript, RxJS, and Angular coding techniques.

Exercise

So far, we haven't implemented a lazy loading component. As a challenge, following the documentation at `https://angular.io/guide/standalone-components`, update `app.route.ts` so that `PageNotFoundComponent` is lazy loaded. After you complete your update, verify that the CLI output correctly shows the new chunked file, and also open up the **Network** tab in DevTools to watch the chunks being downloaded as you navigate the app.

Further reading

- DevTools overview: `https://angular.io/guide/devtools`

- Material Design: `https://m3.material.io`
- *Getting Started with Standalone Components*, Google, August 30, 2023: `https://angular.io/guide/standalone-components`
- Webpack module bundler: `https://webpack.js.org/`

Questions

Answer the following questions as best as possible to ensure you've understood the key concepts from this chapter without googling anything. Do you know if you got all the answers right? Visit `https://angularforenterprise.com/self-assessment` for more:

1. What is the difference between the root module and a feature module?
2. What are the benefits of lazy loading?
3. How's a standalone component different from a module?
4. Why do we create a walking skeleton of our application?
5. What's the benefit of designing around major data entities?
6. Why should we create wikis for our projects?

5

Designing Authentication and Authorization

Designing a high-quality **authentication** and **authorization** system without frustrating the end user is a difficult problem to solve. Authentication is the act of verifying the identity of a user, and authorization specifies the privileges that a user must have to access a resource. Both processes, **auth** for short, must seamlessly work in tandem to address users' needs with varying roles, needs, and job functions.

On today's web, users have a high baseline level of expectations from any auth system they encounter through the browser, so this is an important part of your application to get right the first time. The user should always know what they can and can't do in your application. If there are errors, failures, or mistakes, the user should be informed about why they occurred. As your application grows, it will be easy to miss how an error condition could be triggered. Your implementation should be easy to extend or maintain. Otherwise, this basic backbone of your application will require a lot of maintenance. In this chapter, we will walk through the challenges of creating a great auth UX and implementing a solid baseline experience.

In this chapter, we will implement a token-based auth scheme around the user entity defined in the last chapter. For a robust and maintainable implementation, we will deep dive into **Object-Oriented Programming (OOP)** with abstraction, inheritance, and factories, along with implementing a cache service, a UI service, and an in-memory fake auth service for testing and educational purposes.

In this chapter, we're going to cover the following topics:

- Designing an auth workflow
- TypeScript operators for safe data handling
- Implementing data entities
- Reusable services leveraging OOP concepts
- Creating an auth service
- A cache service using localStorage
- An in-memory auth service
- Logout
- An HTTP interceptor

Technical requirements

The most up-to-date versions of the sample code for the book are on GitHub at the following linked repository. The repository contains the final and completed state of the code. You can verify your progress at the end of this chapter by looking for the end-of-chapter snapshot of code under the `projects` folder.

For *Chapter 5*:

1. Clone the repository `https://github.com/duluca/lemon-mart`.
2. Execute `npm install` on the root folder to install dependencies.
3. The beginning state of the project is reflected at:

```
projects/stage7
```

4. The end state of the project is reflected at:

```
projects/stage8
```

5. Add the stage name to any `ng` command to act only on that stage:

```
npx ng build stage8
```

Note that the `dist/stage8` folder at the root of the repository will contain the compiled result.

Beware that the source code provided in the book and the version on GitHub are likely to be different. The ecosystem around these projects is ever-evolving. Between changes to how Angular CLI generates new code, bug fixes, new versions of libraries, and side-by-side implementations of multiple techniques, there's a lot of variation that's impossible to account for. If you find errors or have questions, please create an issue or submit a pull request on GitHub.

Let's start by going over how a token-based auth workflow functions.

Designing an auth workflow

A well-designed authentication workflow is stateless so that there's no concept of an expiring session. Users can interact with your stateless REST APIs from as many devices and tabs as they wish, simultaneously or over time. A **JSON Web Token** (**JWT**) implements distributed claims-based authentication that can be digitally signed or information-protected and/or encrypted, using a **Message Authentication Code** (**MAC**). This means that once a user's identity is authenticated (that is, a password challenge on a login form), they receive an encoded claim ticket or a token, which can then be used to make future requests to the system without having to reauthenticate the identity of the user.

The server can independently verify the validity of this claim and process the requests without requiring prior knowledge of having interacted with this user. Thus, we don't have to store session information regarding a user, making our solution stateless and easy to scale. Each token will expire after a predefined period, and due to their distributed nature, they can't be remotely or individually revoked; however, we can bolster real-time security by interjecting custom account and user role status checks to ensure that the authenticated user is authorized to access server-side resources.

JWTs implement the **Internet Engineering Task Force** (**IETF**) industry standard RFC 7519, found at `https://tools.ietf.org/html/rfc7519`.

A good authorization workflow enables conditional navigation based on a user's role, so users are automatically taken to the optimal landing screen; routes and UI elements that are not suitable for their roles should not be displayed, and if, by mistake, they try to access a restricted path, they should be prevented from doing so. You must remember that any client-side role-based navigation is merely a convenience and is not meant for security.

This means that every call made to the server should contain the necessary header information, with the secure token, so that the user can be reauthenticated by the server and their role independently verified. Only then will they be allowed to retrieve secured data. By its nature, client-side authentication can't be trusted. All auth logic must be implemented server-side. Implementing password reset screens securely can be especially challenging, since they can be triggered within your web app or via a link embedded into an email/notification. When the modality of interaction increases, the attack surface grows with it. For this reason, I recommend building reset screens with server-side rendering so that both the user and the server can verify that the intended user is interacting with the system. If you're implementing this client-side, you must ensure the server generates a time-limited, one-time-use-only token to pass alongside the new password so that you can be reasonably sure the request is legitimate. Next, let's dive into how you can generate secure tokens.

JWT life cycle

JWTs complement a stateless REST API architecture with an encrypted token mechanism that allows convenient, distributed, and high-performance authentication and authorization of client requests. There are three main components of a token-based authentication scheme:

- **Client-side**: Captures login information and hides disallowed actions for a good UX.
- **Server-side**: Validates that every request is authenticated and has the proper authorization.
- **Auth service**: Generates and validates encrypted tokens and independently verifies the auth status of user requests from a data store.

A secure system presumes that data sent/received between clients (applications and browsers), systems (servers and services), and databases are encrypted using **Transport Layer Security (TLS)**, which is essentially a newer version of the **Secure Sockets Layer (SSL)**. Your REST API must be hosted with a properly configured SSL certificate, serving all API calls over HTTPS so that user credentials are never exposed between the client and the server. Similarly, any database or third-party service call should happen over TLS. This ensures the security of the data in transit.

At rest (when data is in a database), passwords should be stored using a secure one-way hashing algorithm with good salting practices.

Did all the talk of hashing and salting make you think of breakfast? Unfortunately, they're cryptography-related terms. If you want to learn more, check out this article: `https://crackstation.net/hashing-security.htm`.

Sensitive user information, such as **Personally Identifiable Information** (**PII**), should be encrypted at rest with a secure two-way encryption algorithm, unlike passwords. Passwords are hashed, so we verify that the user is providing the same password without the system knowing what the password is. With PII, we must be able to decrypt data to display it to the user. However, since the data is encrypted at rest, if the database is compromised, then the hacked data is worthless.

Following a layered approach to security is critical, as attackers will need to accomplish the unlikely feat of compromising all layers of your security simultaneously to cause meaningful harm to your business.

Fun fact: When you hear about massive data breaches from major corporations, the root cause is a lack of proper implementation of in-transit or at-rest security. Sometimes, this is because it is too computationally expensive to continually encrypt/decrypt data, so engineers rely on being behind firewalls. In that case, once the outer perimeter is breached, as they say, the fox has access to the hen house.

Consider the following sequence diagram, which highlights the life cycle of JWT-based authentication:

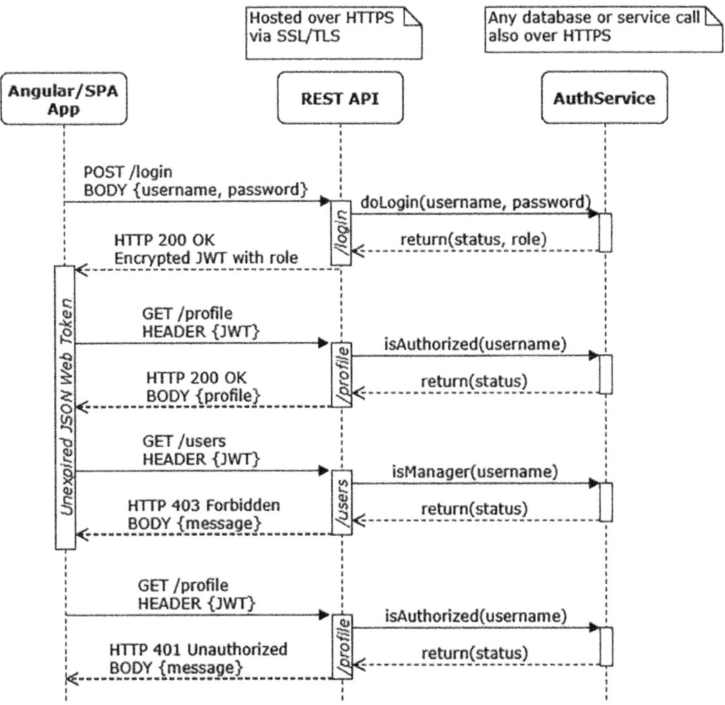

Figure 5.1: The life cycle of JWT-based authentication

Initially, a user logs in by providing their username and password. Once validated, the user's authentication status and role are encrypted in a JWT with an expiration date and time, and it is sent back to the browser.

Our Angular (or any other) application can cache this token in local or session storage securely so that the user isn't forced to log in with every request. This way, we don't resort to insecure practices like storing user credentials in cookies to provide a good UX.

Our technical reviewer, Jurgen Van de Moere, points out that cookies don't necessarily have to be insecure.

See `https://www.youtube.com/watch?v=9ZOpUtQ_4Uk` by Philippe De Ryck, explaining how cookies can be a valid mechanism to store a JWT token in specific cases.

You will get a better understanding of the JWT life cycle when you implement your own auth service later in this chapter. In the following sections, we will design a fully featured auth workflow around the **User** data entity as follows:

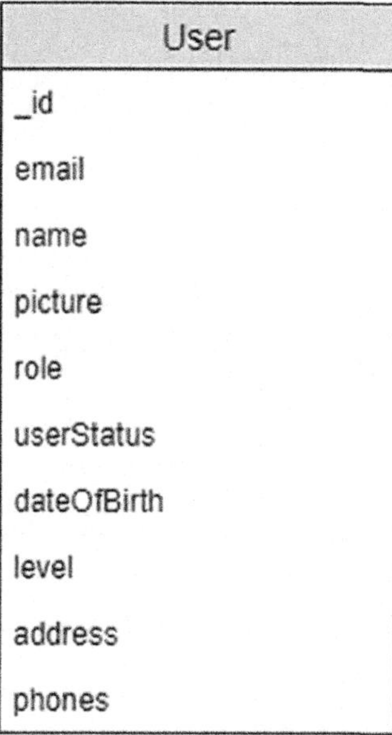

Figure 5.2: The User entity

The **User** entity described is slightly different from our initial entity model. The entity model reflects how data is stored in the database.

The entity is a flattened (or simplified) representation of the user record. Even a flattened entity has complex objects, like a **name**, with properties like first, middle, and last. Furthermore, not all properties are required. Additionally, when interacting with auth systems and other APIs, we may receive incomplete, incorrect, or maliciously formed data, so our code must effectively deal with `null` and `undefined` variables.

Next, let's see how we can leverage TypeScript operators to effectively deal with unexpected data.

TypeScript operators for safe data handling

JavaScript is a dynamically typed language. At runtime, the JavaScript engine executing our code, like Chrome's V8, doesn't know the type of variable we're using. As a result, the engine must infer the type. We can have basic types like `boolean`, `number`, `array`, or `string`, or we can have a complex type, which is essentially a JSON object. In addition, variables can be `null` or `undefined`. In broad terms, `undefined` represents something that hasn't been declared or initialized, and `null` represents the intentional absence of the value of a declared variable.

In strongly typed languages, the concept of `undefined` doesn't exist. Basic types have default values, like a `number` being a zero or a `string` being an empty string. However, complex types can be `null`. A `null` reference means the variable is defined, but there's no value behind it.

The inventor of the `null` reference, Tony Hoare, called it his "billion-dollar mistake."

TypeScript brings the concepts of strongly typed languages to JavaScript, so it must bridge the gap between the two worlds. As a result, TypeScript defines types like `null`, `undefined`, `any`, and `never` to make sense of JavaScript's type semantics. I've added links to relevant TypeScript documentation in the *Further reading* section for a deeper dive into TypeScript types.

As the TypeScript documentation puts it, TypeScript treats `null` and `undefined` differently to match the JavaScript semantics. For example, the union type `string | null` is a different type than `string | undefined` and `string | undefined | null`.

There's another nuance: checking to see whether a value equals `null` using `==` versus `===`. Using the double equals operator, checking that `foo != null` means that `foo` is defined and not `null`. However, using the triple-equals operator, `foo !== null` means that `foo` is not `null` but could be `undefined`. However, these two operators don't consider the truthiness of the variable, which includes the case of an empty string.

These subtle differences have a great impact on how you write code, especially when using the strict TypeScript rules that are applied when you create your Angular application using the `--strict` option. It is important to remember that TypeScript is a compile-time tool and not a runtime tool. At runtime, we're still dealing with the realities of a dynamically typed language. Just because we declared a type to be a string doesn't mean that we will receive a string.

Next, let's see how we can deal with issues related to working with unexpected values.

Null and undefined checking

When working with other libraries or dealing with information sent or received outside of your application, you must deal with the fact that the variable you receive might be `null` or `undefined`.

Outside of your application means dealing with user input, reading from a cookie or `localStorage`, URL parameters from the router, or an API call over HTTP, to name a few examples.

In our code, we mostly care about the truthiness of a variable. This means that a variable is defined, not null, and if it's a basic type, it has a non-default value. Given a `string`, we can check whether the `string` is truthy with a simple `if` statement:

```
example
const foo: string = undefined
if(foo) {
  console.log('truthy')
} else {
  console.log('falsy')
}
```

If `foo` is `null`, `undefined`, or an empty string, the variable will be considered `falsy`. For certain situations, we can use the conditional or ternary operator instead of `if-else`.

The conditional or ternary operator

The conditional or ternary operator has the `?:` syntax. On the left-hand side of the question mark, the operator takes a conditional statement. On the right-hand side, we provide the outcomes for true and false around the colon: `conditional ? true-outcome : false-outcome`. The conditional or ternary operator is a compact way to represent `if-else` conditions and can be very useful to increase the readability of your code base. This operator is not a replacement for an `if-else` block, but it is of great use when using the output of the `if-else` condition.

Consider the following example:

```
example
const foo: string = undefined
let result = ''
if(foo) {
  result = 'truthy'
} else {
  result = 'falsy'
}
console.log(result)
```

The preceding `if-else` block can be rewritten as:

```
example
const foo: string = undefined
console.log(foo ? 'truthy' : 'falsy')
```

In this case, the conditional or ternary operator makes the code more compact and easier to understand. Another common scenario is returning a default value, where the variable is `falsy`.

Next, we consider the null coalescing operator.

The null coalescing operator

The null coalescing operator is `||`. This operator saves us from repetition when the truthy result of the conditional is the same as the conditional itself.

Consider the example where if `foo` is defined, we would like to use the value of `foo`, but if it is `undefined`, we need a default value of `'bar'`:

```
example
const foo: string = undefined
console.log(foo ? foo : 'bar')
```

As you can see, `foo` is repeated twice. We can avoid the duplication by using the null coalescing operator:

```
example
const foo: string = undefined
console.log(foo || 'bar')
```

So, if `foo` is `undefined`, `null`, or an empty string, `bar` will be output. Otherwise, the value of `foo` will be used. But in some cases, we need only to use the default value if the value is `undefined` or `null`.

Let's have a look at the nullish coalescing operator next.

The nullish coalescing operator

The nullish coalescing operator is ??. This operator is like the null coalescing operator, with one crucial difference. Checking the truthiness of a variable is not enough when dealing with data received from an API or user input, where an empty string may be a valid value. As we covered earlier in this section, checking for `null` and `undefined` is not as straightforward as it seems. However, we know that by using the double equals operator, we can ensure that `foo` is defined and not null:

```
example
const foo: string = undefined
console.log(foo != null ? foo : 'bar')
```

In the preceding case, if `foo` is an empty string or another value, we will get the value of the `foo` output. If it is `null` or `undefined`, we will get `'bar'`. A more compact way to do this is by using the nullish coalescing operator:

```
example
const foo: string = undefined
console.log(foo ?? 'bar')
```

The preceding code will yield the same result as the previous example. However, when dealing with complex objects, we need to consider whether their properties are `null` or `undefined` as well. For this, we will consider the optional chaining operator.

Optional chaining

The optional chaining operator is ?. It is like Angular's safe navigation operator. Optional chaining ensures that a variable or property is defined and not `null` before attempting to access a child property or invoke a function. So the statement `foo?.bar?.callMe()` executes without throwing an error, even if `foo` or `bar` is `null` or `undefined`.

Consider the `user` entity, which has a `name` object with properties for `first`, `middle`, and `last`. Let's see what it would take to safely provide a default value of an empty string for a middle name, using the nullish coalescing operator:

```
example
const user = {
  name: {
```

```
      first: 'Doguhan',
      middle: null,
      last: 'Uluca'
    }
  }
  console.log((user && user.name && user.name.middle) ?? '')
```

As you can see, we need to check whether a parent object is `truthy` before accessing a child property. If `middle` is `null`, an empty string is output. Optional chaining makes this task simpler:

```
example
console.log(user?.name?.middle ?? '')
```

Using optional chaining and the nullish coalescing operator together, we can eliminate repetition and deliver robust code that can effectively deal with the realities of JavaScript's dynamic runtime.

So, when designing your code, you must decide whether to introduce the concept of null to your logic or work with default values like empty strings. In the next section, as we implement the User entity, you will see how these choices play out. So far, we have only used interfaces to define the shape of our data. Next, let's build the User entity, leveraging OOP concepts like classes, enums, and abstraction to implement it, along with an auth service.

Let's start simple and see how these patterns are implemented within the context of JavaScript classes and TypeScript fundamentals.

Implementing data entities and interfaces

In this section, I will demonstrate how you can use classes in your own code design to define and encapsulate the behavior of your models, such as the `User` class. Later in this chapter, you will see examples of class inheritance with abstract base classes, which allows us to standardize our implementation and reuse base functionality in a clean and easy-to-maintain manner.

I must point out that OOP has very useful patterns that can increase the quality of your code; however, if you overuse it, then you will start losing the benefits of the dynamic, flexible, and functional nature of JavaScript.

Sometimes, all you need is a bunch of functions in a file, and you'll see examples of that throughout the book.

A great way to demonstrate the value of classes would be to standardize the creation of a default `User` object. We need this because a `BehaviorSubject` object needs to be initialized with a default object. It is best to do this in one place, rather than copy and paste the same implementation in multiple places. It makes a lot of sense for the `User` object to own this functionality instead of an Angular service creating default `User` objects. So, let's implement a `User` class to achieve this goal.

Classes, Interfaces, and Enums

As mentioned, we have only worked with interfaces to represent data. We still want to continue using interfaces when passing data around various components and services. Interfaces are great for describing the kind of properties or functions an implementation has, but they suggest nothing about the behavior of these properties or functions.

With ES2015 (ES6), JavaScript gained native support for classes, which is a crucial concept of the OOP paradigm. Classes are actual implementations of behavior. As opposed to just having a collection of functions in a file, a class can properly encapsulate behavior. A class can then be instantiated as an object using the new keyword.

TypeScript takes the ES2015 (and beyond) implementation of classes and introduces necessary concepts like abstract classes, private, protected, and public properties, and interfaces to make it possible to implement OOP patterns.

We will begin by defining enums and interfaces for the data entities we need, utilizing the best two features of Typescript.

Interfaces help us practice the Dependency Inversion Principle from SOLID design: depend on abstractions, not on concretions. This means between components or services, it is better to pass the interface of an object (an instantiated class) instead of the object itself. This is why every class we define will implement an interface. Further, interfaces are usually the first thing you can start coding in a new project, using them to implement your walking skeleton and API integrations.

Enums help ensure another important rule: never use string literals. Enums are powerful and awesome.

Let's jump in and define the interfaces and enums we need:

1. Define user roles as an `enum` at the location `src/app/auth/auth.enum.ts`:

   ```
   src/app/auth/auth.enum.ts
   export enum Role {
     None = 'none',
   ```

```
  Clerk = 'clerk',
  Cashier = 'cashier',
  Manager = 'manager',
}
```

2. Create a `user.ts` file under the `src/app/user/user` folder.
3. Define a new interface named `IUser` in the `user.ts` file:

src/app/user/user/user.ts

```
import { Role } from '../../auth/auth.enum'
export interface IUser {
  _id: string
  email: string
  name: IName
  picture: string
  role: Role | string
  userStatus: boolean
  dateOfBirth: Date | null | string
  level: number
  address: {
    line1: string
    line2?: string
    city: string
    state: string
    zip: string
  }
  phones: IPhone[]
}
```

Note that every complex property defined on the interface can also be represented as a `string`. In transit, all objects are converted to strings using `JSON.stringify()`. No type of information is included. We also leverage interfaces to represent `Class` objects in memory, which can have complex types. So, our interface properties must reflect both cases using union types. For example, the `role` can either be of type `Role` or `string`. Similarly, `dateOfBirth` can be a `Date` or a `string`.

We define the `address` as an inline type because we don't use the concept of an address outside of this class. In contrast, we define `IName` as its own interface because in *Chapter 8, Recipes – Reusability, Forms, and Caching*, we will implement a separate component for names. We also define a separate interface for phones because they are represented as an array. When developing a form, we need to be able to address individual array elements, like `IPhone`, in the template code.

It is the norm to prepend interface names with a capital `I` so that they can be easily identified. Don't worry; there are no compatibility issues with using the `IPhone` interface on Android phones!

4. In `user.ts`, define the `IName` and `IPhone` interfaces, and implement the `PhoneType` enum:

src/app/user/user/user.ts

```
export interface IName {
  first: string
  middle?: string
  last: string
}
export enum PhoneType {
  None = 'none',
  Mobile = 'mobile',
  Home = 'home',
  Work = 'work',
}
export interface IPhone {
  type: PhoneType
  digits: string
  id: number
}
```

Note that in the `PhoneType` enum, we explicitly defined `string` values. By default, `enum` values are converted into strings as they're typed, which can lead to issues with values stored in a database falling out of sync with how a developer chooses to spell a variable name. With explicit and all lowercase values, we reduce the risk of bugs.

5. Next, define the `User` class, which implements the `IUser` interface:

src/app/user/user/user.ts

```
export class User implements IUser {
  constructor(
    // tslint:disable-next-line: variable-name
    public _id = '',
    public email = '',
    public name = { first: '', middle: '', last: '' } as IName,
    public picture = '',
    public role = Role.None,
    public dateOfBirth: Date | null = null,
    public userStatus = false,
    public level = 0,
    public address = {
      line1: '',
      city: '',
      state: '',
      zip: '',
    },
    public phones: IPhone[] = []
  ) {}
  static Build(user: IUser) {
    if (!user) {
      return new User()
    }

    return new User(
      user._id,
      user.email,
      user.name,
      user.picture,
      user.role as Role,
      typeof user.dateOfBirth === 'string'
        ? new Date(user.dateOfBirth)
        : user.dateOfBirth,
      user.userStatus,
```

```
        user.level,
        user.address,
        user.phones
      )
    }
  }
```

Note that by defining all properties with default values in the constructors as `public` properties, we kill two birds with one stone; otherwise, we would need to define properties and initialize them separately. This way, we achieve a concise implementation.

Using a static `Build` function, we can quickly hydrate the object with data received from the server. We can also implement the `toJSON()` function to customize the serialization behavior of our object before sending the data to the server. But before that, let's add a calculated property.

We can use calculated properties in templates or toast messages to conveniently display values assembled from multiple parts. A great example is extracting a full name from the `name` object as a property in the `User` class.

A calculated property for assembling a full name encapsulates the logic for combining a first, middle, and last name, so you don't have to rewrite this logic in multiple places, adhering to the DRY principle!

6. Implement a `fullName` property getter in the `User` class:

```
src/app/user/user/user.ts
export class User implements IUser {
  ...
  public get fullName(): string {
    if (!this.name) {
      return ''
    }
    if (this.name.middle) {
```

```
      return
        `${this.name.first} ${this.name.middle} ${this.name.last}`
    }
    return `${this.name.first} ${this.name.last}`
  }
}
```

7. Add `fullName` to `IUser` as an optional `readonly` property:

```
src/app/user/user/user.ts
export interface IUser {
  ...
  readonly fullName?: string
}
```

   You can now use the `fullName` property through the `IUser` interface.

8. Implement the `toJSON` function:

```
src/app/user/user/user.ts
export class User implements IUser {
  ...

toJSON(): object {
    const serialized = Object.assign(this)
    delete serialized._id
    delete serialized.fullName
    return serialized
  }
}
```

Note that when serializing the object, we delete the `_id` and `fullName` fields. These are values that we don't want to be stored in the database. The `fullName` field is a calculated property, so it doesn't need storage. The `_id` is normally passed as a parameter in a `GET` or a `PUT` call to locate the record. This avoids mistakes that may result in overwriting the `id` fields of existing objects.

Now that we have the `User data` entity implemented, let's implement the auth service next.

Reusable services leveraging OOP concepts

OOP is an imperative programming style compared to the reactive programming style that RxJS enables. Classes form the bedrock of OOP, whereas observables do the same for reactive programming using RxJS.

I encourage you to become familiar with OOP terminology. Please see the *Further reading* section for some useful resources. You should become familiar with:

- Classes versus objects
- Composition (interfaces)
- Encapsulation (private, protected, and public properties, and property getters and setters)
- Polymorphism (inheritance, abstract classes, and method overriding)

As you know, Angular uses OOP patterns to implement components and services. For example, interfaces implement life cycle hooks such as `OnInit`. We aim to design a flexible auth service that can implement multiple auth providers. In *Chapter 6, Implementing Role-Based Navigation*, we will implement an in-memory provider and a Google Firebase provider. In *Chapter 7, Working with REST and GraphQL APIs*, we will implement two custom providers to interact with our backend and see how **Role-based Access Control** (**RBAC**) is implemented.

By declaring an abstract base class, we can describe the common login and logout behavior of our application, so when we implement another auth provider, we don't have to re-engineer our application.

In addition, we can declare abstract functions, which the implementors of our base class would have to implement, enforcing our design. Any class that implements the base class would also get the benefit of the code implemented in the base class, so we wouldn't need to repeat the same logic in two different places.

The following class diagram reflects the architecture and inheritance hierarchy of our abstract `AuthService`:

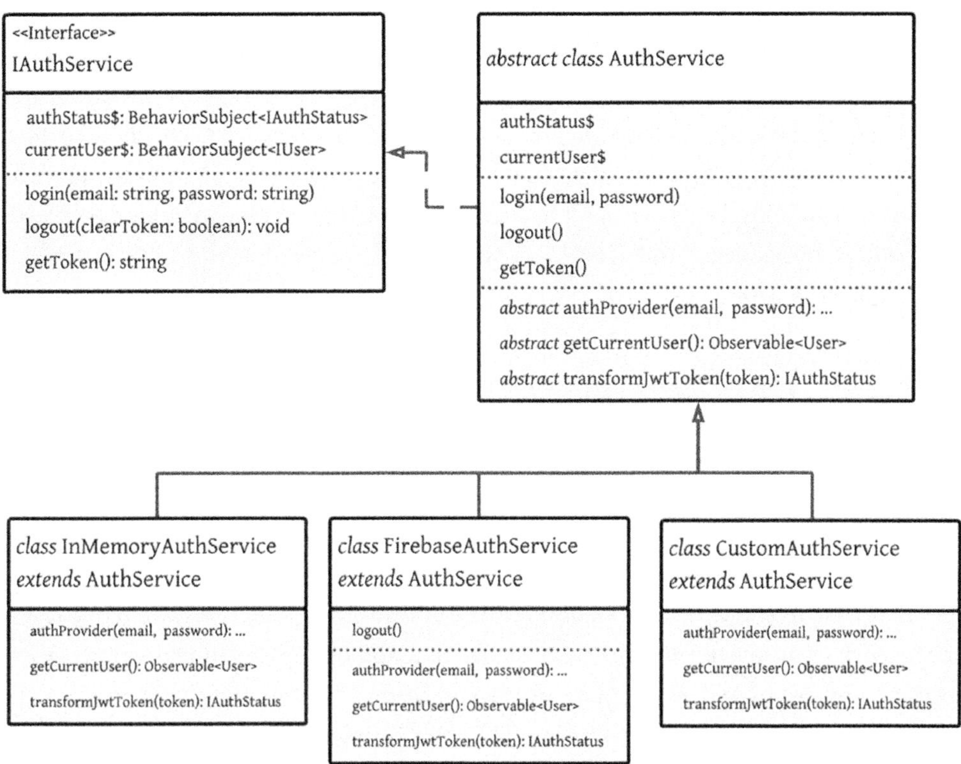

Figure 5.3: The AuthService inheritance structure

`AuthService` implements the interface `IAuthService`, as shown here:

```
export interface IAuthService {
  readonly authStatus$: BehaviorSubject<IAuthStatus>
  readonly currentUser$: BehaviorSubject<IUser>
  login(email: string, password: string): Observable<void>
  logout(clearToken?: boolean): void
  getToken(): string
}
```

The interface reflects the public properties that the service exposes. The service provides the authentication status as the `authStatus$` observable and the current user as `currentUser$`, and it provides three functions, `login`, `logout`, and `getToken`.

`AuthService` requires caching functionality from another service called `CacheService`. Instead of using inheritance to incorporate cache functionality, we can inject it into the base class. Since `AuthService` is an abstract class, it can't be used independently, so we will implement the three auth providers, `InMemoryAuthService`, `FirebaseAuthService`, and `CustomAuthService`, shown at the bottom of the preceding diagram.

Composition is preferred over inheritance, so you must ensure you're using inheritance correctly. Inheritance describes an is-a relationship and composition describes a has-a relationship. In this case, we're using the correct mixture of inheritance and composition because `FirebaseAuthService` is an `AuthService`, and `AuthService` has a `CacheService`.

Note that all three auth services implement all abstract functions. In addition, the `FirebaseAuthService` overrides the base `logout` function to implement its own behavior. All three classes inherit from the same abstract class and expose the same public interface. All three will execute the same auth workflow against different auth servers.

The in-memory auth service doesn't communicate with a server. The service is for demonstration purposes only. It implements fake JWT encoding, so we can demonstrate how the JWT life cycle works.

Let's start by creating the auth service.

Creating an auth service

We will start by creating the abstract auth service and the in-memory service:

1. Add an auth service:

   ```
   $ npx ng g s auth --flat false
   $ npx ng g s auth/inMemoryAuth --skip-tests
   ```

2. Rename `in-memory-auth.service.ts` to `auth.in-memory.service.ts` so that the different auth providers visually group together in File Explorer.

3. Remove the `@Injectable()` decorator of `auth.service.ts` , but keep it on `auth.in-memory.service.ts`.
4. Ensure that `authService` is provided in `app.module.ts` and that `InMemoryAuthService` is used and not the abstract class:

```
src/app/app.module.ts
import { AuthService } from './auth/auth.service'
import { InMemoryAuthService } from './auth/auth.in-memory.service'
...
  providers: [
    {
      provide: AuthService,
      useClass: InMemoryAuthService
    },
    ...
]
```

Creating a separate folder for the service organizes various components related to auth, such as the `enum` definition for the user role. Additionally, we will be able to add an `authService` fake to the same folder for automated testing.

Implement an abstract auth service

Now, let's build an abstract auth service that will orchestrate logins and logouts while encapsulating the logic of managing JWTs, auth status, and information regarding the current user. By leveraging the abstract class, we should be able to implement our own auth service against any auth provider without modifying the internal behavior of our application.

The abstract auth service that we will demonstrate enables rich and intricate workflows. It is a solution that you can drop into your applications without modifying the internal logic. As a result, it is a complicated solution.

This auth service will enable us to demonstrate logging in with an email and password, caching, and conditional navigation concepts based on authentication status and a user's role:

1. Start by installing a JWT decoding library and, to fake authentication, a JWT encoding library:

```
$ npm install jwt-decode
$ npm install -D @types/jwt-decode
```

2. Implement an `IAuthStatus` interface to store decoded user information, a helper interface, and the secure by default `defaultAuthStatus`:

src/app/auth/auth.service.ts

```
import { Role } from './auth.enum'
...
export interface IAuthStatus {
  isAuthenticated: boolean
  userRole: Role
  userId: string
}
export interface IServerAuthResponse {
  accessToken: string
}
export const defaultAuthStatus: IAuthStatus = {
  isAuthenticated: false,
  userRole: Role.None,
  userId: '',
}
...
```

`IAuthStatus` is an interface that represents the shape of a typical JWT that you may receive from your authentication service. It contains minimal information about the user and the user's role. The auth status object can be attached to the header of every REST call to APIs to verify the user's identity. The auth status can be optionally cached in `localStorage` to remember the user's login state; otherwise, they would have to re-enter their password with every page refresh.

In the preceding implementation, we assume the default role of `None`, as defined in the `Role` enum. By not giving any role to the user by default, we're following a least-privileged access model. The user's correct role will be set after they log in successfully with the information received from the auth API.

3. Define the `IAuthService` interface in `auth.service.ts`:

src/app/auth/auth.service.ts

```
export interface IAuthService {
  readonly authStatus$: BehaviorSubject<IAuthStatus>
  readonly currentUser$: BehaviorSubject<IUser>
  login(email: string, password: string): Observable<void>
```

```
  logout(clearToken?: boolean): void
  getToken(): string
}
```

4. Make `AuthService` an `abstract` class, as shown here:

```
export abstract class AuthService
```

5. Implement the interface, `IAuthService`, using VS Code's quick-fix functionality:

```
src/app/auth/auth.service.ts
export abstract class AuthService implements IAuthService {
  authStatus$: BehaviorSubject<IAuthStatus>
  currentUser$: BehaviorSubject<IUser>

  constructor() {}

  login(email: string, password: string): Observable<void> {
    throw new Error('Method not implemented.')
  }
  logout(clearToken?: boolean): void {
    throw new Error('Method not implemented.')
  }
  getToken(): string {
    throw new Error('Method not implemented.')
  }
}
```

6. Implement the `authStatus$` and `currentUser$` properties as `readonly` and initialize our data anchors with their default values:

```
src/app/auth/auth.service.ts
import { IUser, User } from '../user/user/user'
...
export abstract class AuthService implements IAuthService {
  readonly authStatus$ =
    new BehaviorSubject<IAuthStatus>(defaultAuthStatus)
  readonly currentUser$ =
    new BehaviorSubject<IUser>(new User())
  ...
}
```

Note that we removed the type definitions of the properties. Instead, we're letting TypeScript infer the type from the initialization.

You must always declare your data anchors as `readonly` so that you don't accidentally overwrite the data stream by re-initializing a data anchor as a new `BehaviorSubject`. Doing so would render any prior subscribers orphaned, leading to memory leaks, which has many unintended consequences.

All implementors of `IAuthService` must be able to log the user in, transform the token we get back from the server so that we can read and store it, support access to the current user and the auth status, and provide a way to log the user out. We have successfully put in the functions for our public methods and implemented default values for our data anchors, creating hooks for the rest of our application. But so far, we have only defined what our service can do and not how it can do it.

As always, the devil is in the details, and the hard part is the "how." Abstract functions can help us to complete the implementation of a workflow in a service within our application, while leaving the portions of the service that must implement external APIs undefined.

Abstract functions

Auth services that implement the abstract class should be able to support any kind of auth provider and any kind of token transformation while being able to modify behaviors, like user retrieval logic. We must be able to implement login, logout, token, and auth status management without implementing calls to specific services.

By defining abstract functions, we can declare a series of methods that must implement a given set of inputs and outputs—a signature without an implementation. We can then use these abstract functions to orchestrate the implementation of our auth workflow.

The Open/Closed principle drives our design goal here. The `AuthService` will be open to extension through its ability to be extended to work with any kind of token-based auth provider, but it is closed to modification. Once we're done implementing the `AuthService`, we won't need to modify its code to add additional auth providers.

Now, we need to define the abstract functions that our auth providers must implement, as shown in *Figure 5.3* from earlier in the chapter:

- `authProvider(email, password):Observable<IServerAuthResponse>` can log us in via a provider and return a standardized `IServerAuthResponse`
- `transformJwtToken(token): IAuthStatus` can normalize the token a provider returns to the interface of `IAuthStatus`
- `getCurrentUser(): Observable<User>` can retrieve the user profile of the logged-in user

We can then use these functions in our `login`, `logout`, and `getToken` methods to implement the auth workflow:

1. Define the abstract methods that the derived classes should implement as protected properties so that they're accessible in the derived class, but not publicly:

```
src/app/auth/auth.service.ts
...
export abstract class AuthService implements IAuthService {
      protected abstract authProvider(
        email: string,
        password: string
      ): Observable<IServerAuthResponse>
      protected abstract transformJwtToken(token: unknown):
        IAuthStatus
      protected abstract getCurrentUser(): Observable<User>
      ...
}
```

   Leveraging these stubbed-out methods, we can now implement a login method to log a user in and retrieve the currently logged-in user, updating the `authStatus$` and `currentUser$` data streams.

2. Before we move on, implement a `transformError` function to handle errors of different types like `HttpErrorResponse` and `string`, providing them in an observable stream. In a new file named `common.ts` under `src/app/common`, create the `transformError` function:

```
src/app/common/common.ts
import { HttpErrorResponse } from '@angular/common/http'
import { throwError } from 'rxjs'
export function transformError(error: HttpErrorResponse | string) {
```

```
  let errorMessage = 'An unknown error has occurred'
  if (typeof error === 'string') {
    errorMessage = error
  } else if (error.error instanceof ErrorEvent) {
    errorMessage = `Error! ${error.error.message}`
  } else if (error.status) {
    errorMessage =
      `Request failed with ${error.status} ${error.statusText}`
  } else if (error instanceof Error) {
    errorMessage = error.message
  }
  return throwError(errorMessage)
}
```

3. In `auth.service.ts`, implement the `login` method:

```
src/app/auth/auth.service.ts
import * as decode from 'jwt-decode'
import { transformError } from '../common/common'
...
  login(email: string, password: string): Observable<void> {
    const loginResponse$ = this.authProvider(email, password)
      .pipe(
        map((value) => {
          const token = decode(value.accessToken)
          return this.transformJwtToken(token)
        }),
        tap((status) => this.authStatus$.next(status)),
        filter((status: IAuthStatus) => status.isAuthenticated),
        flatMap(() => this.getCurrentUser()),
        map(user => this.currentUser$.next(user)),
        catchError(transformError)
      )
    loginResponse$.subscribe({
      error: err => {
        this.logout()
        return throwError(err)
      },
```

```
    })
    return loginResponse$
  }
```

The `login` method encapsulates the correct order of operations by calling the `authProvider` with the `email` and `password` information, then decoding the received JWT, transforming it, and updating `authStatus$`. Then, `getCurrentUser()` is called only if `status.isAuthenticated` is `true`. Later, `currentUser$` is updated, and finally, we catch any errors using our custom `transformError` function.

We activate the observable stream by calling `subscribe` on it. In the case of an error, we call `logout()` to maintain the correct status of our application and bubble up errors to consumers of `login` by re-throwing the error, using `throwError`.

Now, the corresponding `logout` function needs to be implemented. Logout is triggered by the **Logout** button from the application toolbar in the case of a failed login attempt, as shown earlier, or if an unauthorized access attempt is detected. We can detect unauthorized access attempts by using a router auth guard as the user navigates the application, which is a topic covered later in the chapter.

4. Implement the `logout` method:

src/app/auth/auth.service.ts

```
...
logout(clearToken?: boolean): void {
  setTimeout(() => this.authStatus$.next(defaultAuthStatus), 0)
}
```

We log out by pushing out the `defaultAuthStatus` as the next value in the `authStatus$` stream. Note the use of `setTimeout`, which allows us to avoid timing issues when core elements of the application all change statuses at once.

Think about how the `login` method adheres to the Open/Closed principle. The method is open to extension through the abstract functions `authProvider`, `transformJwtToken`, and `getCurrentUser`. By implementing these functions in a derived class, we can externally supply different auth providers without modifying the `login` method. As a result, the implementation of the method remains closed to modification, thus adhering to the Open/Closed principle.

The true value of creating abstract classes is the ability to encapsulate common functionality in an extensible way.

You may ignore the `getToken` function for now, as we are not yet caching our JWT. Without caching, the user would have to log in with every page refresh. Let's implement caching next.

A cache service using localStorage

We must be able to cache the authentication status of the logged-in user. As mentioned, otherwise, with every page refresh, the user must go through the login routine. We need to update `AuthService` so that it persists the auth status.

There are three main ways to store data:

- `cookie`
- `localStorage`
- `sessionStorage`

Cookies, while they have their use cases, should not be used to store secure data because they can be sniffed or stolen by bad actors. In addition, cookies can store only 4 KB of data and can be set to expire.

`localStorage` and `sessionStorage` are similar. They are protected and isolated browser-side stores that allow the storage of larger amounts of data for your application. Unlike cookies, you can't set an expiration date-time on values stored in either store. Values stored in either store survive page reloads and restores, making them better candidates than cookies for caching information.

The major difference between `localStorage` and `sessionStorage` is how values are persisted across browser tabs. With `sessionStorage`, stored values are removed when the browser tab or window is closed. However, `localStorage` persists across reboots. In most cases, user logins are cached anywhere from minutes to a month or more, depending on your business, so relying on whether the user closes the browser window isn't very useful. Through this process of elimination, I prefer `localStorage` because of its isolation and long-term storage capabilities.

JWTs can be encrypted and include a timestamp for expiration. In theory, this counters the weaknesses of both cookies and `localStorage`. If implemented correctly, either option should be secure for use with JWTs, but `localStorage` is still preferred.

Let's start by implementing a caching service that can provide a centralized caching method for our application. We can then derive from this service to cache our authentication information:

1. Start by creating an abstract `cacheService` that encapsulates the method of caching:

    src/app/common/cache.service.ts

    ```
    @Injectable({ providedIn: 'root' })
    export class CacheService {
      protected getItem<T>(key: string): T | null {
        const data = localStorage.getItem(key)
        if (data != null) {
          try {
            return JSON.parse(data)
          } catch (error) {
            console.error('Parsing error:', error)
            return null
          }
        }
        return null
      }
      protected setItem(key: string, data: object | string) {
        if (typeof data === 'string') {
          localStorage.setItem(key, data)
        }
        localStorage.setItem(key, JSON.stringify(data))
      }
      protected removeItem(key: string) {
        localStorage.removeItem(key)
      }
      protected clear() {
        localStorage.clear()
      }
    }
    ```

    This cache service class can give caching capabilities to any service. While it creates a centralized caching method you can inject into another service, it is not meant to be a centralized value store. You should never use it to synchronize state, so we can avoid introducing side effects and coupling between services and components.

2. Update AuthService to inject the CacheService, which will enable us to implement caching of the JWT in the next section:

   src/app/auth/auth.service.ts

   ```
   ...
   export abstract class AuthService implements IAuthService {
     protected readonly cache = inject(CacheService)
     ...
   }
   ```

Let's go over an example of how to use the base class's functionality by caching the value of the authStatus object:

example

```
authStatus$ = new BehaviorSubject<IAuthStatus>(
  this.getItem('authStatus') ?? defaultAuthStatus
)
constructor() {
  this.authStatus$.pipe(
    tap(authStatus => this.cache.setItem('authStatus', authStatus))
  )
}
```

The technique demonstrated in the example leverages RxJS observable streams to update the cache whenever the value of authStatus$ changes. You can use this pattern to persist any kind of data without cluttering your business logic with caching code. In this case, we wouldn't need to update the login function to call setItem because it already calls this.authStatus.next, and we can just tap into the data stream. This helps with staying stateless and avoiding side effects, by decoupling functions from each other.

Note that we also initialize the BehaviorSubject using the getItem function. Using the nullish coalescing operator, we only use cached data if it is not undefined or null. Otherwise, we provide the default value.

You can implement your own custom cache expiration scheme in the setItem and getItem functions or leverage a service created by a third party.

However, for an additional layer of security, we won't cache the `authStatus` object. Instead, we will only cache the encoded JWT, which contains just enough information, so we can authenticate requests sent to the server.

In the Implementing JWT auth section of *Chapter 7, Working with REST and GraphQL APIs,* we discuss how you should encrypt and verify JWT token validity to avoid token-based exploits.

It is important to understand how token-based authentication works to avoid revealing compromising secrets. Review the JWT life cycle earlier in this chapter to improve your understanding.

Next, let's cache the token.

Caching the JWT

Let's update the authentication service so that it can cache the token:

1. Update `AuthService` to be able to set, get, and clear the token, as shown here:

   src/app/auth/auth.service.ts

   ```
   ...
     protected setToken(jwt: string) {
       this.cache.setItem('jwt', jwt)
     }
     getToken(): string {
       return this.cache.getItem('jwt') ?? ''
     }
     protected clearToken() {
       this.cache.removeItem('jwt')
     }
   ```

2. Call `clearToken` and `setToken` during `login`, and `clearToken` during `logout`, as shown here:

   src/app/auth/auth.service.ts

   ```
   ...
     login(email: string, password: string): Observable<void> {
       this.clearToken()
       const loginResponse$ = this.authProvider(email, password)
         .pipe(
   ```

```
      map(value => {
        this.setToken(value.accessToken)
        const token = decode(value.accessToken)
        return this.transformJwtToken(token)
      }),
      tap((status) => this.authStatus$.next(status)),
      ...
  }
  logout(clearToken?: boolean) {
    if (clearToken) {
      this.clearToken()
    }
    setTimeout(() => this.authStatus$.next(defaultAuthStatus), 0)
  }
```

Every subsequent request will contain the JWT in the request header. You should secure every API to check for and validate the token received. For example, if a user wants to access their profile, the `AuthService` will validate the token to check whether the user is authenticated or not; however, a further database call will still be required to check whether the user is also authorized to view the data. This ensures an independent confirmation of the user's access to the system and prevents any abuse of an unexpired token.

If an authenticated user makes a call to an API where they don't have the proper authorization (say, if a clerk wants to get access to a list of all users), then the `AuthService` will return a `falsy` status, and the client will receive a `403 Forbidden` response, which will be displayed as an error message to the user.

A user can make a request with an expired token; when this happens, a `401 Unauthorized` response is sent to the client. As a good UX practice, we should automatically prompt the user to log in again and let them resume their workflow without any data loss.

In summary, true security is achieved with robust server-side implementation. Any client-side implementation is largely there to enable a good UX around good security practices.

An in-memory auth service

Now, let's implement a concrete version of the auth service that we can use:

1. Start by installing a JWT decoding library and, to fake authentication, a JWT encoding library:

```
$ npm install fake-jwt-sign
```

2. Extend the abstract `AuthService`:

src/app/auth/auth.in-memory.service.ts

```
import { AuthService } from './auth.service'
@Injectable({ providedIn: 'root' })
export class InMemoryAuthService extends AuthService {
  constructor() {
    super()
    console.warn(
      'You're using the InMemoryAuthService. Do not use this service
in production.'
    )
  }
  …
}
```

3. Implement a fake `authProvider` function that simulates the authentication process, including creating a fake JWT on the fly:

src/app/auth/auth.in-memory.service.ts

```
  import { sign } from 'fake-jwt-sign'//For InMemoryAuthService only
...
  protected authProvider(
    email: string,
    password: string
  ): Observable<IServerAuthResponse> {
    email = email.toLowerCase()
    if (!email.endsWith('@test.com')) {
      return throwError(
        'Failed to login! Email needs to end with @test.com.'
      )
    }
    const authStatus = {
      isAuthenticated: true,
```

```
      userId: this.defaultUser._id,
      userRole: email.includes('cashier')
        ? Role.Cashier
        : email.includes('clerk')
        ? Role.Clerk
        : email.includes('manager')
        ? Role.Manager
        : Role.None,
    } as IAuthStatus
    this.defaultUser.role = authStatus.userRole
    const authResponse = {
      accessToken: sign(authStatus, 'secret', {
        expiresIn: '1h',
        algorithm: 'none',
      }),
    } as IServerAuthResponse
    return of(authResponse)
  }
...
```

The `authProvider` implements what would otherwise be a server-side method right in the service, so we can conveniently experiment with the code while fine-tuning our auth workflow. The provider creates and signs a JWT with the temporary `fake-jwt-sign` library so that I can also demonstrate how to handle a properly formed JWT.

Do not ship your Angular application with the `fake-jwt-sign` dependency, since it is meant to be server-side code.

In contrast, a real auth provider would include a `POST` call to a server. See the example code that follows:

```
example
private exampleAuthProvider(
  email: string,
  password: string
): Observable<IServerAuthResponse> { return this.httpClient.
post<IServerAuthResponse>(
```

```
    `${environment.baseUrl}/v1/login`,
    { email: email, password: password }
  )
}
```

It is pretty straightforward, since the hard work is done on the server side. This call can also be made to a third-party auth provider, which I cover in the Firebase authentication recipe later in this chapter.

Note that the API version, v1, in the URL path is defined at the service and not as part of the baseUrl. This is because each API can change versions independently. Login may remain v1 for a long time, while other APIs may be upgraded to v2, v3, and so on.

4. Implementing `transformJwtToken` will be trivial because the login function provides us with a token that adheres to `IAuthStatus`:

   src/app/auth/auth.in-memory.service.ts

   ```
   protected transformJwtToken(token: IAuthStatus):
     IauthStatus {
       return token
     }
   ```

5. Finally, implement `getCurrentUser`, which should return some default user:

   src/app/auth/auth.in-memory.service.ts

   ```
   protected getCurrentUser(): Observable<User> {
     return of(this.defaultUser)
   }
   ```

   Next, provide a `defaultUser` as a private property to the class; what follows is one that I've created.

6. Add a private `defaultUser` property to the `InMemoryAuthService` class:

   src/app/auth/auth.in-memory.service.ts

   ```
   import { PhoneType, User } from '../user/user/user'
   ...
   private defaultUser = User.Build({
     _id: '5da01751da27cc462d265913',
   ```

```
  email: 'duluca@gmail.com',
  name: { first: 'Doguhan', last: 'Uluca' },
  picture: 'https://secure.gravatar.com/
    avatar/7cbaa9afb5ca78d97f3c689f8ce6c985',
  role: Role.Manager,
  dateOfBirth: new Date(1980, 1, 1),
  userStatus: true,
  address: {
    line1: '101 Sesame St.',
    city: 'Bethesda',
    state: 'Maryland',
    zip: '20810',
  },
  level: 2,
  phones: [
    {
      id: 0,
      type: PhoneType.Mobile,
      digits: '5555550717',
    },
  ],
})
```

Congratulations! You've implemented a concrete, but still fake, auth service. Now that you have the in-memory auth service in place, be sure to run your Angular application and ensure no errors are present.

Let's test our auth service by implementing a simple login and logout functionality accessible through the UI.

Simple login

Before we implement a fully-featured `login` component, let's wire up the pre-baked login behavior to the **Login as manager** button we have in the `HomeComponent`. We can test the behavior of our auth service before getting into the details of delivering a rich UI component.

Our goal is to simulate logging in as a manager. To accomplish this, we need to hardcode an email address and a password to log in and, upon successful login, maintain the functionality of navigating to the `/manager` route.

Note that on GitHub, the code sample for this section resides in a file named `home.component.simple.ts` under the folder structure of `projects/stage8`. The alternate file exists for reference purposes only because the code from this section dramatically changes later in the chapter. Ignore the filename difference, as it will not impact your coding for this section.

Let's implement a simple login mechanism:

1. In the `HomeComponent`, implement a `login` function that uses the `AuthService`:

   src/app/home/home.component.ts

   ```
   import { AuthService } from '../auth/auth.service'
   export class HomeComponent implements OnInit {
     constructor(private authService: AuthService) {}
     ngOnInit(): void {}
     login() {
       this.authService.login('manager@test.com', '12345678')
     }
   }
   ```

2. Update the template to remove the `routerLink` and, instead, call the `login` function:

   src/app/home/home.component.ts

   ```
   template: `
       <div fxLayout="column" fxLayoutAlign="center center">
         <span class="mat-display-2">Hello, Limoncu!</span>
         <button mat-raised-button color="primary" (click)="login()">
           Login as Manager
         </button>
       </div>
     `,
   ```

On successful login, we need to navigate to the `/manager` route. We can verify that we're successfully logged in by listening to the `authStatus$` and `currentUser$` observables exposed by the `AuthService`. If `authStatus$.isAuthenticated` is `true` and `currentUser$._id` is a non-empty string, we have a valid login. We can listen to both observables by using RxJS's `combineLatest` operator. Given a valid login condition, we can then use the `filter` operator to reactively navigate to the `/manager` route.

3. Update the `login()` function to implement the login conditional, and upon success, navigate to the `/manager` route:

```
src/app/home/home.component.ts
constructor(
  private authService: AuthService,
  private router: Router
) {}

login() {
  this.authService.login('manager@test.com', '12345678')
combineLatest([
  this.authService.authStatus$, this.authService.currentUser$
])
  .pipe(
    filter(([authStatus, user]) =>
      authStatus.isAuthenticated && user?._id !== ''
    ),
    tap(([authStatus, user]) => {
      this.router.navigate(['/manager'])
    })
  )
  .subscribe()
}
```

Note that we subscribe to the `combineLatest` operator at the end, which is critical in activating the observable streams. Otherwise, our login action will remain dormant unless some other component subscribes to the stream. You only need to activate a stream once.

4. Now, test out the new `login` functionality. Verify that the JWT is created and stored in `localStorage` using the **Chrome DevTools | Application** tab, as shown here:

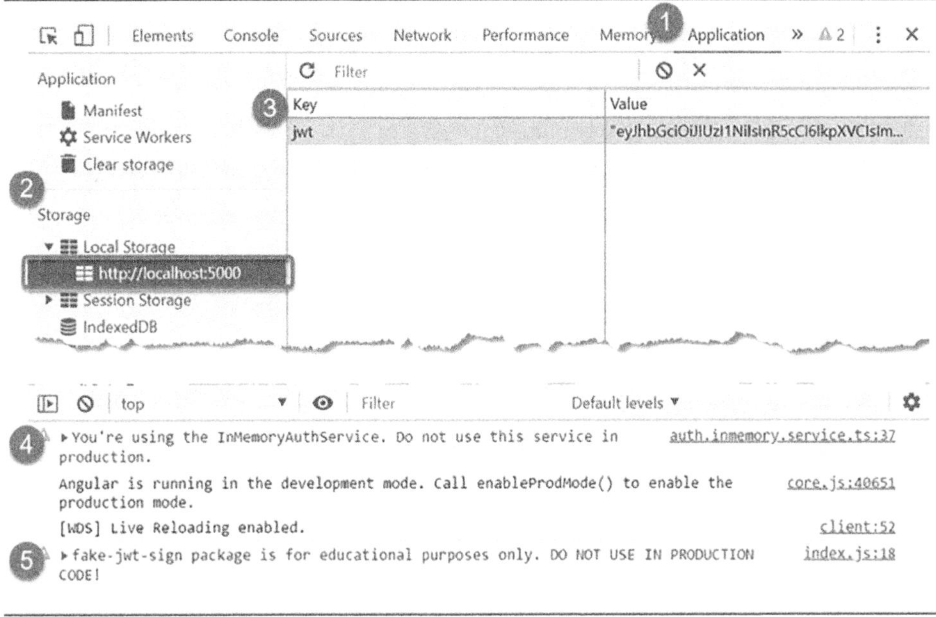

Figure 5.4: DevTools showing Application | Local Storage

You can view **Local Storage** under the **Application** tab. Make sure that the URL of your application is highlighted. In *step 3*, you can see that we have a key named `jwt` with a valid-looking token.

Note *steps 4* and *5*, highlighting two warnings, which, respectively, advise us not to use the `InMemoryAuthService` and the `fake-jwt-sign` package in production code.

Use breakpoints to debug and step through the code to get a more concrete understanding of how `HomeComponent`, `InMemoryAuthService`, and `AuthService` work together to log the user in.

When you refresh the page, note that you're still logged in because we're caching the token in local storage.

Since we're caching the login status, we must also implement a logout experience to complete the auth workflow.

Logout

The logout button on the application toolbar is already wired up to navigate to the `logout` component we created before. Let's update this component so that it can log the user out when navigated to:

1. Implement the `logout` component:

```
src/app/user/logout/logout.component.ts
import { Component, OnInit } from '@angular/core'
import { Router } from '@angular/router'
import { AuthService } from '../../auth/auth.service'
@Component({
  selector: 'app-logout',
  template: `<p>Logging out...</p>`,
})
export class LogoutComponent implements OnInit {
  constructor(private router: Router, private authService:
AuthService) {}
  ngOnInit() {
    this.authService.logout(true)
    this.router.navigate(['/'])
  }
}
```

Note that we explicitly clear the JWT by passing in `true` to the `logout` function. After we call `logout`, we navigate the user back to the home page.

2. Test out the `logout` button.
3. Verify that local storage is cleared after logout.

We have nailed a solid login and logout implementation. However, we're not yet done with the fundamentals of our auth workflow.

Next, we need to consider the expiration status of our JWT.

Resuming a JWT session

It wouldn't be a great UX if you had to log in to Gmail or Amazon every time you visited the site. This is why we cache the JWT, but it would be an equally bad UX to keep you logged in forever. A JWT has an expiration date policy, where the provider can select a few minutes or even months to allow your token to be valid, depending on security needs. The in-memory service creates tokens that expire in one hour, so if a user refreshes their browser window within that frame, we should honor the valid token and let the user continue using the application, without asking them to log back in.

On the flip side, if the token is expired, we should automatically navigate the user to the login screen for a smooth UX.

Let's get started:

1. Update the `AuthService` class to implement a function named `hasExpiredToken` to check whether the token is expired, and a helper function named `getAuthStatusFromToken` to decode the token, as shown here:

   src/app/auth/auth.service.ts

   ```
   ...
     protected hasExpiredToken(): boolean {
       const jwt = this.getToken()
       if (jwt) {
         const payload = decode(jwt) as any
         return Date.now() >= payload.exp * 1000
       }
       return true
     }
     protected getAuthStatusFromToken(): IAuthStatus {
       return this.transformJwtToken(decode(this.getToken()))
     }
   ```

Keep your code DRY! Update the `login()` function to use `getAuthStatusFromToken()` instead.

2. Update the constructor of `AuthService` to check the status of the token:

```
src/app/auth/auth.service.ts
...
constructor() {
  super()
  if (this.hasExpiredToken()) {
    this.logout(true)
  } else {
    this.authStatus$.next(this.getAuthStatusFromToken())
  }
}
```

   If the token is expired, we log the user out and clear the token from `localStorage`. Otherwise, we decode the token and push the auth status to the data stream.

   A corner case to consider here is to also trigger the reloading of the current user in the event of a resumption. We can do this by implementing a new pipe that reloads the current user if activated.

3. First, let's refactor the existing user update logic in the `login()` function to a private property named `getAndUpdateUserIfAuthenticated` so that we can reuse it:

```
src/app/auth/auth.service.ts
...
export abstract class AuthService implements IAuthService {
  private getAndUpdateUserIfAuthenticated = pipe(
    filter((status: IAuthStatus) => status.isAuthenticated),
    flatMap(() => this.getCurrentUser()),
    map((user: IUser) => this.currentUser$.next(user)),
    catchError(transformError)
  )
  ...
  login(email: string, password: string): Observable<void> {
    this.clearToken()
    const loginResponse$ = this.authProvider(email, password)
      .pipe(
        map((value) => {
          this.setToken(value.accessToken)
          const token = decode(value.accessToken)
```

```
          return this.transformJwtToken(token)
        }),
        tap((status) => this.authStatus$.next(status)),
        this.getAndUpdateUserIfAuthenticated
      )
    ...
  }
  ...
}
```

4. In `AuthService`, define an observable property named `resumeCurrentUser$` as a fork of `authStatus$`, and use the `getAndUpdateUserIfAuthenticated` logic:

   src/app/auth/auth.service.ts

   ```
   ...
     protected readonly resumeCurrentUser$ = this.authStatus$.pipe(
       this.getAndUpdateUserIfAuthenticated
     )
   ```

   Once `resumeCurrentUser$` is activated and `status.isAuthenticated` is `true`, then `this.getCurrentUser()` will be invoked and `currentUser$` will be updated.

5. Update the constructor of `AuthService` to activate the pipeline if the token has not expired:

   src/app/auth/auth.service.ts

   ```
   ...
   constructor() {
     if (this.hasExpiredToken()) {
       this.logout(true)
     } else {
       this.authStatus$.next(this.getAuthStatusFromToken())
       // To load user on browser refresh,
       // resume pipeline must activate on the next cycle
       // Which allows for all services to constructed properly
       setTimeout(() => this.resumeCurrentUser$.subscribe(), 0)
     }
   }
   ```

Using the preceding technique, we can retrieve the latest user profile data without dealing with caching issues.

To experiment with token expiration, I recommend creating a faster-expiring token in `InMemoryAuthService`.

As demonstrated earlier in the caching section, it is possible to cache the user profile data using `this.cache.setItem` and the profile data from the cache on the first launch. This would provide a faster UX and cover cases where users may be offline. After the application launches, you could asynchronously fetch fresh user data and update `currentUser$` when new data comes in. You would need to add additional caching and tweak the `getCurrentUser()` logic to get such functionality working. Oh, and you would need a whole lot of testing! It takes a lot of testing to create a high-quality auth experience.

Congratulations! We're done implementing a robust auth workflow! Next, we need to integrate auth with Angular's HTTP client to attach the token to the HTTP header of every request.

An HTTP interceptor

Implement an HTTP interceptor to inject the JWT into the header of every request sent to the API, and gracefully handle authentication failures by asking the user to log back in:

1. Create an `AuthHttpInterceptor` under `auth`:

   src/app/auth/auth.http.interceptor.ts

   ```
   import { HttpHandlerFn, HttpRequest } from '@angular/common/http'
   import { inject } from '@angular/core'
   import { Router } from '@angular/router'
   import { throwError } from 'rxjs'
   import { catchError } from 'rxjs/operators'
   import { environment } from 'src/environments/environment'

   import { UiService } from '../common/ui.service'
   import { AuthService } from './auth.service'

   export function AuthHttpInterceptor(
     req: HttpRequest<unknown>, next: HttpHandlerFn
   ) {
     const authService = inject(AuthService)
   ```

```
    const router = inject(Router)
    const uiService = inject(UiService)

    const jwt = authService.getToken()
    const baseUrl = environment.baseUrl

    if (req.url.startsWith(baseUrl)) {
      const authRequest = req.clone({
        setHeaders: {
          authorization: `Bearer ${jwt}`
        }
      })
      return next(authRequest).pipe(
        catchError((err) => {
          uiService.showToast(err.error.message)
          if (err.status === 401) {
            router.navigate(['/login'], {
              queryParams: {
                redirectUrl: router.routerState.snapshot.url
              },
            })
          }
          return throwError(() => err)
        })
      )
    } else {
      return next(req)
    }
  }
```

Note that `AuthService` is leveraged to retrieve the token, and the `redirectUrl` is set for the `login` component after a `401` error.

Note the if statement `if (req.url.startsWith(baseUrl))` filters out any outgoing requests not made to our API. This way, we don't leak our JWT token to external services.

2. Update `app.config.ts` to provide the interceptor:

```
src/app/app.config.ts
export const appConfig: ApplicationConfig = {
  providers: [
    provideAnimations(),
    provideHttpClient(
      withInterceptors([AuthHttpInterceptor])
    ),
    ...
```

3. Ensure that the interceptor adds the token to requests. To do this, open the **Chrome DevTools | Network** tab, log in, and then refresh the page:

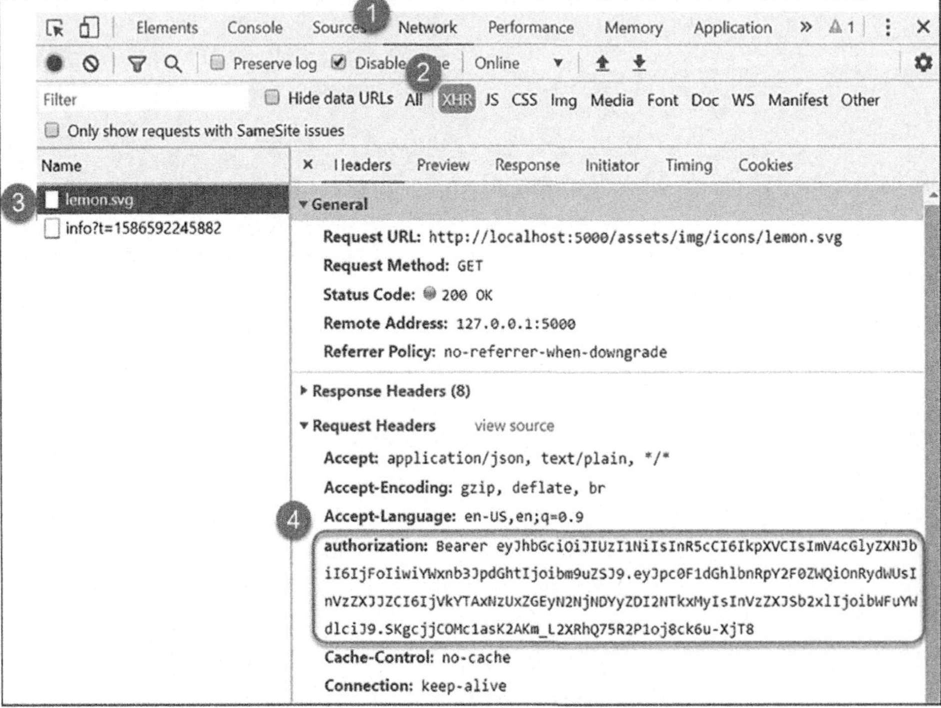

Figure 5.5: The request header for lemon.svg

In *step 4*, you can now observe the interceptor in action. The request for the `lemon.svg` file has the bearer token in the request header.

Now that we have our auth mechanism implemented, let's take advantage of all the supporting code we have written with dynamic UI components and a conditional navigation system, creating a role-based UX in the next chapter.

Summary

You should now have a solid understanding of how JWT works, how to use TypeScript for safe data handling, and how to build extendable services. In this chapter, we defined a `User` object that we can hydrate from or serialize to JSON objects, applying object-oriented class design and TypeScript operators for safe data handling.

We leveraged OOP design principles, using inheritance and abstract classes to implement a base auth service that demonstrates the Open/Closed principle.

We covered the fundamentals of token-based authentication and JWTs so that you don't leak any critical user information. You learned that caching and HTTP interceptors are necessary so that users don't have to input their login information with every request. Following that, we implemented an in-memory auth service that doesn't require any external dependencies, which is great for testing.

Coming up, in *Chapter 6, Implementing Role Based Navigation,* we will build a dynamic UI with navigation and component states reacting to the auth status of the app, using router and auth guards, flex layout media queries, Material components, and a service factory. We will also implement a Firebase auth provider so that you can host your apps on Google Firebase. In *Chapter 7, Working with REST and GraphQL APIs*, we will bring it all together with two custom auth providers that can authenticate against LemonMart Server, using the Minimal MEAN stack.

Further reading

- *Salted Password Hashing - Doing it Right, Defuse Security*, 2019; `https://crackstation.net/hashing-security.htm`.
- *Object-oriented programming*; `https://en.wikipedia.org/wiki/Object-oriented_programming`.
- *TypeScript Classes*; `https://www.typescriptlang.org/docs/handbook/classes.html`.
- *TypeScript Basic Types*; `https://www.typescriptlang.org/docs/handbook/basic-types.html`.
- *TypeScript Advanced Types*; `https://www.typescriptlang.org/docs/handbook/advanced-types.html`.

- *TypeScript 3.7 Features*; `https://www.typescriptlang.org/docs/handbook/release-notes/typescript-3-7.html`.
- *Authentication General Guidelines*; `https://github.com/OWASP/CheatSheetSeries/blob/master/cheatsheets/Authentication_Cheat_Sheet.md`.
- *How to secure your Firebase project even when your API key is publicly available*; paachu, 2019, `https://medium.com/@impaachu/how-to-secure-your-firebase-project-even-when-your-api-key-is-publicly-available-a462a2a58843`.

Questions

Answer the following questions as best as possible to ensure you've understood the key concepts from this chapter without googling anything. Do you know if you got all the answers right? Visit `https://angularforenterprise.com/self-assessment` for more:

1. What's in-transit and at-rest security?
2. What's the difference between authentication and authorization?
3. Explain inheritance and polymorphism.
4. What is an abstract class?
5. What is an abstract method?
6. Explain how the `AuthService` adheres to the Open/Closed principle.
7. How does JWT verify your identity?
8. What is the difference between RxJS's `combineLatest` and `merge` operators?
9. What is a route guard?
10. What does a service factory allow you to do?

Join our community on Discord

Join our community's Discord space for discussions with the authors and other readers:

`https://packt.link/AngularEnterpise3e`

6

Implementing Role-Based Navigation

In *Chapter 5, Designing Authorization and Authentication*, we covered how designing an effective authentication and authorization system is challenging but crucial for user satisfaction. Users expect a high standard from web authentication systems, and any errors should be clearly communicated. As applications grow, their authentication backbone should be easily maintainable and extensible to ensure a seamless user experience.

In this chapter, we will discuss the challenges of creating a great auth UX and implementing a solid baseline experience. We will continue the router-first approach to designing SPAs by implementing the auth experience of LemonMart. In *Chapter 4, Creating a Router-First Line-of-Business App*, we defined user roles, finished our build-out of all major routing, and completed a rough walking-skeleton navigation experience of LemonMart. This means we are well prepared to implement a role-based conditional navigation experience that captures the nuances of a seamless auth experience. We will supplement this with an auth provider using the Google Firebase auth service, which you can leverage in real-world applications.

In this chapter, you will learn about the following topics:

- Dynamic UI components and navigation
- Role-based routing using guards
- A Firebase authentication recipe
- Providing a service using a factory

Technical requirements

The most up-to-date versions of the sample code for the book are on GitHub at the following linked repository. The repository contains the final and completed state of the code. You can verify your progress at the end of this chapter by looking for the end-of-chapter snapshot of code under the `projects` folder.

For *Chapter 6*:

1. Clone the repository `https://github.com/duluca/lemon-mart`.
2. Execute `npm install` on the root folder to install dependencies.
3. You will continue building on `stage8` from the last chapter:

```
projects/stage7
```

4. The end state of the project is reflected at:

```
projects/stage8
```

5. Add the stage name to any `ng` command to act only on that stage:

```
npx ng build stage8
```

Note that the `dist/stage8` folder at the root of the repository will contain the compiled result.

Beware that the source code provided in the book and the version on GitHub are likely to be different. The ecosystem around these projects is ever-evolving. Between changes to how Angular CLI generates new code, bug fixes, new versions of libraries, and side-by-side implementations of multiple techniques, there's a lot of variation that is impossible to account for. If you find errors or have questions, please create an issue or submit a pull request on GitHub.

With the in-memory auth provider in place, let's take advantage of all the supporting code we have written with dynamic UI components and a conditional navigation system for a role-based UX.

Dynamic UI components and navigation

AuthService provides asynchronous auth status and user information, including a user's name and role. We can use all this information to create a friendly and personalized user experience. In this next section, we will implement the LoginComponent so that users can enter their username and password information and attempt a login.

Implementing the login component

The LoginComponent leverages the AuthService we created and implements validation errors using reactive forms.

Remember that in app.config.ts, we provided AuthService using the class InMemoryAuthService. So, during runtime, when AuthService is injected into the LoginComponent, the in-memory service will be used.

The LoginComponent should be designed to be rendered independently of any other component because, during a routing event, if we discover that the user is not properly authenticated or authorized, we will navigate them to this component. We can capture this origination URL as a redirectUrl so that once a user logs in successfully, we can navigate them back to it.

Let's begin:

1. Create a new component named login in the root of your application with inline styles.
2. Let's start by implementing the routes to the LoginComponent:

   src/app/app-routing.modules.ts

   ```
   ...
     { path: 'login', component: LoginComponent },
     { path: 'login/:redirectUrl', component: LoginComponent },
   ...
   ```

Remember that the '**' path must be the last one defined.

3. Using a similar `login` logic to the one we implemented in `HomeComponent`, implement the `LoginComponent` with some styles:

> Don't forget to import the requisite dependent modules into your Angular application for the upcoming steps. This is intentionally left as an exercise for you to locate and import the missing modules.

src/app/login/login.component.ts

```
...
import { AuthService } from '../auth/auth.service'
import { Role } from '../auth/role.enum'
@Component({
  selector: 'app-login',
  templateUrl: 'login.component.html',
  styles: `
      .error { color: red; }
      div[fxLayout] { margin-top: 32px; }
    `,
  standalone: true,
  imports: [
    FlexModule,
    MatCardModule,
    ReactiveFormsModule,
    MatIconModule,
    MatFormFieldModule,
    MatInputModule,
    FieldErrorDirective,
    MatButtonModule,
    MatExpansionModule,
    MatGridListModule,
  ],
})
export class LoginComponent implements OnInit {
  private readonly formBuilder = inject(FormBuilder)
  private readonly authService = inject(AuthService)
  private readonly router = inject(Router)
  private readonly route = inject(ActivatedRoute)
```

```
loginForm: FormGroup
loginError = ''

get redirectUrl() {
  return this.route.snapshot
            .queryParamMap.get('redirectUrl') || ''
}

ngOnInit() {
  this.authService.logout()
  this.buildLoginForm()
}
buildLoginForm() {
  this.loginForm = this.formBuilder.group({
    email: ['', [Validators.required, Validators.email]],
    password: ['', [
      Validators.required,
      Validators.minLength(8),
      Validators.maxLength(50),
    ]],
  })
}
async login(submittedForm: FormGroup) {
  this.authService
    .login(
      submittedForm.value.email,
      submittedForm.value.password
    )
    .pipe(catchError(err => (this.loginError = err)))
  combineLatest([
    this.authService.authStatus$,
    this.authService.currentUser$,
  ])
    .pipe(
      filter(
        ([authStatus, user]) =>
```

```
          authStatus.isAuthenticated && user?._id !== ''
        ),
        first(),
        tap(([authStatus, user]) => {
          this.router.navigate([this.redirectUrl || '/manager'])
        })
      )
      .subscribe()
  }
}
```

We are using the `first` operator to manage the subscription. We ensure that we are logged out when `ngOnInit` is called. We build the reactive form in a standard manner. Finally, the `login` method calls `this.authService.login` to initiate the login process.

We listen to the `authStatus$` and `currentUser$` data streams simultaneously using `combineLatest`. Every time there's a change in each stream, our pipe gets executed. We filter out unsuccessful login attempts. As the result of a successful login attempt, we leverage the router to navigate an authenticated user to their profile. In the case of an error sent from the server via the service, we assign that error to `loginError`.

4. Here's an implementation for a login form to capture and validate a user's `email` and `password` and, if there are any server errors, display them:

Don't forget to import `ReactiveFormsModule` in `app.modules.ts`.

src/app/login/login.component.html

```
<div fxLayout="row" fxLayoutAlign="center">
  <mat-card appearance="outlined" fxFlex="400px">
    <mat-card-header>
      <mat-card-title>
        <div class="mat-headline-5">Hello, Limoncu!</div>
      </mat-card-title>
    </mat-card-header>
    <mat-card-content>
```

```
<form [formGroup]="loginForm" (ngSubmit)="login(loginForm)"
         fxLayout="column">
  <div fxLayout="row" fxLayoutAlign="start center"
          fxLayoutGap="10px">
    <mat-icon>email</mat-icon>
    <mat-form-field fxFlex>
      <input
        matInput
        placeholder="E-mail"
        aria-label="E-mail"
        formControlName="email"
        #email />
      <mat-error [input]="email" [group]="loginForm"
                       appFieldError="invalid">
      </mat-error>
    </mat-form-field>
  </div>
  <div fxLayout="row" fxLayoutAlign="start center"
          fxLayoutGap="10px">
    <mat-icon matPrefix>vpn_key</mat-icon>
    <mat-form-field fxFlex>
      <input
        matInput
        placeholder="Password"
        aria-label="Password"
        type="password"
        formControlName="password"
        #password />
      <mat-hint>Minimum 8 characters</mat-hint>
      <mat-error
        [input]="password"
        [group]="loginForm"
        [appFieldError]=
          "['required', 'minlength', 'maxlength']">
      </mat-error>
    </mat-form-field>
  </div>
```

```
      <div fxLayout="row" class="margin-top">
        @if (loginError) {
          <div class="mat-caption error">
            {{ loginError }}
          </div>
        }
        <div class="flex-spacer"></div>
        <button
          mat-raised-button
          type="submit"
          color="primary"
          [disabled]="loginForm.invalid">
          Login
        </button>
      </div>
    </form>
  </mat-card-content>
</mat-card>
</div>
```

The **Login** button is disabled until the email and password meet client site validation rules. Additionally, `<mat-form-field>` will only display one `mat-error` at a time, unless you create more space for more errors, so be sure to place your error conditions in the correct order.

Once you're done implementing the `LoginComponent`, you can update the home screen to conditionally display or hide the new component we created.

5. Update the `HomeComponent` to clean up the code we added previously so that we can display the `LoginComponent` when users land on the home page of the app:

src/app/home/home.component.ts

```
...
template: `
  @if (displayLogin) {
    <app-login></app-login>
  } @else {
```

```
        <span class="mat-display-3">
          You get a lemon, you get a lemon, you get a lemon...
        </span>
      }
    `,
})
export class HomeComponent {
  displayLogin = true
  constructor() {
  }
}
```

Your application should look like the following screenshot:

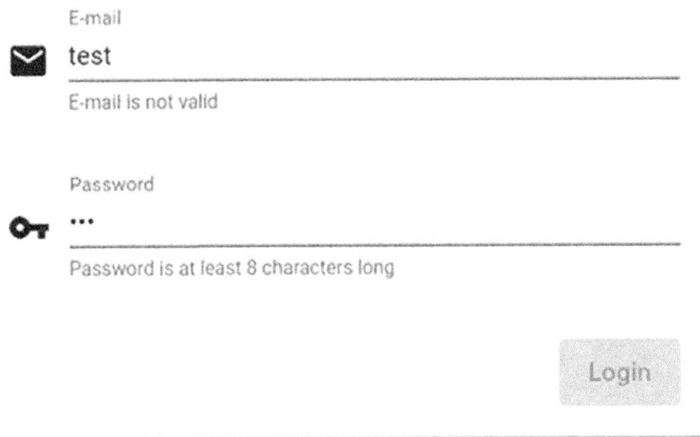

Figure 6.1: LemonMart with login

There's still some work to be done in terms of implementing and showing/hiding the `sidenav` menu, profile, and logout icons, given the user's authentication status.

Conditional navigation

Conditional navigation is necessary to create a frustration-free UX. By selectively showing the elements the user has access to and hiding the ones they don't, we allow the user to confidently navigate through the application.

Let's start by hiding the `LoginComponent` after a user logs into the application:

1. On the `HomeComponent`, inject the `AuthService` into the constructor as a `public` variable:

   src/app/home/home.component.simple.ts

   ```
   ...
   import { AuthService } from '../auth/auth.service'
   ...
   export class HomeComponent {
     constructor(public authService: AuthService) {}
   }
   ```

2. Remove the local variable `displayLogin` because we can directly tap into the auth status in the template using the `async` pipe.
3. Implement a new template using the control flow syntax, along with the `async` pipe, as shown here:

   src/app/home/home.component.ts

   ```
   ...
     template: `
       @if ((authService.authStatus$ | async)?.isAuthenticated) {
         <div>
           <div class="mat-display-4">
             This is LemonMart! The place where
           </div>
           <div class="mat-display-4">
             You get a lemon, you get a lemon, you get a lemon...
           </div>
           <div class="mat-display-4">
             Everybody gets a lemon.
           </div>
         </div>
       } @else {
         <app-login></app-login>
   ```

```
    }
  `,
  standalone: true,
  imports: [LoginComponent, AsyncPipe],
```

Using the `async` pipe avoids errors like `Error: ExpressionChangedAfterItHasBeenCheckedError: Expression has changed after it was checked`. Whenever you see this error, stop using local variables and, instead, use the `async` pipe. It is the reactive thing to do!

4. On the `AppComponent`, we will follow a similar pattern by injecting `AuthService` as a `public` variable:

```
src/app/app.component.ts
import { Component, OnInit } from '@angular/core'
import { AuthService } from './auth/auth.service'
...
export class AppComponent implements OnInit {
  constructor(..., public authService: AuthService) {
  }
  ngOnInit(): void {}
  ...
}
```

5. Update `mat-toolbar` in the template so that we monitor both `authStatus$` and `currentUser$` using the `async` pipe:

```
@if ({
  status: authService.authStatus$ | async,
  user: authService.currentUser$ | async
}; as auth;) {
   <mat-toolbar ...
```

6. Use `@if` to hide all buttons meant for logged-in users:

```
src/app/app.component.ts
@if (auth?.status?.isAuthenticated) {
  <button ... >
```

Now, when a user is logged out, your toolbar should look clean, with no buttons, as shown here:

Figure 6.2: The LemonMart toolbar before a user logs in

7. We can also swap out the generic `account_circle` icon in the `profile` button if the user has a picture:

```
src/app/app.component.ts
import { NgOptimizedImage } from '@angular/common'

styles: `
  .image-cropper {
    border-radius: 50%;
  }
`,
template: `
  ...
  @if (auth?.status?.isAuthenticated) {
    <button mat-mini-fab routerLink="/user/profile"
     matTooltip="Profile" aria-label="User Profile">
    @if (auth?.user?.picture) {
      <img alt="Profile picture" class="image-cropper"
           [ngSrc]="auth?.user?.picture ?? ''"
           width="40px" height="40px" fill />
    }
    @if (!auth?.user?.picture) {
      <mat-icon>account_circle</mat-icon>
    }
  </button>
}
...
`
standalone: true,
  imports: [
    FlexModule,
```

```
    RouterLink,
    NavigationMenuComponent,
    RouterOutlet,
    AsyncPipe,
    MatIconModule,
    MatToolbarModule,
    MatButtonModule,
    MatSidenavModule,
    NgOptimizedImage,
  ],
```

Note the use of the `ngSrc` attribute within the `img` tag, which activates the `NgOptimizedImage` directive. This directive makes it easy to adopt performance best practices for loading images. It has rich features to prioritize or delay the loading of certain images to assist in fast **First Contentful Paint** (**FCP**) scenarios, allow the use of CDNs, and enforce the use of `width` and `height` attributes to prevent layout shifts that can occur when an image loads.

Read more about `NgOptimizedImage` at `https://angular.dev/guide/image-optimization`.

We now have a highly functional toolbar that reacts to the auth status of the application and can also display information that belongs to the logged-in user.

Common validations for forms

Before we move on, we need to refactor the validations for `LoginComponent`. As we implement more forms in *Chapter 8, Recipes – Reusability, Forms, and Caching*, you will realize that it gets tedious very quickly to repeatedly type out form validations in either template or reactive forms. Part of the allure of reactive forms is that they are driven by code, so we can easily extract the validations to a shared class and unit test and reuse them, as follows:

1. Create a `validations.ts` file under the common folder.
2. Implement the email and password validations:

src/app/common/validations.ts

```
import { Validators } from '@angular/forms'
export const EmailValidation = [
```

```
  Validators.required, Validators.email
]
export const PasswordValidation = [
  Validators.required,
  Validators.minLength(8),
  Validators.maxLength(50),
]
```

Depending on your password validation needs, you can use a `RegEx` pattern with the `Validations.pattern()` function to enforce password complexity rules or leverage the OWASP npm package, `owasp-password-strength-test`, to enable passphrases, as well as set more flexible password requirements. See the link to the OWASP authentication general guidelines in the *Further reading* section.

3. Update the `LoginComponent` with the new validations:

src/app/login/login.component.ts

```
import {
  EmailValidation, PasswordValidation
} from '../common/validations'
...
this.loginForm = this.formBuilder.group({
  email: ['', EmailValidation],
  password: ['', PasswordValidation],
})
```

Next, let's encapsulate some common UI behavior in an Angular service.

UI service using environment provider

As we start dealing with complicated workflows, such as the auth workflow, it is important to be able to programmatically display a toast notification for the user. In other cases, we may want to ask for confirmation before executing a destructive action with a more intrusive pop-up notification.

No matter what component library you use, it gets tedious to recode the same boilerplate just to display a quick notification. A UI service can neatly encapsulate a default implementation that can be customized.

In the UI service, we will implement `showToast` and `showDialog` functions that can trigger notifications or prompt users for a decision, allowing us to use them within the code implementing the business logic.

Let's get started:

1. Create a new service named `ui` under `common`.
2. Implement a `showToast` function using `MatSnackBar`:

Check out the documentation for `MatSnackBar` at `https://material.angular.io`.

Since this service could be used by any service, component, or feature module, we can't declare this service in a module context. Since our project is a standalone project, we instead need to implement an **environment provider** so that we can provide the service in the app context defined in `app.config.ts`.

```
src/app/common/ui.service.ts
@Injectable({
  providedIn: 'root',
})
export class UiService {
  constructor(
    private snackBar: MatSnackBar,
    private dialog: MatDialog
  ) {}

  showToast(
    message: string,
    action = 'Close',
    config?: MatSnackBarConfig
) {
    this.snackBar.open(
      message,
      action,
      config || {
```

```
        duration: 7000,
      }
    )
  }
}
```

For a showDialog function using MatDialog, we must implement a basic dialog component.

Check out the documentation for MatDialog at https://material.angular.io.

3. Add a new component named simpleDialog under the common folder with inline templates and styling, skip testing, and a flat folder structure:

app/common/simple-dialog.component.ts

```
import { Component, Inject } from '@angular/core'
import { MAT_DIALOG_DATA, MatDialogRef } from '@angular/material/
dialog'
@Component({
  // prettier-ignore
  template: `
    <h2 mat-dialog-title>{{ data.title }}</h2>
    <mat-dialog-content>
      <p>{{ data.content }}</p>
    </mat-dialog-content>
    <mat-dialog-actions>
      <span class="flex-spacer"></span>
      @if (data.cancelText) {
        <button mat-button mat-dialog-close>
          {{ data.cancelText }}
        </button>
      }
      <button mat-button mat-button-raised color="primary"
        [mat-dialog-close]="true" cdkFocusInitial>
        {{ data.okText }}
      </button>
    </mat-dialog-actions>
```

```
  `,
  standalone: true,
  imports: [MatDialogModule, MatButtonModule],
})
export class SimpleDialogComponent {
  constructor(
    public dialogRef: MatDialogRef<SimpleDialogComponent, boolean>,
    @Inject(MAT_DIALOG_DATA)
    public data: {
      title: string;
      content: string;
      okText: string;
      cancelText: string
    }
  ) {}
}
```

`SimpleDialogComponent` should not have an application selector like `selector: 'app-simple-dialog'`, since we only plan to use it with `UiService`. If auto-generated, remove this property from your component.

4. Now, implement a `showDialog` function using `MatDialog` to display the `SimpleDialogComponent`:

app/common/ui.service.ts

```
...
showDialog(
  title: string,
  content: string,
  okText = 'OK',
  cancelText?: string,
  customConfig?: MatDialogConfig
): Observable<boolean> {
  const dialogRef = this.dialog.open(
    SimpleDialogComponent,
    customConfig || {
      width: '300px',
      data: { title, content, okText, cancelText },
```

```
    }
  )
  return dialogRef.afterClosed()
}
```

ShowDialog returns an Observable<boolean>, so you can implement a follow-on action depending on what selection the user makes. Clicking on **OK** will return true, and **Cancel** will return false.

In SimpleDialogComponent, using @Inject, we can use all variables sent by showDialog to customize the content of the dialog.

5. Add a function named provideUiService as an environment provider at the bottom of UiService:

```
app/common/ui.service.ts
import { importProvidersFrom, makeEnvironmentProviders } from '@
angular/core'

export function provideUiService() {
  return makeEnvironmentProviders([
    importProvidersFrom(MatDialogModule, MatSnackBarModule),
  ])
}
```

makeEnvironmentProviders allows us to wrap the dependencies of Service in an encapsulated object. This way, we don't expose these dependencies to the component using the service. This helps us enforce a decoupled architecture.

6. In app.config.ts, add provideUiService() to the providers array:

```
src/app/app.config.ts
export const appConfig: ApplicationConfig = {
  providers: [
    ...
    provideUiService()
  ]
}
```

7. Update the `login()` function on the `LoginComponent` to display a toast message after login:

src/app/login/login.component.ts
```
import { UiService } from '../common/ui.service'
...
  private readonly uiService = inject(UiService)
  ...
  async login(submittedForm: FormGroup) {
    ...
    tap(([authStatus, user]) => {
      this.uiService.showToast(
        `Welcome ${user.fullName}! Role: ${user.role}`
      )
      ...
    })
  ...
```

Now, a toast message will appear after a user has logged in, as shown here:

Figure 6.3: Material snackbar

The `snackBar` will either take up the full width of the screen or a portion, depending on the size of the browser.

8. Experiment with displaying a dialog instead:

src/app/login/login.component.ts
```
this.uiService.showDialog(
  `Welcome ${user.fullName}!`, `Role: ${user.role}`
)
```

Now that you've verified that both `showToast` and `showDialog` work, which do you prefer?

My rule of thumb between choosing a toast message or a dialog box is that unless the user is about to take an irreversible action, you should choose toast messages over dialogs so that you don't interrupt the user's workflow.

Next, let's implement an application-wide side navigation experience as an alternative to the toolbar-based navigation we already have so that users can switch between modules with ease.

Side navigation

To enhance the user experience, it is essential to enable mobile-first workflows and offer an intuitive navigation mechanism that allows users to access their desired functionality quickly. A side navigation (`SideNav`) bar serves mobile and desktop users equally well. On mobile screens, it can be activated by a triple dash (hamburger) menu, and on a large screen, it can be locked open. To further optimize the experience, we should only show the links a user is authorized to view. We can do this by utilizing the `AuthenticationService` based on the user's current role. We will implement the side navigation mock-up as follows:

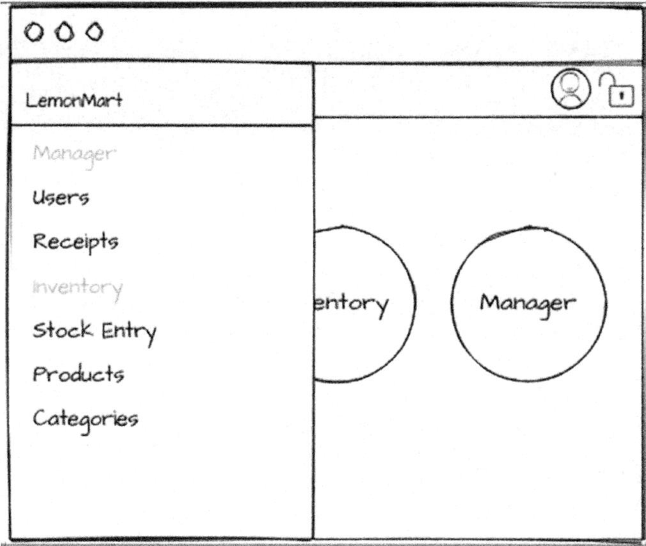

Figure 6.4: Side navigation mock-up

Let's implement the code for the side navigation as a separate component so that it is easier to maintain:

1. In the application's root, create a `NavigationMenu` component with inline templates and styles.

The side navigation isn't technically required until after a user is logged in. However, to be able to launch the side navigation menu from the toolbar, we need to be able to trigger it from `AppComponent`. Since this component will be simple, we will eagerly load it. To do this lazily, Angular does have a Dynamic Component Loader pattern, which has a high implementation overhead that will only make sense if multi-hundred-KB savings are made.

`SideNav` will be triggered from the toolbar, and it comes with a `<mat-sidenav-container>` parent container that hosts the `SideNav` itself and the application's content. So we must render all application content by placing the `<router-outlet>` inside `<mat-sidenav-content>`.

2. In `AppComponent`, define some styles that will ensure that the web application will expand to fill the entire page and remain properly scrollable for desktop and mobile scenarios:

src/app/app.component.ts

```
styles: `
    .app-container {
      display: flex;
      flex-direction: column;
      position: absolute;
      top: 0;
      bottom: 0;
      left: 0;
      right: 0;
    }
    .app-is-mobile .app-toolbar {
      position: fixed;
      z-index: 2;
    }
    .app-sidenav-container {
      flex: 1;
    }
```

```
    .app-is-mobile .app-sidenav-container {
      flex: 1 0 auto;
    }
    mat-sidenav {
      width: 200px;
    }
    .image-cropper {
      border-radius: 50%;
    }
  `,
```

3. Inject the `MediaObserver` service from Angular Flex Layout in `AppComponent`. Also, implement `OnInit`, inject `DestroyRef`, and add a Boolean property named opened:

   ```
   src/app/app.component.ts
   import { MediaObserver } from '@ngbracket/ngx-layout '
   export class AppComponent implements OnInit {
     private destroyRef = inject(DestroyRef)
     opened: boolean
     constructor(
       ...
       public media: MediaObserver
     ) {
     ...
     }
     ngOnInit(): void {
       throw new Error('Method not implemented.')
     }
   }
   ```

   To automatically determine the open/closed status of the side navigation, we need to monitor the media observer and the auth status. When the user logs in, we would like to show the side navigation and hide it when the user logs out. We can do this by assigning opened to the value of `authStatus$.isAuthenticated`. However, if we only consider `isAuthenticated`, and the user is on a mobile device, we will create a less-than-ideal UX. Watching for the media observer's `mediaValue`, we can check whether the screen size is set to extra small or `xs`; if so, we can keep the side navigation closed.

4. Update `ngOnInit` to implement the dynamic side navigation open/closed logic:

src/app/app.component.ts

```
ngOnInit() {
  combineLatest([
    this.media.asObservable(),
    this.authService.authStatus$,
  ])
    .pipe(
      tap(([mediaValue, authStatus]) => {
        if (!authStatus?.isAuthenticated) {
          this.opened = false
        } else {
          if (mediaValue[0].mqAlias === 'xs') {
            this.opened = false
          } else {
            this.opened = true
          }
        }
      }),
      takeUntilDestroyed(this.destroyRef)
    )
    .subscribe()
}
```

By monitoring the media and `authStatus$` streams, we can consider unauthenticated scenarios where the side navigation should not be opened even if there's enough screen space. We also use `takeUntilDestroyed` so that our resources can be cleaned up.

5. Update the template with a responsive `SideNav` that will slide over the content in mobile or push the content aside in desktop scenarios:

src/app/app.component.ts

```
...
// prettier-ignore
template: `
  <div class="app-container">
      @if (
        {
```

```
      status: authService.authStatus$ | async,
      user: authService.currentUser$ | async
    };
    as auth;
  ) {
    <mat-toolbar color="primary" fxLayoutGap="8px"
     class="app-toolbar"
     [class.app-is-mobile]="media.isActive('xs')"
     >
      @if (auth?.status?.isAuthenticated) {
        <button mat-icon-button
          (click)="sidenav.toggle()">
          <mat-icon>menu</mat-icon>
        </button>
      }
  ...
</mat-toolbar>
<mat-sidenav-container class="app-sidenav-container">
  <mat-sidenav #sidenav
    [mode]="media.isActive('xs') ? 'over' : 'side'"
    [fixedInViewport]="media.isActive('xs')"
    fixedTopGap="56" [(opened)]="opened"
  >
    <app-navigation-menu></app-navigation-menu>
  </mat-sidenav>
  <mat-sidenav-content>
    <router-outlet></router-outlet>
  </mat-sidenav-content>
</mat-sidenav-container>
</div>
`,
```

The preceding template leverages the media observer in `@ngbracket/ngx-layout`, a community clone of the deprecated Angular Flex Layout library. We injected `ngx-layout` earlier for a responsive implementation.

You can use the `// prettier-ignore` directive above your template to prevent Prettier from breaking up your template into too many lines, which can hurt readability in certain conditions like this one.

We will implement navigational links in `NavigationMenuComponent`. The number of links in our application will likely grow over time and be subject to various role-based business rules. Therefore, if we were to implement these links in `app.component.ts`, we would risk that file getting too large. In addition, we don't want `app.component.ts` to change very often since changes made there can impact the entire application. It is a good practice to implement the links in a separate component.

6. Implement navigational links in `NavigationMenuComponent`:

src/app/navigation-menu/navigation-menu.component.ts

```
...
  styles: `
      .active-link {
        font-weight: bold;
        border-left: 3px solid green;
      }
      .mat-mdc-subheader {
        font-weight: bold;
      }
  `,
  template: `
    <mat-nav-list>
      <h3 matSubheader>Manager</h3>
      <a mat-list-item
        routerLinkActive="active-link"
        routerLink="/manager/users">
          Users
      </a>
      <a mat-list-item
        routerLinkActive="active-link"
        routerLink="/manager/receipts">
          Receipts
      </a>
```

```
      <h3 matSubheader>Inventory</h3>
      <a mat-list-item
        routerLinkActive="active-link"
        routerLink="/inventory/stockEntry">
          Stock Entry
      </a>
      <a mat-list-item
        routerLinkActive="active-link"
        routerLink="/inventory/products">
          Products
      </a>
      <a mat-list-item
        routerLinkActive="active-link"
        routerLink="/inventory/categories">
          Categories
      </a>
      <h3 matSubheader>Clerk</h3>
      <a mat-list-item
        routerLinkActive="active-link"
        routerLink="/pos">
          POS
      </a>
    </mat-nav-list>
  `,
  standalone: true,
  imports: [MatListModule, RouterLinkActive, RouterLink],
...
```

`<mat-nav-list>` is functionally equivalent to `<mat-list>`, so you can use the documentation of `MatList` for layout purposes. Observe the `subheaders` for **Manager**, **Inventory**, and **Clerk** here:

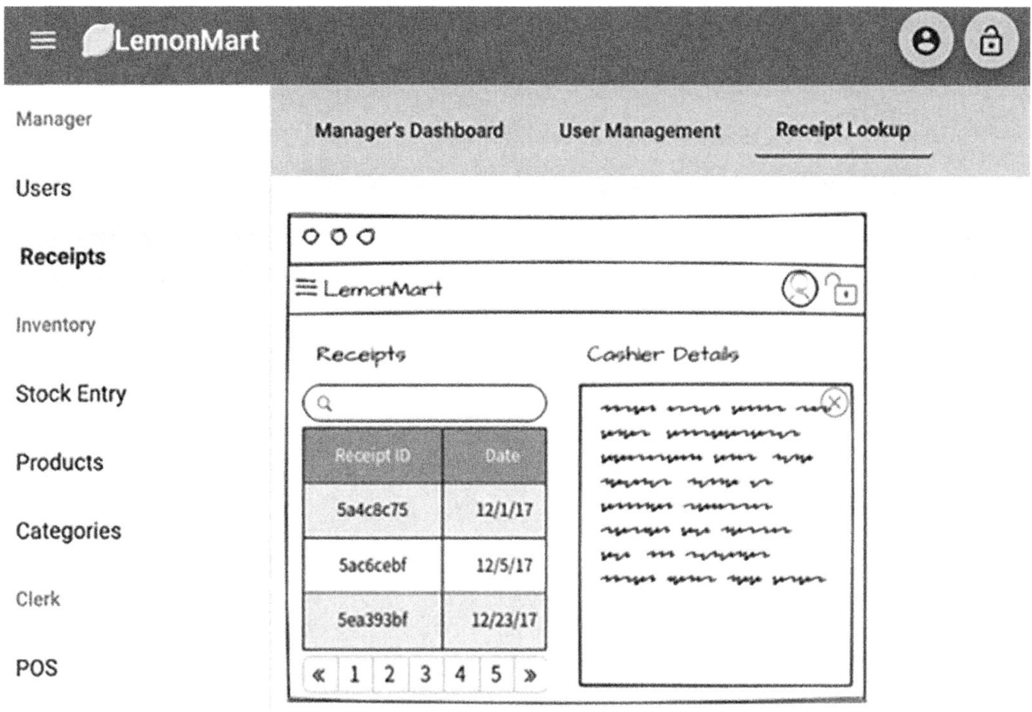

Figure 6.5: The Manager dashboard showing Receipt Lookup on a desktop

`routerLinkActive="active-link"` highlights the selected **Receipts** route, as shown in the preceding screenshot.

Angular Router keeps track of the state of navigation in the app. Based on which link is active, it automatically assigns the appropriate CSS so it can be highlighted as the active one.

You can read more about the router at `https://angular.dev/guide/routing/router-reference`.

Additionally, you can see the difference in appearance and behavior on mobile devices as follows:

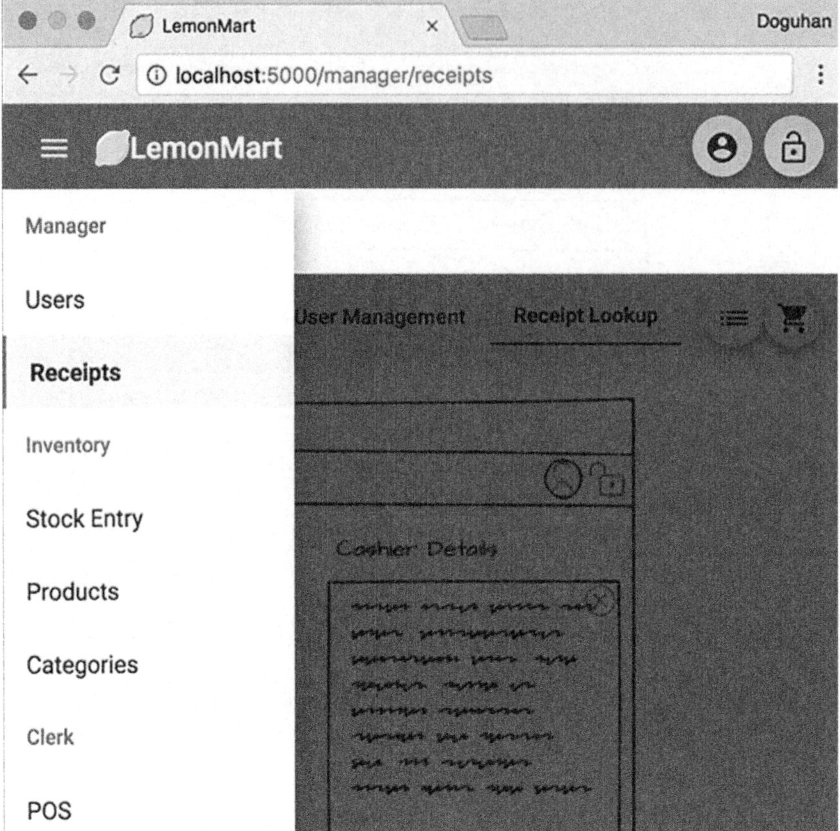

Figure 6.6: The Manager dashboard showing Receipt Lookup on a mobile

Next, let's implement role-based routing.

Role-based routing using guards

This is the most elemental and important part of your application. With lazy loading, we have ensured that only the bare minimum number of assets will be loaded to enable a user to log in.

Once a user logs in, they should be routed to the appropriate landing screen as per their user role, so they're not guessing how they need to use the application. For example, a cashier only needs access to the **point of sale (POS)** screen so that they can check out customers. In this case, cashiers can automatically be routed to that screen.

The following is a mock-up of the POS screen:

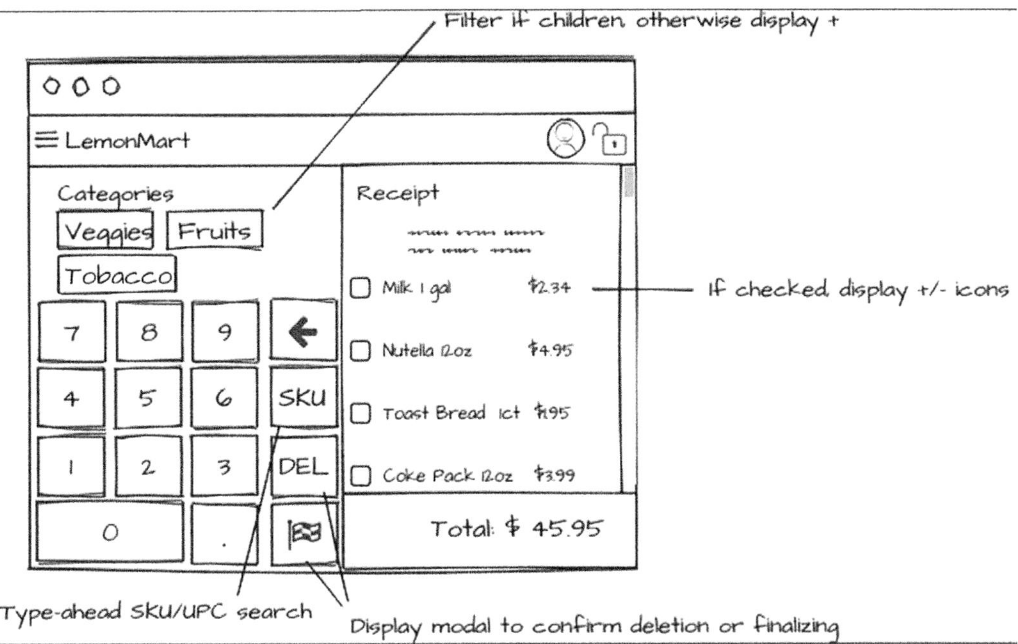

Figure 6.7: A POS screen mock-up

Let's ensure users get routed to the appropriate page after logging in by updating the `LoginComponent`.

Update the `login` logic to each route per role in the function named `homeRoutePerRole`:

```
app/src/login/login.component.ts
async login(submittedForm: FormGroup) {
  ...
    this.router.navigate([
      this.redirectUrl ||
      this.homeRoutePerRole(user.role as Role)
    ])
  ...
}
private homeRoutePerRole(role: Role) {
  switch (role) {
    case Role.Cashier:
      return '/pos'
    case Role.Clerk:
      return '/inventory'
```

```
      case Role.Manager:
        return '/manager'
      default:
        return '/user/profile'
    }
  }
```

Similarly, clerks and managers are routed to their landing screens to access the features they need to accomplish their tasks, as shown earlier. Since we have implemented a default manager role, the corresponding landing experience will be launched automatically.

In the next section, you will learn about route guards, which help check for user authentication and can even load requisite data before a form is rendered. This is crucial in preventing unintentional access to routes that users should not have access to and deterring intentional attempts to breach these restrictions.

Route guards

Route guards enable the further decoupling and reuse of logic and greater control over the component life cycle.

Here are the four major guards you will most likely use:

- `canActivate` and `canActivateChild`: Used for checking auth access to a route
- `canDeactivate`: Used to ask permission before navigating away from a route
- `Resolve`: Allows the pre-fetching of data from route parameters
- `CanLoad`: Allows custom logic to execute before loading feature module assets

Refer to the following sections to discover how to leverage `canActivate` and `canLoad`. The `Resolve` guard will be covered in *Chapter 8, Recipes – Reusability, Forms, and Caching.*

Auth guards

Auth guards enable a good UX by allowing or disallowing accidental navigation to a feature module or a component before the module has loaded, or before any improper data requests have been made to the server. For example, when a manager logs in, they're automatically routed to the `/manager/home` path. The browser will cache this URL, and it would be completely plausible for a clerk to accidentally navigate to the same URL. Angular doesn't know whether a particular route is accessible to a user. Without an `authGuard`, it will happily render the manager's home page and trigger server requests that will fail.

Regardless of the robustness of your frontend implementation, every REST or GraphQL API you implement should also be properly secured with **Role-based Access Control** (**RBAC**) on the server side.

Let's update the router so that `ProfileComponent` can't be activated without an authenticated user, and the `ManagerModule` won't load unless a manager logs in using an `authGuard`:

1. Implement a functional `AuthGuard`:

```
src/app/auth/auth.guard.ts
export const authGuard = (route?: ActivatedRouteSnapshot) => {
  const authService = inject(AuthService)
  const router = inject(Router)
  const uiService = inject(UiService)
  return checkLogin(authService, router, uiService, route)
}
```

Note that all dependencies are being injected inline, using the inject function, which allows dependency injection outside of just the constructor of an `@Injectable` class, in this case, a function.

```
function checkLogin(
  authService: AuthService,
  router: Router,
  uiService: UiService,
  route?: ActivatedRouteSnapshot
): Observable<boolean> {
  return authService.authStatus$.pipe(
    map((authStatus) => {
      const roleMatch = checkRoleMatch(authStatus.userRole, route)
      const allowLogin = authStatus.isAuthenticated && roleMatch
      if (!allowLogin) {
        showAlert(uiService, authStatus.isAuthenticated, roleMatch)
        router.navigate(['login'], {
          queryParams: {
            redirectUrl: router?.getCurrentNavigation()?
```

```
                          .initialUrl.toString(),
          },
        })
      }
      return allowLogin
    }),
    take(1) // the observable must complete for the guard to work
  )
}

function checkRoleMatch(role: Role, route?: ActivatedRouteSnapshot)
{
  if (!route?.data?.['expectedRole']) {
    return true
  }
  return role === route.data['expectedRole']
}

function showAlert(
  uiService: UiService,
  isAuth: boolean,
  roleMatch: boolean
) {
  if (!isAuth) {
    uiService.showToast('You must login to continue')
  }
  if (!roleMatch) {
    uiService.showToast(
      'You do not have the permissions to view this resource'
    )
  }
}
```

2. Use the `canLoad` guard to prevent the loading of a lazily loaded module, such as the `manager's` module:

```
src/app/app.routes.ts
import { authGuard } from './auth/auth.guard'
```

```
...
{
  path: 'manager',
  loadChildren: () => import('./manager/manager.module')
    .then((m) => m.ManagerModule),
  canLoad: [authGuard],
  data: { expectedRole: Role.Manager },
},
...
```

In this instance, when the `ManagerModule` is loaded, `authGuard` will be called during the `canLoad` event, and the `checkLogin` function will verify the authentication status of the user. If the guard returns `false`, the module will not be loaded.

We can go further and provide additional metadata in the route definition, like `expectedRole`, which will be passed into the `checkLogin` function by the `canActivate` event. If a user is authenticated, but their role doesn't match `Role.Manager`, `authGuard` will again return `false`, and the module will not be loaded.

3. Use the `canActivate` guard to prevent the activation of individual components, such as the user's `profile`:

```
src/app/user/user-routing.module.ts
...
{
  path: 'profile', component: ProfileComponent,
  canActivate: [authGuard]
},
...
```

In the case of `user-routing.module.ts`, `authGuard` is called during the `canActivate` event, and the `checkLogin` function controls where this route can be navigated. Since the user is viewing their own profile, there's no need to check the user's role here.

4. Use `canActivate` or `canActivateChild` with an `expectedRole` property to prevent the activation of components by other users, such as `ManagerHomeComponent`:

```
src/app/mananger/manager-routing.module.ts
...
  {
```

```
      path: 'home',
      component: ManagerHomeComponent,
      canActivate: [authGuard],
      data: { expectedRole: Role.Manager },
    },
    {
      path: 'users',
      component: UserManagementComponent,
      canActivate: [authGuard],
      data: { expectedRole: Role.Manager },
    },
    {
      path: 'receipts',
      component: ReceiptLookupComponent,
      canActivate: [authGuard],
      data: { expectedRole: Role.Manager },
    },
  ...
```

Inside `ManagerModule`, we can verify whether the user can access a particular route. We can once again define some metadata, like `expectedRole`, so if a role doesn't match `Role.Manager`, `authGuard` will return `false`, and the navigation will be prevented.

Next, we will review some techniques to implement unit tests to isolate dependencies.

Auth service fake and common testing providers

We need to provide mocked versions of services like `AuthService` or `UiService` using the `commonTestingProviders` function in `common.testing.ts`, using a pattern similar to `commonTestingModules`, which was mentioned in *Chapter 4, Creating a Router-First Line-of-Business App*. This way, we won't have to mock the same objects repeatedly.

Let's create the spy objects using the `autoSpyObj` function from `angular-unit-test-helper` and go over some less obvious changes we need to implement to get our tests passing:

1. Update `commonTestingProviders` in `common.testing.ts`:

```
src/app/common/common.testing.ts
import { autoSpyObj } from 'angular-unit-test-helper'
export const commonTestingProviders: any[] = [
```

```
    { provide: AuthService, useValue: autoSpyObj(AuthService) },
    { provide: UiService, useValue: autoSpyObj(UiService) },
  ]
```

2. Observe the test double provided for the `MediaObserver` in `app.component.spec.ts` and update it to use `commonTestingModules`:

```
src/app/app.component.spec.ts
...
  TestBed.configureTestingModule({
    imports: [...commonTestingModules],
    providers: [
      { provide: MediaObserver, useClass: MediaObserverFake },
...
```

Note how we use the spread syntax, `...`, to expand the `commonTestingModules` within another array. This way, when you need to add more items to the array, it is convenient to do so by just adding a common and another element next to it.

Don't confuse the spread syntax, ..., with this book's use of ellipses, also ..., to represent the existence of surrounding code in the snippets shared.

3. Update the `spec` file for `LoginComponent` to leverage `commonTestingModules` and `commonTestingProviders`:

```
src/app/login/login.component.spec.ts
...
  TestBed.configureTestingModule({
    imports: [... commonTestingModules],
    providers: [... commonTestingProviders],
    declarations: [LoginComponent],
  }).compileComponents()
```

4. Go ahead and apply this technique to all spec files that have a dependency on `AuthService` and `UiService`.

5. The notable exception is services, as in `auth.service.spec.ts`, where you do *not* want to use a test double. Since `AuthService` is the class under test, make sure it is configured as follows:

```
src/app/auth/auth.service.spec.ts
...
TestBed.configureTestingModule({
  imports: [HttpClientTestingModule],
  providers: [AuthService,
  { provide: UiService, useValue: autoSpyObj(UiService) }],
})
```

6. Update `ui.service.spec.ts` with similar considerations.

Remember, don't move on until all your tests pass!

A Firebase authentication recipe

We can leverage our current authentication setup and integrate it with a real authentication service. For this section, you need a free Google and Firebase account. Firebase is Google's comprehensive mobile development platform: `https://firebase.google.com`. You can create a free account to host your application and leverage the Firebase authentication system.

The Firebase console, found at `https://console.firebase.google.com`, allows you to manage users and send a password reset email without implementing a backend for your application. Later, you can leverage Firebase functions to implement APIs in a serverless manner.

Start by adding your project to Firebase using the Firebase console:

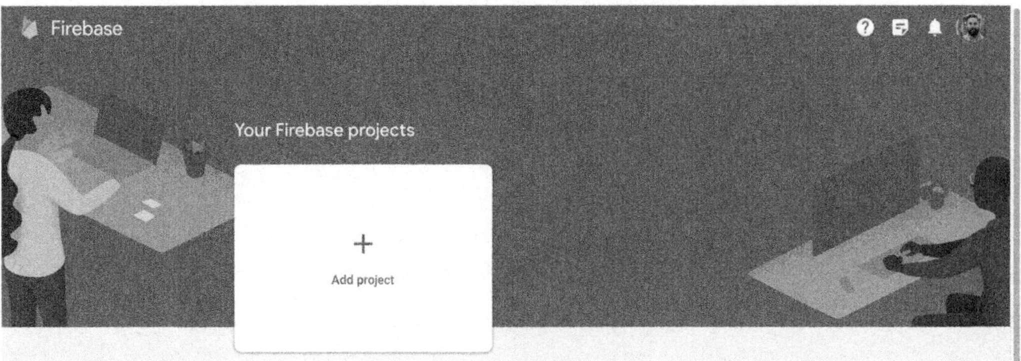

Figure 6.8: The Firebase console

1. Click on **Add project**.
2. Provide your project name.
3. Enable Google Analytics for your project.

It helps to create a Google Analytics account before attempting this, but it should still work. Once your project is created, you should see your project dashboard:

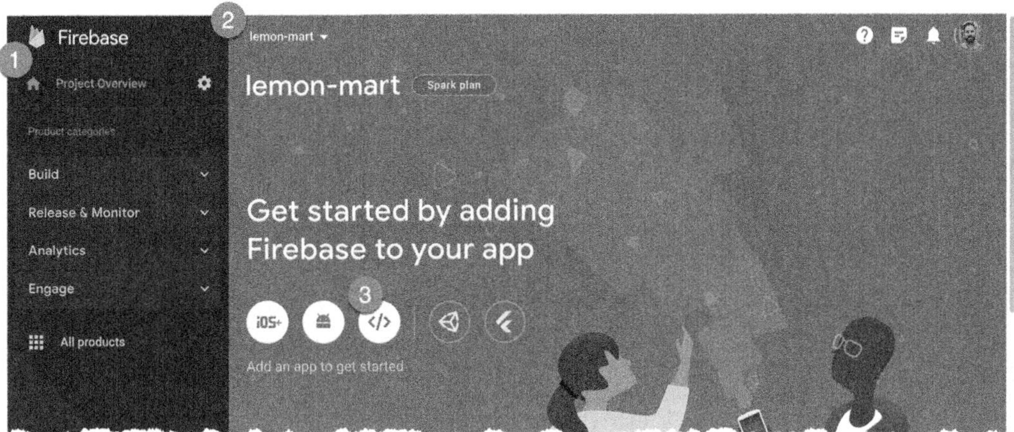

Figure 6.9: The Firebase project overview

On the left-hand side, marked with **1**, you can see a menu of tools and services that you can add to your project. At the top, marked with **2**, you can quickly jump between your projects. Before doing so, you need to add an application to your project.

Create a Firebase application

Your project can include multiple distributions of your application, like web, iOS, and Android versions. In this chapter, we're only interested in adding a web application.

Let's get started:

1. On your project dashboard, click on the web application button to add an application, which is marked with **3** in *Figure 6.9*.
2. Provide an application nickname.
3. Select the option to set up **Firebase Hosting**.
4. Continue by hitting the **Register app** button.
5. Skip over the **Add Firebase SDK** section.

6. Install the Firebase CLI as instructed:

```
$ npm install -g firebase-tools
```

7. Sign in:

```
$ firebase login
```

Make sure your current directory is your project's root folder.

8. Initialize your project:

```
$ firebase init
```

9. Select the **Hosting** option. Don't worry; you can add more features later.
10. Select the project you created as the default, that is, **lemon-mart-007**.
11. Say yes to "Detected an existing Angular codebase in the current directory, should we use this?"

    This will create two new files: `firebase.json` and `.firebaserc`.

12. Build your project for production:

```
$ npx ng build --prod
```

or

```
$ npm run build:prod
```

13. Now, you can deploy your Angular application by executing the following command:

```
$ firebase deploy
```

Your website should be available on a URL similar to `https://lemon-mart-007.firebaseapp.com`, as shown in the terminal.

Add the `.firebase` folder to `.gitignore` so that you don't check in your cache files. The other two files, `firebase.json` and `.firebaserc`, are safe to commit.

Optionally, connect a custom domain name that you own to the account using the Firebase console.

Configuring Firebase authentication

Now, let's configure authentication.

In the Firebase console:

1. Expand the **Build** menu and select **Authentication** from the side navigation:

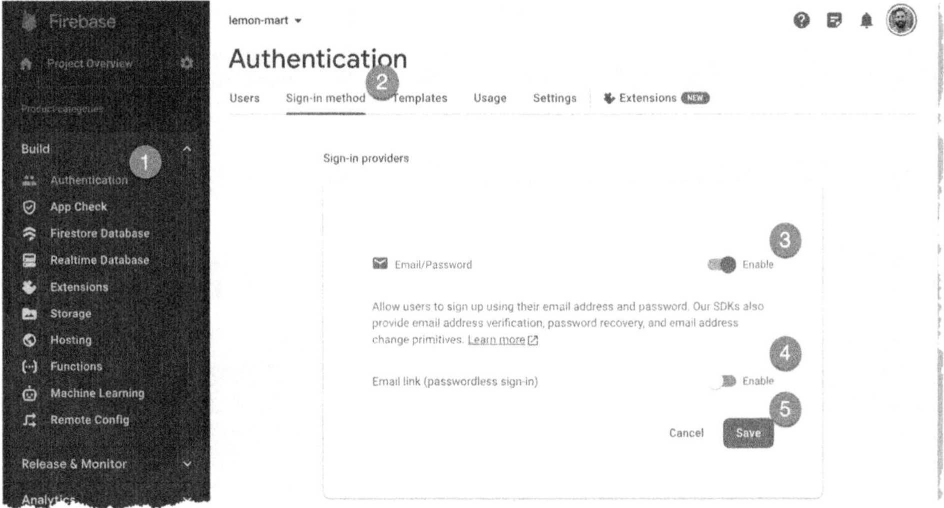

Figure 6.10: The Firebase Authentication page

2. Add a sign-in method; select **Email/Password** as the provider.
3. Enable it.
4. Do not enable the email link.
5. Save your configuration.

You can now see the user management console:

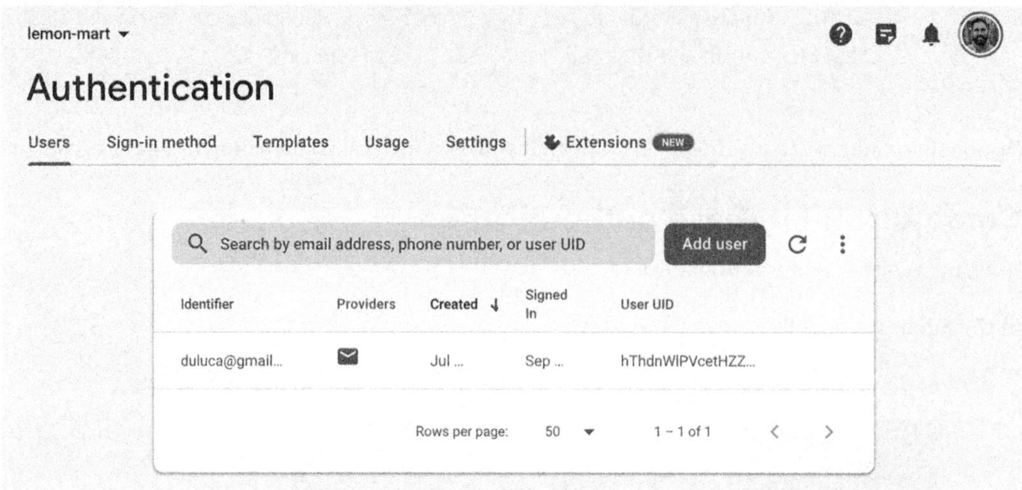

Figure 6.11: The Firebase user management console

It is straightforward and intuitive to operate, so I will leave the configuration of it as an exercise for you.

Adding a Firebase auth provider to Angular

Let's start by adding Angular Fire, the official Firebase library for Angular, to our application:

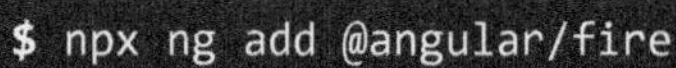

```
$ npx ng add @angular/fire
```

Follow Angular Fire's quick start guide to finish setting up the library with your Angular project, which you can find linked from the `README` file on GitHub at `https://github.com/angular/angularfire`.

1. Ensure Firebase modules are provided in `app.config.ts` as per the documentation.
2. Copy your Firebase `config` object to all of your `environment.ts` files.

Note that any information provided in `environment.ts` is public information. So when you place your Firebase API key in this file, it will be publicly available. There's a small chance that another developer could abuse your API key and run up your bill. To protect yourself from any such attack, check out this blog post by Paachu: *How to secure your Firebase project even when your API key is publicly available* at `https://medium.com/@impaachu/how-to-secure-your-firebase-project-even-when-your-api-key-is-publicly-available-a462a2a58843`.

3. Create a new `FirebaseAuthService`:

```
$ npx ng g s auth/firebaseAuth --lintFix
```

4. Rename the service file `auth.firebase.service.ts`.
5. Be sure to remove `{ providedIn: 'root' }`.
6. Implement Firebase auth by extending the abstract auth service:

src/app/auth/auth.firebase.service.ts

```
import { inject, Injectable } from '@angular/core'
import {
  Auth as FireAuth,
  signInWithEmailAndPassword,
  signOut,
  User as FireUser,
} from '@angular/fire/auth'
import { Observable, of, Subject } from 'rxjs'

import { IUser, User } from '../user/user/user'
import { Role } from './auth.enum'
import {
  AuthService,
  defaultAuthStatus,
  IAuthStatus,
```

```
  IServerAuthResponse,
} from './auth.service'
interface IJwtToken {
  email: string
  iat: number
  exp: number
  sub: string
}

@Injectable()
export class FirebaseAuthService extends AuthService {
  private afAuth: FireAuth = inject(FireAuth)

  constructor() {
    super()
  }

  protected authProvider(
    email: string,
    password: string
  ): Observable<IServerAuthResponse> {
    const serverResponse$ = new Subject<IServerAuthResponse>()

    signInWithEmailAndPassword(this.afAuth, email, password).then(
      (res) => {
        const firebaseUser: FireUser | null = res.user
        firebaseUser?.getIdToken().then(
          (token) => serverResponse$.next({
            accessToken: token
          } as IServerAuthResponse),
          (err) => serverResponse$.error(err)
        )
      },
      (err) => serverResponse$.error(err)
    )

    return serverResponse$
  }
```

```
  protected transformJwtToken(token: IJwtToken): IAuthStatus {
    if (!token) {
      return defaultAuthStatus
    }

    return {
      isAuthenticated: token.email ? true : false,
      userId: token.sub,
      userRole: Role.None,
    }
  }

  protected getCurrentUser(): Observable<User> {
    return of(this.transformFirebaseUser(this.afAuth.currentUser))
  }

  private transformFirebaseUser(firebaseUser: FireUser | null): User
{
    if (!firebaseUser) {
      return new User()
    }

    return User.Build({
      name: {
        first: firebaseUser?.displayName?.split(' ')[0] ||
                 'Firebase',
        last: firebaseUser?.displayName?.split(' ')[1] || 'User',
      },
      picture: firebaseUser.photoURL,
      email: firebaseUser.email,
      _id: firebaseUser.uid,
      role: Role.None,
    } as IUser)
  }

  override async logout() {
    if (this.afAuth) {
```

```
      await signOut(this.afAuth)
    }
    this.clearToken()
    this.authStatus$.next(defaultAuthStatus)
  }
}
```

As you can see, we only had to implement the delta between our already established authentication code and Firebase's authentication methods. We didn't have to duplicate any code, and we had to transform a Firebase `user` object into our application's internal user object.

Note that in `transformFirebaseUser`, we set `role: Role.None` because Firebase authentication doesn't implement the concept of a user role by default. To make the Firebase integration fully functional, you'd have to implement Firebase functions and a Firestore database so that you can store rich user profiles and perform CRUD operations on it. In this case, after authentication, you'd make another call to retrieve the role information. In *Chapter 7, Working with REST and GraphQL APIs*, we cover how to implement this within your custom API.

7. To use Firebase authentication instead of in-memory authentication, update the `AuthService` provider in `app.config.ts`:

```
src/app/app.config.ts
  {
    provide: AuthService,
    useClass: FirebaseAuthService,
  },
```

Once you've completed the steps, add a new user from the Firebase authentication console, and you should be able to log in using real authentication.

Always make sure that you're using HTTPS when transmitting any kind of **Personally Identifiable Information (PII)** or sensitive information (like passwords) over the internet. Otherwise, your information will be logged on to third-party servers or captured by bad actors.

8. Once again, be sure to update your unit tests before moving on:

```
src/app/auth/auth.firebase.service.spec.ts
import {
  HttpClientTestingModule
} from '@angular/common/http/testing'
import { inject, TestBed } from '@angular/core/testing'
import { Auth as FireAuth } from '@angular/fire/auth'

import { UiService } from '../common/ui.service'
import { FirebaseAuthService } from './auth.firebase.service'

const angularFireStub = {
  user: jasmine.createSpyObj('user', ['subscribe']),
  auth: jasmine.createSpyObj('auth',
            ['signInWithEmailAndPassword', 'signOut']),
}

describe('AuthService', () => {
  beforeEach(() => {
    TestBed.configureTestingModule({
      imports: [HttpClientTestingModule],
      providers: [
        FirebaseAuthService,
        UiService,
        { provide: FireAuth, useValue: angularFireStub },
      ],
    })
  })

  it('should be created', inject(
    [FirebaseAuthService],
    (service: FirebaseAuthService) => {
      expect(service).toBeTruthy()
    }
  ))
})
```

Stop! Remove the `fake-jwt-sign` package from your project before deploying a real authentication method.

Congratulations! Your application is integrated with Firebase! Next, let's cover service factories, which can help you to switch the providers of your abstract classes dynamically.

Providing a service using a factory

You can dynamically choose providers during load time, so instead of changing code to switch between authentication methods, you can parametrize environment variables so that different kinds of builds can have different authentication methods. This is especially useful when writing automated UI tests against your application, where real authentication can be difficult, if not impossible, to deal with.

First, we will create an `enum` in `environment.ts` to help define our options, and then we will use that `enum` to choose an auth provider during our application's bootstrap process.

Let's get started:

1. Create a new `enum` called `AuthMode`:

   ```
   src/app/auth/auth.enum.ts
   export enum AuthMode {
     InMemory = 'In Memory',
     CustomServer = 'Custom Server',
     CustomGraphQL = 'Custom GraphQL',
     Firebase = 'Firebase',
   }
   ```

2. Add an `authMode` property in `environment.ts`:

   ```
   src/environments/environment.ts
   ...
     authMode: AuthMode.InMemory,
   ...
   src/environments/environment.prod.ts
   ...
     authMode: AuthMode.Firebase,
   ...
   ```

3. Create an `authFactory` function in a new file under `auth/auth.factory.ts`:

src/app/auth/auth.factory.ts

```
import { environment } from '../../environments/environment'
import { AuthMode } from './auth.enum'
import { FirebaseAuthService } from './auth.firebase.service'
import { InMemoryAuthService } from './auth.in-memory.service'

export function authFactory() {
  switch (environment.authMode) {
    case AuthMode.InMemory:
      return new InMemoryAuthService()
    case AuthMode.Firebase:
      return new FirebaseAuthService()
    case AuthMode.CustomServer:
      throw new Error('Not yet implemented')
    case AuthMode.CustomGraphQL:
      throw new Error('Not yet implemented')
  }
}
```

Note that the factory must import any dependent service, as shown above.

4. Update the `AuthService` provider in `app.config.ts` to use the factory instead:

src/app/app.config.ts

```
  providers: [
    {
      provide: AuthService,
      useFactory: authFactory
    },
```

Note that you can remove imports of `InMemoryAuthService` and `FirebaseAuthService` from `app.config.ts`.

With this configuration in place, whenever you build your application in development configuration, you will use the in-memory auth service, and production (prod) builds will use the Firebase auth service.

Summary

You should now be familiar with how to create high-quality auth experiences. In this chapter, we designed a great conditional navigation experience that you can use in your own applications, by copying the base elements to your project and implementing your own auth provider. We created a reusable UI service so that you can conveniently show alerts in the flow-control logic of your application.

We covered route guards to prevent users from stumbling onto screens they are not authorized to use, and we reaffirmed the point that the real security of your application should be implemented on the server side. You saw how you can use a factory to dynamically provide different auth providers for different environments.

Finally, we implemented a real auth provider with Firebase. In *Chapter 7*, *Working with REST and GraphQL APIs*, we will review LemonMart Server, a full-stack implementation using the minimal MEAN stack with REST and GraphQL APIs. We will complete our authentication journey by learning how to implement a custom auth provider and implement RBAC for both the REST and GraphQL endpoints.

Further reading

- *Angular @if block*: `https://angular.dev/api/core/@if`
- Angular. *CanActivate*. Angular. Retrieved from `https://angular.io/api/router/CanActivate`
- Angular. *CanLoad*. Angular. Retrieved from `https://angular.io/api/router/CanLoad`
- Vasconcelos, V. (2019, October 10). *Angular Router Guards: A Complete Guide*. Angular University. Retrieved from `https://blog.angular-university.io/angular-router-guards/`
- AngularFire. *Getting started with AngularFire authentication*. GitHub. Retrieved from `https://github.com/angular/angularfire/blob/master/docs/auth/getting-started.md`
- Davis, J. (2021, April 12). *Role-Based Authorization in Angular with Firebase*. InDepth. Retrieved from `https://indepth.dev/posts/1305/role-based-firebase-authentication-with-angular-8`

Questions

Answer the following questions as best as possible to ensure you've understood the key concepts from this chapter without googling anything. Do you know if you got all the answers right? Visit `https://angularforenterprise.com/self-assessment` for more:

1. What is the difference between RxJS's `combineLatest` and `merge` operators?
2. Explain the difference between `canActivate` and `canLoad` in the context of Angular route guards.
3. How does dynamic UI rendering improve the user experience in role-based navigation systems?
4. What are the benefits and potential drawbacks of using a service like Firebase Authentication for user management in a web application?
5. Describe a scenario where a service factory can be particularly useful in an Angular application.

7

Working with REST and GraphQL APIs

In *Chapter 1, Angular's Architecture and Concepts*, I introduced you to the wider architecture in which web applications exist, and in *Chapter 3, Architecting an Enterprise App*, we discussed various performance bottlenecks that can impact the success of your app. However, your web app can only perform as well as your full-stack architecture performs. If you're working with an inadequate API design or a slow database, you will spend your time implementing band-aid solutions instead of addressing the root cause of the issues. The moment we move away from the minimalist mindset and start patching holes, we are on our way to constructing a fragile tower that is at risk of collapsing or very expensive to maintain. In short, the choices made in full-stack architecture can profoundly impact the success of your web application. You and your team simply cannot afford to be ignorant of how APIs are designed. Often, the correct way to implement a new feature or fix a performance issue is by redesigning an API endpoint. The **MEAN** stack, using **MongoDB**, **Express**, **Angular**, and **Node.js**, is a popular set of technologies aligned around similar technologies that should ease adoption by web developers. My take on the MEAN stack is minimal MEAN, which prioritizes ease of use, well-being, and effectiveness, the main ingredients for a great **DevEx**.

In the past two chapters, we designed and implemented a **Role-Based Access Control** (**RBAC**) mechanism for our app. In *Chapter 5, Designing Authentication and Authorization*, we dove into security considerations, covered how JWT authentication works, learned how to safely handle data with TypeScript, and tapped into **Object Oriented Programming** (**OOP**) design with inheritance and abstraction to build an extendable auth service. In *Chapter 6, Implementing Role-Based Navigation*, we designed a conditional navigation experience using our auth service and implemented auth providers for custom APIs and Google Firebase.

In this chapter, I'll introduce you to the LemonMart server, which implements JWT auth, REST, and GraphQL APIs. We will use these APIs to implement two custom auth providers in Angular. This will allow you to make authenticated calls to support recipes I will cover in *Chapter 8, Recipes – Reusability, Forms, and Caching, and Caching*, and *Chapter 9, Recipes – Master/Detail, Data Tables, and NgRx*.

This chapter covers a lot of ground. It is designed to serve as a roadmap to the GitHub repository (`https://github.com/duluca/lemon-mart-server`). I cover the architecture, design, and major components of the implementation. I highlight important pieces of code to explain how the solution comes together but avoid going into implementation details. It is more important that you understand why we are implementing various components rather than having a strong grasp of the implementation details. For this chapter, I recommend that you read and understand the server code versus trying to recreate it on your own.

We begin by covering full-stack architecture, the LemonMart server's monorepo design, and how to use Docker Compose to run a three-tier application with a web app, server, and database. Then, we will review REST and GraphQL API design, implementation, and documentation. For REST, we will leverage the **OpenAPI** specification with **SwaggerUI**. For GraphQL, we will leverage **GraphQL schemas** with **Apollo Studio**. Both APIs will be implemented using Express.js and TypeScript. Then, we will cover the implementation of a MongoDB **Object Document Mapper (ODM)** using the DocumentTS library to store users with login credentials. Finally, we will implement a token-based auth function to secure our APIs and the corresponding auth providers in Angular.

In this chapter, you will learn about the following:

- Full-stack architecture
- Working with monorepos
- Designing APIs
- Implementing APIs with Express.js
- A MongoDB ODM with DocumentTS
- Implementing JWT auth
- A custom server auth provider

Technical requirements

The most up-to-date versions of the sample code for the book can be found on GitHub at the following linked repository. The repository contains the final and completed state of the code. This chapter requires the Docker Desktop and Postman applications.

It is critical that you get **lemon-mart-server** up and running on your development environment and have **lemon-mart** communicate with it. Refer to the instructions documented here or in the `README` on GitHub to get your server up and running.

For server-side implementation in *Chapter 7*:

- Clone the `lemon-mart-server` repository using the `--recurse-submodules` option:

```
git clone --recurse-submodules https://github.com/duluca/lemon-mart-server
```

- In the VS Code terminal, execute `cd web-app; git checkout master` to ensure the sub-module from `https://github.com/duluca/lemon-mart` is on the master branch.

Later, in the *Git submodules* section, you can configure the `web-app` folder to pull from your `lemon-mart` server.

- Execute `npm install` in the `root` folder to install dependencies.

Note that running the `npm install` command in the root folder triggers a script, which also installs dependencies under the `server` and `web-app` folders.

- Execute `npm run init:env` in the root folder to configure environment variables in `.env` files.

This command will create two `.env` files, one in the root folder and the other under the `server` folder, to contain your private configuration information. The initial files are generated based on the `example.env` file. You can modify these files later and set your own secure secrets.

- Execute `npm run build` in the root folder, which builds the server and the web app.

Note that the web app is built using a new configuration named `--configuration=lemon-mart-server`, which uses `src/environments/environment.lemon-mart-server.ts`.

- Execute `docker compose up --build` to run containerized versions of the server, web app, and a MongoDB database.

Note that the web app is containerized using a new file named `nginx.Dockerfile`.

- Navigate to `http://localhost:8080` to view the web app.

To log in, click the **Fill** button to populate the email and password fields with the default demo credentials.

- Navigate to `http://localhost:3000` to view the server landing page:

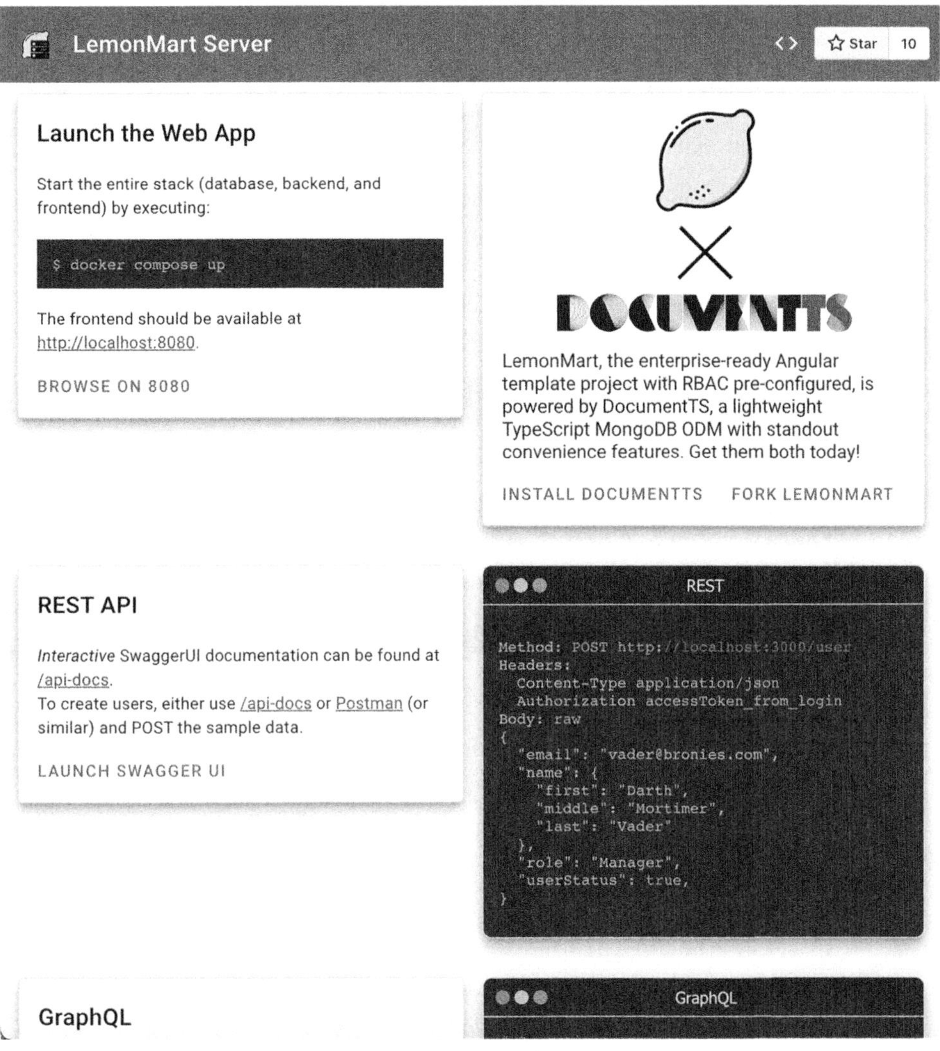

Figure 7.1: LemonMart Server landing page

- Navigate to `http://localhost:3000/api-docs` to view interactive API documentation.
- You can use `npm run start:database` to only start the database, and `npm start` on the `server` folder for debugging.
- You can use `npm run start:backend` to only start the database and the server, and `npm start` on the `web-app` folder for debugging.

For client-side implementations in *Chapter 7*:

- Clone the repository: `https://github.com/duluca/lemon-mart`.
- Execute `npm install` in the root folder to install dependencies.
- The beginning state of the project is reflected at:

```
projects/stage8
```

- The end state of the project is reflected at:

```
projects/stage10
```

- Add the stage name to any `ng` command to act only on that stage:

```
npx ng build stage10
```

Note that the `dist/stage10` folder at the root of the repository will contain the compiled result.

Beware that the source code provided in the book and the version on GitHub are likely to be different. The ecosystem around these projects is ever-evolving. Between changes in how Angular CLI generates new code, bug fixes, new versions of libraries, and side-by-side implementations of multiple techniques, there are a lot of variations that are impossible to account for. If you find errors or have questions, please create an issue or submit a pull request on GitHub.

With your LemonMart server up and running, we are ready to explore the architecture of the MEAN stack. By the end of this section, you should have your own version of LemonMart communicating with the server.

Full-stack architecture

Full-stack refers to the entire stack of software that makes an application work, from databases to servers, APIs, and the web and/or mobile apps that leverage them. The mythical full-stack developer is all-knowing and can comfortably operate in all verticals of the profession. It is next to impossible to specialize in all things *software-related* and to be considered an expert in every given topic. However, to be considered an expert in a single topic, you must also be well-versed in related topics. When learning about a new topic, it is very helpful to keep your tooling and language consistent to absorb new information without additional noise.

For these reasons, I opted to introduce you to the MEAN stack, rather than Spring Boot using Java or ASP.NET using C#. By sticking to familiar tools and languages such as TypeScript, VS Code, npm, GitHub, Jasmine/Jest, Docker, and CircleCI, you can better understand how a full-stack implementation comes together and become a better web developer.

Minimal MEAN

Choosing the **ideal stack** for your project is difficult. First and foremost, your technical architecture should be adequate to meet business needs. For example, if you're trying to deliver an artificial intelligence project with Node.js, you're likely using the wrong stack. Our focus will be on delivering web applications, but beyond that, we have other parameters to consider, including the following:

- Ease of use
- Happiness
- Effectiveness

If your development team will be working on your application for an extended period, it is very important to consider factors beyond compatibility. Your stack, choice of tool, and coding style can have a significant impact if your codebase is easy to use, keeps your developers happy, or makes them feel like effective contributors to the project.

A well-configured stack is key for a great DevEx. This can be the difference between a towering stack of dried-out pancakes or a delicious short stack, with the right amount of butter and syrup.

By introducing too many libraries and dependencies, you can slow down your progress, make your code difficult to maintain, and find yourself in a feedback loop of introducing more libraries to resolve the issues of other libraries. The only way to win this game is to simply not play it.

If you take your time to learn how to work with a few fundamental libraries, you can become a far more effective developer. In essence, you can do more with less. My advice would be to:

- **Think** before you write a single line of code and apply the 80-20 rule.
- **Wait** for libraries and tools to mature, skipping the betas.
- **Fast** by reducing your gluttony for new packages and tools, mastering the fundamentals instead.

Watch my 2017 Ng conference talk entitled *Do More with Less JavaScript* on YouTube at `https://www.youtube.com/watch?v=Sd1aM8181kc`.

This minimalist mindset is the design philosophy behind minimal MEAN. You can review a reference implementation on GitHub at `https://github.com/duluca/minimal-mean`. Refer to the following diagram for the overall architecture:

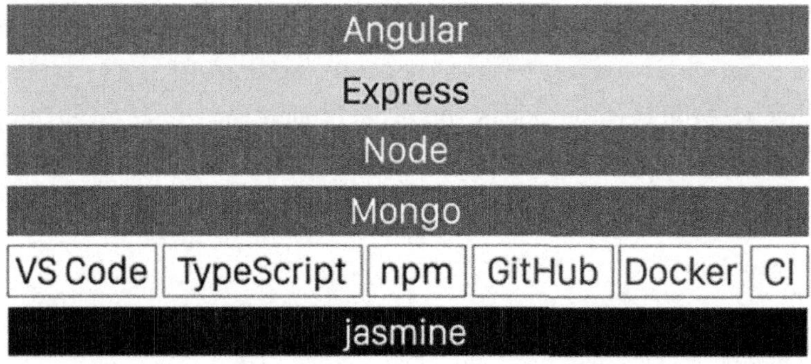

Figure 7.2: Minimal MEAN software stack and tooling

Let's go over the components of the architecture:

- **Angular**: You know this one. Angular is the presentation layer. The output of an Angular build is a set of static files that can be hosted using the minimal Docker container, `duluca/minimal-nginx-web-server`, or `duluca/minimal-node-web-server`.
- **Express.js**: This is our API layer. Express is a fast, unopinionated, and minimalist web framework for Node.js. Express has a vast plugin ecosystem that is almost guaranteed to meet every need. NestJS is built on Express and is a good alternative for well-established teams. In minimal MEAN, we leverage a few Express middleware:

    - `cors`: configures cross-origin resource-sharing settings
    - `compression`: zips packets sent across the wire to lower bandwidth use
    - `morgan`: logs HTTP requests
    - `express.static`: function to serve the content of the `public` folder
    - `graphql`: to host GraphQL endpoint

    You can read more about Express.js at `https://expressjs.com/`

- **Node.js**: This is the server runtime; Express runs on Node so that the business layer will be implemented in Node. Node is a lightweight and efficient JavaScript runtime that uses an event-driven, non-blocking I/O model that suits high-performance and real-time applications. You can increase the reliability of your Node applications by using TypeScript to develop your application.

Node runs everywhere, from fridges to smartwatches. Refer to the blog post by Frank Rosner on non-blocking I/O for a more in-depth explanation of the topic at `https://blog.codecentric.de/en/2019/04/explain-non-blocking-i-o-like-im-five/`.

- **MongoDB**: This is the persistence layer. MongoDB is a document-oriented database with dynamic JSON-like schemas. Read more about MongoDB at `https://www.mongodb.com/`.

The MEAN stack is preferred because it leverages the major benefit of using a JSON-based database, which means that you don't need to transform your data from one format to another, as it crosses the layers of your stack – a major pain point when dealing with .NET, Java, and SQL servers. You can retrieve, display, edit, and update the data using only JSON. In addition, the MongoDB native driver for Node is mature, performant, and capable. I have developed a library called `document-ts`, which aims to simplify interacting with MongoDB by introducing rich document objects that are easy to code. DocumentTS is a very thin TypeScript-based MongoDB helper with optional, rich ODM convenience features. Read more about DocumentTS at `https://github.com/duluca/document-ts`.

Minimal MEAN leverages most of the same tooling and languages we use for Angular development. This enables developers to switch between frontend and backend development with minimal context switching.

NestJS

Minimal MEAN intentionally sticks to the basics, so you can learn more about the underlying technologies. While I have delivered production systems using minimal MEAN for larger teams with varying skill levels, this barebones development experience may not be appropriate. In this case, you may consider NestJS, a popular framework for implementing full-stack Node.js apps. NestJS has a rich feature set with an architecture and coding style resembling Angular.

Feeling adventurous? Create a NestJS app by executing:

```
$ npx @nestjs/cli new your-app-name --strict
```

Nest is built on Express and provides syntactic sugar and concepts to build a scalable backend solution. The framework heavily borrows ideas from Angular to implement dependency injection, guards, interceptors, pipes, modules, and providers. The built-in resource generator can scaffold entity classes, **CRUD** (**Create**, **Retrieve**, **Update**, **Delete**) controllers, **Data Transfer Objects** (**DTOs**), and services.

For example:

```
$ npx nest g resource users
```

When creating a resource, you can choose between creating a REST, GraphQL, microservice, or WebSocket endpoint:

```
? What transport layer do you use?
> REST API
  GraphQL (code first)
  GraphQL (schema first)
  Microservice (non-HTTP)
  WebSockets
```

Nest supports OpenAPI for REST documentation, and GraphQL also supports schema-first and code-first development for GraphQL. For a library with so many features, Nest's explicit Microservice support is welcome, where a fast boot-up time and small framework size are critical for operations. All these features are supported by detailed documentation at `https://docs.nestjs.com/`.

Kudos to Kamil Mysliwiec and Mark Pieszak for creating a great tool and fostering a vibrant community around NestJS. Should you ever need it, you can solicit consulting services at `https://trilon.io/`.

If you visit the documentation site, you may be overwhelmed with the many options on offer. This is why I recommend using a feature-rich library like this after you have mastered the basics with minimal MEAN.

You can read more about NestJS at `https://nestjs.com/`.

Next, let's learn about monorepos, their benefits, and their downsides. I will share how you can combine Nx, Nest, and Angular in a monorepo, and then cover how LemonMart server uses Git submodules to create a monorepo.

Working with monorepos

A **monorepo (monolithic repository)** is a software development strategy to host code from multiple projects in a single repository. This allows for unified versioning, simplified dependency management, and easier code sharing across projects. In a monorepo, developers can jump between projects within the same IDE window and reference code more easily across projects, such as sharing TypeScript interfaces between the frontend and the backend, ensuring that data objects line up every time.

You can enable access to multiple projects in the same IDE window using multi-root workspaces in VS Code, where you can add multiple projects to display in the *Explorer* window. However, a monorepo combines projects at the source control level, allowing us to build them together on our CI server. Read more about multi-root workspaces at `https://code.visualstudio.com/docs/editor/multi-root-workspaces`.

Having access to code from multiple projects makes it possible to commit atomic changes, meaning changes made across projects can be combined into a single commit. This brings a distinct advantage by making it easy to push changes that may otherwise require coordination across multiple repos, deployments, and systems in one place. All processes around maintaining code quality and standards also become simplified. There's one **Pull Request (PR)** to review, one deployment to verify, and one set of checks to enforce.

So why is every project not a monorepo? In large applications, having too many files in the project can become a significant issue. It would require every developer to have top-of-the-line hardware and CI/CD servers to run on expensive, high-performance hardware. In addition, automating the deployment of such a project can become a very complex task. Finally, a new team member joining the team can find it overwhelming.

While monorepos at least date back to the early 2000s, they were impractical to leverage as a strategy for most, except the top tech companies worldwide. In 2019, when Google released the open-source Bazel build tool, itself based on a 2015 internal project called Blaze, the idea became feasible for smaller-scale projects. In the JavaScript, TypeScript, and web app development world, Nx, developed by ex-Googlers, has risen to prominence. In terms of managing, building, and publishing packages, Lerna is a cousin of Nx.

Nx monorepo

As mentioned in *Chapter 3, Architecting an Enterprise App*, Nx is a next-generation build system with first-class monorepo support and powerful integrations. Nx offers an opinionated architecture, which is welcome for large teams and enterprises. Nx also has a cloud offering, where it'll leverage a distributed cache and parallelization to optimize builds without your team investing in complicated infrastructure work.

You can set up a new Nx workspace by executing:

```
$ npx create-nx-workspace@latest
```

Alternatively, you can migrate an existing project by executing the following command in the project folder:

```
$ npx nx@latest init
```

By default, this will give you a monorepo configuration with one app. You can use Nx generators to add libraries that can be shared across components and other modules. By separating code into distinct libraries, multiple people working on the project simultaneously are less likely to have merge conflicts. However, if you follow the router-first architecture and segregate duties between feature modules, you can get similar results. There's more at `https://nx.dev/getting-started`.

The question is, is it worth it? Many experts use it as a standard tool; however, in my pursuit of minimalism, I'm not a fan of bringing a tank to a knife fight. There's a cost to introducing a sophisticated piece of tech like this to a team. There's a steep learning curve to adopt such a tool.

When you layer JavaScript, TypeScript, Git, Nx, Angular, libraries, Node, npm, and other server-side tech on top of each other, the cognitive load required to navigate these tools goes through the roof. Furthermore, each one of these tools requires expertise to correctly configure, maintain, and upgrade them over time.

On modern hardware (at least ones not addled by enterprise-grade *slow-everything-down-so-we-can-make-extra-sure-you-don't-have-a-virus* software installed on it), Angular apps with several hundred components build fast enough. With the adoption of esbuild and Vite, this should improve even further. Nx's distributed cache and centralized dependency management features may tip the scales for you. Always assess your needs carefully before starting a new project; running on autopilot, it's easy to either under- or overestimate your needs.

I want to make one thing crystal clear. If you are working with thousands of components, then Nx is a requirement.

Most Angular monorepos only contain frontend code. To configure a full-stack monorepo using NestJS in an existing Angular workspace, install the Nest schematic and generate a new project within the Nx workspace:

```
$ npm i -D @nrwl/nest
$ npx nx g @nrwl/nest:application apps/your-api
```

You can read more about this at `https://www.thisdot.co/blog/nx-workspace-with-angular-and-nest/`.

Next, let's see how LemonMart server's monorepo is configured.

Git submodules

Git submodules help you share code between multiple repositories while keeping the commits separate. Frontend developers may choose to only work using the frontend repository, whereas full-stack developers will prefer access to all code. Git submodules also provide a convenient way for existing projects to be combined.

Observe the overall structure of the `lemon-mart-server` project, where you are going to have three main folders, as shown here:

```
lemon-mart-server
├───bin
├───web-app (snapshot of lemon-mart)
```

```
├──server
│   package.json
│   README.md
```

The bin folder contains helper scripts or tools, the web-app folder represents your frontend, and server contains the source code for the backend. In our case, the web-app folder is the lemon-mart project. Instead of copying and pasting the code from the existing project, we leverage Git submodules to link two repositories together. The package.json file contains scripts that assist in the initialization, updating, and cleaning up of Git submodules, like modules:update to fetch the latest version of the web app.

I recommend that you perform the following actions on the version of lemon-mart-server that you cloned from GitHub. Otherwise, you will need to create a new project and execute npm init -y to get things started.

To initialize the web-app folder with your project:

1. Update webAppGitUrl with the URL to your own project.
2. Execute webapp:clean to remove the existing web-app folder.
3. Finally, execute the webapp:init command to initialize your project in the web-app folder:

```
$ npm run webapp:init
```

Going forward, execute the modules:update command to update the code in the submodule. To pull the submodules after cloning the repo in another environment, execute npm modules:init. If you ever need to reset the environment and restart, then execute webapp:clean to clean Git's cache and remove the folder.

Note that you can have multiple submodules in your repository. The modules:update command will update all the submodules.

Your web application code is now available in the folder named web-app. Additionally, you should be able to see both projects under VS Code's **SOURCE CONTROL** pane, as shown here:

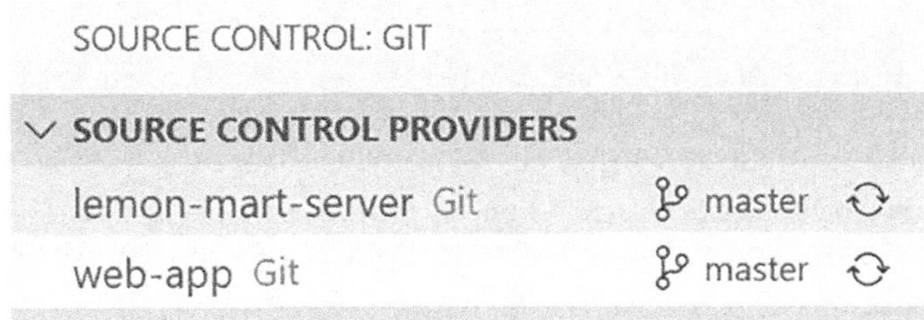

Figure 7.3: VS Code source control providers

Using VS Code's source control, you can independently perform Git actions on either repository.

If things get messy with your submodule, simply `cd` into the submodule directory, execute `git pull`, and then `git checkout main` to restore the main branch. Using this technique, you may check out any branch from your project and submit PRs.

Now that our submodule is ready, let's see how the server project is configured so that we can configure our CI server.

CircleCI config

One of the benefits of using Git submodules is that we can verify that our frontend and backend work in the same CI pipeline. The `config.yml` file implements two jobs, part of the workflow shown here:

`.circleci/config.yml`

```
...
workflows:
  build-and-test-compose:
    jobs:
      - build_server
      - build_webapp
```

The pipeline checks out the code, verifies the security of the packages we're using with `audit-ci`, installs dependencies, checks for styling and linting errors, runs tests, and checks for code coverage levels.

The test commands implicitly build the server code, which is stored under the `dist` folder. In the final step, we move the `dist` folder into the workspace so that we can use it at a later stage.

The CI pipeline will build the server and the web app in parallel, with an option to run the `deploy` job if the jobs succeed on the main branch. There are more details on CI/CD in *Chapter 10, Releasing to Production with CI/CD*.

Next, let's see the difference between RESTful and GraphQL APIs.

Designing APIs

In *Chapter 3, Architecting an Enterprise App*, I cover the importance of a stateless, data-driven design as part of Router-first architecture. As part of this goal, I highlight identifying major data entities that your app will operate around as an important activity. It's no mistake that API design also greatly benefits by designing around major data entities.

In full-stack development, nailing down the API design early on is important. If your frontend and backend teams can agree on major data entities and the shape of those entities, then both teams can agree on a contract to go off and build their own respective pieces of software. In Router-first architecture, I highlight the importance of leveraging TypeScript interfaces to quickly stub out the architecture of your app. Backend teams can conduct similar activities.

A little bit of early design work and agreement ensures integration between these components can be established very early on, and with CI/CD pipelines, we can ensure it doesn't disintegrate.

CI is critical to success. One of the most infamous cases where teams didn't integrate critical systems until too late was the disastrous launch of HealthCare.gov in 2013. Even though 300 people worked on it, and $300,000,000 was spent on this project, it failed. In total, 1.7 billion dollars had to be spent to rescue the project and make it successful. The US federal government can afford to do this. Your enterprise won't be as accepting.

There are further considerations in designing your API, and if frontend and backend developers collaborate closely to achieve shared design goals, the chance of project success is greatly improved.

Some high-level goals are listed as follows:

- Minimize data transmitted between the client and server.
- Stick to well-established design patterns (e.g., pagination API design).
- Design to reduce business logic implementation on the client.
- Design around major data entities.
- Flatten data structures when crossing boundaries.
- Do not expose database keys or foreign key relationships.
- Version endpoints from the get-go.

You should aim to implement all the business logic behind your API surface. The frontend should only contain presentation logic. Any `if` statement implemented by the frontend should also be verified in the backend.

As discussed in *Chapter 1, Angular's Architecture and Concepts,* it is critical to aim for a stateless design in both the backend and frontend. Every request should utilize non-blocking I/O methods and not rely on existing sessions. This is the key to seamlessly scaling your web application code on cloud platforms. Sessions are notorious for scaling out and using a lot of memory.

Whenever you're implementing a project, it is important to limit, if not eliminate, experimentation. This is especially true in full-stack projects. The downstream effect of missteps in API design can be profound and impossible to correct once your application goes live. Proofs of concept are ideal places to experiment and validate ideas and new technologies. Their one great feature is how disposable they are.

Next, let's go over designing REST and GraphQL APIs around major data entities. In this case, we'll review the implementation of an API surrounding users, including authentication. In both cases, we will rely on an API specification language. For REST, we will use the OpenAPI specification, and for GraphQL, the schemas specification, to document the design so that we can concretely communicate the intent of the API to team members. Later, these specs become interactive tools, reflecting the capability of our APIs.

REST APIs

REST (representational state transfer) is commonly used to create stateless, reliable web applications leveraging HTTP methods (verbs) like **GET**, **POST**, **PUT**, and **DELETE**. REST APIs are well defined and static. Like any public API, once released, it is very difficult, if not impossible, to change their interface. It is always possible to extend but hard to optimize for emergent use cases, like mobile or purpose-built apps that need to use the API differently. This usually leads to a great expansion of the API surface as teams implement specific APIs to match new needs. This can lead to maintainability challenges if there are a half-dozen separate codebase to access the same piece of data.

From a frontend developer's perspective, working with APIs they didn't write can be a perplexing experience. Most public APIs and businesses that publish APIs usually resolve this by publishing high-quality documentation and examples. This takes time and money. However, a fast-moving team in an enterprise environment can't afford to wait for such documentation to be manually created.

Enter OpenAPI, aka Swagger. OpenAPI specs can document API names, routes, input and return parameter types, encoding, authentication, request headers, and expected HTTP status codes. This level of detail leaves little room for interpretation of how an API should be consumed, reducing friction and buggy code – all critical ingredients to avoid late-stage integration challenges.

The OpenAPI spec can be defined in the YAML or JSON format. Using this spec file, you can render an interactive UI for your API. Install the Swagger Viewer VS Code extension and preview the `swagger.yaml` file under the `server` folder:

There's also the OpenAPI (Swagger) Editor extension, which is a feature-rich alternative. At the time of publishing, this extension doesn't support OpenAPI version 3.1.0.

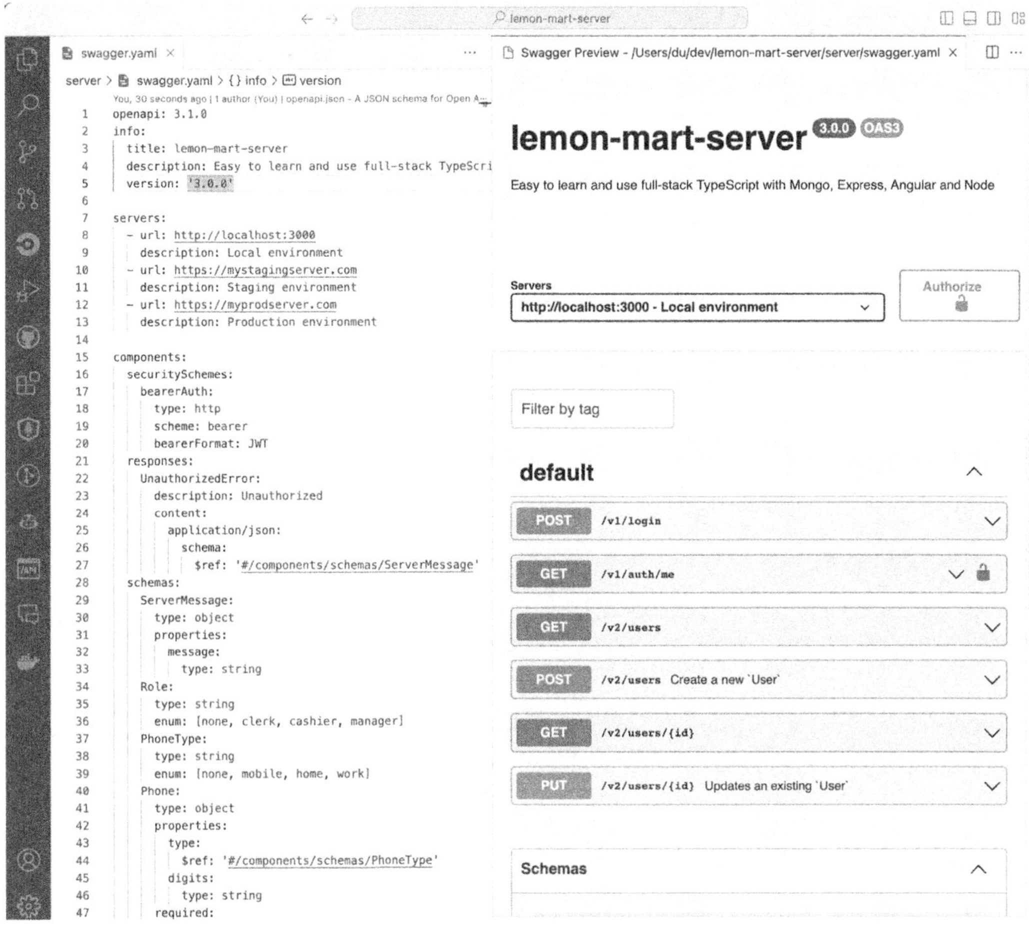

Figure 7.4: Swagger.yaml preview

Using the Swagger UI view, you can try out commands and execute them against your server environment once it's implemented.

OpenAPI Spec

We are using the OpenAPI spec version openapi: 3.1.0. The OpenAPI spec can document metadata about your server, various components of your API, like security schemes, responses, data schemas, and input parameters, and finally, the paths that define your HTTP endpoints.

Let's go over the major components of the `swagger.yaml` file located under the `server` folder:

1. The YAML file starts with general information and target servers:

```
server/swagger.yaml
openapi: 3.1.0
info:
  title: lemon-mart-server
  description: LemonMart API
  version: "3.0.0"
servers:
  - url: http://localhost:3000
    description: Local environment
  - url: https://mystagingserver.com
    description: Staging environment
  - url: https://myprodserver.com
    description: Production environment
```

2. Under `components`, we define common `securitySchemes` and responses, which define the authentication scheme we intend to implement and how the shape of our error message response will appear:

```
server/swagger.yaml
...
components:
  securitySchemes:
    bearerAuth:
      type: http
      scheme: bearer
      bearerFormat: JWT
  responses:
    UnauthorizedError:
      description: Unauthorized
      content:
```

```
        application/json:
          schema:
            $ref: "#/components/schemas/ServerMessage"
          type: string
```

Note the usage of `$ref` to reuse repeating elements. You can see `ServerMessage` being defined here.

3. Under `components`, we define shared data `schemas`, which declare the data entities that we either take in as input or return to the client:

```
server/swagger.yaml
...
  schemas:
    ServerMessage:
      type: object
      properties:
        message:
          type: string
    Role:
      type: string
      enum: [none, clerk, cashier, manager]
    ...
```

4. Under `components`, we define shared `parameters`, making it easy to reuse common patterns such as paginated endpoints:

```
server/swagger.yaml
...
  parameters:
    filterParam:
      in: query
      name: filter
      required: false
      schema:
        type: string
      description: Search text to filter the result set by
...
```

5. Under `paths`, we define REST endpoints, such as a `post` endpoint for the `/login` path:

```
server/swagger.yaml
...
paths:
  /v1/login:
    post:
      description: |
        Generates a JWT, given the correct credentials.
      requestBody:
        required: true
        content:
          application/json:
            schema:
              type: object
              properties:
                email:
                  type: string
                password:
                  type: string
              required:
                - email
                - password
      responses:
        '200': # Response
          description: OK
          content:
            application/json:
              schema:
                type: object
                properties:
                  accessToken:
                    type: string
                description: JWT token that contains userId as
subject, email and role as data payload.
        '401':
          $ref: '#/components/responses/UnauthorizedError'
```

Note that `requestBody` defines input variables that are required with a type of `string`. Under `responses`, we can define how a successful `200` response and an unsuccessful `401` response to a request appear. In the former case, we return an `accessToken`, while in the latter case, we return an `UnauthorizedError`, as defined in *step 2*.

6. Under `paths`, we define the remaining paths:

```
server/swagger.yaml
...
paths:
  /v1/auth/me:
    get: ...
  /v2/users:
    get: ...
    post: ...
  /v2/users/{id}:
    get: ...
    put: ...
```

The OpenAPI spec is powerful, allowing you to define intricate requirements on how users should be able to interact with your API. The OpenAPI spec can be found at `https://spec.openapis.org/oas/latest.html`. It is an invaluable resource while developing your own API definition.

Our overarching goal is to integrate this interactive documentation with our Express.js APIs. Now, let's see how you can implement such an API.

OpenAPI spec with Express

Configuring Swagger with Express is a manual process. But this is a good thing. Forcing yourself to manually document endpoints has a positive side effect. By slowing down, you will get the opportunity to consider your implementation from the perspective of the consumer of the API. This perspective will help you resolve potential issues with your endpoints during development, avoiding annoying, if not costly, rework.

Let's look at an example of how you can directly embed the OpenAPI spec alongside your code in chunks:

```
server/src/v1/routes/authRouter.ts
/**
 * @openapi
 * /v1/auth/me:
 *   get:
 *     description: Gets the `User` object of the logged in user
 *     responses:
 *       '200':
 *         description: OK
 *         content:
 *           application/json:
 *             schema:
 *               $ref: '#/components/schemas/User'
 *       '401':
 *         $ref: '#/components/responses/UnauthorizedError'
 */
router.get('/me', authenticate(), async (_req: Request, res: Response) =>
{
  if (res.locals.currentUser) {
    return res.send(res.locals.currentUser)
  }

  return res.status(401).send({ message: AuthenticationRequiredMessage })
})
```

In this example, we use the `JSDoc` documentation syntax that starts with `/**` and then define the relevant part of the OpenAPI spec right after the `@openapi` identifier. We can still reference components defined elsewhere, as shown with the `$ref` statements to the `User` and `UnauthorizedError` objects.

The major benefit of integrating the spec alongside your code is that the developer knows exactly how the server should respond to a `/me GET` request. If a user exists, we respond with a `User` object; if not, we throw a `401` error that adheres to the shape of the `UnauthorizedError` object. Using some automated tools, we can still generate the same interactive Swagger UI covered earlier, so testers and developers can discover or test the API directly from a web interface.

As the API implementation evolves, this setup makes it easy for developers to keep the spec up to date. By making it easy, we incentivize everyone involved with the desire to keep Swagger UI working because all team members benefit from it. By creating a virtuous cycle, we achieve the ideal of **living documentation**. Normally, initial designs become useless as they grow stale, but instead, we can have an automated and interactive solution that delivers ongoing value.

We are going to use two helper libraries to help us integrate the inline spec into the codebase:

- `swagger-jsdoc`: This allows us to implement OpenAPI specs right on top of the relevant code by using the `@openapi` identifier in a `JSDoc` comment block, generating a `swagger.json` file as output.
- `swagger-ui-express`: This consumes the `swagger.json` file to display the interactive Swagger UI web interface.

Let's explore how Swagger is configured to work with Express.js:

1. The dependencies and type information for TypeScript are shown here:

```
$ npm i swagger-jsdoc swagger-ui-express
$ npm i -D @types/swagger-jsdoc @types/swagger-ui-express
```

2. Let's explore the `docs-config.ts` file, which configures the base OpenAPI definition:

server/src/docs-config.ts

```
import * as swaggerJsdoc from 'swagger-jsdoc'
import { Options } from 'swagger-jsdoc'
import * as packageJson from '../package.json'
const options: Options = {
  swaggerDefinition: {
    openapi: '3.1.0',
    components: {},
    info: {
      title: packageJson.name,
      version: packageJson.version,
      description: packageJson.description,
    },
    servers: [
      {
        url: 'http://localhost:3000',
        description: 'Local environment',
```

```
      },
      {
        url: 'https://mystagingserver.com',
        description: 'Staging environment',
      },
      {
        url: 'https://myprodserver.com',
        description: 'Production environment',
      },
    ],
  },
  apis: [
    '**/models/*.js',
    '**/v1/routes/*.js',
    '**/v2/routes/*. js'
  ],
}
export const specs = swaggerJsdoc(options)
```

Modify the `servers` property to include the location of your testing, staging, or production environments. This allows consumers of your API to test the API using the web interface without additional tooling. Note that the `apis` property informs the code files that `swaggerJsdoc` should parse when constructing the `swagger.json` file. This routine runs during the bootstrapping of the server, which is why we reference the transpiled `.js` files instead of `.ts` files.

3. Bootstrap the `swagger` config in `app.ts`:

```
server/src/app.ts
import * as swaggerUi from 'swagger-ui-express'
import { specs } from './docs-config'
const app = express()
app.use(cors())
...
app.use('/api-docs', swaggerUi.serve, swaggerUi.setup(specs))

app.get('/swagger', function (_req, res) {
  res.json(specs)
})
```

```
...
export default app
```

Specs contain the content of the `swagger.json` file, which is then passed to `swaggerUi`. Then, using the `server` middleware, we can configure `swaggerUi` to host the web interface at `/api-docs`. We can also serve the JSON file from an endpoint to consume it in another tool, at `/swagger`, as shown above.

Even after integrating the spec file alongside the code, developers must manually ensure that the spec and the code match. This process can be automated, including generating TypeScript-based API handlers to prevent coding mistakes.

A community-driven list of high-quality and modern tools for OpenAPI can be found at `https://openapi.tools/`.

Now that you understand how we can design a REST API and create living documentation around it, it's time to learn about GraphQL, which bakes these ideas into its core design.

GraphQL APIs

GraphQL (Graph Query Language), invented at Facebook, is a modern query language for APIs that offers a more flexible, robust, and efficient alternative to the traditional REST API. In GraphQL, instead of HTTP verbs, you write a query to GET data, a mutation to POST, PUT, or DELETE data, and subscriptions to push data in the style of WebSockets. Unlike REST, which exposes a fixed set of endpoints for each resource, GraphQL allows clients to request exactly the data they need, no more and no less. This means clients can shape the responses according to their requirements, leading to fewer over-fetching and under-fetching issues. We no longer need to design the perfect API surface to get optimal results.

In the realm of full-stack development, as touched upon in the *Designing APIs* section, the importance of designing around major data entities cannot be overstated. GraphQL shines in this aspect. Its type system ensures the API shapes around these major data entities, providing a clear contract between the frontend and backend teams. This type system, defined in the GraphQL schema, acts as the contract, specifying the data types that can be fetched and the set of operations available.

For frontend developers, diving into a GraphQL API can be a refreshing experience. The introspective nature of GraphQL means that the schema can be queried for details about itself.

This self-documenting feature ensures that developers always have an up-to-date reference, eliminating the need for separate, manually maintained documentation. This is especially beneficial for agile teams in enterprise settings where waiting for documentation isn't always feasible.

Enter the GraphQL Playground or GraphiQL interactive environments, where developers can test and explore GraphQL queries in real time. Much like Swagger UI for OpenAPI, these tools provide immediate feedback, allowing developers to understand the structure, types, and operations of the API. This hands-on approach reduces the learning curve and fosters a deeper understanding of the API's capabilities.

Next, let's explore how to design GraphQL APIs around major data entities, ensuring that they align with the principles laid out in our Router-first architecture and other best practices.

GraphQL schema

The GraphQL schema is at the heart of any GraphQL API, acting as the contract between the client and the server. It describes the structure and capabilities of the API by defining types and the relationships between the types. These types model the major data entities that the API operates on.

Let's begin by exploring the `graphql.schema` file located under `server/graphql`:

1. Using the type keyword, we can define data objects:

   ```
   server/graphql/graphql.schema
   type User {
     address: Address
     dateOfBirth: String
     email: String!
     id: ID!
     level: Float
     name: Name!
     phones: [Phone]
     picture: String
     role: Role!
     userStatus: Boolean!
     fullName: String
   }
   ```

This `User` type has scalar fields like the `id` and `email` fields, representing primitive value types like `ID`, `String`, `Int`, `Float`, and `Boolean`. The bang symbol `!` indicates these fields are required. We can also define relationships between types, such as `Name` or `Phone`. The square brackets `[]` indicate that `phones` is an array of `Phone` objects.

2. We can also define enums and use them like a scalar type:

   server/graphql/graphql.schema
   ```
   enum Role {
     None
     Clerk
     Cashier
     Manager
   }
   ```

3. Using the reserved type `Query`, we can define how data can be retrieved:

   server/graphql/graphql.schema
   ```
   type Query {
     # Gets a `User` object by id
     # Equivalent to GET /v2/users/{id}
     user(id: ID!): User
   }
   ```

   We can define acceptable arguments and the return type.

4. Using the reserved type `Mutation`, we can define how the state can be modified:

   server/graphql/graphql.schema
   ```
   type Mutation {
     # Generates a JWT, given correct credentials.
     # Equivalent to POST /v1/auth/login
     login(email: String!, password: String!): JWT

     # Create a new `User`
     # Equivalent to POST /v2/users
     createUser(userInput: UserInput!): User
   }
   ```

   We can define a login or a `createUser` method. Note that `createUser` takes an input object, which is required if we want to pass a whole object as an argument.

5. Input objects are declared with the `input` keyword:

   server/graphql/graphql.schema

   ```
   input UserInput {
     address: AddressInput
     dateOfBirth: String
     email: String!
     level: Float
     name: NameInput!
     phones: [PhoneInput]
     picture: String
     role: Role!
     userStatus: Boolean!
   }
   ```

   Note that any related object must also use the input declaration. Output types and input data can't be mixed.

> As you may have noticed, we can also add descriptions to document our API using the # symbol or, optionally, the triple quote """ syntax.

The schema is defined using the GraphQL **Schema Definition Language (SDL)**. You can access the SDL specification at `https://graphql.org/`. It's an essential resource for anyone crafting a well-defined GraphQL API.

Overall, the schema provides a strict contract between the client and the server. It makes explicit the data shapes and capabilities available. Frontend and backend teams can build features in parallel against this contract, and tooling like GraphQL Playground makes the schema interactive.

We will use the Apollo GraphQL library to help construct the schema programmatically in our Express server.

Apollo with Express

Apollo GraphQL is a comprehensive and widely adopted suite of tools and services designed to help developers build, manage, and scale GraphQL applications with ease. Developed by the Meteor Development Group, Apollo has become synonymous with GraphQL development for many developers, due to its robust features and developer-friendly approach. Here's a breakdown of Apollo GraphQL:

- **Apollo Client**: A state-of-the-art GraphQL client that manages local and remote data. It integrates seamlessly with any JavaScript frontend framework, such as React, Vue, or Angular. Apollo Client provides features like caching, optimistic UI updates, and real-time subscriptions, making it easier to fetch, cache, and modify application data.
- **Apollo Server**: A community-driven, open-source GraphQL server that works with any GraphQL schema. Apollo Server provides performance tracing and error tracking and supports schema stitching, allowing for the merging of multiple GraphQL APIs into one unified API.
- **Apollo Client Developer Tools**: Browser extensions offering rich in-browser development experience. Developers can view their GraphQL store, inspect active queries, and interact with their GraphQL server using the built-in GraphiQL IDE.

Apollo provides more advanced dev tools with Apollo Studio as part of its cloud offering. Apollo Federation allows organizations to divide their monolithic GraphQL API into smaller, more maintainable microservices. It provides a means to compose multiple GraphQL services into a single data graph. Apollo Link allows developers to create chainable "links" to handle tasks like logging, request retries, and even offline caching.

In essence, Apollo GraphQL provides a holistic approach to GraphQL development, offering tools and services catering to beginners and advanced users. Whether you're building a small application or scaling a large enterprise system, Apollo's tools ensure great DevEx.

The GraphQL schema and the GraphQL library are inseparable, so we don't have to take extra steps to configure the schema definition to work with the codebase, as we did with OpenAPI.

To generate types from a GraphQL schema, follow the guidance provided at `https://www.apollographql.com/docs/apollo-server/workflow/generate-types/`.

Next, let's see how you can configure your schema and Apollo with Express.js:

1. Install the Apollo server:

```
$ @apollo/server
```

2. Open the `api.graphql.ts` file, which configures the Apollo server:

server/src/graphql/api.graphql.ts

```
...
import { resolvers } from './resolvers'
```

```
const typeDefs = readFileSync('./src/graphql/schema.graphql',
...
export async function useGraphQL(app: Express) {
  const server = new ApolloServer<AuthContext>({
    typeDefs,
    resolvers,
  })

  await server.start()

  ...
  )
}
```

3. Using `node:fs`, we read the schema file into the `typeDefs` object and pass it into a new `ApolloServer` instance along with a reference to the resolvers. Finally, we call `server.start()` and export the `useGraphQL` function.
4. Bootstrap the Apollo server in `index.ts`:

```
server/src/index.ts
import app from './app'
...
async function start() {
  ...
  Instance = http.createServer(app)
  await useGraphQL(app)
      ...
    }
    start()
```

In `index.ts`, right after we create an instance of the Express server, which is defined by the app variable, we call the `useGraphQL` function to start it up. This configuration allows us to implement REST and GraphQL APIs side by side. GraphQL APIs and the interactive Explorer tools can be accessed at `/graphql`, as shown below:

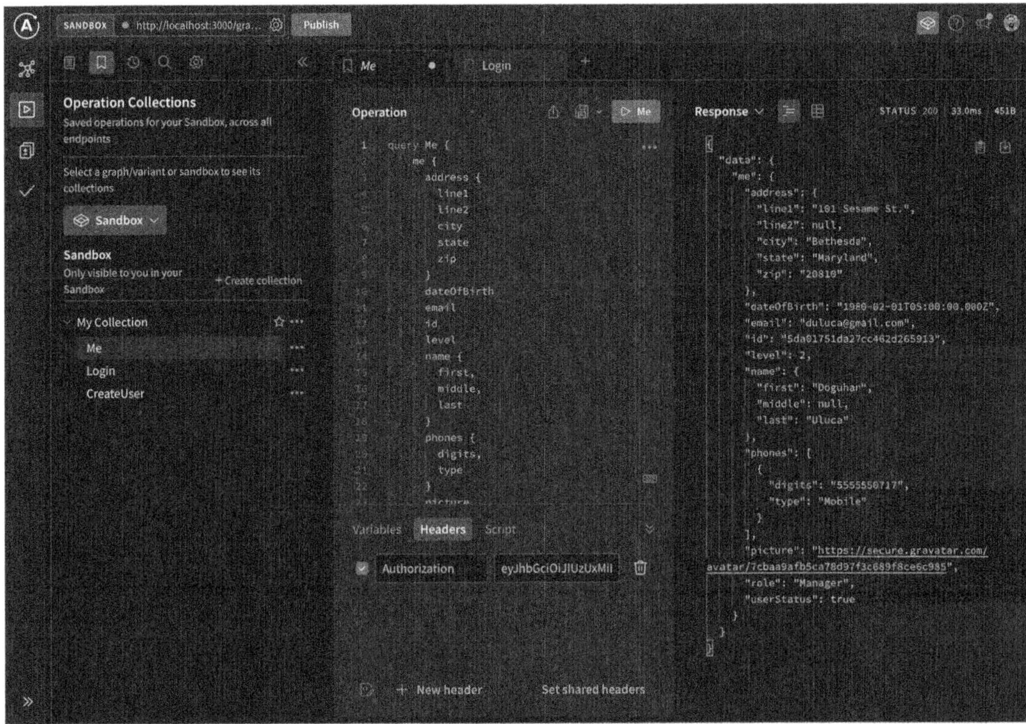

Figure 7.5: GraphQL Explorer

Now that you understand the differences between REST and GraphQL APIs and how we can configure them equivalently with Express.js, let's take a look at the overall architecture of the server.

Implementing APIs with Express.js

Let's go over the architecture and file structure of our backend so that we get an understanding of how the server is bootstrapped, how routing is configured for API endpoints, how public resources are served, and how services are configured.

Review the file structure of our Express server:

```
server/src
├── api.ts
├── app.ts
├── config.ts
├── docs-config.ts
├── graphql
│   ├── api.graphql.ts
│   ├── helpers.ts
│   └── resolvers.ts
├── index.ts
├── models
│   ├── enums.ts
│   ├── phone.ts
│   └── user.ts
├── public
├── services
│   ├── authService.ts
│   └── userService.ts
├── v1
│   ├── index.ts
│   └── routes
│       └── authRouter.ts
└── v2
    ├── index.ts
    └── routes
        └── userRouter.ts
```

Next, we'll review the purpose and the interaction between these files by looking at a component diagram, giving us an overview of the architecture and the dependency tree:

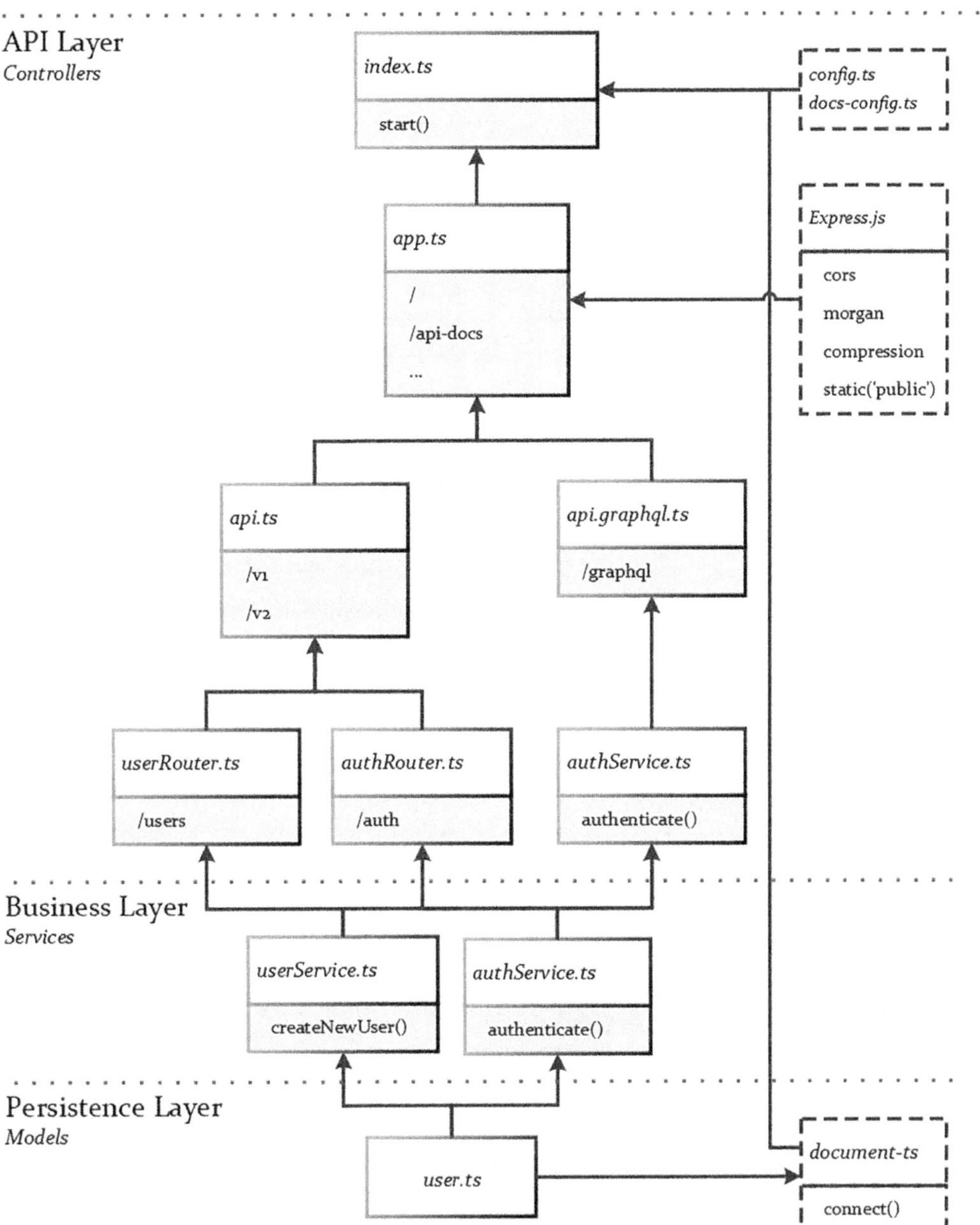

Figure 7.6: Express server architecture

`index.ts` contains a `start` function, which bootstraps the application, leveraging four major helpers:

- `config.ts`: Manages environment variables and settings.
- `app.ts`: Configures Express.js and defines all API paths, and then routers implement the paths and leverage services that contain the business logic. Services use models, such as `user.ts`, to access the database.
- `api.graphql.ts`: Configures GraphQL, resolvers implement queries, and mutators leverage the same services and then resolvers implement queries and mutators and leverage the same services to access the database.
- `document-ts`: Establishes a connection to the database, configures it, and leverages `user.ts` to configure a seed user during startup.

You can see that the components at the top of the diagram are responsible for startup and configuration chores, including configuring API paths, which represent the **API** layer. The **Business** layer should contain most of the business logic for the app, while data access is handled in the **Persistence** layer.

Refer to the following implementation of `index.ts`, which shows a simplified version showing all major components in sequence:

server/src/index.ts

```
...
export let server: http.Server

async function start() {
  await document.connect(config.MongoUri, config.IsProd)
  server = http.createServer(app)
  await useGraphQL(app)

  server.listen(config.Port, async () => {
    console.log(`Server listening on port ${config.Port}...`)
  })
}
start()
```

Note that the last line of code shown, `start()`, is the function call that triggers the server's initialization.

Now, let's investigate how the Express server is set up.

Bootstrapping the server

app.ts configures Express.js, along with serving static assets, routing, and versioning. Express.js leverages middleware functions to integrate with libraries or your code. Middleware are functions that execute during the lifecycle of a request to the Express server. Middleware functions have access to the request and response objects and the following middleware function in the application's request-response cycle. This access allows them to execute any code, make changes, end the request-response cycle, and call the next middleware in the stack. In the code below, cors, logger, and compression are library functions, and later in the chapter, we will go over the implementation of a custom authenticate middleware:

server/src/app.ts

```
import api from './api'
const app = express()
app.use(cors())
app.use(express.json())
app.use(express.urlencoded({ extended: true }))
app.use(logger('dev'))
app.use(compression())
app.use('/', express.static(path.join(__dirname, '../public'), { redirect:
false }))
app.use(api)
export default app
```

In the preceding code, note that configuring Express is straightforward with the `use()` method. First, we configure `cors`, and then `express` parsers, `logger`, and `compression`.

Next, using the `express.static` function, we serve the `public` folder at the root's route, `/`, so that we can display some useful information about our server, as shown in *Figure 7.1* at the beginning of this chapter.

Finally, we configure the router, which is defined in `api.ts`.

REST routes and versioning

`api.ts` configures the Express router. Refer to the following implementation:

server/src/api.ts

```
import { Router } from 'express'
import api_v1 from './v1'
import api_v2 from './v2'
```

```
const api = Router()
// Configure all routes here
api.use('/v1', api_v1)
api.use('/v2', api_v2)
export default api
```

In this case, we have two child routes for v1 and v2. It is critical to always version the APIs you implement. Once an API becomes public, it can be tricky, even impossible sometimes, to simply phase out an API for a newer version. Even minor code changes or slight differences in the API can cause clients to break. You must pay careful attention to only making backward-compatible changes to your API.

At some point, you will need to completely rewrite the endpoint to meet new requirements, performance, and business needs, at which point, you can simply implement a v2 version of your endpoint while leaving the v1 implementation unchanged. This allows you to innovate at the pace you need to while keeping legacy consumers of your app functional.

In short, you should version every API you create. By doing this, you force your consumers to version their HTTP calls to your API. Over time, you can transition, duplicate, and retire APIs under different versions. Consumers then have a choice to call whichever version of the API works for them.

Configuring a route is trivial. Let's see the configuration for v2, as shown:

server/src/v2/index.ts

```
import { Router } from 'express'
import userRouter from './routes/userRouter'
const router = Router()
// Configure all v2 routers here
router.use('/users?', userRouter)
export default router
```

The question mark at the end of /users? means that both /user and /users will work against operations implemented in userRouter. This is a great way to avoid typos while allowing the developer to choose the plurality that makes sense for the operation.

In userRouter, you can implement the GET, POST, PUT, and DELETE operations. Refer to the following implementation:

```
server/src/v2/routes/userRouter.ts
const router = Router()
router.get('/', async (req: Request, res: Response) => {})
router.post('/', async (req: Request, res: Response) => {})
router.get('/:userId', async (req: Request, res: Response) => {})
router.put('/:userId', async (req: Request, res: Response) => {})
export default router
```

In the preceding code, you can observe the use of route parameters. You can consume route parameters through a request object, such as `req.params.userId`.

Note that all routes in the sample code are tagged as `async` because they will all make a database call, which we are going to await. If your route is synchronous, then you don't require the `async` keyword.

Next, let's investigate GraphQL resolvers.

GraphQL resolvers

GraphQL resolvers are implemented in `resolvers.ts`. The GraphQL server performs a breadth-first traversal of the query and recursively calls resolvers to generate the response.

Let me elaborate – when a GraphQL server gets a query, it processes the request layer by layer, starting from the top-level fields and moving horizontally across the structure, like a search that moves across each level of a tree before going deeper, known as breadth-first traversal. For each field it encounters, the server invokes a specific function called a resolver, designed to fetch the data for that field. If a field is complex and contains nested subfields, the resolver for that field will, in turn, call upon other resolvers for each of these subfields. This process repeats itself, descending into the query's hierarchy as needed until all the data for the query is retrieved and can be assembled into the structured response that matches the original query layout.

Refer to the following implementation:

```
server/src/graphql/resolvers.ts
export const resolvers = {
  Query: {
```

```
    me: () => ...,
    user: () => ...,
    users: () => ...,
  },
  Mutation: {
    login: () => ...,
    },
    createUser: () => ...,
    updateUser: () => ...,
  },
```

In the snippet above, we define a resolver function for each query and mutation implemented in the scheme. Each resolver takes in four arguments (`parent`, `args`, `contextValue`, `info`): `parent` can be used to access a parent resolver, `args` contains any input arguments passed in, `contextValue` stores session data useful for auth, and `info` contains metadata about the query itself. Next, let's look at the `type` resolvers:

```
server/src/graphql/resolvers.ts
  User: {
    id: (obj: User) => obj._id.toString(),
    role: (obj: User) => EnumValues.getNameFromValue(Role, obj.role),
    phones: (obj: User) => (obj.phones ? wrapAsArray(obj.phones) : []),
    dateOfBirth: (obj: User) => obj.dateOfBirth?.toISOString(),
  },
  Phone: {
    type: (obj: { type: string }) =>
      EnumValues.getNameFromValue(PhoneType, obj.type),
  },
  Users: {
    data: (obj: Users) => (obj.data ? wrapAsArray(obj.data) : []),
  },
}
```

For non-scalar types, arrays, or enums, we may need to provide a transformation so that GraphQL can appropriately unpack the data retrieved from the database. The good part is we only need to provide a resolver for specific properties of objects that need such manipulation.

Resolvers may seem simple, but they can fulfill very complex needs, e.g., a simple request from a client may involve making multiple service and database calls and collating the results into an efficient response, just so the client can display it.

The atomic nature of resolvers means we only need to implement them once. Next, let's explore how services are configured.

Services

We don't want to implement our business logic in the router files, which represent our API layer. The API layer should largely consist of transforming data and making calls to the business logic layer.

You can implement services using Node.js and TypeScript features. No fancy dependency injection is necessary. The sample application implements two services – `authService` and `userService`.

For example, in `userService.ts`, you can implement a function called `createNewUser`:

server/src/services/userService.ts

```
import { IUser, User } from '../models/user'
export async function createNewUser(userData: IUser):
  Promise<User | boolean> {
  // create user
}
```

`createNewUser` accepts `userData` in the shape of `IUser`, and when it is done creating the user, it returns an instance of `User`. We can then use this function in our router as follows:

server/src/v2/routes/userRouter.ts

```
import { createNewUser } from '../../services/userService'
router.post('/', async (req: Request, res: Response) => {
  const userData = req.body as IUser
  const success = await createNewUser(userData)
```

```
  if (success instanceof User) {
    res.send(success)
  } else {
    res.status(400).send({ message: 'Failed to create user.' })
  }
})
```

We can await the result of `createNewUser` and, if successful, return the created object as a response to the POST request.

Note that even though we cast `req.body` as `IUser`, this is only a development time comfort feature. At runtime, the consumer may pass any number of properties to the body. Careless handling of request parameters is one of the primary ways your code can be maliciously exploited.

Congratulations! Now, you have a good understanding of how our Express server works. Next, let's look at how to connect to MongoDB.

MongoDB ODM with DocumentTS

DocumentTS acts as an **ODM**, implementing a layer of models to enable rich and customizable interaction with database objects. ODM is the document-based database equivalent of an **Object Relational Mapper** (**ORM**) in relational databases. Think of Hibernate or Entity Framework. If you're not familiar with these concepts, I recommend that you do further research before moving on.

To get started, you can check out the following article, *MongoDB ORMs, ODMs, and Libraries*, at `https://www.mongodb.com/developer/products/mongodb/mongodb-orms-odms-libraries`.

At its core, DocumentTS leverages the Node.js driver for MongoDB. The makers of MongoDB implement this driver. It guarantees the best performance and feature parity with new MongoDB releases, whereas third-party libraries often lag in supporting new features. By using the `database.getDbInstance` method, you can access the native driver directly. Otherwise, you will access Mongo through the models that you implement. Refer to the following diagram for an overview:

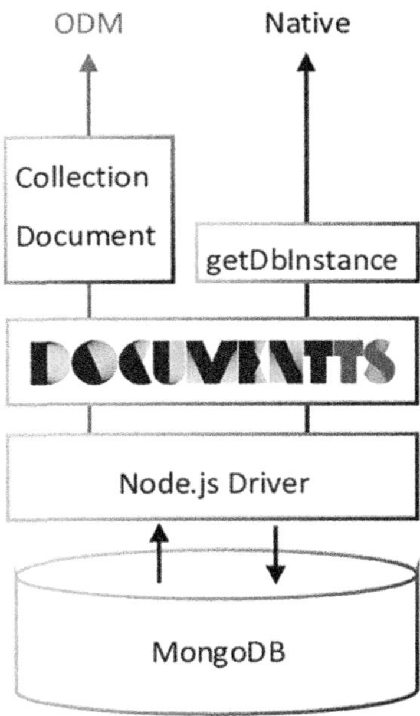

Figure 7.7: DocumentTS overview

You can read more about MongoDB's Node.js driver at `https://mongodb.github.io/node-mongodb-native/`.

For more details on how DocumentTS works and the configuration details, refer to the project wiki on GitHub at `https://github.com/duluca/document-ts/wiki`. The wiki covers connecting to the database, defining models that implement `IDocument`, and configuring serialization and deserialization of data. Models allow calculated properties like `fullName` to be included in client responses while excluding fields like passwords. Passwords are also prevented from being saved to the database in clear text.

The overview continues by demonstrating how to create indexes and query the database with aggregation. It creates a unique index on email, so duplicate emails cannot be registered. A weighted text index assists in filtering query results. DocumentTS aims to provide a convenient yet optional layer on top of the native MongoDB driver to help build fully async web applications. Developers are directly exposed to the MongoDB driver, so they learn how to work with the database instead of just the library.

Let's see how you can fetch data using the new user model.

Implementing JWT auth

In *Chapter 5, Designing Authentication and Authorization,* we discussed implementing a JWT-based authentication mechanism. In LemonMart, you implemented a base auth service that can be extended for custom authentication services.

We'll leverage three packages for our implementation:

- `jsonwebtoken`: Used to create and encode JWTs
- `bcryptjs`: Used to hash and salt a user's password before saving it in the database, so we never store a user's password in plain text
- `uuid`: A generated universally unique identifier that is useful when resetting a user's password to a random value

A hash function is a consistently repeatable, one-way encryption method, which means you get the same output every time you provide the same input, but even if you have access to the hashed value, you cannot readily figure out what information it stores. We can, however, compare whether the user has entered the correct password by hashing the user's input and comparing the hash of their input to that of the stored hash of their password.

The auth service hashes user passwords before storing them and compares hashed passwords on login. The `createJwt` function generates a JWT access token upon successful login. The authenticate middleware decodes the JWT and loads the user into the response stream for authenticated endpoints.

Note the vagueness of the incorrect email/password messages in the code. This is done so that bad actors cannot fish the system to exploit the authentication system.

For password hashing, the `User` model's `setPassword` method uses bcrypt's `genSalt` and `hash` functions. The `comparePassword` method compares the hashed stored password with the hashed user input. This ensures passwords are never stored in plain text.

The login API endpoint finds the user by email, calls `comparePassword` to validate the password, and, on success, calls `createJwt` to generate a signed JWT with user details like email, role, etc. The JWT is returned to the client as the `accessToken`:

```
// Example of hashing and salting password
user.setPassword = async (password) => {
  const salt = await bcrypt.genSalt(10);
  return await bcrypt.hash(password, salt);
}
```

The authenticate middleware decodes the JWT, finds the user by the encoded `id`, and injects the user into `res.locals.currentUser`. Authenticated endpoints like `/me` can conveniently access the user's info. It also handles role-based access by checking options like `requiredRole`:

```
// Example of JWT-based login
router.post('/login', async (req, res) => {
  const user = await User.findByEmail(req.body.email);
  if (user && user.comparePassword(req.body.password)) {
    const accessToken = createJwt(user);
    return res.send({accessToken});
  }
  return res.status(401).send('Invalid credentials');
})
```

When retrieving a user by email, remember that emails are case-insensitive, so you should always convert the input to lowercase. You can improve this implementation further by validating the email and stripping any white space, script tags, or even rogue Unicode characters. Consider using libraries such as `express-validator` or `express-sanitizer`.

Authenticating middleware

The `authenticate` function is a middleware we can use in our API implementations to ensure that only authenticated users with appropriate permissions can access an endpoint. Remember that real security is achieved in your backend implementation, and this `authenticate` function is your gatekeeper.

`authenticate` takes a nullable `options` object to verify the current user's role with the `requiredRole` property, so if an API is configured as shown below, only a manager can access that API:

```
authenticate({ requiredRole: Role.Manager })
```

In certain cases, we want a user to be able to update their own records but also allow managers to update everyone else's records. In this case, we leverage the permitIfSelf property, as shown here:

```
authenticate({
    requiredRole: Role.Manager,
    permitIfSelf: {
      idGetter: (req: Request) => req.body._id,
      requiredRoleCanOverride: true,
    },
  }),
```

In this case, if the _id of the updated record matches the current user's _id, then the user can update their own record. Since requiredRoleCanOverride is set to true, a manager can update any record. If it were set to false, this wouldn't be allowed. By mixing and matching these properties, you can cover a vast majority of your gatekeeping needs.

Note that idGetter is a function delegate so that you can specify how the _id property should be accessed when the authenticate middleware executes.

See the following example implementation of a simplified authenticate middleware and its usage:

The full implementation can be found at server/src/services/auth.service.ts.

```
// Authenticate middleware
function authenticate(options) {
  return async (req, res, next) => {
    const user = await decodeAndFindUser(req.headers.authorization);
    if (user) {
      // Check role if required
      if (options.requiredRole && user.role !== options.requiredRole) {
        return res.status(403).send("Forbidden");
      }

      // Attach user to response
```

```
        res.locals.user = user;

        return next();
      } else {
        return res.status(401).send('Unauthenticated');
      }
    }
  }

  // Usage in RESTful route
  router.get('/me', authenticate(), (req, res)
    => res.send(res.locals.user)
  )
```

The `authenticate` method is implemented as Express.js middleware. It can read the request header for an authorization token, verify the validity of the JWT provided, load the current user, and inject it into the response stream, so an authenticated API endpoint can conveniently access the current user's information. This is shown by the `me` API above. If successful, the middleware calls the `next()` function to yield control back to Express. If unsuccessful, then the API can't be called.

Note that `authenticateHelper` returns useful error messages, so users aren't confused if they try to execute an action they're not permitted to execute.

In GraphQL, authentication and authorization are handled separately. At the Express.js level, we apply the `authenticate` middleware to the `/graphql` route. However, for explorer, introspection, and login functions to work, we must create exceptions to the rule. See the code below, which implements this logic:

```
// GraphQL authentication
app.use('/graphql', authenticate({
    authOverridingOperations: ['Login']
  })
)

// Usage in GraphQL resolver
me: (parent, args, contextValue) => authorize(contextValue),
```

See `server/src/graphql/resolvers.ts` to see the full implementation of the auth in action.

The `authOverridingOperations` property signals to `authenticate` that it should permit calls for introspection and the `Login` function. All other calls to other GraphQL functions will now be authenticated with the authentication context available in resolvers. In the resolvers, we can use the `authorize` method (located at `server/src/graphql/helpers.ts`) to check if the requestor can see the resource they're trying to access. The `contextValue` stores the session context similar to how `res.local` works in Express.

Next, let's implement two custom auth providers, one for REST and another for GraphQL.

Custom server auth provider

Now that you understand the auth implementation in our server, we can implement a custom auth provider in LemonMart, as covered in *Chapter 6, Implementing Role-Based Navigation*:

You must implement this custom auth provider in your Angular app.

The code sample for this section is in the `projects/stage10` folder in the `lemon-mart-app` app or `web-app` folder.

1. Start by creating a `baseUrl` variable in `environment.ts` so that we can connect to your server.
2. In `environment.ts` and `environment.prod.ts`, implement a `baseUrl` variable.
3. Also, select `authMode` as `AuthMode.CustomServer`:

```
web-app/src/environments/environment.ts
web-app/src/environments/environment.prod.ts
export const environment = {
  ...
  baseUrl: 'http://localhost:3000',
  authMode: AuthMode.CustomServer,
```

4. Install a helper library to programmatically access TypeScript enum values:

```
$ npm i ts-enum-util
```

5. Implement the RESTful custom authentication provider using `HttpClient`, as shown here:

web-app/src/app/auth/auth.custom.service.ts

```
import { $enum } from 'ts-enum-util'
...
@Injectable(@Injectable({ providedIn: 'root' }))
export class CustomAuthService extends AuthService {
  private httpClient: HttpClient = inject(HttpClient)

  protected authProvider(
    email: string,
    password: string
  ): Observable<IServerAuthResponse> {
    return this.httpClient.post<IServerAuthResponse>
      (`${environment.baseUrl}/v1/auth/login`, {
        email,
        password,
      })
      .pipe(first())
  }

  protected transformJwtToken(token: IJwtToken): IAuthStatus {
    return {
      isAuthenticated: token.email ? true : false,
      userId: token.sub,
      userRole: $enum(Role)
        .asValueOrDefault(token.role, Role.None),
      userEmail: token.email,
      userPicture: token.picture,
    } as IAuthStatus
  }

  protected getCurrentUser(): Observable<User> {
    return this.httpClient
      .get<IUser>(`${environment.baseUrl}/v1/auth/me`)
```

```
          .pipe(
          first(),
          map((user) => User.Build(user)),
            catchError(transformError)
          )
    }
  }
```

6. The `authProvider` method calls our `/v1/auth/login` method, and `getCurrentUser` calls `/v1/auth/me` to retrieve the current user.

Ensure that calls to `login` methods always happen on HTTPS. Otherwise, you will send user credentials on the open internet. This is ripe for eavesdroppers on public Wi-Fi networks to steal user credentials.

7. Implement the GraphQL custom authentication provider using Apollo Client, as shown here:

web-app/src/app/auth/auth.graphql.custom.service.ts

```
import { GET_ME, LOGIN } from './auth.graphql.queries'
...
@Injectable({ providedIn: 'root' })
export class CustomGraphQLAuthService extends AuthService {
  private apollo: Apollo = inject(Apollo)

  protected authProvider(
    email: string,
    password: string
  ): Observable<IServerAuthResponse> {
    return this.apollo
      .mutate<{ login: IServerAuthResponse }>({
        mutation: LOGIN,
        variables: {
          email,
          password,
        },
      })
      .pipe(
```

```
        first(),
        map((result) =>
          result.data?.login as IServerAuthResponse
        )
      )
    }

  protected transformJwtToken(token: IJwtToken): IAuthStatus {
    return {
      isAuthenticated: token.email ? true : false,
      userId: token.sub,
      userRole: $enum(Role).asValueOrDefault(
        token.role,
        Role.None
      ),
      userEmail: token.email,
      userPicture: token.picture,
    } as IAuthStatus
  }

  protected getCurrentUser(): Observable<User> {
    return this.apollo
      .watchQuery<{ me: IUser }>({
        query: GET_ME,
      })
      .valueChanges.pipe(
        first(),
        map((result) => User.Build(result.data.me))
      )
  }
}
```

Note that the `LOGIN` mutation and `Me` query are implemented in `auth.graphql.queries.ts`. Otherwise, they take up too much space for the service code to be readable.

8. Update `authFactory` to return the new provider for the `AuthMode.CustomServer` option:

```
web-app/src/app/auth/auth.factory.ts
export function authFactory() {
  ...
  case AuthMode.CustomServer:
    return new CustomAuthService()
  case AuthMode.CustomGraphQL:
    return new CustomGraphQLAuthService()
}
```

9. Start your web app to make sure that things are working.

Congratulations! You now grasp how code works across the entire software stack, from the database to the front and back ends.

Summary

In this chapter, we covered full-stack architecture. You learned about building a minimal MEAN stack. You now know how to create a monorepo for a full-stack application and configure a Node.js server with TypeScript. You learned about monorepos, containerizing a Node.js server, and declaratively defining infrastructure with Docker Compose. Using Docker Compose with CircleCI, we saw how you can verify your infrastructure in a CI environment.

You learned how to design a RESTful API using OpenAPI and GraphQL using Apollo, set up an Express.js app, and configure it such that you can generate interactive documentation for your APIs. You learned about the benefits of using DocumentTS with MongoDB.

You then implemented a JWT-based authentication service with an `authenticate` middleware to secure API endpoints and allow for RBAC. Finally, you implemented two custom authentication providers in Angular. For REST, we used `HttpClient`, and for GraphQL, Apollo Client.

The next two chapters will explore Angular recipes to create forms and data tables. In *Chapter 8, Recipes – Reusability, Forms, and Caching*, and *Chapter 9, Recipes – Master/Detail, Data Tables, and NgRx*, we will tie everything together by sticking to a decoupled component architecture, smartly choosing between creating user controls and components and maximizing code reuse, with various TypeScript, RxJS, NgRx, and Angular coding techniques.

For the rest of the book, you will want your LemonMart server and MongoDB instance up and running to verify the correct functionality of your forms and tables as you implement them.

Exercise

You secured your endpoints using the `authenticate` middleware. You configured Postman to send a valid token so that you can communicate with your secured endpoints. By way of an exercise, try removing the `authenticate` middleware and calling the same endpoint with and without a valid token. Re-add the middleware, and then try the same thing again. Observe the different responses you get from the server.

Further reading

- *What is DX? (Developer Experience)*, Albert Cavalcante, 2019, `https://medium.com/@albertcavalcante/what-is-dx-developer-experience-401a0e44a9d9`
- *Overview of Blocking versus Non-Blocking*, 2023, `https://nodejs.org/en/docs/guides/blocking-vs-non-blocking/`
- *Explain Non-Blocking I/O like I'm Five, Frank Rosner*, 2019, `https://blog.codecentric.de/en/2019/04/explain-non-blocking-i-o-like-im-five/`
- *OpenAPI Specification*, 2023, `https://swagger.io/docs/specification`
- *Serialization*, 2023, `https://en.wikipedia.org/wiki/Serialization`
- *JSON*, 2023, `https://en.wikipedia.org/wiki/JSON`
- *Aggregation in MongoDB*, 2023, `https://docs.mongodb.com/manual/aggregation`
- *Apollo Authentication*, 2023, `https://www.apollographql.com/docs/react/networking/authentication`
- *Setting Up Authentication and Authorization with Apollo Federation*, 2023, `https://www.apollographql.com/blog/backend/auth/setting-up-authentication-and-authorization-apollo-federation/`
- *Apollo Built-in error codes*, 2023, `https://www.apollographql.com/docs/apollo-server/data/errors#built-in-error-codes`
- *Apollo Router & Gateway architecture*, 2023, `https://www.apollographql.com/docs/federation/building-supergraphs/router`

Questions

Answer the following questions to ensure you've understood the key concepts from this chapter without googling anything. Do you know if you got all the answers right? Visit `https://angularforenterprise.com/self-assessment` for more:

1. What are the main components that make for a great developer experience?
2. What is a `.env` file?
3. What is the purpose of the `authenticate` middleware?
4. How does Docker Compose differ from using the Dockerfile?
5. What is an ODM? How does it differ from an ORM?
6. What is middleware?
7. What are the uses of the OpenAPI spec?
8. How would you refactor code for the `/v2/users/{id} PUT` endpoint in `userRouter.ts` so that the code is reusable?
9. What are the major differentiators between REST and GraphQL?
10. What are the similarities between OpenAPI and the GraphQL schema?

Join our community on Discord

Join our community's Discord space for discussions with the authors and other readers:

`https://packt.link/AngularEnterpise3e`

8

Recipes – Reusability, Forms, and Caching

In the next two chapters, we will complete most of the implementation of LemonMart and round out our coverage of the router-first approach. In this chapter, I will reinforce the idea of a decoupled component architecture by creating a *reusable* and *routable* component that supports data binding. We will use **Angular directives** to reduce boilerplate code and leverage classes, interfaces, enums, validators, and pipes to maximize code reuse with TypeScript and ES features.

In addition, we will create a **multi-step form** that architecturally scales well and supports a responsive design. Then, we will differentiate between user controls and components by introducing a **lemon rater** and a reusable form part that encapsulates the name object.

This chapter covers a lot of ground. It is organized in a recipe format, so you can quickly refer to a particular implementation when working on your projects. I will cover the implementations' architecture, design, and major components. I will highlight important pieces of code to explain how the solution comes together. Leveraging what you've learned so far, I expect you to fill in routine implementation and configuration details. However, you can always refer to the GitHub project if you are stuck.

In this chapter, you will learn about the following topics:

- Implementing CRUD services with caching
- Multi-step responsive forms
- Reusing repeating template behavior with directives
- Calculated properties and DatePicker

- Typeahead support
- Dynamic form arrays
- Creating shared components
- Reviewing and saving form data
- Scalable form architecture with reusable parts
- Input masking
- Custom controls with `ControlValueAccessor`
- Layouts using a grid list
- Restoring cached data

Technical requirements

The most up-to-date versions of the sample code for the book are on GitHub at the repository linked in the following steps. The repository contains the final and completed state of the code. You can verify your progress at the end of this chapter by looking at the end-of-chapter snapshot of the code under the `projects` folder.

For *Chapter 8*:

Be sure that **lemon-mart-server** is up and running. Refer to *Chapter 7, Working with REST and GraphQL APIs*.

1. Clone the repo at `https://github.com/duluca/lemon-mart`.
2. Execute `npm install` in the root folder to install the dependencies.
3. The beginning state of the project is reflected at:

   ```
   projects/stage10
   ```

4. The end state of the project is reflected at:

   ```
   projects/stage11
   ```

5. Add the stage name to any `ng` command to act only on that stage:

   ```
   npx ng build stage11
   ```

Note that the `dist/stage11` folder at the root of the repository will contain the compiled result.

Beware that the source code provided in the book and the version on GitHub will likely differ. The ecosystem around these projects is ever-evolving. Between changes to how Angular CLI generates new code, bug fixes, new versions of libraries, or side-by-side implementations of multiple techniques, there's a lot of variation impossible to account for. If you find errors or have questions, please create an issue or submit a pull request on GitHub.

Let's start with implementing a user service to retrieve data and build a form to display and edit profile information. Later, we will refactor this form to abstract out its reusable parts.

Implementing CRUD services with caching

We need a service that can perform CRUD operations on a user so that we can implement a user profile. However, the service must be robust enough to withstand common errors. After all, it is very bad UX when users unintentionally lose the data they typed. Form data can be reset due to circumstances outside of a user's control, like a network or validation error, or user errors, like hitting the back or refresh button by mistake. We will create a user service leveraging the `CacheService` we built in *Chapter 5, Designing Authentication and Authorization*, so keep a copy of user data in `localStorage` while the server processes it. The service will implement the following interface and, as always, reference the abstract `IUser` interface over the concrete user implementation:

```
export interface IUserService {
  getUser(id: string): Observable<IUser>
  updateUser(id: string, user: IUser): Observable<IUser>
  getUsers(
    pageSize: number,
    searchText: string,
    pagesToSkip: number
  ): Observable<IUsers>
}
```

Before creating the service, start **lemon-mart-server** and set your application's `AuthMode` to `CustomServer`.

You can use `npm run start:backend` to start the database and the server.

In this section, we will implement the `getUser` and `updateUser` functions. We will implement `getUsers` in *Chapter 9, Recipes – Master/Detail, Data Tables, and NgRx,* to support pagination with a data table.

Start by creating the user service:

1. Create a `UserService` under `src/app/user/user`.
2. Declare the `IUserService` interface from the preceding snippet, excluding the `getUsers` function.
3. Ensure the `UserService` class implements `IUserService`.
4. Inject the `CacheService`, `HttpClient`, and `AuthService`, as shown here:

src/app/user/user/user.service.ts

```
export interface IUserService {
  getUser(id: string): Observable<Iuser>
  updateUser(id: string, user: Iuser): Observable<Iuser>
}
@Injectable({
  providedIn: 'root',
})
export class UserService implements IUserService {
  private readonly cache = inject(CacheService)
  private readonly httpClient = inject(HttpClient)
  private readonly authService = inject(AuthService)

  getUser(id: string): Observable<IUser> {
    throw new Error('Method not implemented.')
  }
  updateUser(id: string, user: IUser): Observable<IUser> {
    throw new Error('Method not implemented.')
  }
}
```

5. Implement the getUser function, as shown here:

```
src/app/user/user/user.service.ts
getUser(id: string | null): Observable<IUser> {
  if (id === null) {
    return throwError('User id is not set')
  }
  return this.httpClient.get<IUser>(
    `${environment.baseUrl}/v2/user/${id}`
  )
}
```

We provide a getUser function that can load any user's profile information. Note that the security for this function is provided in the server implementation with the authenticate middleware. The requestor can either get their profile or will need to be a manager. We use getUser with a resolve guard later in the chapter.

Updating the cache

Implement updateUser, which accepts an object that implements the IUser interface so that data can be sent to a PUT endpoint:

```
src/app/user/user/user.service.ts
updateUser(id: string, user: IUser): Observable<IUser> {
  if (id === '') {
    return throwError('User id is not set')
  }
  // cache user data in case of errors
  this.cache.setItem('draft-user', Object.assign(user, { _id: id }))
  const updateResponse$ = this.httpClient
    .put<IUser>(`${environment.baseUrl}/v2/user/${id}`, user)
    .pipe(map(User.Build), catchError(transformError))
  updateResponse$.subscribe(
    (res) => {
      this.authService.currentUser$.next(res)
      this.cache.removeItem('draft-user')
    },
    (err) => throwError(err)
  )
  return updateResponse$
}
```

Note how the cache service is used with `setItem` to save user-entered data if the `put` call fails. When the call succeeds, we remove the cached data using `removeItem`. Also, note how we hydrate a user returned from the server as a `User` object with `map(User.Build)`, which calls the constructor of `class User`.

Hydrate is a common term for populating an object with data from a database or a network request. For example, the `User` JSON object we pass between components or receive from the server fits the `IUser` interface but is not the `class User` type. We serialize objects to JSON using the `toJSON` method. When we hydrate and instantiate a new object from JSON, we reverse and deserialize the data.

It is important to highlight that you should always stick to interfaces, not concrete implementations like `User` when passing data around. This is the **D** in **SOLID** – the **Dependency Inversion Principle**. Referencing concrete implementations like `User` creates a lot of risk because they change a lot, whereas an abstraction such as `IUser` will seldom change. After all, you wouldn't solder a lamp directly to the electrical wiring in the wall. Instead, you solder the lamp to a plug and then use the plug to get the electricity you need.

With this code completed, `UserService` can now be used for basic CRUD operations.

Multi-step responsive forms

Overall, forms are a different beast than the rest of your application, and they require special architectural considerations. I don't recommend over-engineering your form solution with dynamic templates or route-enabled components. By definition, the different parts of a form are tightly coupled. From the perspectives of maintainability and ease of implementation, creating one giant component is a better strategy than using some of the aforementioned strategies and over-engineering.

We will implement a multi-step input form to capture user profile information in a single component. I will be covering my recommended technique to split forms up into multiple components later in the chapter, in the *Reusable form parts and scalability* section.

Since the implementation of the form changes dramatically between this section and later in the chapter, you can find the code for the initial version on GitHub at `projects/stage11/src/app/user/profile/profile.initial.component.ts` and `projects/stage11/src/app/user/profile/profile.initial.component.html`.

We will also make this multi-step form responsive for mobile devices using media queries:

1. Let's start by adding some helper data that will help us display an input form with options:

```
src/app/user/profile/data.ts
export interface IUSState {
  code: string
  name: string
}
export function USStateFilter(value: string): IUSState[] {
  return USStates.filter((state) => {
    return (
      (state.code.length === 2 &&
       state.code.toLowerCase() === value.toLowerCase()) ||
       state.name.toLowerCase().indexOf(value.toLowerCase()) === 0
    )
  })
}
const USStates = [
  { code: 'AK', name: 'Alaska' },
  { code: 'AL', name: 'Alabama' },
  ...
  { code: 'WY', name: 'Wyoming' },
]
```

2. Add new validation rules to `common/validations.ts`:

```
src/app/common/validations.ts
...
export const OptionalTextValidation = [
  Validators.minLength(2),
  Validators.maxLength(50)
]
export const RequiredTextValidation =
  OptionalTextValidation.concat([Validators.required])
export const OneCharValidation = [
  Validators.minLength(1),
  Validators.maxLength(1)
]
```

```
export const USAZipCodeValidation = [
  Validators.required,
  Validators.pattern(/^\d{5}(?:[-\s]\d{4})?$/),
]
export const USAPhoneNumberValidation = [
  Validators.required,
  Validators.pattern(/^\D?(\d{3})\D?\D?(\d{3})\D?(\d{4})$/),
]
```

3. Now, implement `profile.component.ts` as follows:

src/app/user/profile/profile.component.ts

```
import { Role } from '../../auth/auth.enum'
import { $enum } from 'ts-enum-util'
import { IName, IPhone, IUser, PhoneType } from '../user/user'
...
@Component({
  selector: 'app-profile',
  templateUrl: './profile.component.html',
  styleUrls: ['./profile.component.css'],
})
export class ProfileComponent implements OnInit {
  Role = Role
  PhoneType = PhoneType
  PhoneTypes = $enum(PhoneType).getKeys()
  formGroup: FormGroup
  states$: Observable<IUSState[]>
  userError = ''
  currentUserId: string

  constructor(
    private formBuilder: FormBuilder,
    private uiService: UiService,
    private userService: UserService,
    private authService: AuthService
  ) {}
  private destroyRef = inject(DestroyRef)
```

```
  ngOnInit() {
    this.buildForm()
    this.authService.currentUser$.pipe(
      filter((user) => user !== null),
      tap((user) => {
        this.currentUserId = user._id
        this.buildForm(user)
      }),
      takeUntilDestroyed(this.destroyRef)
    ).subscribe()
  }
  private get currentUserRole() {
    return this.authService.authStatus$.value.userRole
  }
  buildForm(user?: IUser) {}
  ...
}
```

Upon load, we request the current user from `authService`, but this might take a while, so we first build an empty form with `this.buildForm()` as the first statement. We also store the user's ID in the `currentUserId` property, which we will need later when implementing the save functionality.

Note that we filter out `null` or `undefined` users so that we don't try to build the form in an invalid state.

The implementation above introduces a UX issue in the case where `authService.currentUser$` is retrieved from an API. If the API takes over half a second (really, 340 ms) to return the data, there'll be a noticeable pop-up of new information on the form. This will overwrite any text the user may have already entered.

To prevent this, we could disable and reenable the form once the information is received. However, this component isn't aware of where the information comes from; it merely subscribes to `authService.currentUser$`, which may or may not ever return a value. Even if we could reliably tell that we are receiving data from an API, we would have to implement a bespoke solution in every component.

Using an `HttpInterceptor`, we can globally detect when API calls are triggered and completed; we can expose a `signal` where components can individually subscribe to display a loading spinner, or we can leverage the `UiService` to launch a global loading spinner to block the UI while data is retrieved from the server. In *Chapter 9, Recipes – Master/Detail, Data Tables, and NgRx*, I cover how to implement a global spinner.

A global spinner is the ultimate 80–20 solution. However, you may find that a global spinner is a non-starter in large applications with dozens of components continuously retrieving data. Complex UI requires expensive UX solutions. In this case, you will indeed want to implement a component-level spinner. This is demonstrated in the *Data tables with pagination* section of *Chapter 9, Recipes – Master/Detail, Data Tables, and NgRx.*

Later in this chapter, we will implement a resolve guard to load a user based on their `userId`, provided on a route to increase the reusability of this component.

Form controls and form groups

As you may recall, `FormControl` objects are the most elemental parts of a form, usually representing a single input field. We can use `FormGroup` to group together a collection of related `FormControl` objects, such as the individual first, middle, and last parts of a person's name. `FormGroup` objects can also group together a mix of `FormControl`, `FormGroup`, and `FormArray` objects. The latter object allows us to have dynamically repeating elements. `FormArray` is covered later in the chapter in the *Dynamic form arrays* section.

Our form has many input fields, so we will use a `FormGroup` created by `this.formBuilder.group` to house our various `FormControl` objects. Additionally, children `FormGroup` objects will allow us to maintain the correct shape of the data structure.

Since the implementation of the form changes dramatically between this section and later in the chapter, you can find the code for the initial version on GitHub at `projects/stage11/src/app/user/profile/profile.initial.component.ts` and `projects/stage11/src/app/user/profile/profile.initial.component.html`.

Start building the `buildForm` function, as follows:

```
src/app/user/profile/profile.component.ts
```

```
...
  buildForm(user?: IUser) {
    this.formGroup =
    this.formBuilder.group({
      email: [
        {
          value: user?.email || '',
          disabled: this.currentUserRole !== Role.Manager,
        },
        EmailValidation,
      ],
      name: this.formBuilder.group({
        first: [user?.name?.first || '', RequiredTextValidation],
        middle: [user?.name?.middle || '', OneCharValidation],
        last: [user?.name?.last || '', RequiredTextValidation],
      }),
      role: [
        {
          value: user?.role || '',
          disabled: this.currentUserRole !== Role.Manager,
        },
        [Validators.required],
      ],
      dateOfBirth: [user?.dateOfBirth || '', Validators.required],
      address: this.formBuilder.group({
        line1: [user?.address?.line1 || '', RequiredTextValidation],
        line2: [user?.address?.line2 || '', OptionalTextValidation],
        city: [user?.address?.city || '', RequiredTextValidation],
        state: [user?.address?.state || '', RequiredTextValidation],
        zip: [user?.address?.zip || '', USAZipCodeValidation],
      }),
    })
  }
```

`buildForm` optionally accepts an `IUser` to prefill the form. Otherwise, all fields are set to their default values. The `formGroup` property itself is the top-level `FormGroup`. Various `FormControls` are added to it, such as `email`, with validators attached to them as needed.

Note how `name` and `address` are their own `FormGroup` objects. This parent-child relationship ensures the proper structure of the form data, when serialized to JSON, which fits the structure of `IUser` in a manner that the rest of our application and server-side code can utilize.

You will complete the implementation of the `formGroup` independently by following the sample code provided for the chapter. I will review sections of the code piece by piece over the next few sections to explain certain key capabilities.

Stepper and responsive layout

Angular Material's stepper ships with the `MatStepperModule`. The stepper allows form inputs to be broken up into multiple steps so that the user is not overwhelmed with processing dozens of input fields simultaneously. The user can still track their place in the process, and as a side effect, as the developer, we break up our `<form>` implementation and enforce validation rules on a step-by-step basis, or create optional workflows where certain steps can be skipped or required. As with all Material user controls, the stepper has been designed with a responsive UX. In the next few sections, we will implement three steps covering different form-input techniques in the process:

1. Account information:
    - Input validation
    - Responsive layout with media queries
    - Calculated properties
    - `DatePicker`
2. Contact information:
    - Typeahead support
    - Dynamic form arrays
3. Review:
    - Read-only views
    - Saving and clearing data

Let's start by adding the Angular material dependencies:

1. Import the following Material modules in `profile.component.ts`:

```
MatAutocompleteModule,
MatButtonModule,
MatDatepickerModule,
```

```
MatFormFieldModule,
MatIconModule,
MatInputModule,
MatListModule,
MatNativeDateModule,
MatOptionModule,
MatRadioModule,
MatSelectModule,
MatStepperModule,
MatToolbarModule,
```

2. Import other supporting modules:

```
FlexModule,
ReactiveFormsModule,
...
```

3. Implement a horizontal stepper with a form containing the first step:

```
src/app/user/profile/profile.component.html
<mat-toolbar color="accent">
<h5>User Profile</h5>
</mat-toolbar>
<mat-horizontal-stepper #stepper="matHorizontalStepper">
  <mat-step [stepControl]="formGroup">
    <form [formGroup]="formGroup">
      <ng-template matStepLabel>Account Information</ng-template>
      <div class="stepContent">
        ...
      </div>
    </form>
  </mat-step>
</mat-horizontal-stepper>
```

4. Now, start implementing the name row of the `Account Information` step in place of the ellipses in the preceding step:

```
src/app/user/profile/profile.component.html
<div fxLayout="row" fxLayout.lt-sm="column"
     [formGroup]="formGroup.get('name')" fxLayoutGap="10px">
```

```
<mat-form-field appearance="outline" fxFlex="40%">
  <input matInput placeholder="First Name"
         aria-label="First Name" formControlName="first">
    @if (formGroup.get('name.first')?.hasError('required'))
    {
       <mat-error>First Name is required</mat-error>
    }
    @if (formGroup.get('name.first')?.hasError('minLength'))
    {
      <mat-error>Must be at least 2 characters</mat-error>
    }
    @if (formGroup.get('name.first')?.hasError('maxLength'))
    {
      <mat-error>Can't exceed 50 characters</mat-error>
    }
</mat-form-field>
<mat-form-field appearance="outline" fxFlex="20%">
  <input matInput placeholder="MI"
    aria-label="Middle Initial" formControlName="middle">
    @if (formGroup.get('name.middle')?.hasError('invalid'))
    {
      <mat-error>Only initial</mat-error>
    }
</mat-form-field>
<mat-form-field appearance="outline" fxFlex="40%">
  <input matInput placeholder="Last Name"
    aria-label="Last Name" formControlName="last">
    @if (formGroup.get('name.last')?.hasError('required'))
    {
      <mat-error>Last Name is required</mat-error>
    }
```

```
        @if (formGroup.get('name.last')?.hasError('minLength'))
        {
          <mat-error>Must be at least 2 characters</mat-error>
        }
        @if (formGroup.get('name.last')?.hasError('maxLength'))
        {
          <mat-error>Can't exceed 50 characters</mat-error>
        }
    </mat-form-field>
  </div>
```

5. Take your time understanding how the stepper and the form configuration work so far. You should see the first row render, pulling in data from the **lemon-mart-server**:

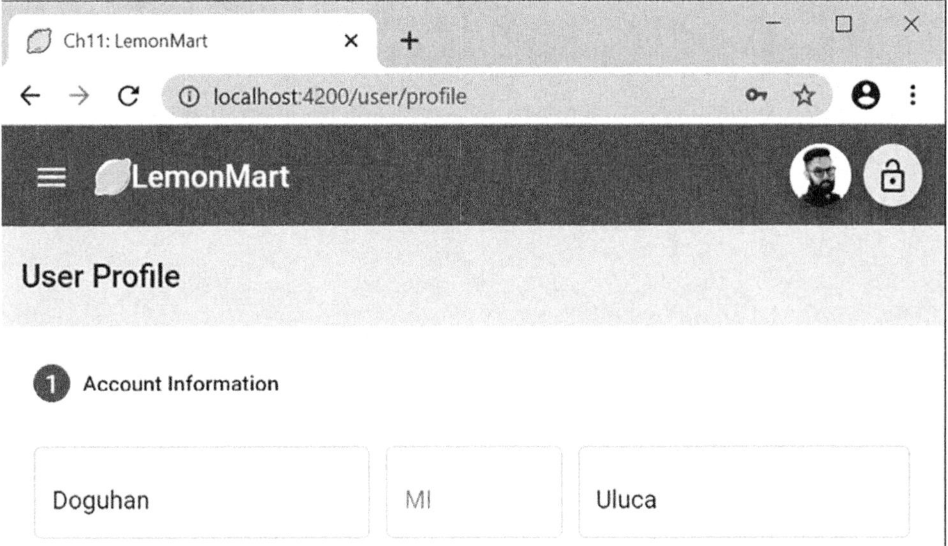

Figure 8.1: Multi-step form – step 1

Note that adding `fxLayout.lt-sm="column"` to a row with `fxLayout="row"` enables a responsive layout for the form, as shown here:

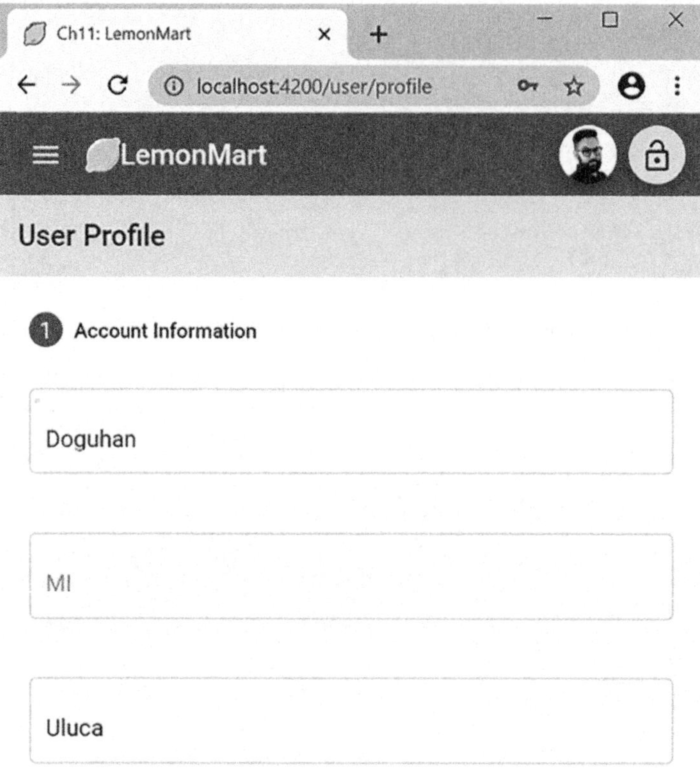

Figure 8.2: Multi-step form on mobile

Before we move on to how to implement the **Date of Birth** field, let's reevaluate our strategy by implementing error messages.

Reusing repeating template behavior with directives

In the previous section, we implemented a `mat-error` element for every validation error for every field part of the `name` object. This quickly adds up to seven elements for three fields. In *Chapter 5, Designing Authentication and Authorization*, we implemented `common/validations.ts` to reuse validation rules. We can reuse the behavior we implement within `mat-error`, or any other `div` for that matter, using an attribute directive.

Attribute directives

In *Chapter 1, Angular's Architecture and Concepts,* I mentioned that Angular components represent the most basic unit of an Angular app. With components, we define custom HTML elements that can reuse features and functionality represented by a template and some TypeScript code. Conversely, a directive augments the capabilities of an existing element or component. In a sense, a component is a super directive that augments basic HTML capabilities.

With this view in mind, we can define three kinds of directives:

- Components
- Structural directives
- Attribute directives

Basically, components are directives with templates; this is the most common type of directive you will use. Structural directives modify the DOM by adding or removing elements, `*ngIf` and `*ngFor` being the canonical examples.

As of Angular 17, you can use the @-syntax to implement control flow and deferrable views, replacing `*ngIf` and `*ngFor` in favor of `@if` or `@for`, respectively. See the code snippet below for an example:

```
@if (user.isHuman) {
  <human-profile [data]="user" />
} @else if (user.isRobot) {
  <!-- robot users are rare, so load their profiles lazily -->
  @defer {
    <robot-profile [data]="user" />
  }
} @else {
  <p>The profile is unknown!
}
```

Finally, attribute directives allow you to define new attributes to add to HTML elements or components, adding new behavior.

Let's implement an attribute directive that can encapsulate field-level error behavior.

Field error attribute directive

Imagine using a directive to reduce repetitive elements to display field errors. Consider the following example using the first name field as an example:

```
example
<mat-form-field appearance="outline" fxFlex="40%">
  <mat-label>First Name</mat-label>
  <input matInput aria-label="First Name" formControlName="first" #name />
  <mat-error [input]="name" [group]="formGroup.get('name')"
    [appFieldError]="ErrorSets.RequiredText">
  </mat-error>
</mat-form-field>
```

We have the standard layout structure for a Material form field, but only a single `mat-error` element exists. There are three new properties on `mat-error`:

- `input` binds to the HTML input element that was tagged with `#name`, using a template reference variable so that we can tap into the blur event of the input element and read the `placeholder`, `aria-label`, and `formControlName` properties.
- `group` binds to the parent FormGroup object that contains the form control, so by using the `formControlName` property from input, we can retrieve the `formControl` object while avoiding extra code.
- `appFieldError` binds to an array of validation errors that must be checked against the `formControl` object, such as `required`, `minlength`, `maxlength`, and `invalid`.

Using the preceding information, we can craft a directive that can render one or more lines of error messages inside the `mat-error` element, effectively replicating the verbose method we used in the previous section.

Let's go ahead and create an attribute directive named `FieldErrorDirective`:

1. Create `FieldErrorDirective` under `src/app/user-controls`.
2. Define the directive's selector as a bindable attribute named `appFieldError`:

```
src/app/user-controls/field-error/field-error.directive.ts
@Directive({
  selector: '[appFieldError]',
})
```

3. Outside of the directive, define two new types named `ValidationError` and `ValidationErrorTuple`, which define the kinds of error conditions we will deal with and a structure that will allow us to attach a custom error message to the error type:

   src/app/user-controls/field-error/field-error.directive.ts
   ```
   export type ValidationError =
     'required' | 'minlength' | 'maxlength' | 'invalid'

   export type ValidationErrorTuple = {
     error: ValidationError;
     message: string
   }
   ```

4. Like the way we grouped validations, let's define two sets of commonly occurring error conditions so that we don't have to type them out over and over again:

   src/app/user-controls/field-error/field-error.directive.ts
   ```
   export const ErrorSets: { [key: string]: ValidationError[] } = {
     OptionalText: ['minlength', 'maxlength'],
     RequiredText: ['minlength', 'maxlength', 'required'],
   }
   ```

5. Next, let's define the `@Input` targets for the directive:

   src/app/user-controls/field-error/field-error.directive.ts
   ```
   export class FieldErrorDirective implements OnDestroy, OnChanges {
     @Input() appFieldError:
       | ValidationError
       | ValidationError[]
       | ValidationErrorTuple
       | ValidationErrorTuple[]
     @Input() input: HTMLInputElement | undefined
     @Input() group: FormGroup
     @Input() fieldControl: AbstractControl | null
     @Input() fieldLabel: string | undefined
   ```

Note that we already went over the purpose of the top three attributes. `fieldControl` and `fieldLabel` are optional attributes. If `input` and `group` are specified, the optional attributes can be auto-populated. Since they are class-wide variables, it made sense to expose them if the user wants to override the default behavior of the directive. This is an easy win to create flexible and reusable controls.

6. Import the element reference in the `constructor`, which can be later used by a `renderErrors` function to display error in the inner HTML of the `mat-error` element:

src/app/user-controls/field-error/field-error.directive.ts

```
private readonly nativeElement: HTMLElement
constructor(private el: ElementRef) {
  this.nativeElement = this.el.nativeElement
}
renderErrors(errors: string) {
  this.nativeElement.innerText = errors
}
```

7. Implement a function that can return canned error messages, depending on the error type:

src/app/user-controls/field-error/field-error.directive.ts

```
getStandardErrorMessage(error: ValidationError): string {
  const label = this.fieldLabel || 'Input'
  switch (error) {
    case 'required':
      return `${label} is required`
    case 'minlength':
      return `${label} must be at least ${
        this.fieldControl?.getError(error)?.requiredLength ?? 2
      } characters`
    case 'maxlength':
      return `${label} can\'t exceed ${
        this.fieldControl?.getError(error)?.requiredLength ?? 50
      } characters`
    case 'invalid':
```

```
        return `A valid ${label} is required`
    }
  }
```

Note that we can dynamically extract the required `minlength` or `maxlength` from the `fieldControl`, greatly reducing the number of custom messages we need to generate.

8. Implement the algorithm that can loop through all the elements in `appFieldError` and the errors that need to be displayed in an array, using the `getStandardErrorMessage` method:

src/app/user-controls/field-error/field-error.directive.ts

```
updateErrorMessage() {
    const errorsToDisplay: string[] = []
    const errors = Array.isArray(this.appFieldError)
      ? this.appFieldError
      : [this.appFieldError]
    errors.forEach(
      (error: ValidationError
            | { error: ValidationError; message: string }) => {
        const errorCode =
          typeof error === 'object' ? error.error : error
        const message =
          typeof error === 'object'
            ? () => error.message
            : () => this.getStandardErrorMessage(errorCode)
        const errorChecker =
          errorCode === 'invalid'
            ? () => this.fieldControl?.invalid
            : () => this.fieldControl?.hasError(errorCode)
        if (errorChecker()) {
          errorsToDisplay.push(message())
        }
      }
    )
    this.renderErrors(errorsToDisplay.join('<br>'))
  }
```

Ultimately, we can display the error messages using the `renderErrors` method.

Note the use of function delegates, a technique that allows functions to be passed around and used as variables. Since this code will execute hundreds of times a minute, it is important to avoid unnecessary invocations. Function delegates help organize our code better while deferring the execution of their logic unless absolutely necessary. This pattern of coding allows for memorization techniques to enhance performance further. Refer to the *Further reading* section for more details.

9. Now, initialize the `fieldControl` property, which represents a `formControl`. We will listen to the `valueChanges` events of the control, and if the validation status is invalid, then we execute our custom `updateErrorMessage` logic to display error messages:

src/app/user-controls/field-error/field-error.directive.ts

```
private controlSubscription: Subscription | undefined
ngOnDestroy(): void {
  this.unsubscribe()
}
unsubscribe(): void {
  this.controlSubscription?.unsubscribe()
}
initFieldControl() {
    if (this.input && this.group) {
      const controlName = this.input.
        getAttribute('formControlName') ?? ''
      this.fieldControl =
        this.fieldControl || this.group.get(controlName)
      if (!this.fieldControl) {
        throw new Error(
          `[appFieldError] couldn't bind to control ${controlName}`
        )
      }
      this.unsubscribe()
      this.controlSubscription = this.fieldControl?.valueChanges
        .pipe(
          filter(() => this.fieldControl?.status === 'INVALID'),
```

```
          tap(() => this.updateErrorMessage())
        )
        .subscribe()
    }
  }
```

Note that since we're subscribing to `valueChanges`, we must also unsubscribe. We unsubscribe once with `ngOnDestroy` and again right before subscribing. This is because `initFieldControl` may be called multiple times. If we don't clear the prior subscription, it will result in a memory leak and related performance issues.

Additionally, if we can't bind to a `fieldControl`, we throw an error message, which usually points to a coding error.

10. Finally, we configure all major attributes with the `ngOnChanges` event, which triggers any time an `@Input` attribute is updated. This ensures that, in the case where form elements could be dynamically added or removed, we will always consider the newest values. We call `initFieldControl` to start listening to value changes, implement an `onblur` event handler that triggers `updateErrorMessage()` for the HTML input element, and assign the value of `fieldLabel`:

src/app/user-controls/field-error/field-error.directive.ts

```
  ngOnChanges(changes: SimpleChanges): void {
    this.initFieldControl()
    if (changes.input.firstChange) {
      if (this.input) {
        this.input.onblur = () => this.updateErrorMessage()
        this.fieldLabel =
          this.fieldLabel ||
          this.input.placeholder ||
          this.input.getAttribute('aria-label') ||
          ''
      } else {
        throw new Error(
          `appFieldError.[input] couldn't bind to any input element`
        )
```

```
      }
    }
  }
```

Note that if we can't bind to an HTML `input` element, this usually means that the developer simply forgot to wire things up correctly. In this case, we throw a new `Error` object, which generates a helpful stack trace in the console, so you can pinpoint the location where the error occurs in the template.

This wraps up the implementation of the directive. Now, we need to package the directive in a module named `field-error.module.ts`:

src/app/user-controls/field-error/field-error.directive.ts

```
  @NgModule({
  imports: [CommonModule, ReactiveFormsModule],
  declarations: [FieldErrorDirective],
  exports: [FieldErrorDirective],
})
export class FieldErrorModule {}
```

Now, go ahead and use the directive in our existing forms:

1. Import the module in `app.module.ts` and `user.module.ts`.
2. Update `profile.component.html` with the new directive.
3. Update `login.component.html` with the new directive.

Be sure to define `ErrorSets` as a public property variable in the `component` class so that you can use it in the template.

Test your forms to ensure that our validation messages are displayed as expected and there are no console errors.

Congratulations! You've learned how to inject new behavior into other elements and components using directives. By doing this, we can avoid a lot of repeated code and standardize error messages across our app.

Before moving on, finish implementing the form by looking at the implementation on GitHub. You can find the code for the form template at `projects/stage11/src/app/user/profile/profile.initial.component.html` and the `component` class at `projects/stage11/src/app/user/profile/profile.initial.component.ts`.

Do not include the `app-lemon-rater` and `app-view-user` elements, and remove the `mask` attribute from the phone number, which we will implement later in the chapter.

Here, you can see the User Profile as it appears on LemonMart:

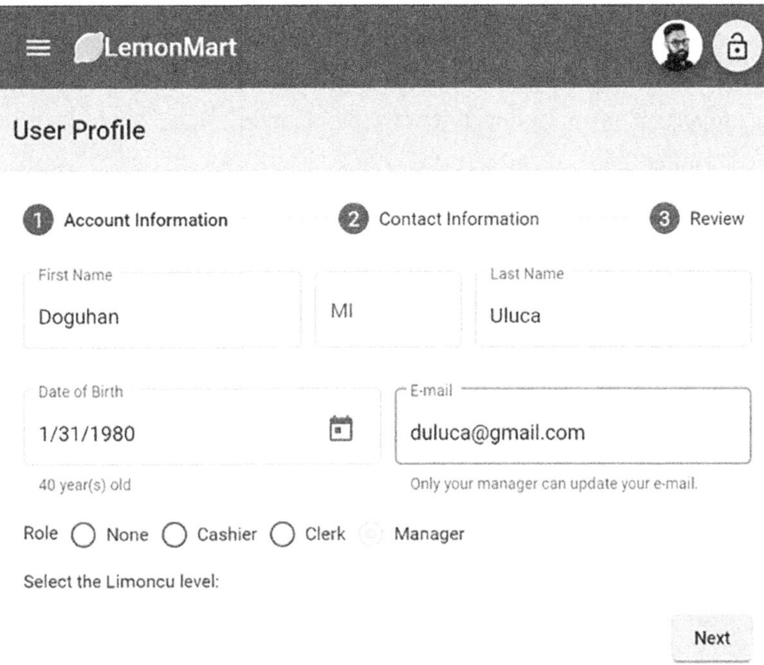

Figure 8.3: Profile component in a mostly completed state

Next, we will review the `profile` component and see how the **Date of Birth** field works.

Calculated properties and DatePicker

We can display calculated properties based on user input. For example, to display a person's age based on their date of birth, introduce class properties that calculate the age and display it as follows:

src/app/user/profile/profile.component.ts

```
now = new Date()
get dateOfBirth() {
  return this.formGroup.get('dateOfBirth')?.value || this.now
}
get age() {
  return this.now.getFullYear() - this.dateOfBirth.getFullYear()
}
```

The implementation for the age property getter is not the most performant option. To calculate the age, we call the `getFullYear()` function of `this.now` and `this.dateOfBirth`. As a property referenced in the template, Angular's change detection algorithm will call age up to 60 times per second, mixed with other elements on the screen, which can lead to major performance issues. You can resolve this issue by creating a **pure custom pipe** so that Angular understands only to check the age property if one of its dependent values changes.

You can read more about pure pipes at `https://angular.dev/guide/pipes/change-detection`.

Another option would be to use **computed signals**. Like calculated properties, computed signals are read-only signals that derive their value from other signals.

We could rewrite the code above like below:

```
now = new Date()
dateOfBirth =
  signal(
   this.formGroup.get('dateOfBirth')?.value || this.now
  )
age = computed(() =>
  this.now.getFullYear() - this.dateOfBirth().
getFullYear())
```

We create `dateOfBirth` as a **signal** and age as a **computed signal**. With this setup, age will be updated if and only if `dateOfBirth` changes. As you can see, the implementation is straightforward, and Angular's change detection algorithm will do the right thing by default.

Except for one wrinkle! Due to the absence of **signal-based components** and the requisite `FormGroup` support, we can't readily use `dateOfBirth` or age in reactive forms.

This helps you appreciate how big a change signals are for Angular. Read more at `https://angular.dev/guide/signals#computed-signals`.

To validate a date within the last hundred years, implement a `minDate` class property:

src/app/user/profile/profile.component.ts

```
minDate = new Date(
  this.now.getFullYear() - 100,
  this.now.getMonth(),
  this.now.getDate()
)
```

The usage of the calculated properties in the template looks like this:

src/app/user/profile/profile.component.html

```
<mat-form-field appearance="outline" fxFlex="50%">
  <mat-label>Date of Birth</mat-label>
  <input matInput aria-label="Date of Birth" formControlName="dateOfBirth"
    [min]="minDate" [max]="now" [matDatepicker]="dateOfBirthPicker" #dob />
  @if (formGroup.get('dateOfBirth')?.value) {
    <mat-hint> {{ age }} year(s) old </mat-hint>
  }
  <mat-datepicker-toggle matSuffix [for]="dateOfBirthPicker">
  </mat-datepicker-toggle>
  <mat-datepicker #dateOfBirthPicker></mat-datepicker>
  <mat-error [input]="dob" [group]="formGroup"
    [appFieldError]=
      "{error: 'invalid', message: 'Date must be within the last 100 years'}">
  </mat-error>
</mat-form-field>
```

Refer to the highlighted `[min]` and `[max]` attributes in the preceding snippet to apply the hundred-year date range.

The `DatePicker` in action appears as follows:

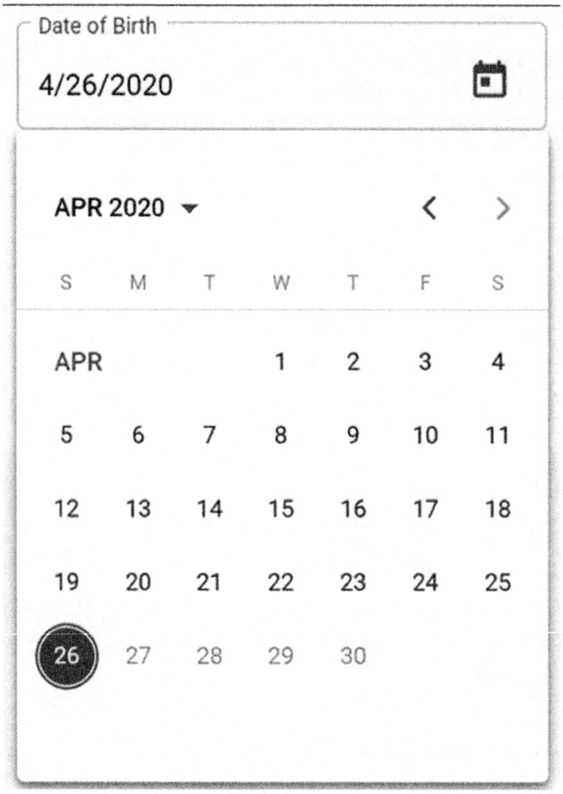

Figure 8.4: Selecting a date with DatePicker

Note that dates beyond April 26, 2020 are grayed out. After the date is selected, the calculated age is displayed as follows:

Figure 8.5: Calculated age property

Now, let's move on to the next step, **Contact Information**, and see how we can enable a convenient way to display and input the state portion of the address field.

Typeahead support

In buildForm, we set a listener on address.state to support a typeahead filtering drop-down experience:

src/app/user/profile/profile.component.ts

```
const state = this.formGroup.get('address.state')
if (state != null) {
  this.states$ = state.valueChanges.pipe(
    startWith(''),
    map((value) => USStateFilter(value))
  )
}
```

On the template, implement mat-autocomplete, bound to the filtered states array with an async pipe:

src/app/user/profile/profile.component.html

```
...
<mat-form-field appearance="outline" fxFlex="30%">
  <mat-label>State</mat-label>
  <input type="text" aria-label="State" matInput formControlName="state"
    [matAutocomplete]="stateAuto" #state />
  <mat-autocomplete #stateAuto="matAutocomplete">
    @for (state of states$ | async; track state) {
      <mat-option [value]="state.name">
        {{ state.name }}
      </mat-option>
    }
  </mat-autocomplete>
  <mat-error [input]="state" [group]="formGroup.get('address')"
    appFieldError="required">
  </mat-error>
</mat-form-field>
...
```

Here's how it looks when a user enters the character V:

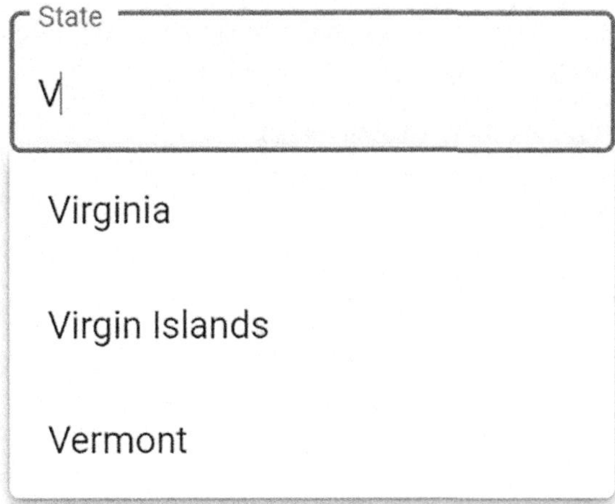

Figure 8.6: Dropdown with typeahead support

In the next section, let's enable the input of multiple phone numbers.

Dynamic form arrays

Note that the phones property is an array, potentially allowing for many inputs. We can implement this by building a FormArray with the this.formBuilder.array function. We also define several helper functions to make it easier to build the FormArray:

- buildPhoneFormControl helps to build FormGroup objects of individual entries.
- buildPhoneArray creates as many FormGroup objects as needed, or if the form is empty, it creates an empty entry.
- addPhone adds a new empty FromGroup object to the FormArray.
- get phonesArray() is a convenient property to get the phones control from the form.

Let's see how the implementation comes together:

src/app/user/profile/profile.component.ts

```
...
phones: this.formBuilder.array(this.buildPhoneArray(user?.phones || [])),
...
  private buildPhoneArray(phones: IPhone[]) {
    const groups = []
    if (phones?.length === 0) {
```

```
      groups.push(this.buildPhoneFormControl(1))
    } else {
      phones.forEach((p) => {
        groups.push(
          this.buildPhoneFormControl(p.id, p.type, p.digits)
        )
      })
    }
    return groups
      }
  private buildPhoneFormControl(
    id: number, type?: string, phoneNumber?: string
  ) {
    return this.formBuilder.group({
      id: [id],
      type: [type || '', Validators.required],
      digits: [phoneNumber || '', USAPhoneNumberValidation],
  })
}
...
```

`buildPhoneArray` supports the initialization of a form with a single phone input or by filling it with the existing data, working in tandem with `buildPhoneFormControl`. The latter function comes in handy when a user clicks on an **Add** button to create a new row for the entry:

src/app/user/profile/profile.component.ts

```
...
addPhone() { this.phonesArray.push(
this.buildPhoneFormControl(
  this.formGroup.get('phones').value.length + 1)
)
}
get phonesArray(): FormArray {
  return this.formGroup.get('phones') as FormArray
}
...
```

The phonesArray property getter is a common pattern that makes accessing certain form properties easier. However, in this case, it is also necessary because get('phones') must be typecast to FormArray so that we can access the length property on it on the template:

src/app/user/profile/profile.component.html

```
...
<mat-list formArrayName="phones">
  <h2 mat-subheader>Phone Number(s)
    <button mat-button (click)="addPhone()">
      <mat-icon>add</mat-icon>
      Add Phone
    </button>
  </h2>
  @for (position of phonesArray.controls; track position; let i = $index)
  {
    <mat-list-item [formGroupName]="i">
      <mat-form-field appearance="outline" fxFlex="100px">
        <mat-label>Type</mat-label>
        <mat-select formControlName="type">
          @for (type of PhoneTypes; track type) {
            <mat-option [value]="convertTypeToPhoneType(type)">
              {{ type }}
            </mat-option>
          }
        </mat-select>
    </mat-form-field>
    <mat-form-field appearance="outline" fxFlex fxFlexOffset="10px">
      <mat-label>Number</mat-label>
      <input matInput type="text" formControlName="digits"
        aria-label="Phone number" prefix="+1" />
        @if (phonesArray.controls[i].invalid &&
              phonesArray.controls[i].touched) {
          <mat-error>A valid phone number is required</mat-error>
        }
    </mat-form-field>
    <button fxFlex="33px" mat-icon-button
      (click)="phonesArray.removeAt(i)">
      <mat-icon>delete</mat-icon>
```

```
      </button>
    </mat-list-item>
    }
  </mat-list>
  ...
```

Note the highlighted `convertTypeToPhoneType` function, which converts a `string` to `enum PhoneType`.

Also highlighted in the preceding code block is how the `remove` function is implemented inline in the template, making it easier to read and maintain.

Let's see how the dynamic array should be working:

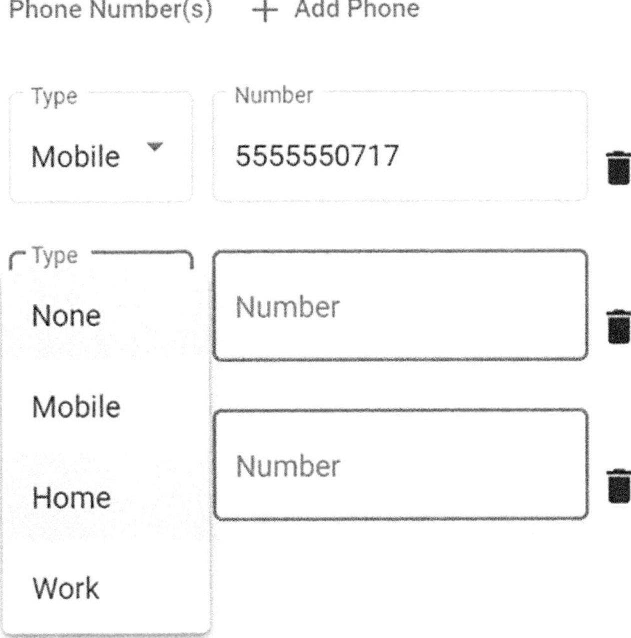

Figure 8.7: Multiple inputs using FormArray

Now that we're done inputting data, we can move on to the last step of the stepper, **Review**. However, as was mentioned earlier, the **Review** step uses the `<app-view-user>` directive to display its data. Let's build that view first.

Creating shared components

Here's a minimal implementation of the `<app-view-user>` directive, a prerequisite for the **Review** step.

Create a new `viewUser` component under the `user` folder structure, as follows:

```
src/app/user/view-user/view-user.component.ts
import { AsyncPipe, DatePipe } from '@angular/common'
import {
  Component, inject, Input, OnChanges, SimpleChanges
} from '@angular/core'
import { MatButtonModule } from '@angular/material/button'
import { MatCardModule } from '@angular/material/card'
import { MatIconModule } from '@angular/material/icon'
import { Router } from '@angular/router'

import { IUser, User } from '../user/user'
@Component({
  selector: 'app-view-user',
  template: `
    @if (currentUser) {
      <div>
        <mat-card appearance="outlined">
          <mat-card-header>
            <div mat-card-avatar>
              <mat-icon>account_circle</mat-icon>
            </div>
            <mat-card-title>{{ currentUser.fullName }}</mat-card-title>
            <mat-card-subtitle>{{ currentUser.role }}</mat-card-subtitle>
          </mat-card-header>
          <mat-card-content>
            <p><span class="mat-input bold">E-mail</span></p>
            <p>{{ currentUser.email }}</p>
            <p><span class="mat-input bold">Date of Birth</span></p>
            <p>{{ currentUser.dateOfBirth | date: 'mediumDate' }}</p>
          </mat-card-content>
          @if (editMode) {
```

```
            <mat-card-actions>
              <button mat-button mat-raised-button
(click)="editUser(currentUser._id)">
                Edit
              </button>
            </mat-card-actions>
          }
        </mat-card>
      </div>
    }
  `,
  styles: `
    .bold {
      font-weight: bold;
    }
`,
  standalone: true,
  imports: [MatCardModule, MatIconModule, MatButtonModule, AsyncPipe,
DatePipe],
})
export class ViewUserComponent implements OnChanges {
  private readonly router = inject(Router)

  @Input() user!: IUser
  currentUser = new User()

  get editMode() {
    return !this.user
  }

  ngOnChanges(changes: SimpleChanges): void {
    this.currentUser = User.Build(changes['user'].currentValue)
  }
  editUser(id: string) {
    this.router.navigate(['/user/profile', id])
  }
}
```

The preceding component uses input binding with `@Input` to get user data compliant with the `IUser` interface from an outside component. We implement the `ngOnChanges` lifecycle hook, which fires whenever the bound data changes. In this event, we hydrate the simple JSON object stored in the `user` property as an instance of the `User` class with `User.Build`.

We then assign the `User` object to the property `this.currentUser`. Even if we wanted to, we couldn't directly bind to the user property, because calculated properties such as `fullName` can only work if data is hydrated into an instance of the `User` class. Angular 17.1 introduces signal-based inputs in developer preview. We could define user like `user = input<IUser>()` and leverage effect and a computed signal to streamline our implementation. In the current state of our code, we incur a heavy change detection penalty given the number of properties we're binding to. However in signal-based component there would be no such penalty. I look forward to refactoring this component, when signal-based components are released.

Now, we are ready to complete the multi-step form.

Reviewing and saving form data

On the last step of the multistep form, users should be able to review and then save the form data. As a good practice, a successful `POST` request will return the data that was saved back to the browser. We can then reload the form with the information received back from the server:

```
src/app/user/profile/profile.component.ts
...
async save(form: FormGroup) {
    this.userService
      .updateUser(this.currentUserId, form.value)
      .pipe(first())
      .subscribe({
        next: (res: IUser) => {
          this.patchUser(res)
          this.formGroup.patchValue(res)
          this.uiService.showToast('Updated user')
        },
        error: (err: string) => (this.userError = err),
      })
  }
...
```

Note that `updateUser` returns the saved value of the user. It is possible that the database returns a different version of `user` than what we had before, so we use `formGroup.patchValue` to update the data powering the form. The form automatically updates to reflect any changes.

If there are errors when saving the data, they'll be set to `userError` to be displayed on the form. Before saving the data, we present it in a compact format with the reusable `app-view-user` component, which we can bind the form data to:

src/app/user/profile/profile.component.html

```
...
<mat-step [stepControl]="formGroup">
  <form [formGroup]="formGroup" (ngSubmit)="save(formGroup)">
    <ng-template matStepLabel>Review</ng-template>
    <div class="stepContent">
      Review and update your user profile.
      <app-view-user [user]="formGroup.getRawValue()"></app-view-user>
    </div>
    <div fxLayout="row" class="margin-top">
      <button mat-button matStepperPrevious>Back</button>
      <div class="flex-spacer"></div>
      @if (userError) {
        <div class="mat-caption error">{{ userError }}</div>
      }
      <button mat-button color="warn" (click)="stepper.reset()">
        Reset
      </button>
      <button mat-raised-button matStepperNext color="primary"
        type="submit" [disabled]="formGroup.invalid">
        Update
      </button>
    </div>
  </form>
</mat-step>
...
```

Note that we use `formGroup.getRawValue()` to extract the JSON of the form data. See how we bind `userError` to display error messages. Also, the **Reset** button uses `stepper.reset()`, which can conveniently reset all the user input.

This is how the final product should appear:

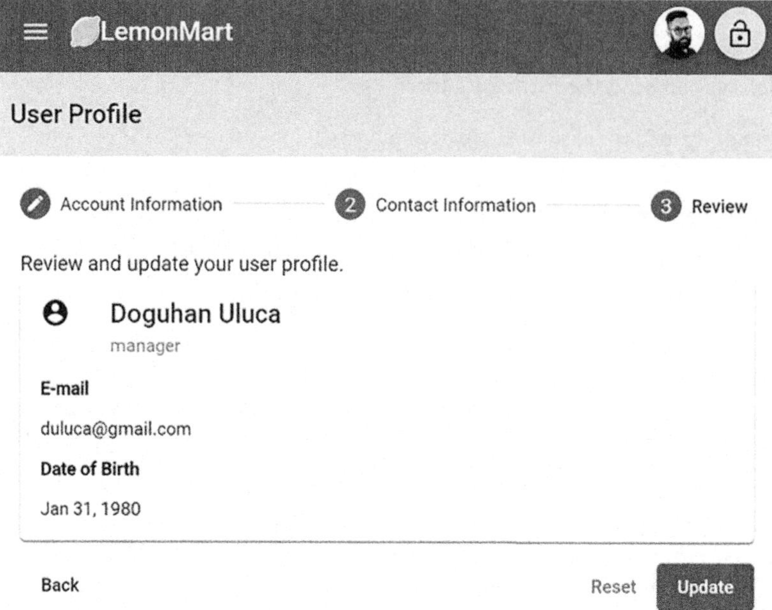

Figure 8.8: Review step

Now that the user profile input is done, we are about halfway to our eventual goal of creating a master/detail view where a **Manager** can click on a user and view their profile details. We still have a lot more code to add, and along the way, we have fallen into a pattern of adding lots of boilerplate code to load the requisite data for a component.

Next, let's refactor our form to make our code reusable and scalable, so even if our form has dozens of fields, the code is still maintainable, and we don't introduce an exponential cost increase to make changes.

Scalable form architecture with reusable parts

As mentioned in the introduction to the *Multi-step responsive forms* section, forms are tightly coupled beasts that can grow large, and using the wrong architectural pattern to scale your implementation can cause significant issues when implementing new features or maintaining existing ones.

To demonstrate how you can break up your form into multiple parts, we will refactor it to extract the highlighted section in the following screenshot, the name `FormGroup`, as its own component. The technique to accomplish this is the same as you'd use when you want to put each step of your form into a separate component:

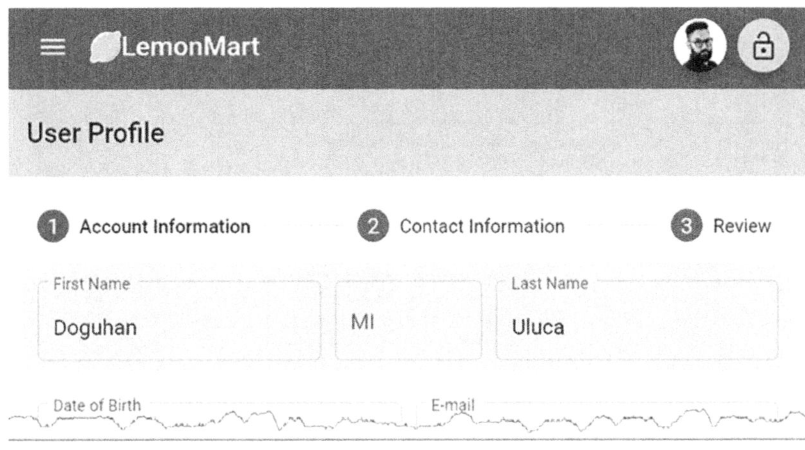

Figure 8.9: User profile's name part highlighted

By making the name `FormGroup` reusable, you will also learn about how you can reuse the business logic that you build into that `FormGroup` in other forms. We will extract the name `FormGroup` logic into a new component named `NameInputComponent`. In doing so, we also have an opportunity to extract some reusable form functionality to a `BaseFormComponent` as an `abstract class`.

There are going to be several components that are working together here, including `ProfileComponent`, `ViewUserComponent`, and `NameInputComponent`. We need all the values in these three components to be up to date as the user enters them.

`ProfileComponent` will own the master form to which we'll need to register any child form. Once we do this, all the form validation techniques you've learned so far will still apply.

This is a key way to make your form able to scale across many components and continue to be easy to work with, without introducing unnecessary validation overhead. Hence, it is useful to review the different interactions between these objects to solidify your understanding of the asynchronous and decoupled nature of their behavior:

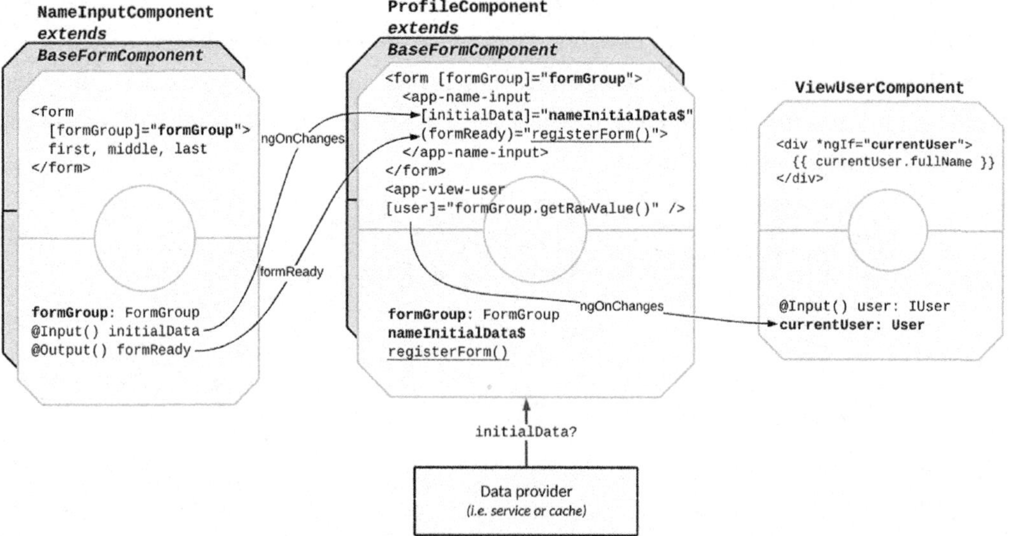

Figure 8.10: Form component interactions

In this section, we combine many of the concepts you've learned throughout the book. Utilize the preceding diagram to understand how the various form components interact.

In the preceding diagram, properties in bold indicate data binding. Underlined function elements indicate event registrations. Arrows show the points of connection between the components.

The workflow begins with the instantiation of `ProfileComponent`. The `OnInit` event of the component begins building the `formGroup` object, while asynchronously loading any potential `initialData` that may need to be patched into the forms. Refer to the preceding diagram for a visual representation of `initialData` coming in from a service or cache.

`NameInputComponent` is used in the `ProfileComponent` form as `<app-name-input>`. To synchronize `initialData` with the `NameInputComponent`, we bind a `nameInitialData$` subject using the `async` pipe, since `initialData` comes in asynchronously.

NameInputComponent implements the OnChanges lifecycle hook, so whenever nameInitialData$ updates, its value is patched into the NameInputComponent form.

Like ProfileComponent, NameInputComponent also implements the OnInit event to construct its formGroup object. Since this is an asynchronous event, NameInputComponent needs to expose a formReady event that ProfileComponent can subscribe to. Once the formGroup object is ready, we emit the event and the registerForm function on ProfileComponent triggers. registerForm adds the formGroup object of NameInputComponent as a child element to the parent formGroup on ProfileComponent.

ViewUserComponent is used in the ProfileComponent form as <app-view-user>. When the values in the parent form change, we need <app-view-user> to stay current. We bind to the user property on ViewUserComponent, which implements OnChanges to receive updates. Every time there is an update, the User object is hydrated from the IUser object, so calculated fields such as fullName can continue working. The updated User is then assigned to currentUser, bound to the template..

We will begin by building a BaseFormComponent, which NameInputComponent and ProfileComponent will then implement.

Abstract form component

We can share common functionality and standardize the implementation of all components that implement a form by implementing a base abstract class. An abstract class cannot be instantiated on its own because it wouldn't make sense to do so, since it will not have a template, making it useless on its own.

Note that BaseFormComponent is just a class and not an Angular component.

BaseFormComponent will standardize the following:

- @Input initialData and disable as binding targets
- The @Output formReady event
- formGroup, and the FormGroup to be used in the template's buildForm function to build the formGroup

With the preceding assumptions, the base class can provide some generic functionality:

- `patchUpdatedData` can update the data (partially or fully) in the `formGroup` without rebuilding it.
- `registerForm` and `deregisterForm` can register or deregister child forms.
- `deregisterAllForms` can automatically deregister any registered child form.
- `hasChanged` can determine whether `initialData` has changed, given a `SimpleChange` object provided by the `ngOnChange` event handler.
- `patchUpdatedDataIfChanged` leverages `hasChanged` and uses `patchUpdatedData` to update the data if, and only if, there has been an update to `initialData` and `formGroup` is already initialized.

Create a new class, `BaseFormComponent`, under `src/common` as follows:

src/app/common/base-form.class.ts

```
import { EventEmitter, Input, Output, SimpleChange, SimpleChanges }
  from '@angular/core'
import { AbstractControl, FormGroup } from '@angular/forms'
export abstract class BaseFormComponent<TFormData extends object> {
  @Input() initialData: TFormData
  @Input() disable: boolean
  @Output() formReady: EventEmitter<AbstractControl>
  formGroup: FormGroup
  private registeredForms: string[] = []
  constructor() {
    this.formReady = new EventEmitter<AbstractControl>(true)
  }
  abstract buildForm(initialData?: TFormData): FormGroup
  patchUpdatedData(data: object) {
    this.formGroup.patchValue(data, { onlySelf: false })
  }
  patchUpdatedDataIfChanged(changes: SimpleChanges) {
    if (this.formGroup && this.hasChanged(changes.initialData)) {
      this.patchUpdatedData(this.initialData)
    }
  }
  emitFormReady(control: AbstractControl | null = null) {
    this.formReady.emit(control || this.formGroup)
  }
```

```
  registerForm(name: string, control: AbstractControl) {
    this.formGroup.setControl(name, control)
    this.registeredForms.push(name)
  }
  deregisterForm(name: string) {
    if (this.formGroup.contains(name)) {
      this.formGroup.removeControl(name)
    }
  }
  protected deregisterAllForms() {
    this.registeredForms.forEach(() => this.deregisterForm(name))
  }
  protected hasChanged(change: SimpleChange): boolean {
    return change?.previousValue !== change?.currentValue
  }
}
```

Let's implement `NameInputComponent` using the `BaseFormComponent`.

Implementing a reusable form part

Start by identifying the name `FormGroup` in the `profile` component code and template files:

1. The following is the name `FormGroup` implementation:

   src/app/user/profile/profile.component.ts

   ```
   ...
   name: this.formBuilder.group({
     first: [user?.name?.first || '', RequiredTextValidation],
     middle: [user?.name?.middle || '', OneCharValidation],
     last: [user?.name?.last || '', RequiredTextValidation],
   }),
   ...
   ```

Note that when we move these validation rules to a new component, we still want them to be in effect when determining the overall validation status of the parent form. We achieve this using the `registerForm` function we implemented in the previous section. Once our new `FormGroup` is registered with the existing one, they work the same way as before our refactor.

1. Next is the name `FormGroup` template:

```
src/app/user/profile/profile.component.html
...
<div fxLayout="row" fxLayout.lt-sm="column"
  [formGroup]="formGroup.get('name')" fxLayoutGap="10px">
  <mat-form-field appearance="outline" fxFlex="40%">
    <mat-label>First Name</mat-label>
    <input matInput aria-label="First Name"
           formControlName="first" #name />
    ...
</div>
...
```

   You will be moving most of this code to the new component.

2. Create a new `NameInputComponent` under the `user` folder.
3. Extend the class from `BaseFormComponent`.
4. Inject `FormBuilder` into the `constructor`:

For components with small or limited pieces of functionality, I prefer creating them with an inline template and styling so that it is easier to change the code from one place.

```
src/app/user/name-input/name-input.component.ts
export class NameInputComponent extends BaseFormComponent<IName> {
  constructor(private formBuilder: FormBuilder) {
    super()
  }
  buildForm(initialData?: IName): FormGroup {
    throw new Error("Method not implemented.");
  }
  ...
}
```

Remember that the base class already implements the `formGroup`, `initialData`, `disable`, and `formReady` properties, so you don't need to redefine them.

Note that we must implement the `buildForm` function, since it was defined as abstract. This is a great way to enforce standards across developers. Also, note that the implementing class can override any base function provided by simply redefining the function with the `override` keyword. You'll see this in action when we refactor the `ProfileComponent`.

5. Implement the `buildForm` function.
6. Set the `name` property part of the `formGroup` in `ProfileComponent` to `null`:

```
src/app/user/name-input/name-input.component.ts
export class NameInputComponent implements OnInit {
  ...
  buildForm(initialData?: IName): FormGroup {
    const name = initialData
    return this.formBuilder.group({
      first: [name?.first : '', RequiredTextValidation],
      middle: [name?.middle : '', OneCharValidation],
      last: [name?.last : '', RequiredTextValidation],
    })
  }
```

7. Implement the template by bringing over the content from `ProfileComponent`:

```
src/app/user/name-input/name-input.component.ts
template: `
    <form [formGroup]="formGroup">
      <div fxLayout="row" fxLayout.lt-sm="column"
        fxLayoutGap="10px">
        ...
      </div>
    </form>
  `,
```

8. Implement the `ngOnInit` event handler:

```
src/app/user/name-input/name-input.component.ts
ngOnInit() {
  this.formGroup = this.buildForm(this.initialData)
  this.formReady.emit(this.formGroup)
}
```

Getting the `ngOnInit` event handler's implementation right in every `BaseFormComponent` implementation is critical. The preceding example is fairly standard behavior for any `child` component you may implement.

Note that the implementation in `ProfileComponent` will be a bit different.

9. Implement the `ngOnChanges` event handler, leveraging the base `patchUpdatedDataIfChanged` behavior:

src/app/user/name-input/name-input.component.ts

```
ngOnChanges(changes: SimpleChanges) {
  this.disable ?
    this.formGroup?.disable() : this.formGroup?.enable()
  this.patchUpdatedDataIfChanged(changes)
}
```

Note that in `patchUpdatedDataIfChanged`, setting `onlySelf` to `false` will cause the parent form also to update. You can override the function if you'd like to optimize this behavior.

Now, you have a fully implemented `NameInputComponent` that you can integrate into `ProfileComponent`.

To verify your `ProfileComponent` code going forward, refer to `projects/stage11/src/app/user/profile/profile.component.ts` and `projects/stage11/src/app/user/profile/profile.component.html`.

Before you begin using `NameInputComponent`, perform the following refactors.

10. Refactor `ProfileComponent` to extend `BaseFormComponent` and conform to its default values as needed.
11. Define a readonly `nameInitialData$` property with the `BehaviorSubject<IName>` type, and initialize it with empty strings.
12. Replace the content in `ProfileComponent` with the new `<app-name-input>` component:

src/app/user/profile/profile.component.html

```
<mat-horizontal-stepper #stepper="matHorizontalStepper">
```

```
  <mat-step [stepControl]="formGroup">
    <form [formGroup]="formGroup">
      <ng-template matStepLabel>Account Information</ng-template>
        <div class="stepContent">
          <app-name-input [initialData]="nameInitialData$ | async"
            (formReady)="registerForm('name', $event)">
          </app-name-input>
        </div>
        ...
      </ng-template>
    </form>
  </mat-step>
  ...
</mat-horizontal-stepper>
```

Note that the base form component function, `registerForm`, is leveraged here.

13. Ensure that your `ngOnInit` is implemented correctly:

Note that some additional refactors are present on the updated `ProfileComponent`, such as the `patchUser` function seen in the following snippet. Don't miss these updates when you update your component.

src/app/user/profile/profile.component.ts

```
ngOnInit() {
  this.formGroup = this.buildForm()
  this.authService.currentUser$
    .pipe(
      filter((user) => user != null),
      tap((user) => this.patchUser(user)),
      takeUntilDestroyed(this.destroyRef)
    )
    .subscribe()
}
```

It is important to update the current form's data with `pathUpdatedData`, as well as `nameInitialData$`, when there's an update to `initialData`.

14. Ensure that `ngOnDestroy` is implemented correctly:

```
src/app/user/profile/profile.component.ts
  ngOnDestroy() {
    this.deregisterAllForms()
  }
```

You can leverage the base class functionality to deregister from all child forms automatically.

Next, let's learn about masking user input to increase our data quality.

Input masking

Masking user input is an input UX tool and also a data quality one. I'm a fan of the `ngx-mask` library, which makes it easy to implement input masking in Angular. We will demonstrate input masking by updating the phone number input field, ensuring that users input a valid phone number, as shown in the following screenshot:

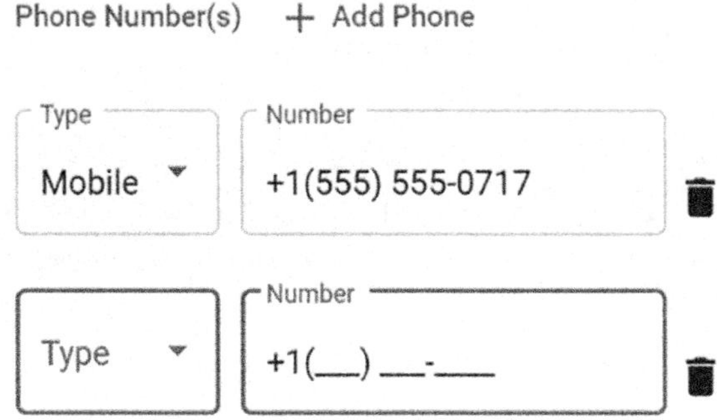

Figure 8.11: Phone number field with input masking

Set up your input masking as follows:

1. Install the library via npm with `npm i ngx-mask`.
2. Either use the environment provider, `provideEnvironmentNgxMask()`, in `app.config.ts` or `provideNgxMask()` in your feature module, `user.module.ts`.
3. Import the `NgxMaskDirective` in `profile.component.html`:
4. Update the `number` field in `ProfileComponent` as follows:

```
src/app/user/profile/profile.component.html
<mat-form-field appearance="outline" fxFlex fxFlexOffset="10px">
  <mat-label>Number</mat-label>
  <input matInput type="text" formControlName="number"
```

```
        prefix="+1" mask="(000) 000-0000" [showMaskTyped]="true" />
        @if (phonesArray.controls[i].invalid &&
             phonesArray.controls[i].touched) {
          <mat-error>A valid phone number is required</mat-error>
        }
    </mat-form-field>
```

And it's that simple. You can learn more about the module and its capabilities on GitHub at `https://github.com/JsDaddy/ngx-mask`.

Custom controls with ControlValueAccessor

So far, we've learned about forms using standard form controls and input controls provided by Angular Material. However, it is possible for you to create custom user controls. If you implement the `ControlValueAccessor` interface, then your custom controls will play nicely with forms and the `ControlValueAccessor` interface's validation engine.

We will be creating the custom rater control shown in the following screenshot and will place it as a control on the first step of `ProfileComponent`:

Figure 8.12: The lemon rater user control

User controls are inherently highly reusable, tightly coupled, and customized components to enable rich user interactions. Let's implement one.

Implementing a custom rating control

The Lemon Rater will dynamically highlight the number of lemons selected as the user interacts with the control in real time. As such, creating a high-quality custom control is an expensive endeavor. However, it is entirely worthwhile to spend the effort on elements of your application that define your brand and/or make up the core of the UX.

The Lemon Rater is a modified version of Jennifer Wadella's Galaxy Rating App sample found at `https://github.com/tehfedaykin/galaxy-rating-app`. I highly recommend watching Jennifer's Ng-Conf 2019 talk on `ControlValueAccessor`, linked in the *Further reading* section.

Set up your custom rating control as follows:

1. Generate a new component called `LemonRater` under the `user-controls` folder.
2. In `LemonRater`, implement the `ControlValueAccess` interface:

src/app/user-controls/lemon-rater/lemon-rater.component.ts

```
export class LemonRaterComponent implements ControlValueAccessor {
  disabled = false
  private internalValue: number
  get value() {
    return this.internalValue
  }
  onChanged: any = () => {}
  onTouched: any = () => {}
  writeValue(obj: any): void {
    this.internalValue = obj
  }
  registerOnChange(fn: any): void {
    this.onChanged = fn
  }
  registerOnTouched(fn: any): void {
    this.onTouched = fn
  }
  setDisabledState?(isDisabled: boolean): void {
    this.disabled = isDisabled
  }
}
```

3. Add the `NG_VALUE_ACCESSOR` provider with the `multi` property set to `true`. This will register our component with the form's change events, so form values can be updated when the user interacts with the rater:

src/app/user-controls/lemon-rater/lemon-rater.component.ts

```
@Component({
  selector: 'app-lemon-rater',
  templateUrl: 'lemon-rater.component.html',
  styleUrls: ['lemon-rater.component.css'],
  providers: [
    {
```

```
      provide: NG_VALUE_ACCESSOR,
      useExisting: forwardRef(() => LemonRaterComponent),
      multi: true,
    },
  ],
  standalone: true,
  imports: [NgClass],
```

`forwardRef` allows us to refer to components not yet defined. There's more at `https://angular.dev/api/core/forwardRef`.

4. Implement a custom rating scheme with a function, allowing us to set the selected rating based on user input:

src/app/user-controls/lemon-rater/lemon-rater.component.ts

```
export class LemonRaterComponent implements ControlValueAccessor {
  @ViewChild('displayText', { static: false }) displayTextRef!:
ElementRef
  disabled = false

  private internalValue!: number
  get value() {
    return this.internalValue
  }

  ratings = Object.freeze([
    {
      value: 1,
      text: 'no zest',
    },
    {
      value: 2,
      text: 'neither a lemon or a lime ',
    },
    {
      value: 3,
      text: 'a true lemon',
```

```
    },
  ])
  ...
  setRating(lemon: any) {
    if (!this.disabled) {
      this.internalValue = lemon.value
      this.ratingText = lemon.text
      this.onChanged(lemon.value)
      this.onTouched()
    }
  }
  setDisplayText() {
    this.setSelectedText(this.internalValue)
  }
  private setSelectedText(value: number) {
    this.displayTextRef.nativeElement.textContent =
      this.getSelectedText(value)
  }
  private getSelectedText(value: number) {
    let text = ''
    if (value) {
      text = this.ratings
        .find((i) => i.value === value)?.text || ''
    }
    return text
  }
}
```

Note that by using `@ViewChild`, we're getting the HTML element named `#displayText` (highlighted in the following template). Using `setSelectText`, we replace the `textContent` of the element.

5. Implement the template, referring to the sample code for the contents of the svg tag:

```
src/app/user-controls/lemon-rater/lemon-rater.component.html
<i #displayText></i>
<div class="lemons" [ngClass]="{'disabled': disabled}">
  @for (lemon of ratings; track lemon) {
```

```
    <svg width="24px" height="24px" viewBox="0 0 513 513"
         [attr.title]="lemon.text" class="lemon rating"
         [ngClass]="{'selected': lemon.value <= value}"
         (mouseover)=
           "displayText.textContent = !disabled ? lemon.text : ''"
         (mouseout)="setDisplayText()"
         (click)="setRating(lemon)"
    >
    ...
    </svg>
  }
</div>
```

The three most important attributes in the template are `mouseover`, `mouseout`, and `click`. The `mouseover` attribute displays the text for the rating the user is currently hovering over, `mouseout` resets the display text to the selected value, and `click` calls the `setRating` method we implemented to record the user's selection. However, the control can have even richer user interactivity by highlighting the number of lemons when the user hovers over a rating or selects it. We will accomplish this via some CSS magic.

6. Implement the CSS for the user control:

src/app/user-controls/lemon-rater/lemon-rater.component.css

```
.lemons {
  cursor: pointer;
}
.lemons:hover .lemon #fill-area {
  fill: #ffe200 !important;
}
.lemons.disabled:hover {
  cursor: not-allowed;
}
.lemons.disabled:hover .lemon #fill-area {
  fill: #d8d8d8 !important;
}
.lemons .lemon {
  float: left; margin: 0px 5px;
}
.lemons .lemon #fill-area {
```

```
  fill: #d8d8d8;
}
.lemons .lemon:hover~.lemon #fill-area {
  fill: #d8d8d8 !important;
}
.lemons .lemon.selected #fill-area {
  fill: #ffe200 !important;
}
.lemons .dad.heart #ada {
  fill: #6a0dad !important;
}
```

The most interesting bit is with `.lemons .lemon:hover~.lemon #fill-area`. Note that the operator ~ , or the general sibling combinator, selects a range of elements so that a dynamic number of lemons will be highlighted as the user hovers over them.

`#fill-area` refers to a `<path>` defined within the lemon `.svg`, allowing the lemon's color to be adjusted dynamically. I had to manually inject this ID field into the `.svg` file.

Now, let's see how you can use this new user control in a form.

Using custom controls in forms

We will use the lemon rater in the `profile` component to capture the Limoncu level of the employee.

Limoncu is a Turkish word for a person who grows or sells lemons, and it is also LemonMart's proprietary employee engagement and performance measurement system.

Let's integrate the lemon rater:

1. Start by importing the `LemonRaterComponent` in `profile.component.ts`.

2. Ensure that the level form control is initialized in `buildForm`:

src/app/user/profile/profile.component.ts
```
buildForm(initialData?: IUser): FormGroup {
  ...
  level: [user?.level || 0, Validators.required],
  ...
}
```

3. Insert the lemon rater as the last element of the first `mat-step`, inside the `form` element:

src/app/user/profile/profile.component.html
```
<div fxLayout="row" fxLayout.lt-sm="column" class="margin-top"
fxLayoutGap="10px">
  <mat-label class="mat-body-1">Select the Limoncu level:
    <app-lemon-rater formControlName="level">
    </app-lemon-rater>
  </mat-label>
</div>
```

We integrate with the custom control by implementing `formControlName` like any other control.

Congratulations! You should have a working custom control that is integrated with your form.

Layouts using a grid list

The Flex Layout library is great for laying out content using CSS Flexbox. Angular Material provides another mechanism to lay out content, using CSS Grid with its Grid List functionality. A good way to demonstrate this functionality is by implementing a helpful list of fake login information in the `LoginComponent`, demonstrated here:

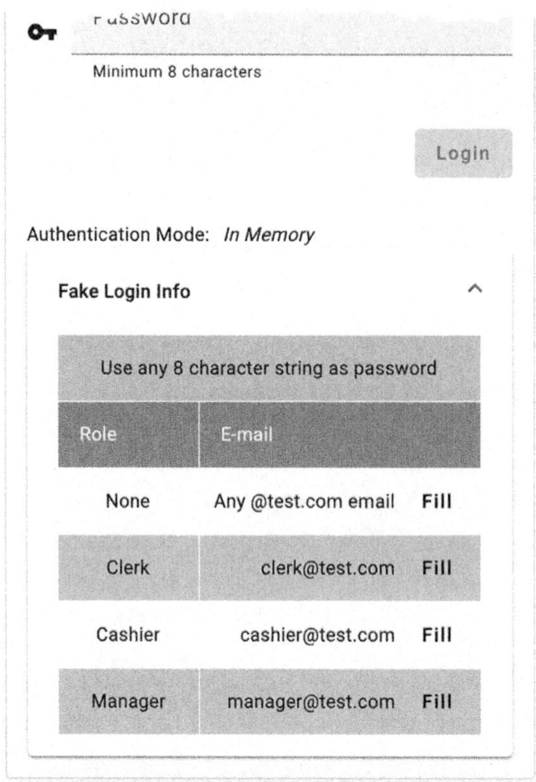

Figure 8.13: Login helper with the grid list

Implement your list as follows:

1. Start by defining a `roles` property that is an array of all the roles:

```
src/app/login/login.component.ts
roles = Object.keys(Role)
```

2. Import `MatExpansionModule` and `MatGridListModule` in **`login.component.ts`**.
3. Implement a new `mat-card-content` below the existing one:

```
src/app/login/login.component.html
<div fxLayout="row" fxLayoutAlign="center">
  <mat-card fxFlex="400px">
    <mat-card-header>
      <mat-card-title>
        <div class="mat-headline">Hello, Limoncu!</div>
```

```
        </mat-card-title>
      </mat-card-header>
      <mat-card-content>
        ...
      </mat-card-content>
      <mat-card-content>
      </mat-card-content>
    </mat-card>
  </div>
```

4. Inside the new `mat-card-content`, put in a label to display the authentication mode:

```
src/app/login/login.component.html
<div fxLayout="row" fxLayoutAlign="start center" fxLayoutGap="10px">
  <span>Authentication Mode: </span><i>{{ authMode }}</i>
</div>
```

5. Beneath the label, implement an expansion list:

```
src/app/login/login.component.html
<mat-accordion>
  <mat-expansion-panel>
    <mat-expansion-panel-header>
        <mat-panel-title>
          Fake Login Info
        </mat-panel-title>
    </mat-expansion-panel-header>
    ...
  </mat-expansion-panel>
</mat-accordion>
```

6. After `mat-expansion-panel-header`, in the area marked with ellipses in the preceding step, implement a table of roles and email addresses, along with some hint text regarding password length, using `mat-grid-list`, as shown in the following code block:

```
src/app/login/login.component.html
<mat-grid-list cols="3" rowHeight="48px" role="list">
  <mat-grid-tile [colspan]="3" role="listitem"
  style="background: pink">
    Use any 8 character string as password
```

```
    </mat-grid-tile>
    <mat-grid-tile>
      <mat-grid-tile-header>Role</mat-grid-tile-header>
    </mat-grid-tile>
    <mat-grid-tile [colspan]="2">
      <mat-grid-tile-header>E-mail</mat-grid-tile-header>
    </mat-grid-tile>
    @for (role of roles; track role; let oddRow = $odd) {
      <div>
        <mat-grid-tile
          role="listitem"
          [style.background]="oddRow ? 'lightGray' : 'white'">
          {{ role }}
        </mat-grid-tile>
        <mat-grid-tile
          [colspan]="2"
          role="listitem"
          [style.background]="oddRow ? 'lightGray' : 'white'">
          <div fxFlex fxLayoutAlign="end center">
            @if (role.toLowerCase() === 'none') {
              <div>Any &#64;test.com email</div>
            } @else {
              {{ role.toLowerCase() }}&#64;test.com
            }
            <button
              mat-button
              (click)="
                this.loginForm.patchValue({
                  email: role.toLowerCase() + '@test.com',
                  password: 'whatever'
                })
              ">
              Fill
            </button>
          </div>
        </mat-grid-tile>
      </div>
```

```
  }
</mat-grid-list>
```

We use `colspan` to control the width of each row and cell. We leverage `fxLayoutAlign` to right-align the contents of the **E-mail** column. We use `@if; @else` control flow operators to selectively display content. Finally, a **Fill** button helps us to populate the login form with fake login information.

In your application, you can use an expansion panel to communicate password complexity requirements to your users.

You can read more about expansion panels at `https://material.angular.io/components/expansion` and Grid List at `https://material.angular.io/components/grid-list/overview`.

Restoring cached data

At the beginning of the chapter, when implementing the `updateUser` method in `UserService`, we cached the `user` object in case of any errors that may wipe out user-provided data:

```
src/app/user/user/user.service.ts
updateUser(id: string, user: IUser): Observable<IUser> {
  ...
  This.cache.setItem('draft-user', user)
  ...
}
```

Consider a scenario where the user may be temporarily offline when they attempt to save their data. In this case, our `updateUser` function will save the data.

Let's see how we can restore this data in `ProfileComponent` when loading the user profile:

1. Start by adding functions named `loadFromCache` and `clearCache` to the `ProfileComponent` class:

   ```
   src/app/user/profile.component.ts
   private loadFromCache(): Observable<User | null> {
     let user = null
     try {
       const draftUser = this.cache.getItem('draft-user')
       if (draftUser != null) {
   ```

```
      user = User.Build(JSON.parse(draftUser))
    }
    if (user) {
      this.uiService.showToast('Loaded data from cache')
    }
  } catch (err) {
    this.clearCache()
  }
  return of(user)
}
clearCache() {
  this.cache.removeItem('draft-user')
}
```

After loading the data, we parse the data into a JSON object, using `JSON.parse`, and then hydrate the `User` object with `User.Build`.

2. Update the template to call the `clearCache` function so that when the user resets the form, we also clear the cache:

src/app/user/profile.component.html

```
<button mat-button color="warn"
    (click)="stepper.reset(); clearCache()">
  Reset
</button>
```

3. Update `ngOnInit` to conditionally load data from the cache or the latest `currentUser$` from `authService`:

src/app/user/profile.component.ts

```
ngOnInit() {
  this.formGroup = this.buildForm()
  combineLatest([
        this.loadFromCache(),
        this.authService.currentUser$,
      ])
        .pipe(
        takeUntilDestroyed(this.destroyRef),
```

```
          filter(
            ([cachedUser, me]) =>
              cachedUser != null || me != null
          ),
          tap(
            ([cachedUser, me]) =>
              this.patchUser(cachedUser || me)
          )
        )
        .subscribe()
}
```

We leverage the `combineLatest` operator to combine the outputs of `loadFromCache` and `currentUser$`. We check that one of the streams returns a non-null value. If a cached user exists, it precedes the value received from `currentUser$`.

You can test your cache by setting the network status of your browser to offline, as shown here:

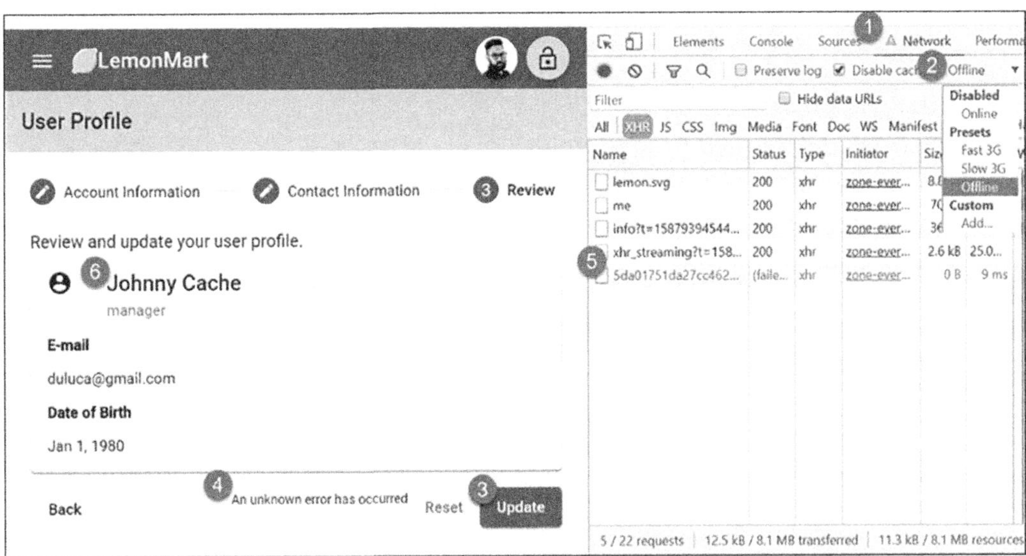

Figure 8.14: Offline network status

Set the network status of your browser to offline as follows:

1. In Chrome DevTools, navigate to the **Network** tab.
2. Select **Offline** in the dropdown marked as **2** in the preceding screenshot.
3. Update the form data, such as the name, and hit **Update**.

4. You'll see an error reading **An unknown error has occurred**, displayed at the bottom of the form.
5. You'll see that your PUT request has failed in the **Network** tab.
6. Now, refresh your browser window, and observe that the new name you entered is still present.

Refer to the following screenshot, which shows the toast notification you get after loading data from the cache:

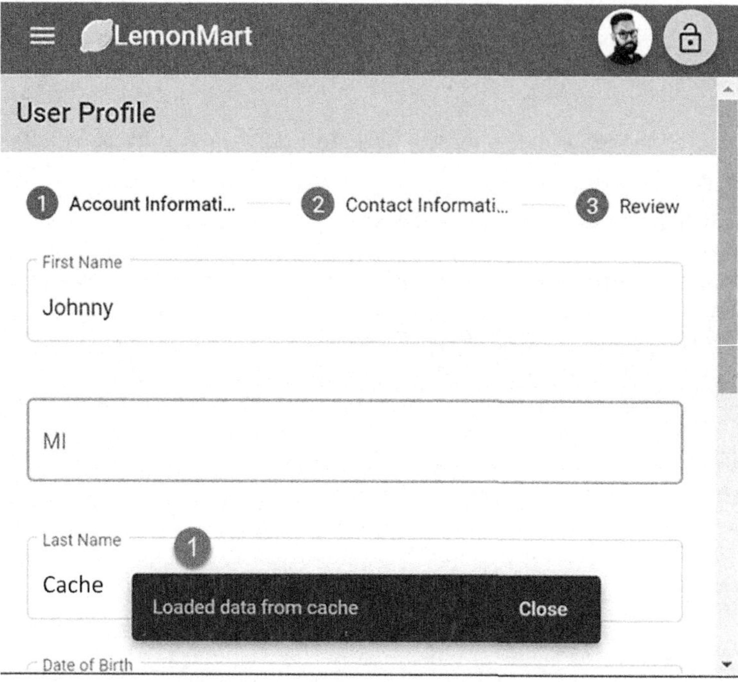

Figure 8.15: Data loaded from the cache

Implementing a great caching UX is incredibly challenging. I provided a rudimentary method to show what is possible. However, many edge cases can impact how caching in your application works.

In my case, the cache stubbornly sticks around until we successfully save the data to the server. This may be frustrating for some users.

Congratulations! You've successfully implemented a sophisticated form to capture data from your users!

Exercise

Practice new concepts like signals and `@defer` in Angular by updating `UserService` and the multi-step `ProfileComponent` form:

- Update `UserService` and its related components to use `signal` instead of `BehaviorSubject`.
- Use `@defer` to delay the rendering of conditional views.
- Implement an expansion panel in `LoginComponent` to communicate password complexity requirements to your users.

Summary

This chapter covered forms, directives, and user control-related functionality for LemonMart. Using data binding, we created reusable components that can be embedded within another component. We showed that you can use PUT to send data to a server and cache data input by a user. We also created a multi-step input form that is responsive to changing screen sizes. We removed the boilerplate code from our components by leveraging reusable form parts, a base form class to house common functionality, and an attribute directive to encapsulate field-level error behavior and messages.

We created dynamic form elements with a date picker, typeahead support, and form arrays. We implemented interactive controls with input masking and the lemon rater. Using the `ControlValueAccessor` interface, we integrated the lemon rater seamlessly with our form. We showed that we can scale the size and complexity of our forms linearly by extracting the name as its form section. Additionally, we covered building layouts using a grid list.

In the next chapter, we will further enhance our components to orchestrate them using the router. We will also implement a master/detail view and a data table and explore NgRx as an alternative to RxJS/BehaviorSubject.

Further reading

- *Reactive forms*, 2024: `https://angular.dev/guide/forms/reactive-forms`
- *Attribute directives*, 2024: `https://angular.dev/guide/directives/attribute-directives`
- *Meet Angular's New Control Flow*, 2023: `https://blog.angular.io/meet-angulars-new-control-flow-a02c6eee7843`
- *rxweb: Good way to show the error messages in Angular Reactive Forms*, Ajay Ojha, 2019: `https://medium.com/@oojhaajay/rxweb-good-way-to-show-the-error-messages-in-angular-reactive-forms-c27429f51278`

- *The Control Value Accessor*, Jennifer Wadella, 2019: `https://www.youtube.com/watch?v=kVbLSN0AW-Y`
- *CSS Combinators*, 2020: `https://developer.mozilla.org/en-US/docs/Web/CSS/CSS_Selectors#Combinators`
- *Memoization in JavaScript*, Sumit Kumar Singh, 2023: `https://designtechworld.medium.com/memoization-in-javascript-282d5fad29c8`
- *Why you should never use function calls in Angular template expressions,* Jurgen Van de Moere, 2019: `https://medium.com/showpad-engineering/why-you-should-never-use-function-calls-in-angular-template-expressions-e1a50f9c0496`

Questions

Answer the following questions as best as possible to ensure you've understood the key concepts from this chapter without googling anything. Do you know if you got all the answers right? Visit `https://angularforenterprise.com/self-assessment` for more:

1. What is the difference between a component and a user control?
2. What is an attribute directive?
3. What is the `@`-syntax?
4. What is the purpose of the `ControlValueAccessor` interface?
5. What is serialization, deserialization, and hydration?
6. What does it mean to patch values on a form?
7. How do you associate two independent `FormGroup` objects with each other?

9

Recipes – Master/Detail, Data Tables, and NgRx

In this chapter, we complete the router-first architecture implementation on LemonMart by implementing the top three most used features in business applications: master/detail views, data tables, and state management. I will demonstrate data tables with server-side pagination, highlighting the integration between the frontend and backend using LemonMart and LemonMart Server.

We will leverage the router orchestration concept to orchestrate how our components load data or render. We will then use resolve guards to reduce boilerplate code when loading data before navigating to a component. We will use auxiliary routes to lay out components through the router configuration and reuse the same component in multiple contexts.

We will then dive into NgRx using the LocalCast Weather app and explore NgRx Signal Store with LemonMart, so you can become familiar with more advanced application architecture concepts in Angular. By the end of this chapter, we will have touched upon the major functionality that Angular and Angular Material offer – only the good parts, if you will.

This chapter covers a lot of ground. It is organized in a recipe format, so you can quickly refer to a particular implementation when working on your projects. I cover the architecture, design, and major components of the implementation and highlight important pieces of code to explain how the solution comes together. Leveraging what you've learned, I expect the reader to fill in routine implementation and configuration details. However, you can always refer to the GitHub repo if you get stuck.

In this chapter, you will learn about the following topics:

- Loading data with resolve guard
- Reusing components with binding and route data
- Master/detail view using auxiliary routes
- Data tables with pagination
- NgRx store and effects
- NgRx ecosystem
- Implementing a global spinner
- Configuring server proxies with the Angular CLI

Technical requirements

The most up-to-date versions of the sample code for the book are on GitHub at the repository linked in the following list. The repository contains the final and completed state of the code. You can verify your progress at the end of this chapter by looking for the end-of-chapter snapshot of code under the `projects` folder.

For *Chapter 9*:

Be sure that **lemon-mart-server** is up and running. Refer to *Chapter 7, Working with REST and GraphQL APIs*.

1. Clone the repositories at `https://github.com/duluca/local-weather-app` and `https://github.com/duluca/lemon-mart`.
2. Execute `npm install` on the root folder to install dependencies.
3. The beginning state of the project is reflected at:

```
projects/stage11
```

4. The end state of the project is reflected at:

```
projects/stage12
```

5. Add the stage name to any `ng` command to act only on that stage:

```
npx ng build stage12
```

Note that the `dist/stage12` folder at the root of the repository will contain the compiled result.

In *Chapter 8, Recipes – Reusability, Forms, and Caching*, we created a `ViewUserComponent` with an `editUser` function. We need this functionality later in the chapter when implementing a master/detail view in the system, where a manager can see all users in the system and edit them. Before enabling the `editUser` functionality, we need to ensure that the `ViewUserComponent` component alongside the `ProfileComponent` can load any user given their ID.

In the next couple of sections, we will learn about resolve guards to simplify our code and reduce the amount of boilerplate. Let's start by implementing a resolve guard we can use for both components.

Loading data with resolve guard

A resolve guard is a different kind of router guard, as mentioned in *Chapter 6, Implementing Role-Based Navigation*. A resolve guard can load necessary data for a component by reading record IDs from `route` parameters, asynchronously loading the data, and having it ready when the component activates and initializes.

The major advantages of a resolve guard include reusability of the loading logic, a reduction of boilerplate code, and the shedding of dependencies because the component can receive the data it needs without having to import any service:

1. Create a new `user.resolve.ts` class under `user/user`:

```
src/app/user/user/user.resolve.ts
import { inject } from '@angular/core'
import { ActivatedRouteSnapshot, ResolveFn } from '@angular/router'
import { catchError, map } from 'rxjs/operators'

import { transformError } from '../../common/common'
import { User } from './user'
import { UserService } from './user.service'

export const userResolver: ResolveFn<User> = (route:
ActivatedRouteSnapshot) => {
  return inject(UserService)
```

```
      .getUser(route.paramMap.get('userId'))
      .pipe(map(User.Build), catchError(transformError))
  }
```

Similar to the `updateUser` method in `UserService`, we use `map(User.Build)` to hydrate the `user` object, so it is ready to be used when a component loads data from the `route` snapshot, as we'll see next.

2. Modify `user-routing.module.ts` to add a new path, `profile/:userId`, with a route resolver and the `canActivate authGuard`:

src/app/user/user-routing.module.ts

```
...
{
    path: 'profile/:userId',
    component: ProfileComponent,
    resolve: {
      user: userResolver,
    },
    canActivate: [authGuard],
  },
  ...
```

When combined with an auth guard, the `resolve` function won't be executed until the guard succeeds.

3. Update the `profile` component to load the data from the `route` if it exists:

src/app/user/profile/profile.component.ts

```
...
  constructor(
    ...
    private route: ActivatedRoute
  ) {
    super()
  }
```

```
  private readonly destroyRef = inject(DestroyRef)

  ngOnInit() {
    this.formGroup = this.buildForm()
    if (this.route.snapshot.data['user']) {
      this.patchUser(this.route.snapshot.data['user'])
    } else {
       combineLatest(
        [this.loadFromCache(),
         this.authService.currentUser$]
       )
      .pipe(
        takeUntilDestroyed(this.destroyRef),
        filter(
          ([cachedUser, me]) =>
            cachedUser != null || me != null
        ),
        tap(
          ([cachedUser, me]) =>
           this.patchUser(cachedUser || me)
        )
      )
      .subscribe()
    }
  }
```

We first check whether a user is present in the `route` snapshot. If so, we call `patchUser` to load this user. Otherwise, we fall back to our conditional cache-loading logic.

Note that the `patchUser` method also sets the `currentUserId` and `nameInitialDate$` Observables and calls the `patchUpdateData` base to update the form data.

You can verify that the resolver is working by navigating to the profile with your user ID. Using the out-of-the-box settings, this URL will look something like `http://localhost:4200/user/profile/5da01751da27cc462d265913`.

Reusing components with binding and route data

Now, let's refactor the `viewUser` component so that we can reuse it in multiple contexts. User information is displayed in two places in the app per the mock-ups created.

The first place is the **Review** step of the user profile that we implemented in the previous chapter. The second place is on the user management screen on the `/manager/users` route, as follows:

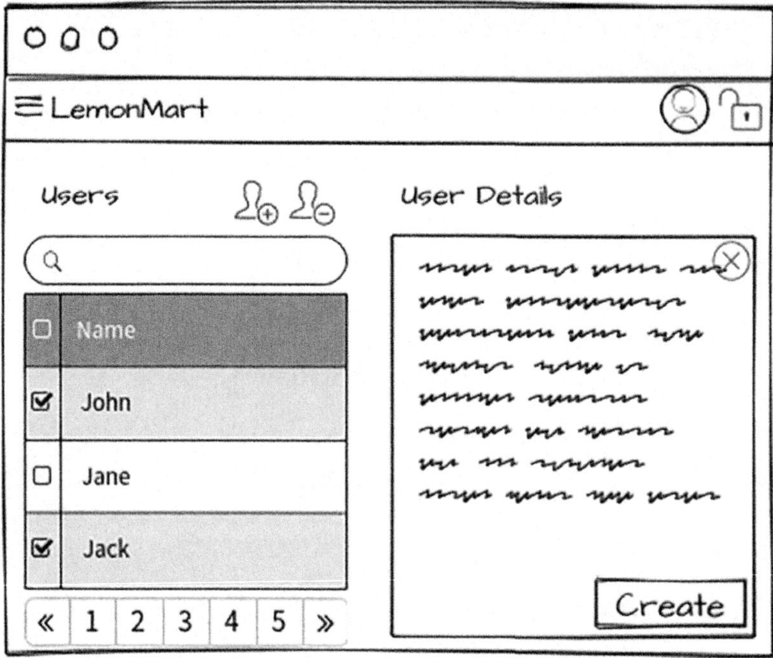

Figure 9.1: Manager user management mock-up

To maximize code reuse, we must ensure that our shared `ViewUser` component can be used in both contexts.

In the first use case, we bind the current user to the **Review** step of the multi-step input form. In the second use case, the component will need to load its data using a resolve guard, so we don't need to implement additional logic to achieve our goal:

1. Update the `viewUser` component to inject the `Router` and `ActivatedRoute`. In `ngOnInit` we need to set `currentUser` from the route in and subscribe to future route change events to apply updates to the user using a helper function `assignUserFromRoute` and unsubscribe from the event in `ngOnDestroy`:

   src/app/user/view-user/view-user.component.ts

   ```
   ...
   export class ViewUserComponent
     implements OnInit, OnChanges, OnDestroy {
   ```

```
  private readonly route = inject(ActivatedRoute)
  private readonly router = inject(Router)
  private routerEventsSubscription?: Subscription
  ...

  ngOnInit() {
    // assignment on initial render
    this.assignUserFromRoute()

    this.routerEventsSubscription =
      this.router.events.subscribe((event) => {
      // assignment on subsequent renders
      if (event instanceof NavigationEnd) {
        this.assignUserFromRoute()
      }
    })
  }

  private assignUserFromRoute() {
    if (this.route.snapshot.data['user']) {
      this.currentUser = this.route.snapshot.data['user']
    }
  }

  ngOnDestroy(): void {
    this.routerEventsSubscription?.unsubscribe()
  }

  ...
}}
```

`ngOnInit` will only fire once when the component is initialized within another component or loaded within the router context. If any data for the route has been resolved, we update `currentUser`. When the user wants to view another user, a new navigation event will occur with a different user ID. Since Angular will reuse the component, we must subscribe to router events to react to subsequent user changes. In this case, in case of a `NavigationEnd` event, if the route has resolved user data, we again update `currentUser`.

We now have three independent events to update and handle data. Within the parent component context, `ngOnChanges` handles updates to the `@Input` value and updates `currentUser` if `this.user` has been bound to. The code we added above handles the remaining two cases with router context on the first navigation and subsequent navigation events.

Since LemonMart is bootstrapped as a standalone application and `viewUser` is a standalone component, we can use this component across multiple lazy-loaded modules without additional orchestration.

If you're not using standalone components, you must wrap this component inside a `SharedComponentsModule` and import that module in your lazy-loaded modules. You can find an example implementation in the GitHub history of the project.

With the key pieces in place, let's begin implementing the master/detail view.

Master/detail view using auxiliary routes

The true power of router-first architecture comes to fruition with auxiliary routes, where we can influence the layout of components solely through router configuration, allowing for rich scenarios where we can remix the existing components into different layouts. Auxiliary routes are routes that are independent of each other where they can render content in named outlets that have been defined in the markup, such as `<router-outlet name="master">` or `<router-outlet name="detail">`. Furthermore, auxiliary routes can have their parameters, browser history, children, and nested auxiliaries.

In the following example, we will implement a basic master/detail view using auxiliary routes:

1. Implement a simple component with two named outlets defined:

src/app/manager/user-management/user-management.component.ts

```
template: `
  <div class="h-pad">
    <router-outlet name="master"></router-outlet>
    <div style="min-height: 10px"></div>
    <router-outlet name="detail"></router-outlet>
  </div>
`
```

2. Add a new `userTable` component under `manager`.
3. Update `manager-routing.module.ts` to define the auxiliary routes:

   src/app/manager/manager-routing.module.ts

   ```
     ...
       {
         path: 'users',
         component: UserManagementComponent,
         children: [
           {
             path: '', component: UserTableComponent,
              outlet: 'master'
           },
           {
             path: 'user',
             component: ViewUserComponent,
             outlet: 'detail',
             resolve: {
               user: userResolver,
             },
           },
         ],
         canActivate: [authGuard],
         canActivateChild: [authGuard],
         data: {
           expectedRole: Role.Manager,
         },
       },
   ...
   ```

   This means that when a user navigates to `/manager/users`, they'll see the `UserTableComponent`, because it is implemented with the default path.

4. Provide `UserResolve` in `manager.module.ts` since `viewUser` depends on it.

5. Implement a temporary button in `userTable`:

```
src/app/manager/user-table/user-table.component.html
<button
  mat-icon-button
  [routerLink]="[
    '../users',
    { outlets: { detail: ['user', { userId: row._id }] } }
  ]"
  [skipLocationChange]="true">
  <mat-icon>visibility</mat-icon>
</button>
```

The `skipLocationChange` directive navigates without pushing a new record into history. So, if the user views multiple records and hits the **Back** button, they will be taken back to the previous screen instead of having to scroll through the records they viewed first.

Imagine that a user clicks on a **View detail** button like the one defined previously – then, `ViewUserComponent` will be rendered for the user with the given `userId`. In the next screenshot, you can see what the **View Details** button will look like after we implement the data table in the next section:

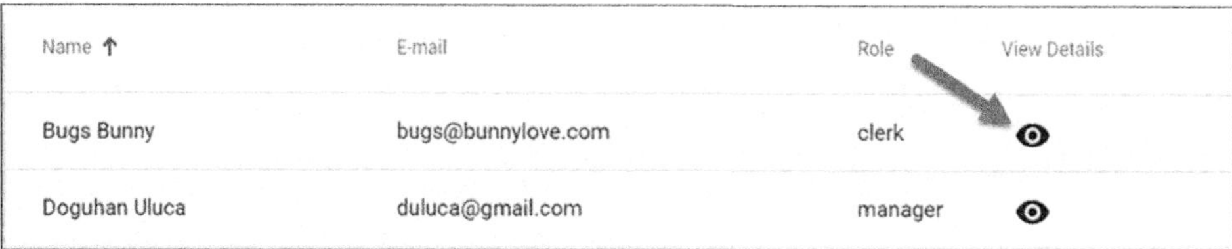

Figure 9.2: View Details button

You can have as many combinations as possible and alternative components defined for the master and detail, allowing for the infinite possibilities of dynamic layouts. However, setting up the `routerLink` can be a frustrating experience. Depending on the exact condition, you must either supply or not supply all or some outlets in the link.

For example, in the preceding scenario, consider this alternative implementation, where the master outlet is explicitly defined:

```
['../users', {
  outlets: {
    master: [''], detail: ['user', {userId: row.id}]
  }
}],
```

The router will not correctly parse this route and silently fail to load. If it is `master: []` it will work. This comes down to how pattern matching happens on empty routes; while this makes logical sense in the framework code, it doesn't make intuitive sense for developers using the APIs.

Now that we've completed the implementation of the resolve guard for `ViewUserComponent`, you can use Chrome DevTools to see the data being loaded correctly.

Before debugging, ensure that the **lemon-mart-server** we created in *Chapter 7, Working with REST and GraphQL APIs*, is running.

6. In **Chrome DevTools**, set a breakpoint right after `this.currentUser` is assigned, as shown:

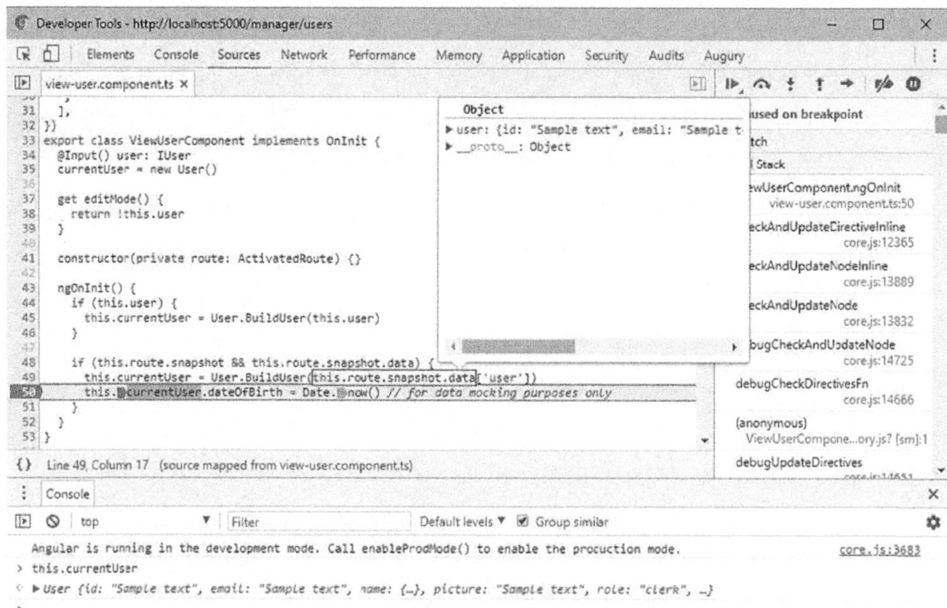

Figure 9.3: Dev Tools debugging ViewUserComponent

You will observe that `this.currentUser` is correctly set without any boilerplate code for loading data inside the `ngOnInit` function, showing the true benefit of a resolve guard. `ViewUserComponent` is the detail view; now, let's implement the master view as a data table with pagination.

Data tables with pagination

We have created the scaffolding to lay out our master/detail view. In the master outlet, we will have a paginated data table of users, so let's implement `UserTableComponent`, which will contain a `MatTableDataSource` property named `dataSource`. We will need to be able to fetch user data in bulk using standard pagination controls such as `pageSize` and `pagesToSkip` and narrow down the selection further with user-provided search text.

Let's start by adding the necessary functionality to `UserService`:

1. Implement a new `IUsers` interface to describe the data structure of the paginated data:

```
src/app/user/user/user.service.ts
...
export interface IUsers {
```

```
  data: IUser[]
  total: number
}
```

2. Update the interface for UserService with a getUsers function:

src/app/user/user/user.service.ts

```
...
export interface IUserService {
  getUser(id: string): Observable<IUser>
  updateUser(id: string, user: IUser): Observable<IUser>
  getUsers(pageSize: number, searchText: string,
    pagesToSkip: number): Observable<IUsers>
}
export class UserService implements IUserService {
...
```

3. Add getUsers to UserService:

src/app/user/user/user.service.ts

```
...
getUsers(
    pageSize: number,
    searchText = '',
    pagesToSkip = 0,
    sortColumn = '',
    sortDirection: '' | 'asc' | 'desc' = 'asc'
  ): Observable<IUsers> {
    const recordsToSkip = pageSize * pagesToSkip
    if (sortColumn) {
      sortColumn =
        sortDirection === 'desc' ? `-${sortColumn}` : sortColumn
    }
    return this.httpClient.get<IUsers>(
      `${environment.baseUrl}/v2/users`, {
        params: {
          filter: searchText,
          skip: recordsToSkip.toString(),
          limit: pageSize.toString(),
```

```
          sortKey: sortColumn,
        },
      })
    }
...
```

Note that the `sort` direction is indicated by the keywords `asc` for ascending and `desc` for descending. When sorting a column in ascending order, we pass the column name as a parameter to the server. We prepend the column name with a minus sign to sort a column in descending order.

4. Set up `UserTable` with pagination, sorting, and filtering:

src/app/manager/user-table/user-table.component.ts

```
...
@Component({
  selector: 'app-user-table',
  templateUrl: './user-table.component.html',
  styleUrls: ['./user-table.component.css'],
})
export class UserTableComponent implements AfterViewInit {
  @ViewChild(MatPaginator) paginator!: MatPaginator
  @ViewChild(MatSort) sort!: MatSort

  private skipLoading = false
  private readonly userService = inject(UserService)
  private readonly router = inject(Router)
  private readonly activatedRoute = inject(ActivatedRoute)
  private readonly destroyRef = inject(DestroyRef)

  readonly refresh$ = new Subject<void>()

  readonly demoViewDetailsColumn = signal(false)

  items$!: Observable<Iuser[]>
  displayedColumns = computed(() => [
    'name',
    'email',
```

```
    'role',
    ...(this.demoViewDetailsColumn() ? ['_id'] : []),
  ])

  isLoading = true
  resultsLength = 0
  hasError = false
  errorText = ''
  selectedRow?: Iuser

  search = new FormControl<string>('', OptionalTextValidation)

  resetPage(stayOnPage = false) {
    if (!stayOnPage) {
      this.paginator.firstPage()
    }
    // this.outletCloser.closeOutlet('detail')
    this.router.navigate([
      '../users',
      { outlets: { detail: null } }
    ], {
      skipLocationChange: true,
      relativeTo: this.activatedRoute,
    })
    this.selectedRow = undefined
  }

  showDetail(userId: string) {
    this.router.navigate([
      '../users',
      { outlets: { detail: ['user', { userId: userId }] } }
    }],
      {
        skipLocationChange: true,
        relativeTo: this.activatedRoute,
      }
    )
```

```
}

ngAfterViewInit() {
  this.sort.sortChange
    .pipe(
      tap(() => this.resetPage()),
      takeUntilDestroyed(this.destroyRef)
    )
    .subscribe()

  this.paginator.page
    .pipe(
      tap(() => this.resetPage(true)),
      takeUntilDestroyed(this.destroyRef)
    )
    .subscribe()

  if (this.skipLoading) {
    return
  }

  setTimeout(() => {
    this.items$ = merge(
      this.refresh$,
      this.sort.sortChange,
      this.paginator.page,
      this.search.valueChanges.pipe(
        debounceTime(1000),
        tap(() => this.resetPage())
      )
    ).pipe(
      startWith({}),
      switchMap(() => {
        this.isLoading = true
        return this.userService.getUsers(
          this.paginator.pageSize,
          this.search.value as string,
```

```
            this.paginator.pageIndex,
            this.sort.active,
            this.sort.direction
          )
        }),
        map((results: { total: number; data: IUser[] }) => {
          this.isLoading = false
          this.hasError = false
          this.resultsLength = results.total
          return results.data
        }),
        catchError((err) => {
          this.isLoading = false
          this.hasError = true
          this.errorText = err
          return of([])
        }),
        takeUntilDestroyed(this.destroyRef),

      )
    })
  }
}
```

We define and initialize various properties to support loading paginated data. `items$` stores the observable stream that defines what data is displayed on the data table. `displayedColumns`, a computed signal, defines the columns for the table. To dynamically show or hide columns we can defined a toggle using a signal, such as `demoViewDetailsColumn`. Since this signal is referenced within the computed signal, when it updates the computed signal will also be updated., which will then be reflected on the table. `paginator` and `sort` provide pagination and sorting preferences . `search` provides the text we need to filter our results by.

`resetPage` helps rewind the pagination to the first page and hide the detail view. This is useful after a search, pagination, or sort event, otherwise the detail view of a random record will be displayed.

`showDetail` uses the router to display the detail view of a selected record in the named outlet `detail`. Later in this section, we will go over a version of the same link implemented in the template. I purposefully included both options, so you can see how both are implemented.

I purposefully left the following code commented out in the code base:

```
// this.outletCloser.closeOutlet('detail')
```

I found in certain instances the router may not be able to gracefully close an outlet. `OutletCloserService`, found in the `common` folder, can close any outlet from any context without fuss.

The reference to the original version by Andrew Scott is at `https://stackblitz.com/edit/close-outlet-from-anywhere`.

The magic happens in `ngAfterViewInit`. We first subscribe to `sort` and `paginator` change events, so we can properly reset the table. Next, we use the `merge` method within a `setTimeout` call, as highlighted in the preceding snippet, to listen for changes in pagination, sorting, and filter properties that impact what data needs to be displayed. If one property changes, the whole pipeline is triggered.

Why is the `setTimeout` necessary? Since we use references to paginator and sort extracted from the template, we must use the `ngAfterViewInit` lifecycle hook. However, at this point, Angular has already set the `dataSource` property for the Material data table component. If we re-assign it with the `merge` operator, we'll get NG0100 `ExpressionChangedAfterItHasBeenCheckedError`. Using `setTimeout` pushes the reassignment into the next change detection cycle, avoiding the error.

This is similar to how we implemented the login routine in `AuthService`. The pipeline contains a call to `this.userService.getUsers`, which will retrieve users based on the pagination, sorting, and filter preferences passed in. Results are then piped into the `this.items$` Observable, which the data table subscribes to with an `async` pipe to display the data.

There's no need to subscribe to `this.items$`, because the Material data table already subscribes to it internally. If you subscribe, every call to the server will be made twice.

However, you must take care to place the `takeUntilDestroyed` call as the last element in the pipe. Otherwise, you could leak subscriptions merged after the call.

Read more about it at `https://cartant.medium.com/rxjs-avoiding-takeuntil-leaks-fb5182d047ef`.

5. Import the following modules:

src/app/manager/user-table/user-table.component.ts

```
imports: [
  AsyncPipe,
  FlexModule,
  FormsModule,
  MatButtonModule,
  MatFormFieldModule,
  MatIconModule,
  MatInputModule,
  MatPaginatorModule,
  MatProgressSpinnerModule,
  MatSlideToggleModule,
  MatSortModule,
  MatTableModule,
  MatToolbarModule,
  ReactiveFormsModule,
  RouterLink,
],
```

6. Implement the CSS for `userTable`:

src/app/manager/user-table/user-table.component.scss

```
.loading-shade {
  position: absolute;
```

```
  top: 0;
  left: 0;
  bottom: 56px;
  right: 0;
  background: rgba(0, 0, 0, 0.15);
  z-index: 1;
  display: flex;
  align-items: center;
  justify-content: center;
}

.filter-row {
  min-height: 64px;
  padding: 8px 24px 0;
}

.full-width {
  width: 100%;
}

.mat-mdc-paginator {
  background: transparent;
}

/* row selection styles */
.mat-mdc-row .mat-mdc-cell {
  border-bottom: 1px solid transparent;
  border-top: 1px solid transparent;
  cursor: pointer;
}

.mat-mdc-row:hover .mat-mdc-cell {
  border-color: currentColor;
  background-color: #efefef;
}

.selected {
```

```
  font-weight: 500;
  background-color: #efefef;
}
```

The styles below the comment `/* row selection styles */` assist in the material ripple effect when individual rows are clicked.

7. Finally, implement the `userTable` template:

src/app/manager/user-table/user-table.component.html

```
<div fxLayout="row" fxLayoutAlign="end">
  <mat-slide-toggle
    [checked]="demoViewDetailsColumn()"
    (change)="demoViewDetailsColumn.set($event.checked)">
    Demo 'View Details' Column
  </mat-slide-toggle>
</div>
<div class="filter-row">
  <form style="margin-bottom: 32px">
    <div fxLayout="row">
      <mat-form-field class="full-width">
        <mat-icon matPrefix>search</mat-icon>
        <input matInput placeholder="Search"
               aria-label="Search" [formControl]="search" />
        <mat-hint>Search by e-mail or name</mat-hint>
        @if (search.invalid) {
          <mat-error>
            Type more than one character to search
          </mat-error>
        }
      </mat-form-field>
    </div>
  </form>
</div>
<div class="mat-elevation-z8">
  @if (isLoading) {
    <div class="loading-shade">
```

```
    <mat-spinner></mat-spinner>
  </div>
}
@if (hasError) {
  <div class="error">
    {{ errorText }}
  </div>
}
<mat-table
  class="full-width"
  [dataSource]="items$"
  matSort
  matSortActive="name"
  matSortDirection="asc"
  matSortDisableClear>
  <ng-container matColumnDef="name">
    <mat-header-cell *matHeaderCellDef mat-sort-header>
      Name
    </mat-header-cell>
    <mat-cell *matCellDef="let row">
      {{ row.fullName }}
    </mat-cell>
  </ng-container>
  <ng-container matColumnDef="email">
    <mat-header-cell *matHeaderCellDef mat-sort-header>
      E-mail
    </mat-header-cell>
    <mat-cell *matCellDef="let row">
      {{ row.email }}
    </mat-cell>
  </ng-container>
  <ng-container matColumnDef="role">
    <mat-header-cell *matHeaderCellDef mat-sort-header>
      Role
    </mat-header-cell>
    <mat-cell *matCellDef="let row">
      {{ row.role }}
```

```
      </mat-cell>
    </ng-container>
    <ng-container matColumnDef="_id">
      <mat-header-cell *matHeaderCellDef>
        View Details
      </mat-header-cell>
      <mat-cell *matCellDef="let row"
                style="margin-right: 8px">
        <button
          mat-icon-button
          [routerLink]="[
            '../users',
            {
              outlets: { detail: ['user', { userId: row._id }]
            }
          }]"
          [skipLocationChange]="true">
          <mat-icon>visibility</mat-icon>
        </button>
      </mat-cell>
    </ng-container>
    <mat-header-row *matHeaderRowDef="displayedColumns()">
    </mat-header-row>
    <mat-row
      matRipple
      (click)="selectedRow = row;
        demoViewDetailsColumn() ? 'noop' : showDetail(row._id)"
      [class.selected]="selectedRow === row"
      *matRowDef="let row; columns: displayedColumns()">
    </mat-row>
  </mat-table>
  <mat-toolbar>
    <mat-toolbar-row>
      <button mat-icon-button (click)="refresh$.next()">
        <mat-icon title="Refresh">refresh</mat-icon>
      </button>
      <span class="flex-spacer"></span>
```

```
      <mat-paginator [pageSizeOptions]="[5, 10, 25, 100]"
                     [length]="resultsLength">
      </mat-paginator>
    </mat-toolbar-row>
  </mat-toolbar>
</div>
```

Note the implementation of the `loading-shade` style, which places a spinner over the table while loading data. This is an example of a localized spinner. Later in the *Implementing a global spinner with NgRx/SignalState section,* I cover how we can implement a global version. Most very large applications will require a localized spinner to avoid excessive full-screen interruptions caused by a global spinner.

We bind `items$` to `dataSource` to activate the Observable. Below, the `mat-icon-button` with `[routerLink]="['../users', { outlets: { detail: ['user', { userId: row._id }] } }]"` uses the context row variable to assign a URL that will display `ViewUserComponent` in the `detail` outlet. `skipLocationChange` ensures that the URL in the browser won't be updated with the outlet information.

Note that using the relative URL `'../users'` in the `routerLink`, as shown above, allows the `UserTableComponent` to be decoupled from the context of the manager feature module. This way, the component could be reused under other contexts like `/owner/users` or `/ceo/users` instead of being hard coded to `/manager/users`.

Setting up the router within lazy-loaded modules and named outlets could be error-prone.

You can enable the router's debug mode by modifying the root provider in `app.config.ts` by adding the `withDebugTracing` function as shown:

```
provideRouter(routes, withDebugTracing()),
```

Further on, the `matRipple` directive enables a Material Design ripple when a row is clicked. Right after this, we implement the click handlers. By default, clicking on a row will display the detail view using the `showDetail` function; otherwise, users will click on a view button on the rightmost column.

Finally, observe the click on the refresh button, which causes an update in the `refresh$` Observable. This will be picked up by the merge pipeline we implemented in the component.

With just the master view in place, the table is as shown in the following screenshot (make sure you've updated to the latest version of Angular):

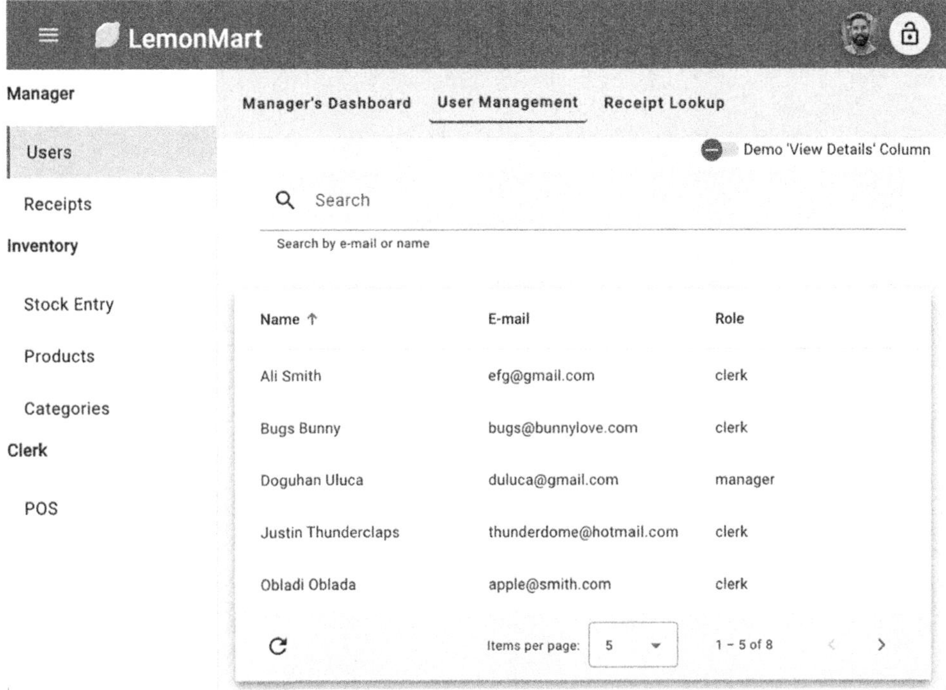

Figure 9.4: User table

If you click on a row, `ViewUserComponent` will get rendered in the detail outlet using the `showDetails` function, as shown:

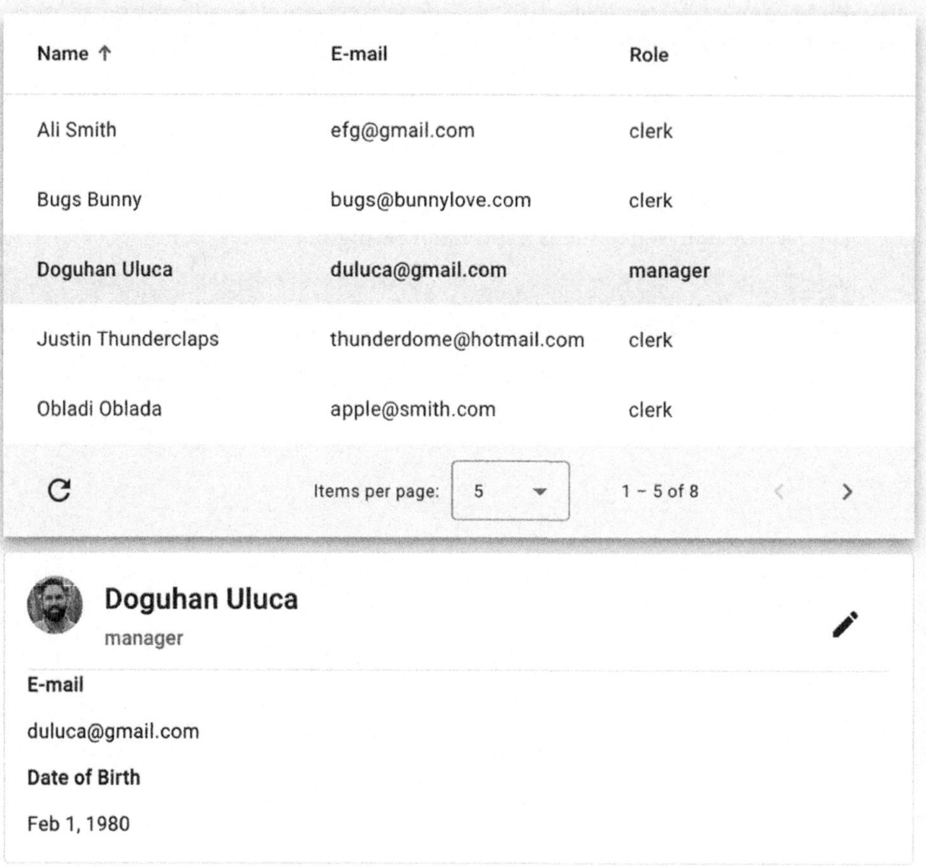

Figure 9.5: Master/detail view with row click

Note how the row is highlighted to indicate selection. If you flip the **Demo 'View Details' Column** option on the top right, you will unhide the **View Details** column.

If you click on the **View** icon, `ViewUserComponent` will get rendered in the detail outlet using `routerLink` in the template, as shown:

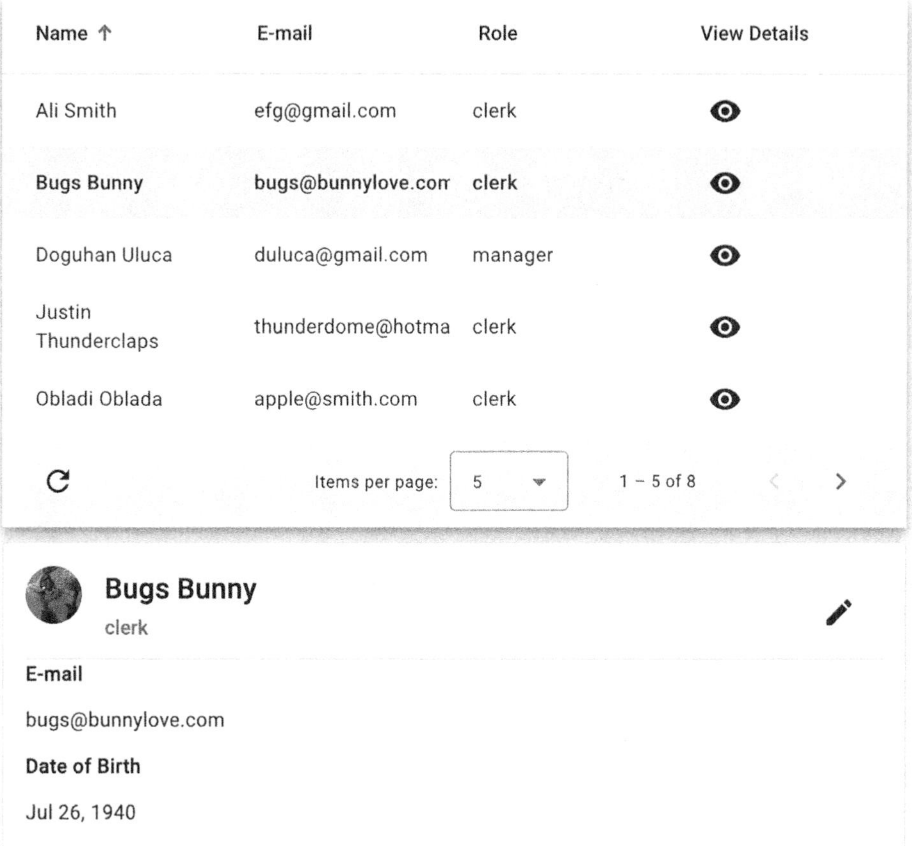

Figure 9.6: Master/detail view icon click

In the previous chapter, we implemented the **Edit** button, represented by the pencil icon in the top right, passing the `userId` to the `UserProfile` to edit and update the data.

8. Click on the **Edit** button to be taken to the `ProfileComponent`, edit the user record, and verify that you can update another user's record.
9. Confirm that you can view the updated user record in the data table.

This demonstration of data tables with pagination completes the major functionality of LemonMart for this book. Before moving on, make sure all the tests have passed.

For the unit tests, I import concrete implementations of `NameInputComponent` or `ViewUserComponent` instead of using the `createComponentMock` function from `angular-unit-test-helper`. This is because `createComponentMock` is not sophisticated enough to bind data to child components. In the *Further reading* section, I've included a blog post by Aiko Klostermann that covers testing Angular components with `@Input()` properties.

With the heavy lifting of the implementation completed, we can now explore alternative architectures, tools, and libraries to better understand the best ways to architect Angular apps for various needs. Next, let's explore NgRx.

NgRx store and effects

As covered in *Chapter 1, Angular's Architecture and Concepts*, the NgRx library brings reactive state management to Angular based on RxJS. State management with NgRx allows developers to write atomic, self-contained, and composable pieces of code, creating actions, reducers, and selectors. This kind of reactive programming isolates side effects in state changes. NgRx is an abstraction layer over RxJS to fit the **Flux pattern**.

There are four major elements of NgRx:

- **Store**: The central location where state information is persisted. You implement a reducer to store a state transition in the store and a selector to read data out of the store. These are atomic and composable pieces of code.

  A view (or user interface) displays data from the store by using a selector.

- **Action**: Unique events that happen throughout your app.

Actions are triggered from a view with the purpose of dispatching them to the store.

- **Dispatcher**: This is a method to send actions to the store.

Reducers in the store listen for dispatched actions.

- **Effect**: This is a combination of an action and a dispatcher. Effects are usually used for actions that are not triggered from a view.

Let's revisit the following Flux pattern diagram, which now highlights an **Effect**:

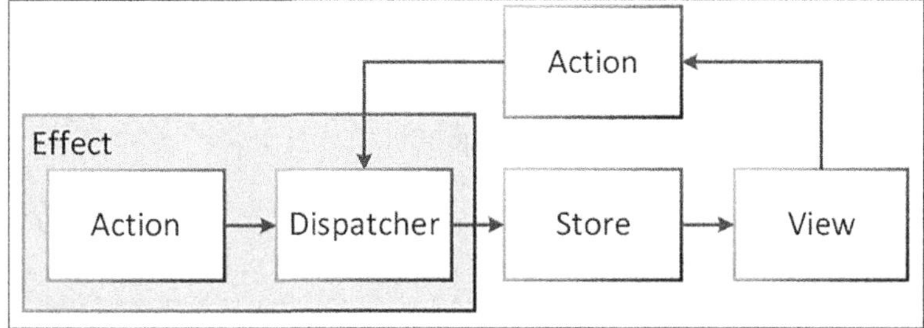

Figure 9.7: Flux pattern diagram

Let's demonstrate how NgRx works by going over a concrete example. To keep it simple, we will leverage the LocalCast Weather app.

Implementing NgRx for LocalCast Weather

We will implement NgRx to execute the search functionality in the LocalCast Weather app. Consider the following architecture diagram:

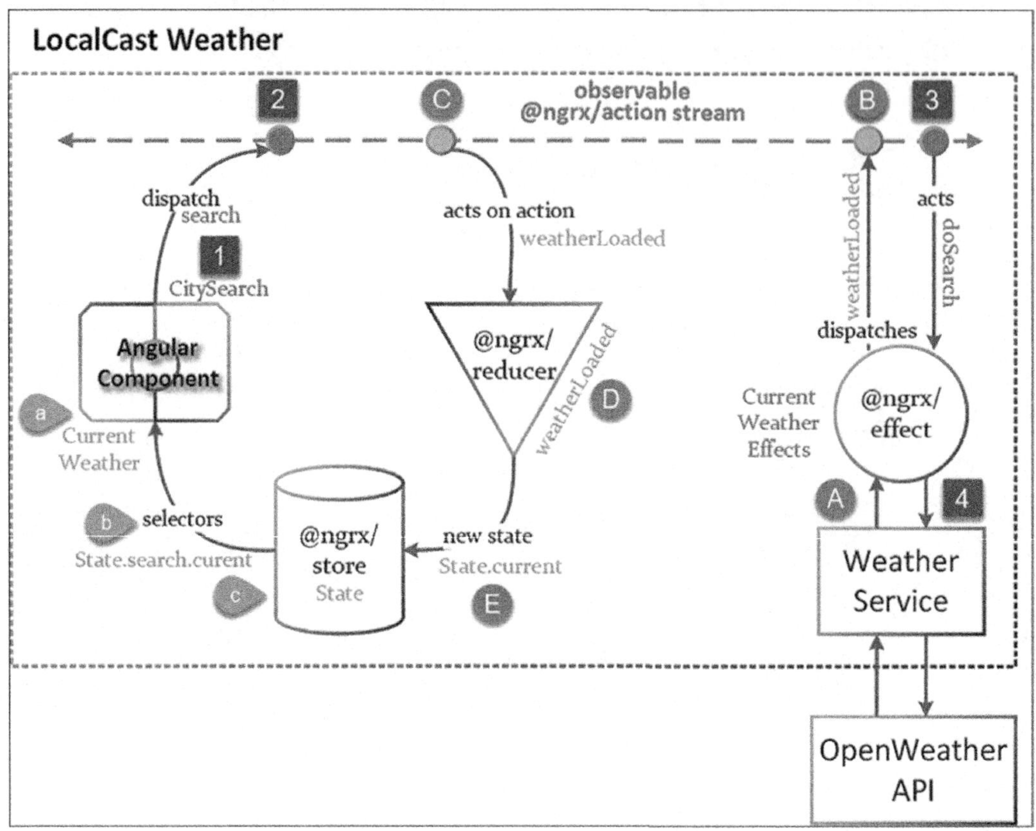

Figure 9.8: LocalCast Weather architecture

We will use the NgRx store and effects libraries to achieve our implementation. NgRx store actions are reflected in the diagram in light gray with a `WeatherLoaded` reducer and the app state. At the top, actions are represented as a stream of various data objects, either dispatching actions or acting on dispatched actions, enabling us to implement the **Flux pattern** introduced in *Chapter 1, Angular's Architecture and Concepts*. The NgRx effects library extends the Flux pattern by isolating side effects in its model without littering the store with temporary data.

The effects workflow, represented in dark gray in *Figure 9.8*, begins with *step 1*:

1. `CitySearchComponent` dispatches the `search` action.

2. The `search` action appears on the Observable `@ngrx/action` stream (or data stream).
3. `CurrentWeatherEffects` acts on the `search` action to perform a search.
4. `WeatherService` performs the search to retrieve current weather information from the **OpenWeather API**.

Store actions, represented in light gray, begin with *step A* (uppercase A):

a. `CurrentWeatherEffects` dispatches the `weatherLoaded` action.
b. The `weatherLoaded` action appears on the Observable data stream, labeled `@ngrx/action` stream.
c. The `weatherLoaded` reducer acts on the `weatherLoaded` action.
d. The `weatherLoaded` reducer transforms the weather information to be stored as the new state.
e. The new state is a persisted `search` state, part of the `appStore` state.

Note that there's a parent-level `appStore` state containing a child `search` state. I intentionally retained this setup to demonstrate how the parent-level state scales as you add different kinds of data elements to the store.

Finally, a view (an Angular component) reads from the store, beginning with *step a* (lowercase a):

a. The `CurrentWeather` component subscribes to the `selectCurrentWeather` selector using the `async` pipe.
b. The `selectCurrentWeather` selector listens for changes to the `store.search.current` property in the `appStore` state.
c. The `appStore` state retrieves the persisted data.

Using an NgRx selector is like writing a query to read data stored in a database. The database, in this case, is the store.

Using NgRx, when a user searches for a city, the actions to retrieve, persist, and display that information on `CurrentWeatherComponent` happen automatically via individual composable and immutable elements.

Comparing BehaviorSubject and NgRx

We will implement NgRx alongside `BehaviorSubject` so you can see the differences in implementing the same feature. To do this, we will need a slide toggle to switch between the two strategies:

> This section uses the **local-weather-app** repo. You can find the code samples for this chapter under the `projects/stage12` folder.
>
> Note that the main app under the `src` folder uses a button toggle to switch between `Signals`, `BehaviorSubject`, and `NgRx`.

1. Start by implementing a `<mat-slide-toggle>` element on `CitySearchComponent`, as shown in the following screenshot:

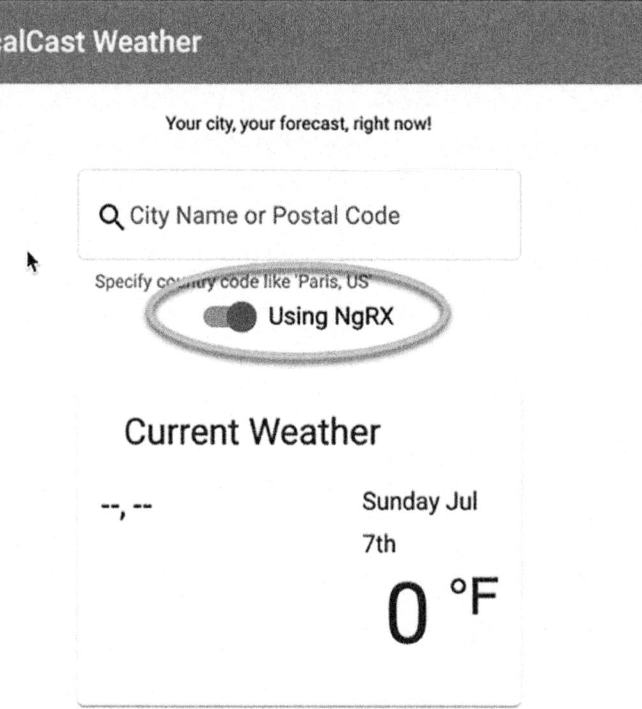

Figure 9.9: LocalCast Weather slide toggle

Ensure the field is backed by a property on your component named `useNgRx`.

2. Refactor the `doSearch` method to extract the `BehaviorSubject` code into its own function named `behaviorSubjectBasedSearch`.

3. Stub out a function called ngRxBasedSearch:

```
src/app/city-search/city-search.component.ts
doSearch(searchValue: string) {
  const userInput = searchValue.split(',').map((s) => s.trim())
  const searchText = userInput[0]
  const country = userInput.length > 1 ? userInput[1] : undefined
  if (this.useNgRx) {
    this.ngRxBasedSearch(searchText, country)
  } else {
    this.behaviorSubjectBasedSearch(searchText, country)
  }
}
```

We will be dispatching an action from the ngRxBasedSearch function that you just created.

Setting up NgRx

You can add the NgRx Store package with the following command:

```
$ npx ng add @ngrx/store
```

This will create a reducers folder with an `index.ts` file in it. Now add the NgRx `effects` package:

```
$ npx ng add @ngrx/effects --minimal
```

We use the `--minimal` option here to avoid creating unnecessary boilerplate.

Next, install the NgRx schematics library so you can take advantage of generators to create the boilerplate code for you:

```
$ npm i -D @ngrx/schematics
```

Implementing NgRx can be confusing due to its highly decoupled nature, which may necessitate some insight into the library's inner workings.

The sample project under `projects/stage12` configures `@ngrx/store-devtools` for debugging.

If you would like to be able to `console.log` NgRx actions for debugging or instrumentation during runtime, you can use a MetaReducer as described in the NgRx documentation, `https://ngrx.io/guide/store/metareducers`.

Defining NgRx actions

Before we can implement effects or reducers, we first need to define the actions our app will be able to execute. For LocalCast Weather, there are two types of actions:

- `search`: Fetches the current weather for the city or zip code that's being searched
- `weatherLoaded`: Indicates that new current weather information has been fetched

Create an action named `search` by running the following command:

```
$ npx ng generate @ngrx/schematics:action search --group --creators
```

Take the default options when prompted.

The `--group` option groups actions under a folder named `action`. The `--creators` option uses creator functions to implement actions and reducers, which is a more familiar and straightforward way to implement these components.

Now, let's implement the two actions using the `createAction` function, providing a name and an expected list of input parameters:

src/app/action/search.actions.ts

```
import { createAction, props, union } from '@ngrx/store'
import { ICurrentWeather } from '../interfaces'
export const SearchActions = {
  search: createAction(
    '[Search] Search',
    props<{ searchText: string; country?: string }>()
  ),
  weatherLoaded: createAction(
    '[Search] CurrentWeather loaded',
    props<{ current: ICurrentWeather }>()
  ),
```

```
}
const all = union(SearchActions)
export type SearchActions = typeof all
```

The search action has the name '[Search] Search' and has searchText and an optional country parameter as inputs. The weatherLoaded action follows a similar pattern. At the end of the file, we create a union type of actions, so we can group them under one parent type to use in the rest of the application.

Notice that action names are prepended by [Search]. This convention helps developers visually group related actions together during debugging.

Now that our actions are defined, we can implement the effect to handle the search action and dispatch a weatherLoaded action.

Implementing NgRx effects

As mentioned earlier, effects let us change the stored state without necessarily storing the event data causing the change. For example, we want our state only to have weather data, not the search text itself. Effects allow us to do this in one step, rather than forcing us to use an intermediate store for the searchText and a far more complicated chain of events to turn that into weather data.

Otherwise, we would have to implement a reducer in between. We first need to store this value in the NgRx store, then retrieve it from a service, and finally dispatch a weatherLoaded action. The effect will make it simpler to retrieve data from the service.

Now let's add CurrentWeatherEffects to our app:

```
$ npx ng generate @ngrx/schematics:effect currentWeather --module=app.
module.ts --root --group --creators
```

Take the default options when prompted.

You will have a new current-weather.effects.ts file under the effects folder.

Once again, `--group` is used to group effects under a folder of the same name. `--root` registers the effect in `app.module.ts` and we use creator functions with the `--creators` option.

In the `CurrentWeatherEffects` file, start by implementing a private `doSearch` method:

src/app/effects/current-weather.effects.ts

```
private doSearch(action: { searchText: string; country?: string }) {
  return this.weatherService.getCurrentWeather(
    action.searchText,
    action.country
  ).pipe(
    map((weather) =>
      SearchActions.weatherLoaded({ current: weather })
    ),
    catchError(() => EMPTY)
  )
}
```

Note that we're choosing to ignore errors thrown with the `EMPTY` function. You can surface these errors to the user with a `UiService` like the one you've implemented for LemonMart.

This function takes an action with search parameters, calls `getCurrentWeather`, and upon receiving a response, dispatches the `weatherLoaded` action, passing in the current weather property.

Now let's create the effect itself, so we can trigger the `doSearch` function:

src/app/effects/current-weather.effects.ts

```
getCurrentWeather$ = createEffect(() =>
  this.actions$.pipe(
    ofType(SearchActions.search),
    exhaustMap((action) => this.doSearch(action))
  )
)
```

This is where we tap into the Observable action stream, `this.actions$`, and listen to actions of the `SearchAction.search` type. We then use the `exhaustMap` operator to register for the emitted event.

Due to its unique nature, `exhaustMap` won't allow another search action to be processed until the `doSearch` function completes dispatching its `weatherLoaded` action.

Impact of RxJS operators on actions

In the preceding example, I used the `exhaustMap` operator. This is not necessarily the correct RxJS operator for this use case, `switchMap` is. I selected `exhaustMap` with the express purpose of limiting the number of API calls generated toward a free resource, which can aggressively rate limit requests.

Let's explore four RxJS operators we can choose from:

1. `mergeMap`: Allows for handling multiple actions in parallel, ideal for scenarios where each action's effect is independent and doesn't need to be synchronized.
2. `concatMap`: Processes actions in sequence, starting the next one only after the previous action is complete, ensuring actions are handled in the order they were dispatched, which is useful for maintaining consistency in state updates.
3. `switchMap`: On receiving a new action, it cancels the previous one and switches to the new one, which is suitable for use cases like search bar inputs where only the latest action (e.g., user input) is relevant.
4. `exhaustMap`: Ignores new actions if one is already being processed, making it useful for avoiding duplicate or conflicting requests, such as multiple submissions of the same form.

With `exhaustMap`, if actions are created rapidly before the `doSearch` function completes, the actions that haven't been processed will be dropped. So, if actions *a*, *b*, *c*, *d*, and *e* are created, but `doSearch` completes between when *c* and *d* were created, then actions *b*, *c*, and *e* are never processed, but action *d* will be. API calls for *b*, *c*, and *e* are never made. Only a `weatherLoaded` action for *d* is dispatched. While we avoid making unnecessary API calls for results users will never see, the end state will confuse the user.

Using `mergeMap`, all search actions are processed in parallel, API calls made, and `weatherLoaded` actions dispatched. So, if actions *a*, *b*, *c*, *d*, and *e* are created rapidly. The user may see flashes of results from all actions, but the last one displayed will be *e*.

With `concatMap`, actions are processed sequentially. Considering actions *a*, *b*, *c*, *d*, and *e*, the API call for *b* isn't made until after the `weatherLoaded` action is dispatched for *a* and the result is rendered. This will happen for each action until the weather for *e* is displayed.

With `switchMap`, API calls will be made with each action. However, only the last action will be dispatched, so the user will only see the last action displayed.

So, from a UX perspective, switchMap is functionally the correct implementation. You could also implement a loading spinner or disable user input while data is processed to prevent expensive API calls.

Ultimately, depending on your use case and UX needs, consider a different RxJS operator. Not all dispatched actions result in a screen that needs to be rendered. If you wanted to retain all data input, you could process actions in a service worker background thread and update a notification panel or a badge with a counter in your app.

Implementing reducers

With the weatherLoaded action triggered, we need a way to ingest the current weather information and store it in our appStore state. Reducers will help us handle specific actions, creating an isolated and immutable pipeline to store our data predictably.

Let's create a search reducer:

```
$ npx ng generate @ngrx/schematics:reducer search
    --reducers=reducers/index.ts --group --creators
```

Take the default options. Here, we use --group to keep files organized under the reducers folder and --creators to leverage the creator style of creating NgRx code. We also specify the location of our parent appStore state at reducers/index.ts with --reducers, so our new reducer can be registered with it.

You may observe that reducers.index.ts has been updated to register the new search.reducer.ts. Let's implement it step by step.

In the search state, we will be storing the current weather, so implement the interface to reflect this:

```
src/app/reducers/search.reducer.ts
export interface State {
  current: ICurrentWeather
}
```

Now let's specify the initialState. This is similar to how we need to define a default value of a signal or BehaviorSubject. Refactor the WeatherService to export a const defaultWeather: ICurrentWeather object that you can use to initialize BehaviorSubject and initialState:

```
src/app/reducers/search.reducer.ts
```

```
export const initialState:
  State = {
      current: defaultWeather,
  }
```

Finally, implement `searchReducer` to handle the `weatherLoaded` action using the on operator:

```
src/app/reducers/search.reducer.ts
const searchReducer = createReducer(
  initialState,
  on(SearchActions.weatherLoaded, (state, action) => {
    return {
      ...state,
      current: action.current,
    }
  })
)
```

We register for the `weatherLoaded` action, unwrap the stored data, and pass it into the `search` state.

This is, of course, a very simplistic case. However, it is easy to imagine a more complicated scenario where we may need to flatten or process a piece of data received and store it in an easy-to-consume manner. Isolating such logic in an immutable way is the key value proposition of utilizing a library like NgRx.

Registering with Store using selector

We need `CurrentWeatherComponent` to register with the `appStore` state for updated current weather data.

Start by dependency injecting the `appStore` state and registering the selector to pluck current weather from the `State` object:

```
src/app/current-weather/current-weather.component.ts
import * as appStore from '../reducers'
export class CurrentWeatherComponent {
  current$: Observable<ICurrentWeather>
  constructor(private store: Store<appStore.State>) {
    this.current$ =
      this.store.pipe(select((state: State) => state.search.current))
```

```
  }
  ...
}
```

We listen to state change events that flow through the store. Using the `select` function, we can implement an inline select to get the data we need.

We can refactor this a bit and make our selector reusable by using a `createSelector` to create a `selectCurrentWeather` property on `reducers/index.ts`:

```
src/app/reducers/index.ts
export const selectCurrentWeather = createSelector(
  (state: State) => state.search.current,
  current => current
)
```

As the number of TypeScript interfaces and NgRx selectors increases, you should break them into separate files and organize your code better.

In addition, since we want to maintain the continued operation of `BehaviorSubject`, we can implement a `merge` operator in `CurrentWeatherComponent` to listen to both `WeatherService` updates and `appStore` state updates:

```
src/app/current-weather/current-weather.component.ts
import * as appStore from '../reducers'
  constructor(
    private weatherService: WeatherService,
    private store: Store<appStore.State>
  ) {
    this.current$ = merge(
      this.store.pipe(select(appStore.selectCurrentWeather)),
      this.weatherService.currentWeather$
    )
  }
```

Now that we can listen to store updates, let's implement the final puzzle piece: dispatching the search action.

Dispatching store actions

We need to dispatch the search action so that our search effect can fetch the current weather data and update the store. Earlier in this chapter, you implemented a stubbed function called `ngRxBasedSearch` in the `CitySearchComponent`.

Let's implement `ngRxBasedSearch`:

src/app/city-search/city-search.component.ts

```
ngRxBasedSearch(searchText: string, country?: string) {
  this.store.dispatch(SearchActions.search({ searchText, country }))
}
```

Don't forget to inject the `appState` store into the component!

And that's it! Now you should be able to run your code and test to see whether it all works.

As you can see, NgRx brings a lot of sophisticated techniques to the table to create ways to make data transformations immutable, well defined, and predictable. However, this comes with considerable implementation overhead.

Use your best judgment to determine whether you need the Flux pattern in your Angular app. The frontend application code can often be made much simpler by implementing RESTful APIs that return flat data objects, with complicated data manipulations handled server side, reducing, if not eliminating, the need for tools like NgRx.

Unit testing reducers and selectors

You can implement unit tests for the `weatherLoaded` reducer and the `selectCurrentWeather` selector in `search.reducer.spec.ts`:

src/app/reducers/search.reducer.spec.ts

```
import { SearchActions } from '../actions/search.actions'
import { defaultWeather } from '../weather/weather.service'
import { fakeWeather } from '../weather/weather.service.fake'
import { selectCurrentWeather } from './index'
import { initialState, reducer } from './search.reducer'
describe('Search Reducer', () => {
```

```
    describe('weatherLoaded', () => {
      it('should return current weather', () => {
        const action = SearchActions.weatherLoaded({ current: fakeWeather })
        const result = reducer(initialState, action)
        expect(result).toEqual({ current: fakeWeather })
      })
    })
  })
  describe('Search Selectors', () => {
    it('should selectCurrentWeather', () => {
      const expectedWeather = defaultWeather
      expect(selectCurrentWeather({
        search: { current: defaultWeather }
      })).toEqual(
        expectedWeather
      )
    })
  })
```

These unit tests are straightforward and will ensure that no unintentional changes to the data structure can happen within the store.

Unit testing components with MockStore

You need to update the tests for `CurrentWeatherComponent` so that we can inject a mock `Store` into the component to test the value of the `current$` property.

Let's look at the delta of what needs to be added to the spec file to configure the mock store:

src/app/current-weather/current-weather.component.spec.ts

```
import { MockStore, provideMockStore } from '@ngrx/store/testing'
describe('CurrentWeatherComponent', () => {
  ...
  let store: MockStore<{ search: { current: ICurrentWeather } }>
  const initialState = { search: { current: defaultWeather } }
  beforeEach(async(() => {
    ...
    TestBed.configureTestingModule({
```

```
      imports: [AppMaterialModule],
      providers: [
        ...
        provideMockStore({ initialState }),
      ],
    }).compileComponents()
    ...
    store = TestBed.inject(Store) as any
  }))
...
})
```

We can now update the `'should get currentWeather from weatherService'` test to see whether `CurrentWeatherComponent` works with a mock store:

```
src/app/current-weather/current-weather.component.spec.ts
it('should get currentWeather from weatherService', (done) => {
  // Arrange
  store.setState({ search: { current: fakeWeather } })
  weatherServiceMock.currentWeather$.next(fakeWeather)
  // Act
  fixture.detectChanges() // triggers ngOnInit()
  // Assert
  expect(component.current$).toBeDefined()
  component.current$.subscribe(current => {
    expect(current.city).toEqual('Bethesda')
    expect(current.temperature).toEqual(280.32)
    // Assert on DOM
    const debugEl = fixture.debugElement
    const titleEl: HTMLElement =
      debugEl.query(By.css('.mat-title')).nativeElement
    expect(titleEl.textContent).toContain('Bethesda')
    done()
  })
})
```

The mock store allows us to set the store's current state, which in turn allows the selector to call in the constructor to fire and grab the provided fake weather data.

`TestBed` is not a hard requirement for writing unit tests in Angular, a topic covered well at `https://angular.dev/guide/testing`. My colleague and reviewer of the 2nd edition, Brendon Caulkins, contributed a bedless `spec` file for this chapter, named `current-weather.component.nobed.spec.ts`. He cites significant performance increases when running the tests, with fewer imports and less maintenance, but a higher level of care and expertise required to implement the tests. If you're on a large project, consider skipping `TestBed`.

The sample code on GitHub is under the `projects/stage12` folder.

Go ahead and update the remainder of your tests, and do not move on until they all start passing.

NgRx ecosystem

Now that you understand NgRx better beyond just theory, let's examine the different available options within the ecosystem.

Here are some popular options from the community, including sibling packages from NgRx:

- **NgRx/Data**, a gentle introduction to NgRx with simplified entity management
- **NgRx/ComponentStore**, a component-scoped version of NgRx/Store with less boilerplate
- **NgRx/SignalStore**, the next generation of state management in Angular
- **Akita**, a reactive state management offering tailor-made for JS applications
- **Elf**, a reactive store with magical powers

Let's explore these options.

NgRx/Data

If NgRx is a configuration-based framework, NgRx Data is a convention-based sibling of NgRx. NgRx Data automates the creation of stores, effects, actions, reducers, dispatches, and selectors. If most of your application actions are **CRUD** (**Create**, **Retrieve**, **Update**, and **Delete**) operations, then NgRx Data can achieve the same result as NgRx with much less code needing to be written.

`@ngrx/data` works in tandem with the `@ngrx/entity` library. Together they offer a rich feature set, including transactional data management.

NgRx Data may be a much better introduction to the Flux pattern for you and your team, allowing an easy ramp-up for the full NgRx framework. Unfortunately, NgRx Data is no longer recommended for new projects.

As of version 17, NgRx Data is officially in maintenance mode, and it's not recommended for new projects or adding to existing projects.

You can read more about it at `https://ngrx.io/guide/data`.

You can add NgRx Data to your project by executing the following commands:

```
$ npx ng add @ngrx/store -minimal
$ npx ng add @ngrx/effects -minimal
$ npx ng add @ngrx/entity
$ npx ng add @ngrx/data
```

So, should you implement NgRx Data in your next app? It depends, but probably not, given its maintenance mode status. Since the library is an abstraction layer on top of NgRx, you may find yourself lost and restricted if you don't have a good understanding of the internals of NgRx. However, the library holds much promise for reducing boilerplate code regarding entity data management and CRUD operations.

If you're doing lots of CRUD operations in your app, you may save time, but be careful to limit the scope of your implementation to the areas that need it. As the NgRx documentation highlights, NgRx Data lacks many capabilities of a full-featured entity management system, like deep entity cloning, server-side querying, relationships, key generation, and non-normalized server responses.

For a full-featured entity management library, consider BreezeJS `https://www.getbreezenow.com/breezejs`. However, beware that Breeze doesn't adhere to reactive, immutable, and redux principles as NgRx does.

Next, let's investigate ComponentStore for a less demanding and more focused application of the Flux pattern.

NgRx/ComponentStore

NgRx ComponentStore offers a lightweight, reactive state management solution ideal for local state within components or modules.

It's designed to manage local state without needing a global store, maintaining a clean separation of concerns, and making components simple and maintainable. This approach is particularly useful for complex components with many local states and interactions, as it allows for push-based services that manage this state with the component's lifecycle, supporting reusability and independent instances.

You can implement the data source of your paginated data table using `ComponentStore`, similar to how this is done with Elf. Check out this excellent two-part blog post by Pierre Bouillon: `https://dev.to/this-is-angular/handling-pagination-with-ngrx-component-stores-1j1p`.

In contrast, NgRx Store manages a global shared state and is beneficial for larger applications requiring scalability, multiple effects, and DevTools integration. ComponentStore, while less scalable and with many updaters and effects, ensures type safety, performance, and ease of testing, allowing for a more encapsulated and component-specific state management.

The choice between `ComponentStore` and `Store` hinges on the application's size, component dependencies, state longevity, and business requirements, among other factors.

Read more about ComponentStore at `https://ngrx.io/guide/component-store`.

You can add ComponentStore to your project by executing the following:

```
$ npx ng add @ngrx/component-store
```

In short, `ComponentStore` is an alternative to the "Service with a Subject" approach we've covered in the book. However, with Angular's architecture shifting toward Signals, you may want to skip the `ComponentStore` and implement `SignalStore` instead.

NgRx/Signals

I introduced you to signals in the *Using Angular signals* section of *Chapter 2, Forms, Observables, Signals, and Subjects*. NgRx/Signals is a self-contained library offering a reactive state management solution alongside a suite of utilities for working with Angular Signals. It's architected for simplicity, presenting an intuitive API for developers. Its lightweight nature ensures minimal load on applications while maintaining high performance.

The library champions declarative programming, fostering clean and concise code. It facilitates the crafting of autonomous components that are easily integrated, promoting scalable and flexible applications. Additionally, it enforces type safety, mitigating errors early in the development cycle.

The library includes the following:

- SignalStore is a robust state management system bringing the best of both worlds from NgRx/Store and NgRx/ComponentStore.
- SignalState is a streamlined utility for managing state within Angular components and services overtaking any need for self-managed signal properties in service.
- `rxMethod` provides opt-in usage to interact with Observables. Useful for interacting with existing code.
- `withEntities` is an entity management plugin offering an efficient approach to facilitate CRUD operations for managing entities.

We will investigate SignalState and SignalStore in depth in the upcoming sections.

Read more about NgRx Signals at `https://ngrx.io/guide/signals`.

You can add SignalStore to your project by executing:

```
$ npx ng add @ngrx/signals
```

Let's round up our state management ecosystem tour with some popular non-NgRx options, Akita and Elf.

Akita

Akita is a state management solution combining Flux, Redux, and RxJS concepts into the Observable Data Store model, favoring immutability and streaming data. It emphasizes simplicity, reduces boilerplate code, and is accessible to developers at all levels due to its moderate learning curve. Akita adopts object-oriented principles, making it intuitive for those familiar with OOP, and enforces a consistent structure to guide and standardize team development practices.

Akita is built around RxJS/`BehaviorSubject` and provides specialized classes for state management, such as `Store`, `Query`, and `EntityStore`. Like NgRx, Akita exposes state changes as RxJS Observables and utilizes the update method for state mutations, enabling an OOP style for state management.

It's worthwhile to experiment with Akita if you're looking for a simpler solution with built-in entity management, plugins for state history, server-side pagination, more OOP versus functional, and, overall, less boilerplate code.

You can learn more about Akita at `https://opensource.salesforce.com/akita/`.

Elf

Elf is the most magical option of the bunch. It's a newer state management library for Angular that aims to simplify reactivity and state mutations with a minimalistic API, focusing on ergonomics and ease of use. It uses modern RxJS patterns for state management, enabling fine-grained control over state changes and reactivity. Elf is designed to be lightweight and straightforward, offering a simpler alternative to the more comprehensive NgRx suite.

Elf is modular, fully tree-shakable, and provides first-class support for the following:

- **Request cache** to prevent redundant API calls.
- **Entities** such as NgRx/Data or Akita.
- **State persistence** for offline-first applications.
- **State history** for easy undo/redo functionality.
- **Advanced pagination** to optimize fetching and caching of paginated data
- Elf integrates features and best practices for building reactive web apps with statement management and makes them easy. While features like pagination support can be implemented using NgRx/ComponentStore, the built-in pagination caching support is impressive. In addition, Elf has a plugin to sync state across browser tabs, enabling truly advanced state management.
- Given the number of built-in and high-quality features that ship with Elf, it is a standout solution that may be the right option for your next project. You can learn more about Elf at `https://ngneat.github.io/elf/`.

We've covered the nuances of the NgRx ecosystem. Let's learn how you can configure proxies with Angular to deal with convention-based state management libraries that expect a certain way to access server-side data.

Configuring server proxies with the Angular CLI

Some state management libraries, especially convention-based entity stores like NgRx Data, make assumptions about accessing server-side data. In the case of NgRx Data, the library wants to access the REST API via the `/api` path hosted on the same port as your Angular app. We must leverage the Angular CLI's proxy feature to accomplish this during development.

Normally, HTTP requests are sent to our web server, and our API server should have the same URL. However, during development, we usually host both applications on two different ports of `http://localhost`. Certain libraries, including NgRx Data, require that HTTP calls be on the same port. This creates a challenge for creating a frictionless development experience. For this reason, the Angular CLI ships with a proxy feature with which you can direct the `/api` path to a different endpoint on your localhost. This way, you can use one port to serve your web app and your API requests:

1. Create a `proxy.conf.json` file under `src`, as shown:

If you're working in the **lemon-mart-server** monorepo, this will be `web-app/src`.

```
proxy.conf.json
{
  "/api": {
    "target": "http://localhost:3000",
    "secure": false,
    "pathRewrite": {
       "^/api": ""
    }
  }
}
```

2. Register the proxy with `angular.json`:

```
angular.json
...
"serve": {
  "builder": "@angular-devkit/build-angular:dev-server",
  "options": {
    "browserTarget": "lemon-mart:build",
    "proxyConfig": "proxy.conf.json"
  },
  ...
}
```

Now the server that is started when you run `npm start` or `ng serve` can rewrite the URLs of any call made to the `/api` route with `http://localhost:3000`. This is the port that **lemon-mart-server** runs by default.

Use the correct port number and child route if your API is running on a different port.

Implementing a global spinner with NgRx/SignalState

In the *Multi-step responsive forms* section of *Chapter 8, Recipes – Reusability, Forms, and Caching*, and the *Data tables with pagination* section earlier in this chapter, I discussed the differences between localized spinners and global ones. A global spinner is the ultimate 80-20 solution to paper over UX issues stemming from UI elements not being ready for interaction while data loads. However, this will cause excessive full-screen interruptions in large applications with multiple on-screen components or background service workers loading data. In that case, most components will require local spinners instead.

With that in mind, let's go after the 80-20 solution. We can use an `HttpInterceptor` to detect when an API call is made within the application. This allows us to show or hide a global spinner. However, if multiple calls are made concurrently, we must keep track of this, otherwise the global spinner may behave erratically. With NgRx/SignalState, we can keep track of the number of calls without introducing the local state in a service.

NgRx/SignalState

SignalState is a lightweight utility provided by `@ngrx/signals` for managing signal-based state in Angular components and services in a concise and minimalistic manner. It is used to create and operate on small slices of state directly in your component class, service, or a standalone function. You can provide a deeply nested signal of the object properties.

SignalState should be used within a component or service to manage simple state. The library offers the following functions:

- `signalState` is a utility function that takes the initial state of the store and defines the shape of the state.
- `patchState` updates the stored value.

Read more about NgRx SignalState at `https://ngrx.io/guide/signals/signal-state`.

We start by adding `signalState`, `computed signal`, `showLoader`, and `hideLoader` functions to `UiService`:

1. Modify UiService as shown:

src/app/common/ui.service.ts

```
@Injectable({ providedIn: 'root' })
export class UiService {
  ...
  private readonly loadState = signalState({
    count: 0,
    isLoading: false
  })
  isLoading = computed(() => this.loadState.isLoading())

  showLoader() {
    if (this.loadState.count() === 0) {
      patchState(this.loadState, () => ({ isLoading: true }))
    }
    patchState(this.loadState, (state) => ({
      count: state.count++
    }))}

  hideLoader() {
    patchState(this.loadState, (state) => ({
      count: state.count–
    }))
    if (this.loadState.count() === 0) {
      patchState(this.loadState, () => ({ isLoading: false }))
    }
  }
  ...
}
```

We start by defining a private `signalState` and initializing the `count` and `isLoading` properties. The state should always be encapsulated within the boundaries it's being used to avoid uncontrolled side effects. As we cover in the next section, SignalStore is a more robust solution to manage side effects. However, we want `isLoading` to be publicly available, so a UI component can bind it to hide or display the spinner. So, we implement a `computed` signal, which acts as a selector to return the current value of `isLoading` in a read-only manner.

`patchState` is a utility function that provides a type-safe way to perform immutable updates on pieces of state. We use it to update the values of `count` and `isLoading`, whenever `show` or `hide` functions are called.

2. Next, implement `LoadingHttpInterceptor` under `src/common` to call the `show` and `hide` methods:

src/common/loading.http.interceptor.ts

```
export function LoadingHttpInterceptor(
  req: HttpRequest<unknown>, next: HttpHandlerFn) {
  const uiService = inject(UiService)
  uiService.showLoader()
  return next(req).pipe(finalize(() =>
                          uiService.hideLoader()))
}
```

We inject `UiService` and call `showLoader` to increment the count by one. We then set up the finalize operator, so when the API call is finished `hideLoader` is called to decrement the count by one. So, whenever a loader function is called and the count is equal to zero, we know we either need to show or hide the spinner.

Don't forget to provide the new interceptor in `app.config.ts`.

3. Now, create a `LoadingOverlayComponent` under common and use `isLoading` to show or hide a spinner:

src/common/loading-overlay.component.ts

```
@Component({
  selector: 'app-loading-overlay',
```

```
template: `
  @if (uiService.isLoading()) {
    <div class="overlay">
      <div class="center">
        <img alt="loading" class="spinner"
                  src="assets/img/icons/lemon.svg" />
      </div>
    </div>
  }
`,
styles: `
  .overlay {
    position: fixed;
    width: 100%;
    height: 100%;
    left: 0;
    top: 0;
    background-color: rgba(255, 255, 255, 0.65);
    z-index: 9999;
  }
  .spinner {
    display: block;
    width: 48px;
    height: 48px;
    animation-name: spin;
    animation-duration: 1.00s;
    animation-iteration-count: infinite;
    animation-timing-function: ease-in-out;
  }

  @keyframes spin {
    0% { transform: rotate(0deg); }
    100% { transform: rotate(360deg); }
  }
  .center {
      position: absolute;
      top: 50%;
```

```
        left: 50%;
        transform: translate(-50%, -50%);
      }
    `,
    standalone: true,
    encapsulation: ViewEncapsulation.ShadowDom,
  })
  export class LoadingOverlayComponent {
    readonly uiService = inject(UiService)
  }
```

We inject and use the computed `isLoading` signal from `UiService`. With the `@if` flow control, the spinner will be shown or hidden depending on whether `isLoading` is set to true or false.

The use of `ViewEncapsulation.ShadowDom` in Angular allows component styles to be encapsulated within a Shadow DOM. By default, Angular uses an emulated mode to scope styles to components. However, the Shadow DOM encapsulation provides more robust support for dynamic CSS features.

4. Finally, update `app.component.ts` to import and place the new component at the top of the template:

```
src/app/app.component.ts
template: `
    <app-loading-overlay></app-loading-overlay>
    <div class="app-container">
    ...
```

5. Give it a try. A glorious lemon spinner will take over the screen whenever an API call is made.

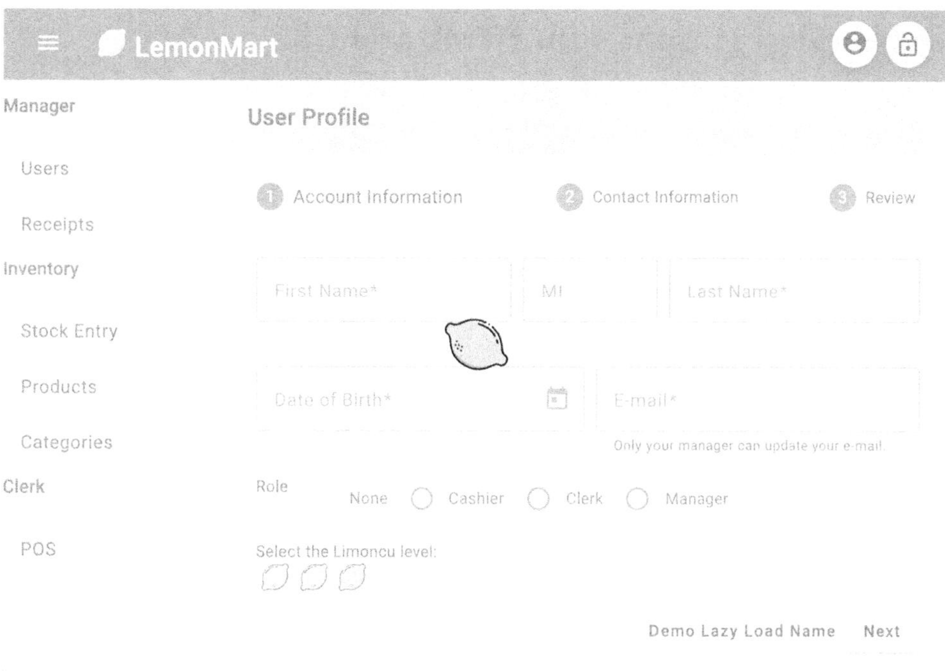

Figure 9.10: LemonMart's lemon spinner

6. This resolves the data pop-in issues in the user profile form mentioned in *Chapter 8, Recipes – Reusability, Forms, and Caching.*

Are your API calls happening too quickly to appreciate the spinner?

In **lemon-mart-server**, you can add a two-second delay:

server/src/v1/routes/authRouter.ts

```
router.get('/me', authenticate(), async (_req, res) => {
  await setTimeout(2000)
...
```

Or you can slow things down in your browser's DevTools **Network** tab by changing the **No Throttling** dropdown to **Fast 3G** or **Slow 3G**.

Pre-loading screens with HTML and CSS

If you follow the tip from the previous section and slow down the network speed of your browser to **Slow 3G** and **Disable caching**, you'll notice that it takes forever and a half for anything to be shown on screen. In *Chapter 3, Architecting an Enterprise App*, I covered how to implement **Server-side Rendering** (**SSR**) to overcome such issues. However, that may not always be an option or may be overkill. Using simple HTML and CSS we can implement an easy solution to present an attractive and dynamic loading screen to entertain bored users staring at your app on a slow network.

Let's start by adding the CSS in LemonMart:

1. Create `spinner.css` under `src/assets/styles`. Copy the contents from LemonMart's GitHub repo at `https://github.com/duluca/lemon-mart/blob/main/src/assets/styles/spinner.css`.
2. Update `index.html` to import the stylesheet and place the necessary HTML inside the `<app-root>` element:

```
src/index.html
<head>
  ...
  <link href="assets/styles/spinner.css" rel="stylesheet" />
</head>
<body class="mat-typography mat-app-background">
    <app-root>
      <div class="spinner-background">
        <div class="spinner-container">
          <svg class="spinner" width="65px" height="65px"
            viewBox="0 0 66 66">
            <circle class="path" fill="none" stroke-width="6"
              stroke-linecap="round" cx="33" cy="33" r="30">
            </circle>
          </svg>
          <h2 class="animate-text">Loading</h2>
        </div>
      </div>
    </app-root>
</body>
```

When Angular launches, the contents of `<app-root>` will be replaced by your application.

Note that this pre-loading screen is designed to be minimal and should come up instantly on screen. However, you will notice it still can take up to 6 seconds to display. This is because Angular prioritizes the global `styles.scss` file for loading first. If you're using Angular Material, this adds 165 KB of content, which takes almost 6 seconds to load in **Slow 3G**. However, this is still much better in the context of a 50-second total loading time.

3. Restart your Angular app and you should see the pre-loading screen:

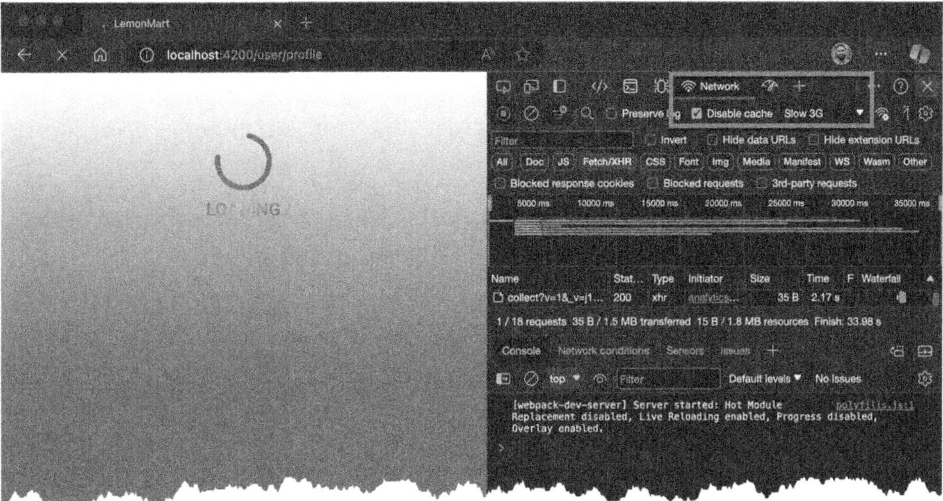

Figure 9.11: Preloading screen on slow networks

Now that you understand how to work with a state slice using NgRx/SignalState, let's dive into the excellent NgRx/SignalStore library next. In fact, it's so good that it inspired me to rewrite the LocalCast Weather app to be nearly Observable and RxJS operator-free with zero subscribe calls or async pipes.

Rewriting Angular apps with NgRx/SignalStore

With Observables, the best subscription is the one you don't have to make. Throughout this book, we used the `async pipe`, `take(1)`, `takeUntilDestroyed`, and `unsubscribe` in `ngOnDestroy` to try and manage them. The sample code for this book has been through many reviews by various practitioners and experts over a period of six years. Every review highlighted some oversight or bug with the RxJS code.

The 3rd edition of the book provides a 99% bug-free implementation. I could never claim 100% due to the insane complexity of the RxJS ecosystem.

I take pride in not taking the easy way out. I do my best to provide realistic and complete examples for you, not just counters and to-do lists. However, these are still highly controlled and small-sized projects compared to what happens in real life. You rarely have time to go back and reevaluate your entire project. Mistakes get compounded over time. This is a sad reality of working with RxJS. It's wonderful for what it does, but 95+ percent of code written doesn't require the flexibility and reactivity the tool brings. Most code is about retrieving some data from an API once and displaying it. Signals with async/await-driven promises make this kind of code straightforward to write.

RxJS and signal helpers

Several important functions will help you transition away from Observables and RxJS:

- **JavaScript promises** are a construct that allows for asynchronous operations, providing a way to handle the eventual success value or failure reason.
- **JavaScript async/await** is syntactic sugar in JavaScript that allows you to write asynchronous code in a synchronous fashion, built on top of promises.
- **RxJS Interop** `toSignal` creates a signal that tracks the value of an Observable, like the async pipe in templates but more flexible. Similar to async pipe, `toSignal` manages the subscription for us, so there's no need to use subscribe, `takeUntil`, or unsubscribe. There's also `toObservable`, which is a useful bridge during the transition.
- `ChangeDetectionStrategy.OnPush` is a strategy that tells Angular to run change detection on a component only when its input properties change, improving performance by reducing the number of checks. You will need to set the `changeDetection` property of your components to this until Signal-based components arrive.
- `lastValueFrom` is a utility function that converts an Observable to a promise that resolves with the last value emitted by the Observable. This operator also manages the subscription for us. There's also `firstValueFrom`, but you probably won't need that one. This conversation will be necessary until Angular implements promise-based APIs to modules such as `HttpClient`, `Router`, `FormControl`, etc.

RxJS Interop is in developer preview.

You can read more about it at `https://angular.dev/guide/signals/rxjs-interop`.

State management remains key to managing the complexity of large applications. Let's see how NgRx SignalStore can help with the transition.

NgRx/SignalStore

SignalStore is a fully featured state management solution built around declarative programming, ensuring clean and concise code. SignalStore is for managing larger stores with complex state as opposed to SignalState, which is designed to contain simple state within a single component or service.

Read more about NgRx SignalStore at `https://ngrx.io/guide/signals/signal-store`.

SignalStore can provided at the root level or component level. The library offers the following functions:

- `signalStore` is a utility function for managing larger and more complex pieces of state in an application.
- `withState` takes the initial state of the store and defines the shape of the state.
- `withComputed` derives computed properties from existing pieces of state in the store.
- `withMethods` contains custom functions (store methods) that are exposed publicly to operate on the store with a well-defined API. `withMethods` can use `patchState` and injected services to update the store.
- `withHooks` are called when the store is created or destroyed, allowing for fetching data to initialize the store or updating state.
- `withEntities` is an extension to facilitate CRUD operations for managing entities. It is like `@ngrx/entity` but not the same.

Read more about NgRx SignalStore entities at `https://ngrx.io/guide/signals/signal-store/entity-management`.

Also, see advanced use cases with custom store features at `https://ngrx.io/guide/signals/signal-store/custom-store-features`.

Let's see how we can apply SignalStore to LocalCast Weather. The diagram below is a recreation of the one from the *Implementing NgRx for LocalCast Weather* section earlier in this chapter.

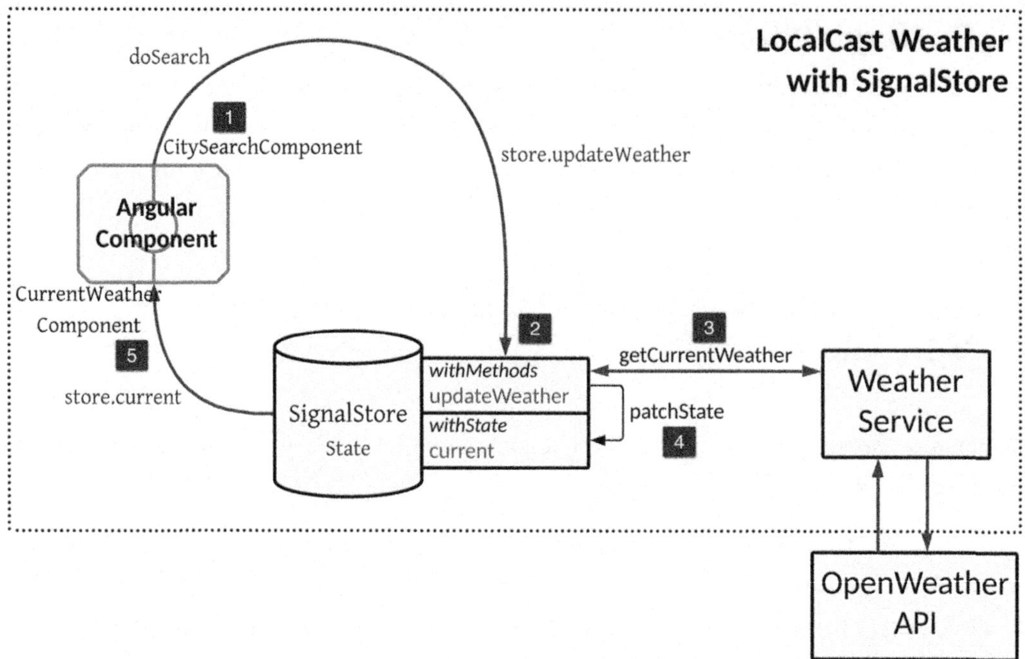

Figure 9.12: LocalCast Weather architecture

Upon initial inspection, SignalStore appears simpler than the NgRx store implementation. That's because the inherent reactivity of signals is baked into Angular. You must remember this invisible thread that makes the magic work beneath the surface of this implementation.

The workflow, represented in dark gray in *Figure 9.12*, begins with *step 1*:

1. `CitySearchComponent` triggers the `doSearch` method, which in turn calls `store.updateWeather`.
2. `withMethods` activates the `updateWeather` function, which has an injected reference to `WeatherService` and calls `getCurrentWeather` from it.
3. `updateWeather` awaits the result from `getCurrentWeather`, which retrieves the current weather information from **OpenWeather**, and uses `patchState` to update `store.current`.
4. `CurrentWeatherComponent` is bound to `store.current`, so when the value updates, the template is automatically updated.

Now that we understand how SignalStore operates conceptually, let's take a tour of the new code base.

Refactoring RxJS and NgRx code

We will review the refactored LocalCast Weather app to examine how the code was rewritten to be simpler and more concise using signals and SignalStore.

The source code for this section is under `projects/signal-store` on the `local-weather-app` repository at `https://github.com/duluca/local-weather-app/tree/main/projects/signal-store`.

You can run the project by executing:

```
$ npx ng serve --project signal-store
```

Run Cypress tests with:

```
$ npx ng run signal-store:cypress-run --spec "cypress/e2e/app.cy.ts,cypress/e2e/simple-search.cy.ts"
```

NgRx Store to SignalStore

Let's start with the Store implementation under `projects/signal-store/src/app/store`:

projects/signal-store/src/app/store/weather.store.ts

```
export const WeatherStore = signalStore(
  {
    providedIn: 'root',
  },
  withState({
    current: defaultWeather,
  }),
  withMethods((store, weatherService = inject(WeatherService)) => ({
    async updateWeather(searchText: string, country?: string) {
      patchState(store, {
        current: await weatherService.getCurrentWeather(
          searchText,
          country
        ),
      })
```

```
    },
  }))
)
```

`withState` defines and initializes the store. `withMethods` implements the `updateWeather` function, which encapsulates the behavior for updating the current weather. This function used to be in `WeatherService` but has now been moved into the store. Arguably, this should have been the case for the NgRx Store implementation; however, with an overall simpler architecture, it is easier to see that any potential side effect is best implemented in the store.

Services from Observables to Signals

We must update API calls to return a Promise instead of an Observable. I first updated `PostalCodeService`:

projects/signal-store/src/app/postal-code/postal-code.service.ts

```
export class PostalCodeService implements IPostalCodeService {
  private readonly httpClient = inject(HttpClient)

  resolvePostalCode(postalCode: string): Promise<IPostalCode> {
    const uriParams = new HttpParams()
      .set('maxRows', '1')
      .set('username', environment.username)
      .set('postalcode', postalCode)

    const httpCall$ = this.httpClient.get<IPostalCodeData>(
      `${environment.baseUrl}${environment.geonamesApi}.geonames.org/
postalCodeSearchJSON`,
      { params: uriParams }
    )

    return lastValueFrom(httpCall$).then((data) =>
      data.postalCodes?.length > 0 ?
        data.postalCodes[0] : defaultPostalCode
    )
  }
}
```

`resolvePostalCode` now returns `Promise<IPostalCode>`. We store the Observable from `httpClient.get` as a local `httpCall$` variable, which is then wrapped by `lastValueFrom`. In the process, we also removed the pipe, which implemented `mergeMap` and `defaultIfEmpty` to clean up the received data. We must implement a similar functionality in the `then` function. As shown previously, `then` behaves similarly to a `tap` function.

Next, let's look at `WeatherService`:

projects/signal-store/src/app/weather/weather.service.ts

```
export class WeatherService implements IWeatherService {
  private readonly httpClient = inject(HttpClient)
  private readonly postalCodeService = inject(PostalCodeService)

  async getCurrentWeather(
    searchText: string, country?: string): Promise<ICurrentWeather> {
    const postalCode = await
      this.postalCodeService.resolvePostalCode(searchText)

    if (postalCode && postalCode !== defaultPostalCode) {
      return this.getCurrentWeatherByCoords({
        latitude: postalCode.lat,
        longitude: postalCode.lng,
      })
    } else {
      const uriParams = new HttpParams().set(
        'q',
        country ? `${searchText},${country}` : searchText
      )

      return this.getCurrentWeatherHelper(uriParams)
    }
  }

  private getCurrentWeatherHelper(
    uriParams: HttpParams): Promise<ICurrentWeather> {
    uriParams = uriParams.set('appid', environment.appId)
```

```
    const httpCall$ = this.httpClient.get<ICurrentWeatherData>(
      `${environment.baseUrl}api.openweathermap.org/data/2.5/weather`,
      { params: uriParams }
    )
    return lastValueFrom(httpCall$).then(
          (data) => this.transformToICurrentWeather(data))
  }
```

getCurrentWeather is now an async function to await the result of postalCodeService.resolvePostalCode. The logic inside the switchMap to handle the response from resolvePostalCode is now a simple if-else statement with less nesting. getCurrentWeatherHelper has been refactored similar to how we refactored resolvePostalCode.

Most importantly, there's no longer a BehaviorSubject, a signal, or any code that remains in the service that updates the value of currentWeather.

Components from Observables to Signals

With the services updated, we can now complete the refactor and update the components to use signals.

Let's start with CitySearchComponent:

```
projects/signal-store/src/app/city-search/city-search.component.ts
@Component({
  selector: 'app-city-search',
  ...
  changeDetection: ChangeDetectionStrategy.OnPush,
})
export class CitySearchComponent {
  private readonly store = inject(WeatherStore)

  search = new FormControl(
    '',
    [Validators.required, Validators.minLength(2)]
  )

  readonly searchSignal = toSignal(
    this.search.valueChanges.pipe(
      filter(() => this.search.valid),
```

```
      debounceTime(1000)
    )
  )

  constructor() {
    effect(() => {
      this.doSearch(this.searchSignal())
    })
  }

  doSearch(searchValue?: string | null) {
    if (typeof searchValue !== 'string') return
    const userInput = searchValue.split(',').map((s) => s.trim())
    const searchText = userInput[0]
    const country = userInput.length > 1 ? userInput[1] : undefined

    this.store.updateWeather(searchText, country)
  }
}
```

We first set the `changeDetection` strategy to be `OnPush`. Next, we wrap `search.valueChanges` in a `toSignal` function to convert the Observable to a signal. This is notably the only pipe remaining in the app. The main reason is because of the `debounceTime` operator. See the tip box for more. We then use the `effect` function to react to changes pushed to `searchSignal`, which triggers `doSearch`, which in turn calls `store.updateWeather`. As we covered earlier, `store.updateWeather` will end up updating the `store.current` signal. Notably, we no longer reference `WeatherService` from this component, and no template changes were needed.

Filter and debounce are the only RxJS operators left in LocalCast Weather. Currently, there aren't operators for signals. You can check out how a debounced signal function might work in this Stack Overflow answer `https://stackoverflow.com/a/76597576/178620`. However, as the author An Nguyen notes, it's complicated code, and it's better to use a well-tested library for now.

Next, let's look at `CurrentWeatherComponent`:

`projects/signal-store/src/app/current-weather/current-weather.component.ts`

```
@Component({
  selector: 'app-current-weather',
  ...
  changeDetection: ChangeDetectionStrategy.OnPush,
})
export class CurrentWeatherComponent {
  readonly store = inject(WeatherStore)
  ...
}
```

The most remarkable change happens within `CurrentWeatherComponent`. We set `changeDetection` as before, but now we only have to inject `WeatherStore`. That's it:

```
projects/signal-store/src/app/current-weather/
current-weather.component.html
<div fxLayout="row">
  <div fxFlex="66%" class="mat-headline-6 no-margin" data-testid="city">
    {{ store.current().city }},
    {{ store.current().country }}
  </div>
  ...
```

In the template, we can remove the null guard because the signal is always initialized. Then we simply bind to `store.current()` signal. This, of course, requires a rather annoying refactoring of the template. We have to update every reference to `current` with `store.current()`. This could have been avoided by introducing a local variable named `current` and then using an `effect` to listen to updates on `store.current()`. However, with that configuration, you wouldn't get the benefits of the granular change detection that `signal` and `OnPush` offer.

I expect when Signal-based components arrive, we will be able to write code similar to how async pipe works:

```
@if (store.current() as current)
```

This will be a tremendous help in avoiding annoying template rewrites.

And with the component updates done, the application refactor is complete. There are other subtle changes around the app code. You will notice a lot less imports and providers.

In my opinion, the signal-only code is easier to understand and maintain; far superior to the RxJS alternative. I hope you enjoyed this glimpse into Angular's future.

Summary

In this chapter, we completed going over all major Angular app design considerations using router-first architecture, along with our recipes, to implement a line-of-business app easily. We reviewed how to edit existing users, leverage a resolve guard to load user data, and hydrate and reuse a component in different contexts.

We implemented a master/detail view using auxiliary routes and demonstrated how to build data tables with pagination. We then learned how to implement NgRx/Store and NgRx/SignalStore using **local-weather-app**. We covered the available options within the NgRx ecosystem, including NgRx/Data, NgRx/ComponentStore, Akita, and Elf, and the differences between those options, so you can make informed decisions about what to include in your project.

We also implemented a pre-loading animation, so your app looks responsive when loading in slow connections. We also implemented a global spinner within the app to handle data pop-in-related UX issues. Finally, we took a peek into Angular's signal-based future by touring a full refactor of **local-weather-app** using SignalStore and developer preview features.

Using the router-first design, architecture, and implementation approach, we tackled our application's design with a high-level understanding of what we wanted to achieve. We saw the power of router orchestration by demonstrating the use of router outlets and reusing the same component in two different contexts. By identifying code reuse opportunities early on, we optimized our implementation strategy to implement reusable components ahead of time without running the risk of grossly over-engineering our solution.

In the next chapter, we learn about containerization using Docker and deploying your apps to the cloud. Docker allows powerful workflows that can greatly improve development experiences while allowing you to implement your server configuration as code, putting the final nail in the coffin of the developer's favorite excuse when their software breaks: "But it works on my machine!"

Exercises

1. Update `UserTableComponent` and related services in **lemon-mart** to leverage Elf entities and pagination to enable optimized handling of requests.
2. Follow the guide on `https://ngneat.github.io/elf/docs/features/pagination`.

3. Rewrite your Angular app with NgRx/SignalStore to be nearly Observable and RxJS operator-free with zero subscribe calls or async pipes.
4. If you think this is a hilarious exercise tacked on toward the end of the book, give me a shoutout on my GitHub profile at `https://github.com/duluca`.

Further reading

- *Testing Angular Components With @Input()*, Aiko Klostermann, 2017, available at `https://medium.com/better-programming/testing-angular-components-with-input-3bd6c07cfaf6`
- *What is NgRx?*, 2020, available at `https://ngrx.io/docs`
- *NgRx Testing*, 2020, available at `https://ngrx.io/guide/store/testing`
- *@ngrx/data*, 2020, available at `https://ngrx.io/guide/data`
- *NgRx: Action Creators redesigned*, Alex Okrushko, 2019, available at `https://medium.com/angular-in-depth/ngrx-action-creators-redesigned-d396960e46da`
- *Simplifying Frontend State Management with Observable Store*, Dan Wahlin, 2019, available at `https://blog.codewithdan.com/simplifying-front-end-state-management-with-observable-store/`
- *Handling pagination with NgRx component stores*, Pierre Bouillon, 2023, `https://dev.to/this-is-angular/handling-pagination-with-ngrx-component-stores-1j1p`
- *Navigating the Nuances of toSignal in Angular: What to Know*, Netanel Basal, 2023, `https://netbasal.com/navigating-the-nuances-of-tosignal-in-angular-what-to-know-e4d6a4b5dfaf`
- *A Guide to Angular Signals With Practical Use Cases*, Arman Murzabulatov, 2023, `https://hackernoon.com/a-guide-to-angular-signals-with-practical-use-cases-part-1`
- *The Power of @ngrx/signalstore: A Deep Dive Into Task Management*, Peter Eijgermans, 2024, `https://dzone.com/articles/the-power-of-ngrxsignalstore-a-deep-dive-into-task`
- *How to Implement a Global Loader in Angular*, Faizan Shaikh , 2023, `https://blog.bitsrc.io/how-to-implement-a-global-loader-in-angular-df111a2c43d9`
- *RxJS: Avoiding takeUntil Leaks*, Nicholas Jamieson, 2018, `https://cartant.medium.com/rxjs-avoiding-takeuntil-leaks-fb5182d047ef`
- *Comprehensive Guide to Higher-Order RxJS Mapping Operators: switchMap, mergeMap, concatMap (and exhaustMap)*, Angular University, 2023, `https://blog.angular-university.io/rxjs-higher-order-mapping`

Questions

Answer the following questions as best as possible to ensure you've understood the key concepts from this chapter without googling anything. Do you know if you got all the answers right? Visit `https://angularforenterprise.com/self-assessment` for more:

1. What is a resolve guard?
2. What are the benefits of router orchestration?
3. What is an auxiliary route?
4. How does NgRx differ from using RxJS/Subject?
5. What's the value of NgRx Data?
6. In `UserTableComponent`, why do we use `readonly isLoadingResults$: BehaviorSubject<Boolean>` over a simple Boolean to drive the loading spinner?

Join our community on Discord

Join our community's Discord space for discussions with the authors and other readers:

`https://packt.link/AngularEnterpise3e`

10

Releasing to Production with CI/CD

Ship it or it never happened! If you don't publish your code, you create zero value. This motivation to ship your work is prevalent in many industries. However, delivering a piece of work to someone else or opening it up to public scrutiny can be terrifying. In software engineering, delivering anything is difficult; delivering something to production is even more difficult.

Check out my 2018 talk, *Ship It or It Never Happened: The Power of Docker, Heroku, and CircleCI*, at `https://bit.ly/ship-it-or-it-never-happened`.

We live in an era of moving fast and breaking things. However, the latter part of that statement rarely works in an enterprise. You can live on the edge and adopt the YOLO lifestyle, but this doesn't make good business sense.

```
--yolo          Skips cleanup and testing
```

Figure 10.1: A creative CLI option for a tool

In an enterprise project, code has to go through numerous quality gates before it can be merged. In this chapter, we will cover **Continuous Integration** (**CI**) pipelines leveraging GitHub flow and CircleCI, which help teams achieve frequent, reliable, high-quality, and flexible releases.

Frequent and reliable releases are only possible if we have a set of automated tests that can quickly verify the correctness of our code for us. Automated testing is critical to ensure your changes don't introduce regressions. So, we will go over the importance of writing unit tests and **end-to-end (e2e)** tests with Cypress.

To move fast without breaking things, we need to implement **Continuous Deployment (CD)** using DevOps best practices such as **Infrastructure as Code (IaC)**, so we can verify the correctness of our running code more often.

In this chapter, we will cover deploying Angular apps using CLI tools, then go over a Docker-based approach to implement IaC that can be run on most CI services and cloud providers, allowing you to achieve repeatable builds and deployments from any CI environment to any cloud provider. Working with flexible tools, you will avoid overspecializing in one service and keep your configuration management skills relevant across different CI services.

This book leverages CircleCI as the CI server. Other notable CI servers are Jenkins, Azure DevOps, and the built-in mechanisms within GitLab and GitHub.

This chapter covers:

- Automated testing
- Continuous integration
- Deploying to the cloud
- DevOps
- Containerizing web apps using Docker
- Working with containers in the cloud
- Continuous deployment
- Code coverage reports

Technical requirements

The following software is required to follow along with this chapter:

- Docker Desktop Community version 4+
- Docker Engine CE version 24+
- CircleCI account

- Vercel account
- Firebase account
- Coveralls account

The most up-to-date versions of the sample code for the book are on GitHub at the repositories linked in the following list. The repository contains the final and completed state of the code. Follow the instructions below to find out how to verify your progress as you go through the sections of this chapter.

For *Chapter 10*:

1. Clone the repositories `https://github.com/duluca/local-weather-app` and `https://github.com/duluca/lemon-mart`.
2. Execute `npm install` on the root folder to install dependencies.

   `package.json` contains builds scripts.

   Note that the `.circleci` folder contains extra YAML files.

For **local-weather-app**:

a. `.circleci/config.stage4.yml` represents a simple CI pipeline.
b. `.circleci/config.stage9.yml` adds CD with target deployment to Vercel.
c. `.circleci/config.yml` shows an advanced pipeline with parallel builds and automated Cypress tests.

For **lemon-mart**:

a. `.circleci/config.stage9.yml` adds CD with target deployment to Vercel.
b. `.circleci/config.docker-integration.yml` demonstrates a container within a container setup with multi-stage Dockerfiles and an AWS ECS Fargate deployment.
c. `.circleci/config.yml` shows an advanced pipeline with parallel builds and automated Cypress tests.

Beware that the source code provided in the book and the version on GitHub will likely differ. Cloud services are ever-evolving and changing. If you find errors or have questions, please create an issue or submit a pull request on GitHub.

First, let's understand why automated testing is critical to delivering quality solutions via CI/CD pipelines.

Automated testing

As developers, we integrate code from various sources into our solutions. This can be from coffee-fueled, long, and tiring code sessions, a copy-pasted StackOverflow answer, a snippet from a blog post, an npm package, or a major library like Angular. We are expected to deliver quality results within the confines of an estimate we threw out there. In these conditions, bugs inevitably end up in our code. When deadlines, ambition, or ill-fated architectural decisions intersect with the regular cadence of coding, things only get worse.

Automated tests ensure that the code we write is correct and it stays correct. We rely on CI/CD pipelines for repeatable processes that are not prone to human error, but the pipeline is only as good as the quality of the automated tests we write.

Angular has two main categories of tests, unit and e2e tests. Unit tests are meant to be fast and easy to create and execute, and e2e tests are slower and more expensive. However, there's a problem: Angular unit tests are not unit tests.

To understand why, we need a deep dive into unit testing fundamentals to familiarize you with the benefits of test-driven development and cover principles like FIRST and SOLID.

Unit testing

Unit testing is crucial to ensure that the behavior of your application doesn't unintentionally change over time. Unit tests will enable you and your team to continue making changes to your application without introducing changes to previously verified functionality. Developers write unit tests, where each test is scoped to test only the code in the **Function Under Test** (**FUT**) or **Class Under Test** (**CUT**). Unit tests should be plentiful, automated, and fast. You should write unit tests alongside the original code. If they are separated from the implementation, even by a day or two, you will start forgetting the details of your code. Because of that, you may forget to write tests for potential edge cases.

Unit tests should adhere to the FIRST principle:

- Fast
- Isolated
- Repeatable
- Self-verifying
- Timely

A unit test should be fast, taking only milliseconds to run, so we can have thousands of them running in just a few minutes. For fast tests to be possible, a unit test should be isolated. It shouldn't talk to a database, make requests over the network, or interact with the DOM. Isolated tests are going to be repeatable so that every run of the test returns the same result. Predictability means we can assert the correctness of a test without relying on any outside environment, which makes our tests self-verifying. As mentioned earlier, you should write unit tests promptly; otherwise, you lose the benefits of writing unit tests.

It is possible to adhere to the FIRST principle if your tests focus only on a single FUT/CUT. But what about other classes, services, or parameters we must pass into the FUT/CUT? A unit test can isolate the behavior of the FUT/CUT by leveraging test doubles. A test double allows us to control outside dependencies, so instead of injecting an `HttpService` to your component, you may inject a fake or mocked `HttpService`. Using test doubles, we can control the effects of outside dependencies and create fast and repeatable tests.

How much testing is enough testing? You should have at least as much test code as production code. If you don't, then you're nowhere near writing enough tests.

See the *Further reading* section for literature going back 20+ years on this.

Unit tests aren't the only kind of tests you can create, but they are by far the kind you should create the most of. Consider the three kinds of tests you can create: unit, integration, and UI.

As we've said, unit tests only focus on one FUT/CUT at a time. Integration tests test the integration of various components so that they can include database calls, network requests, and interaction with the DOM. Due to their nature, integration tests are slow to run and must be frequently maintained. Increases in runtime and maintenance mean that integration tests are more expensive than unit tests over time. UI tests test the application as if a user were using it, filling in fields, clicking buttons, and observing the expected outcome.

You may imagine that these tests are the slowest and most fragile kind of tests. The UI of an application changes frequently, and it is very tough to create repeatable tests with UI testing.

We can leverage integration and UI testing to create acceptance tests. Acceptance tests are written to automate the business acceptance of our functionality. Angular's e2e tests are a way to create acceptance tests.

We can visualize the pros and cons of the three major classes of automated testing with Mike Cohn's testing pyramid, shown as follows:

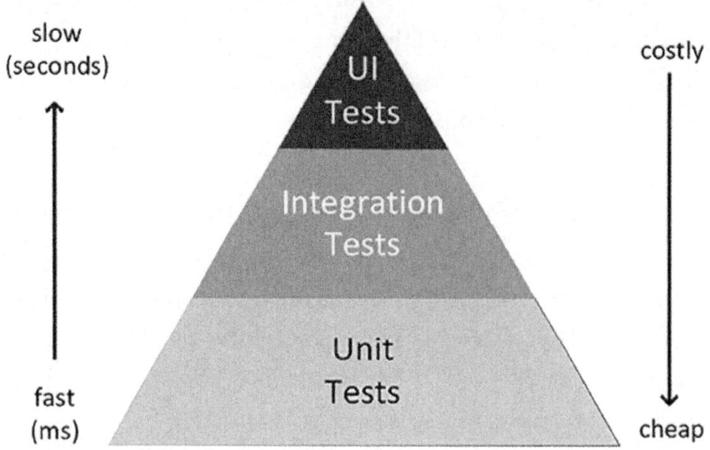

Figure 10.2: Mike Cohn's testing pyramid

The testing pyramid effectively summarizes the relative amount of tests of each kind we should create for our applications while considering their speed and cost.

Given the description and expectations of unit tests, you can now begin understanding why **Angular unit tests are not really unit tests**. As I explained in the *Component architecture* section of *Chapter 1, Angular's Architecture and Concepts*, an Angular component consists of a component class and a template. To truly test a component, we must interact with the DOM. This is why Angular tests must utilize `TestBed` to execute. Further, the dependency injection can be very cumbersome to configure and mock. Ultimately, `TestBed` is slow and fragile compared to true unit tests.

Consider using Spectator to simplify your Angular tests. Spectator aims to help you get rid of all the boilerplate grunt work, focusing on readable and streamlined unit tests.

More info can be found at `https://github.com/ngneat/spectator`.

Standalone components are much easier to configure because they define their dependencies, and we no longer need to introduce modules to `TestBed`.

What does all this mean for Angular? Within this reality, unit testing a component is a waste of time. You should extract all business logic into services and functions and test those thoroughly. Hopefully, future updates to the Angular unit testing setup will change this situation.

Cypress component tests are a great way to integration test individual components' functionality. Follow the instructions in the next section to set Cypress up for your project.

More information about component testing is at `https://docs.cypress.io/guides/component-testing/angular/overview`.

Beginning with Angular 17.1, you can swap out the Karma test runner with the modern **Web Test Runner**. You can set it up with the following instructions:

```
$ npm i -D @web/test-runner
```

Update `angular.json` with:

```
"test": {
  "builder": "@angular-devkit/build-angular:web-test-runner"
}
```

You can read more at `https://modern-web.dev/docs/test-runner/overview`.

To test UI and template logic, Angular e2e tests will deliver the best bang for the buck, and now you can configure Cypress as the default e2e provider for your application.

Cypress e2e tests

While unit tests focus on isolating the CUT, e2e tests are about integration testing. I highly recommend that you configure Cypress as your e2e provider by executing:

```
$ npx ng add @cypress/schematic
```

You can read more about the Cypress integration at `https://www.npmjs.com/package/@cypress/schematic`.

Cypress allows you to easily create tests for your modern web applications, debug them visually, and automatically run them in your CI builds. You can read more about Cypress at `https://www.cypress.io/`.

e2e tests allow you to write **Automated Acceptance Tests (AATs)** from the perspective of a user interacting with your application in a browser. Cypress tests are easy to create and run. By using the `data-testid` attribute on HTML components, you can make them less fragile.

You can find sample Cypress tests for **local-weather-app** and **lemon-mart** under the `cypress` folder.

You can execute the tests in development by executing:

```
$ npx ng e2e
```

For CI, you can use the following commands:

```
$ npx ng run local-weather-app:cypress-run
$ npx ng run lemon-mart:cypress-run
```

In `local-weather-app`, check out the `cypress/e2e/app.cy.ts` file:

cypress/e2e/app.cy.ts

```
import '../support/commands'

describe('LocalCast Weather', () => {
  beforeEach(() => {
    cy.visit('/')
  })

  it('has the correct title', () => {
    cy.byTestId('title').should('have.text', 'LocalCast Weather')
  })
})
```

In the `cypress/support/commands.ts file`, I implemented a helper function called `byTestId`, which finds an HTML element containing the `data-testid` attribute with the given name. In this case, `cy.byTestId("title")` will find the following element:

src/app/app.component.ts

```
<span data-testid="title">LocalCast Weather</span>
```

The test will work even if the element moves around on the page. Using test IDs makes it easy and convenient to write more dependable tests.

Building robust and maintainable e2e code requires some additional concepts like Page Objects. You can learn more about Page Objects at `https://docs.cypress.io/guides/end-to-end-testing/protractor-to-cypress#Using-Page-Objects` and other best practices at `https://docs.cypress.io/guides/references/best-practices`.

Next, let's set up CI to ensure that our tests always run before we deploy the app to production.

Continuous integration

Before pushing your code to production, you should enable CI. This simple tool helps ensure we don't ship broken code to production by executing automated tasks, including the execution of tests, every time we make changes to our code.

CircleCI

CircleCI makes it easy to get started, with a free tier and excellent documentation for beginners and pros alike. If you have unique enterprise needs, CircleCI can be brought on-premises, behind corporate firewalls, or as a private deployment in the cloud.

CircleCI has pre-baked build environments for the virtual configuration of free setups, but it can also run builds using Docker containers, making it a solution that scales to the user's skills and needs:

1. Create a CircleCI account at `https://circleci.com/`.
2. Navigate to **Projects** to add a new project.
3. Search for `local-weather-app` and click on **Set Up Project**.
4. Follow the on-screen prompts to create a sample `.yml` file. Hello World or Node.js works, but you will replace the content anyway.

This section uses the **local-weather-app** repo. The `config.yml` file for this section is named `.circleci/config.stage4.yml`.

5. Copy the following .yml content into the file:

```
.circleci/config.yml
version: 2.1
orbs:
  browser-tools: circleci/browser-tools@1
  cypress: cypress-io/cypress@3
commands:
  install:
    description: 'Install project dependencies'
    steps:
      - checkout
      - restore_cache:
          keys:
            - node_modules-{{ checksum "package-lock.json" }}
      - run: npm install
      - save_cache:
          key: node_modules-{{ checksum "package-lock.json" }}
          paths:
            - node_modules
  lint:
    description: 'Check for code style and linting errors'
    steps:
      - run: npm run style
      - run: npm run lint
  build_and_test:
    description: 'Builds and tests Angular project'
    steps:
      - run: npx ng build --configuration production
      - attach_workspace:
          at: ~/
      - browser-tools/install-chrome
      - browser-tools/install-chromedriver
      - run: npx ng test --watch=false --code-coverage
  store:
    description: 'Stores build_and_test artifacts'
    steps:
      - store_test_results:
```

```
          path: ./test_results
      - store_artifacts:
          path: ./coverage
jobs:
  run_build_and_test:
    docker:
      - image: cimg/node:lts-browsers
    working_directory: ~/repo
    steps:
      - install
      - cypress/install
      - lint
      - build_and_test
      - run: npx ng run local-weather-app:cypress-run
      - store
workflows:
  build-and-test:
    jobs:
      - run_build_and_test
```

6. Select **Commit** and **Run**.
7. CircleCI should run on a new branch.

If everything goes well, you should have a passing, *green* build. If not, you will see a failed, *red* build.

When you have a green build, you can leverage CircleCI to enforce the execution of your automated pipeline with every code push. GitHub flow allows us to control how code flows into our repositories.

GitHub flow

The main reason we're developing software is to deliver value. In automating the way we deliver software, we are creating a value delivery stream. It is easy to deliver broken software; however, to reliably deliver value, each change to the code base should flow through a stream of checks and balances.

With control gates, we can enforce standards, make our quality control process repeatable for every team member, and have the ability to isolate changes. If something goes wrong or the work doesn't live up to your standards, you can easily discard the proposed changes and restart.

GitHub flow is an essential part of defining a value delivery stream and implementing control gates. As GitHub puts it, *"GitHub flow is a lightweight, branch-based workflow that supports teams and projects where deployments are made regularly."*

GitHub flow consists of six steps, as shown in the following graphic from GitHub:

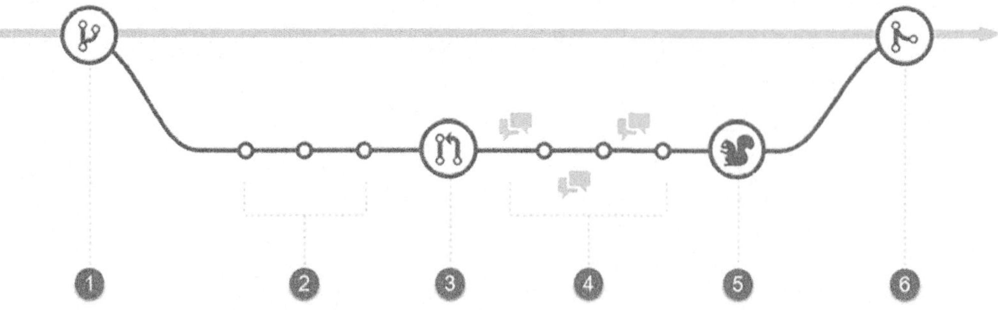

Figure 10.3: GitHub flow diagram

1. **Branch** – always add new code for a bug or a feature in a new branch
2. **Commit** – make multiple commits to your branch
3. **Create a pull request** – signal the readiness of your work to your team members and view CI results in a pull request
4. **Discuss and review** – request a review of your code changes, address general or line-level comments, and make necessary modifications
5. **Deploy** – optionally test your code on a test server or staging server with the ability to roll back to the main branch
6. **Merge** – apply your changes to the main branch

You can use GitHub flow to ensure that only high-quality code ends up in the main branch. A solid foundation sets other team members up for success when making changes. You must restrict push access to the main branch to enforce GitHub flow.

Let's enable branch protection for the main branch:

1. Navigate to the GitHub **Settings** tab for your project.
2. Select **Branches** from the left navigation pane.
3. If a rule exists for your main branch, click the **Edit** or **Add rule** button.
4. Enter `main` as the branch name pattern.

5. Enable the following options:

   a. Require a pull request before merging.

   b. Require approvals from at least one peer.

   c. Dismiss stale pull request approvals.

   d. Require status checks to pass before merging.

   e. Require branches to be up to date before merging.

   f. Require linear history.

6. Search for `CircleCI` and select the CI job that must succeed, in this case: `run_build_and_test`

7. After you've saved your changes, you should see your new rule on the **Branches** page as shown:

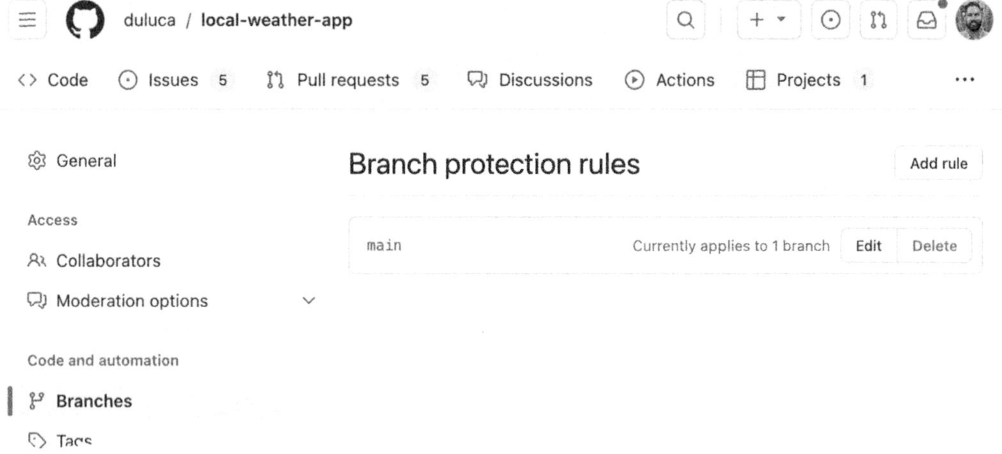

Figure 10.4: GitHub Branches

You are no longer able to commit code to your main branch directly. To commit code, you first need to create a branch from the main branch, commit your changes to the new branch, and create a pull request using the new branch when you're ready. If you're unfamiliar with `git` commands, you can use GitHub Desktop to assist you with these operations. See the handy **Branch** menu in GitHub Desktop here:

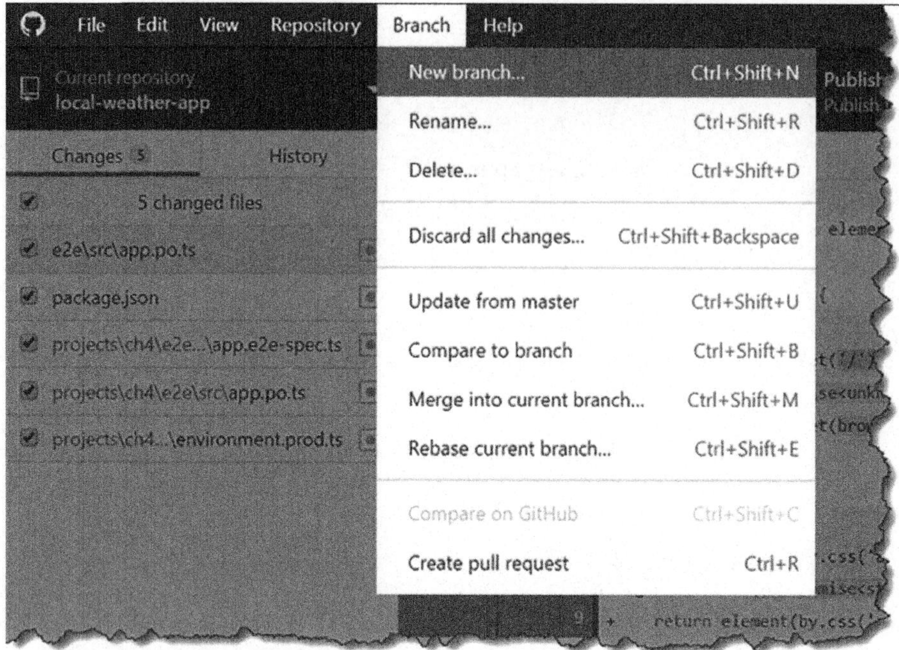

Figure 10.5: GitHub Desktop Branch menu

After creating a pull request, you can now observe checks running against your branch. Now that we have CircleCI configured, if everything went well, you should be able to merge a pull request, as shown:

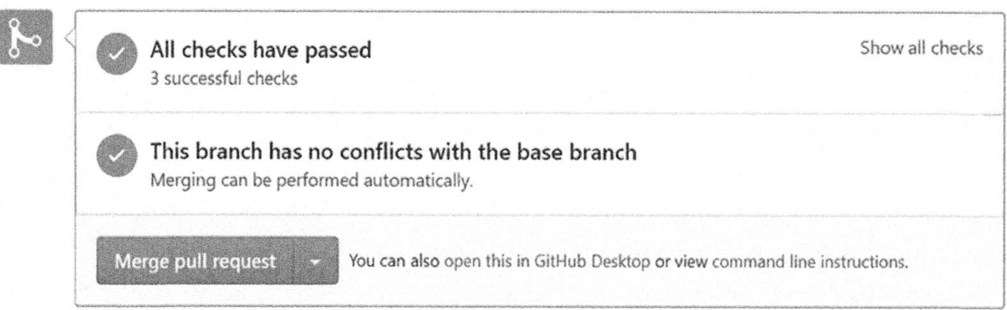

Figure 10.6: GitHub.com status checks passing

When the checks fail, you are forced to fix any issues before you can merge the new code. Also, you may run into merge conflicts if a team member merged to the main branch while you were working on your branch. In this case, you may use GitHub Desktop's **Update from master** feature for your branch to catch up with the latest main branch.

Observe the state of a failing pull request in the following image:

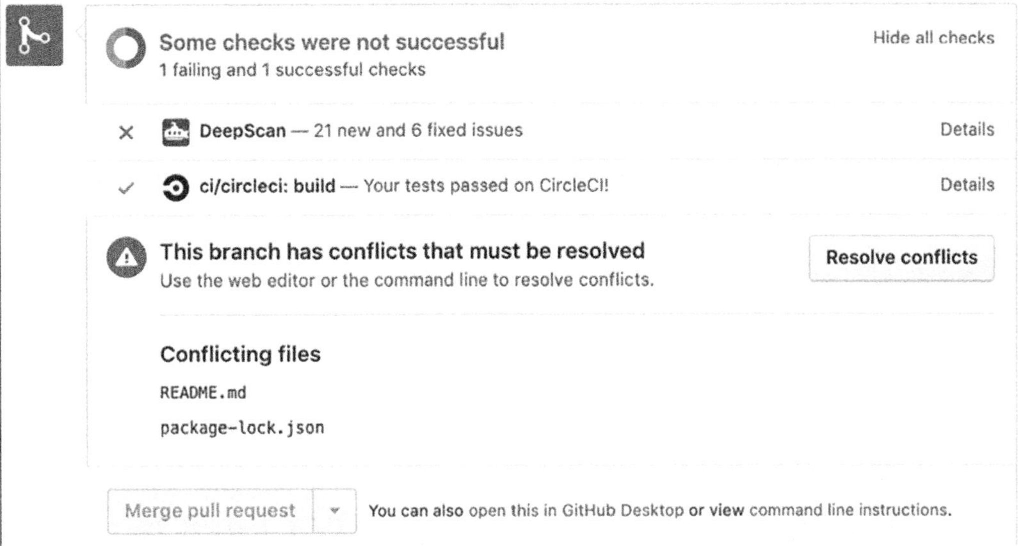

Figure 10.7: GitHub.com status checks failing

Note that I have an additional check, DeepScan, which runs additional tests against my code base. You can register your repository with DeepScan at `https://deepscan.io`. Later in the chapter, I demonstrate how you can enforce unit test code coverage using Coveralls.

For more information, refer to `https://guides.github.com/introduction/flow`.

Now that we have ensured that our automated checks are being enforced, we can be reasonably sure that we won't push a broken app to production. Next, let's learn how we can deploy our app to the cloud.

Deploying to the cloud

If delivering something to production is difficult from a coding perspective, it is very complicated to do it right from an infrastructure perspective. Deploying solutions in the full-fledged versions of Azure, AWS, and Google Cloud is complicated. To deliver quick results, we can leverage cloud services that can serve the `dist` folder of our Angular app within minutes.

One such service is Vercel, and another is Firebase, which can leverage the `ng deploy` command.

Vercel

Vercel, `https://vercel.com`, is a multi-cloud service that enables real-time global deployments of applications directly from the CLI. Vercel works with static files, Node.js, PHP, Go applications, and any custom stack of software you're willing to write a custom builder for, making it quite straightforward. Vercel has a free tier that you can use to deploy the `dist` folder of your Angular applications very quickly.

Install the `vercel` package to your project and run the `login` command:

```
$ npm i -D vercel
$ npx vercel login
```

Follow the on-screen prompts to complete the login process. Now, let's configure the `publish` script.

Deploying static files

After you build an Angular project, the build output resides in the `dist` folder. The files in this folder are considered static files; all a web server needs to do is deliver these files to a client browser, unmodified, and then the browser executes your code dynamically.

This means that any web server can serve up your Angular project. However, `vercel` makes it exceedingly easy and free to pull off.

This section uses the **local-weather-app** repository.

Let's begin deploying your Angular app using Vercel's static file hosting capabilities:

1. Add two new scripts to `package.json`, as shown:

```
package.json
...
"prevercel:publish": "npm run build:prod",
"vercel:publish":
  "vercel deploy --prod dist/local-weather-app --yes"
```

2. Execute `npm run vercel:publish`.
3. Follow the on-screen commands to accept first-use settings.

In the terminal window, observe that the Angular project is built first and then uploaded to vercel:

```
$ npm run vercel:publish
...
Build at: 2023-11-07T03:51:23.229Z - Hash: d6b1388088df7136 - Time:
5403ms
...
✅ Production: https://local-weather-hhk9xi3wz-duluca.vercel.app
[1s] to clipboard] [4s]
```

4. Follow the URL displayed on the screen to see that your app has been successfully deployed.

And you're done! Congratulations, your Angular app is live on the internet!

Firebase

Firebase, `https://firebase.google.com/`, is an app development platform that helps you build and grow apps and games users love. It is backed by Google and trusted by millions of businesses around the world.

In the Firebase authentication recipe section of *Chapter 6, Implementing Role-Based Navigation*, you created a Firebase app for LemonMart and deployed your app using **firebase deploy**. We will leverage the account you created to deploy LemonMart to Firebase hosting using the new `ng deploy` command instead.

ng deploy

`ng deploy` is a new CLI command that helps cloud services offer seamless integration with Angular, so you can easily deploy your app to the cloud.

Now let's configure the LemonMart project using `@angular/fire`.

This section uses the **lemon-mart** repository.

Execute the following command and make sure to select `ng deploy -- hosting`:

```
$ npx ng add @angular/fire
◉ ng deploy -- hosting
```

This will create a deploy configuration in angular.json and add or update existing Firebase configuration files.

For LemonMart, I modified angular.json so it would automatically build using the Firebase authentication mode:

```
angular.json
...
"deploy": {
  "builder": "@angular/fire:deploy",
  "options": {
    "version": 2,
    "browserTarget": "lemon-mart:build:firebase"
  }
}
```

The Firebase configuration is defined under the **Configurations** options, and it uses environment.firebase.ts to build the app.

I also modified firebase.json to deploy dist/lemon-mart, because the repository is configured as a multi-project Angular app. However, you shouldn't need to modify the auto-generated files.

Execute the following command to deploy:

```
$ npx ng deploy
...
Build at: 2023-11-07T04:27:36.842Z - Hash: ad999f95a270f4e6 - Time: 14141ms
=== Deploying to 'lemon-mart-007'...
...
✓ Deploy complete!

Project Console: https://console.firebase.google.com/project/lemon-mart-007/overview
Hosting URL: https://lemon-mart-007.web.app
```

Follow the URL on the screen to see that your app has been successfully deployed.

ng deploy offers a better integrated and simpler option compared to using platform-specific CLI commands. Working with CLI commands is great, but one command that works on one machine can easily fail on another. IaC is the only way high-performing enterprise teams can deliver high-quality code with speed. However, to get there, we first need to understand what DevOps is.

DevOps

DevOps is the marriage of development and operations. It is well established for development that code repositories like Git track every code change. In operations, there has long been a wide variety of techniques to track changes to environments, including scripts and various tools that aim to automate the provisioning of operating systems and servers.

How often have you heard the saying, "It works on my machine"? Developers often use that line as a joke. Still, it is often the case that software that works perfectly well on a test server ends up running into issues on a production server due to minor differences in configuration.

Earlier, we discussed how GitHub flow can enable us to create a value delivery stream. We always branch from the main branch before making a change, enforce that change to go through our CI pipeline, and, once we're reasonably sure that our code works, merge back to the main branch. See the following diagram:

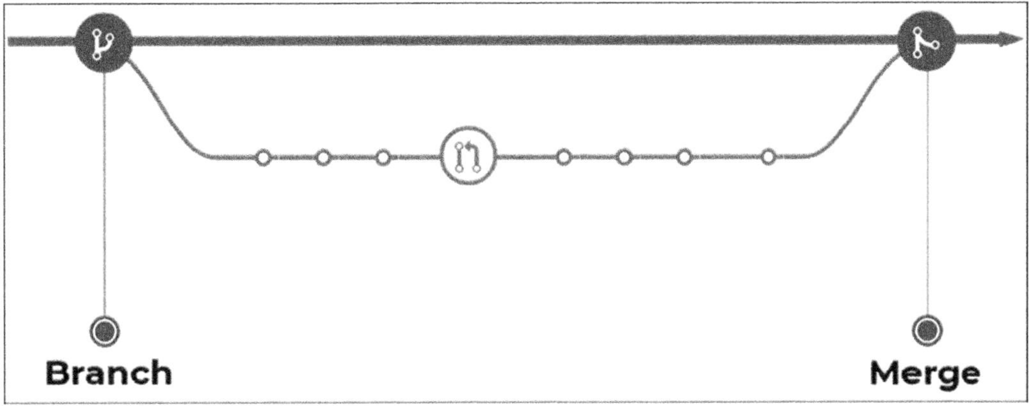

Figure 10.8: Branching and merging

Remember, your main branch should always be deployable, and you should frequently merge your work with the main branch.

Docker allows us to define the software and the specific configuration parameters that our code depends on in a declarative manner using a special file named a Dockerfile. Similarly, CircleCI allows us to define the configuration of our CI environment in a `config.yml` file. By storing our configuration in files, we can check the files alongside our code. We can track changes using Git and enforce them to be verified by our CI pipeline.

By storing the definition of our infrastructure in code, we achieve IaC, we also achieve repeatable integration, so no matter what environment we run our infrastructure in, we should be able to stand up our full-stack app with a one-line command.

You may remember that in *Chapter 1, Angular's Architecture and Concepts*, we covered how TypeScript covers the JavaScript feature gap. Like TypeScript, Docker covers the configuration gap, as demonstrated in the following diagram:

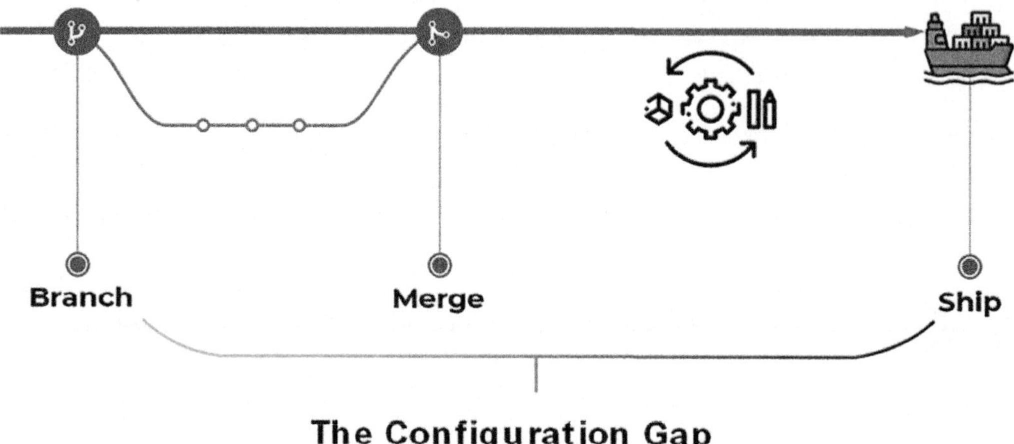

Figure 10.9: Covering the configuration gap

By using Docker, we can be reasonably sure that our code, which worked on our machine during testing, will work the same way when we ship it.

In summary, DevOps brings operations closer to development, where it is cheaper to make changes and resolve issues. So, DevOps is primarily a developer's responsibility, but it is also a way of thinking that the operations team must be willing to support. Let's dive deeper into Docker.

Containerizing web apps using Docker

Docker, which can be found at `https://docker.io`, is an open platform for developing, shipping, and running applications. Docker combines a lightweight container virtualization platform with workflows and tooling that help manage and deploy applications. The most obvious difference between **Virtual Machines** (**VMs**) and Docker containers is that VMs are usually dozens of gigabytes in size and require gigabytes of memory, whereas containers take up megabytes in terms of disk and memory size requirements. Furthermore, the Docker platform abstracts away host **Operating System** (**OS**)-level configuration settings, so every piece of configuration that is needed to successfully run an application is encoded within a human-readable format.

Anatomy of a Dockerfile

A Dockerfile consists of four main parts:

- **FROM** – where we can inherit from Docker's minimal "scratch" image or a pre-existing image
- **SETUP** – where we configure software dependencies to our requirements
- **COPY** – where we copy our built code into the operating environment
- **CMD** – where we specify the commands that will bootstrap the operating environment

Bootstrap refers to a set of initial instructions that describe how a program loads or starts up.

Consider the following visualization of the anatomy of a Dockerfile:

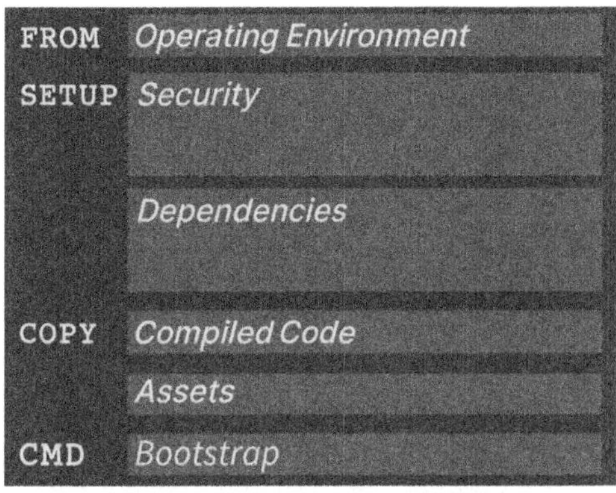

Figure 10.10: Anatomy of a Dockerfile

A concrete representation of a Dockerfile is demonstrated in the following code:

Dockerfile

```
FROM duluca/minimal-nginx-web-server:1-alpine
COPY /dist/local-weather-app /var/www
CMD 'nginx'
```

You can map the `FROM`, `COPY`, and `CMD` parts of the script to the visualization. We inherit from the `duluca/minimal-nginx-web-server` image using the `FROM` command. Then, we copy the compiled result of our app from our development machine or build environment into the image using the `COPY` (or, alternatively, the `ADD`) command. Finally, we instruct the container to execute the nginx web server using the `CMD` (or, alternatively, the `ENTRYPOINT`) command.

Note that the preceding `Dockerfile` doesn't have a distinct `SETUP` part. `SETUP` doesn't map to an actual `Dockerfile` command but represents a collection of commands you can execute to set up your container. In this case, all the necessary setup was done by the base image, so there are no additional commands to run.

Common `Dockerfile` commands are `FROM`, `COPY`, `ADD`, `RUN`, `CMD`, `ENTRYPOINT`, `ENV`, and `EXPOSE`. For the full `Dockerfile` reference, refer to `https://docs.docker.com/engine/reference/builder/`.

The `Dockerfile` describes a new container that inherits from a container named `duluca/minimal-nginx-web-server`. This is a container that I published on Docker Hub, which inherits from the `nginx:alpine` image, which itself inherits from the `alpine` image. The `alpine` image is a minimal Linux operating environment that is only 5 MB in size. The `alpine` image itself inherits from `scratch`, which is an empty image. See the inheritance hierarchy demonstrated in the following diagram:

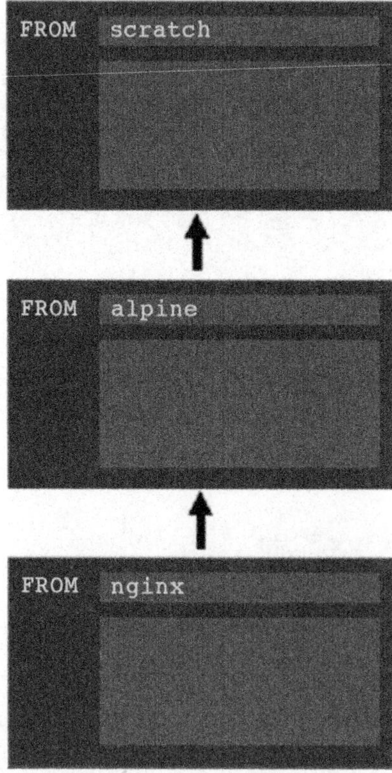

Figure 10.11: Docker inheritance

The `Dockerfile` then copies the contents of the `dist` folder from your development environment into the container's `www` folder, as shown in the following diagram:

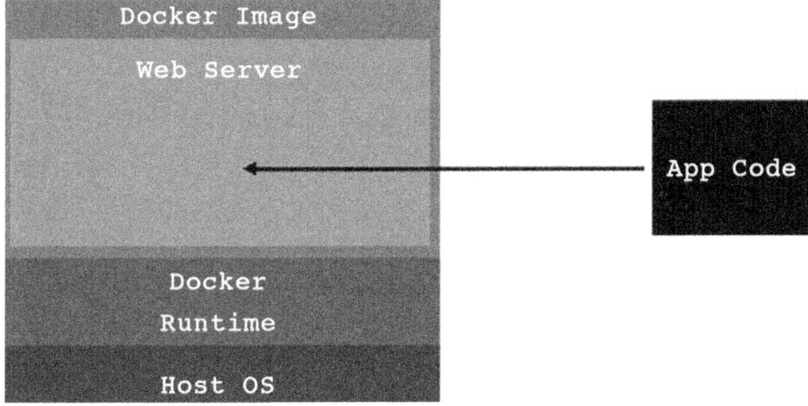

Figure 10.12: Copying code into a containerized web server

In this case, the parent image is configured with an `nginx` server to act as a web server to serve the content inside the `www` folder. At this point, our source code is accessible from the internet but lives inside layers of secure environments. Even if our app has a vulnerability of some kind, it would be tough for an attacker to harm the systems we are operating on. The following diagram demonstrates the layers of security that Docker provides:

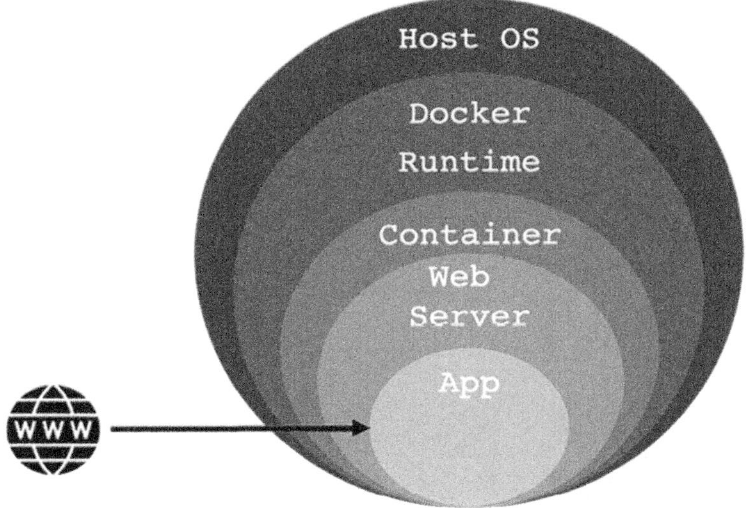

Figure 10.13: Docker security

In summary, at the base layer, our host OS, such as Windows or macOS, runs the Docker runtime, which will be installed in the next section. The Docker runtime can run self-contained Docker images, which the aforementioned Dockerfile defines. `duluca/minimal-nginx-web-server` is based on the lightweight Linux operating system, Alpine. Alpine is a completely pared-down version of Linux that doesn't come with any GUI, drivers, or even most of the CLI tools you may expect from a Linux system. As a result, the OS is only ~5 MB in size. We then inherit from the `nginx` image, which installs the web server, which itself is around a few megabytes in size. Finally, our custom `nginx` configuration is layered over the default image, resulting in a tiny ~7 MB image. The `nginx` server is configured to serve the contents of the `/var/www` folder. In the `Dockerfile`, we merely copy the contents of the `/dist` folder in our development environment and place it into the `/var/www` folder. We will later build and execute this image, which will run our `nginx` web server containing the output of our `dist` folder. I have published a similar image named `duluca/minimal-node-web-server`, which clocks in at ~15 MB.

`duluca/minimal-node-web-server` can be more straightforward to work with, especially if you're not familiar with `nginx`. It relies on an `Express.js` server to serve static content. Most cloud providers provide concrete examples using Node and Express, which can help you narrow down any errors. In addition, `duluca/minimal-node-web-server` has HTTPS redirection support baked into it. You can spend a lot of time trying to set up an `nginx` proxy to do the same thing when all you need to do is set the `ENFORCE_HTTPS` environment variable in your `Dockerfile`. See the following sample Dockerfile:

```
Dockerfile
FROM duluca/minimal-node-web-server:lts-alpine
WORKDIR /usr/src/app
COPY dist/local-weather-app public
ENTRYPOINT [ "npm", "start" ]
ENV ENFORCE_HTTPS=xProto
```

You can read more about the options `minimal-node-web-server` provides at `https://github.com/duluca/minimal-node-web-server`.

As we've now seen, the beauty of Docker is that you can navigate to `https://hub.docker.com`, search for `duluca/minimal-nginx-web-server` or `duluca/minimal-node-web-server`, read its `Dockerfile`, and trace its origins all the way back to the original base image that is the foundation of the web server. I encourage you to vet every Docker image you use in this manner to understand what exactly it brings to the table for your needs.

You may either find it overkill or that it has features you never knew about that can make your life a lot easier.

Note that the parent images should pull a specific tag of `duluca/minimal-nginx-web-server`, which is `1-alpine`. Similarly, `duluca/minimal-node-web-server` pulls from `lts-alpine`. These evergreen base packages always contain the latest version 1 of `nginx` and Alpine or an LTS release of Node. In Docker Hub, I have pipelines to automatically update both images when a new base image is published. So, you will get the latest bug fixes and security patches whenever you pull these images.

Having an evergreen dependency tree removes the burden on you as the developer to hunt down the latest version of a Docker image. Alternatively, if you specify a version number, your images will not be subject to any potential breaking changes. However, it is better to remember to test your images after a new build than never update your image and, potentially, deploy compromised software. After all, the web is ever-changing and will not slow down for you to keep your images up to date.

Just like npm packages, Docker can bring great convenience and value, but you must take care to understand the tools you are working with.

Installing Docker

To be able to build and run containers, you must first install the Docker execution environment on your computer. You can download Docker Desktop at `https://www.docker.com/products/docker-desktop/`. Follow the instructions on the screen to complete the installation.

Setting up npm scripts for Docker

Now, let's configure some Docker scripts for your Angular apps that you can use to automate your container's building, testing, and publishing. I have developed a set of scripts called **npm scripts for Docker** that works on Windows 10 and macOS. You can get the latest version of these scripts and automatically configure them in your project by executing the following command.

Run the following command on both the **local-weather-app** and **lemon-mart** projects now!

Install the npm scripts for Docker task:

```
$ npx mrm npm-docker
```

After you execute the mrm scripts, we're ready to take a deep dive into the configuration settings using the Local Weather app as an example.

Building and publishing an image to Docker Hub

Next, let's ensure that your project is configured correctly so we can containerize it, build an executable image, and publish it to Docker Hub, allowing us to access it from any build environment.

This section uses the **local-weather-app** repository.

You will need to take the following steps:

1. Sign up for a Docker Hub account at `https://hub.docker.com/`.
2. Create a public (free) repository for your application.
3. In `package.json`, add or update the `config` property with the following configuration properties:

   package.json

   ```
   ...
   "config": {
     "imageRepo": "[namespace]/[repository]",
     "imageName": "custom_app_name",
     "imagePort": "0000",
     "internalContainerPort": "3000"
   },
   ...
   ```

   `namespace` will be your Docker Hub username. You will define what your repository will be called during creation. An example image `repository` variable should look like `duluca/localcast-weather`. The image name is for easy identification of your container while using Docker commands such as `docker ps`. I will just call mine `localcast-weather`. The `imagePort` property will define which port should be used to expose your application from inside the container. Since we use port `4200` for development, pick a different one, like `8080`. `internalContainerPort` defines the port that your web server is mapped to. This will mostly be port `3000` for Node servers and, for `nginx` servers, `80`. Refer to the documentation of the base container you're using.

4. Let's review the Docker scripts added to `package.json` by the `mrm` task from earlier. The following section presents an annotated version of the scripts added, explaining each entry.

Note that with `npm` scripts, the `pre` and `post` keywords are used to execute helper scripts before or after executing a given script. Scripts are intentionally broken into smaller pieces to make them easier to read and maintain.

- The `build` script is as follows:

package.json

```
...
  "scripts": {
    ...
    "predocker:build": "npm run build",
    "docker:build": "cross-conf-env docker image build --platform
linux/amd64,linux/arm64 . -t $npm_package_config_imageRepo:$npm_
package_version",
    "postdocker:build": "npm run docker:tag",
    ...
```

Note that the following `cross-conf-env` command ensures the script executes equally well in macOS, Linux, and Windows environments.

- `npm run docker:build` will build your Angular application in the `pre` script, then build the Docker image using the `docker image build` command, and tag the image with a version number in the `post` script.

In my project, the `pre` command builds my Angular application in prod mode and runs a test to ensure that I have an optimized build with no failing tests.

My `pre` command looks like this:

```
"predocker:build": "npm run build:prod && npm test --
--watch=false"
```

- The `tag` script is as follows:

package.json

```
    ...
    "docker:tag": " cross-conf-env docker image tag $npm_package_
config_imageRepo:$npm_package_version $npm_package_config_
imageRepo:latest",
    ...
```

- `npm run docker:tag` will tag an already built Docker image using the version number from the `version` property in `package.json` and the latest tag.
- The `stop` script is as follows:

package.json

```
    ...
    "docker:stop": "cross-conf-env docker stop $npm_package_config_
imageName || true",
    ...
```

- `npm run docker:stop` will stop the image if it's currently running, so the `run` script can execute without errors.
- The `run` script is as follows:

package.json

```
    ...
    "docker:run": "run-s -c docker:stop docker:runHelper",
    "docker:runHelper": "cross-conf-env docker run -e NODE_ENV=local
--rm --name $npm_package_config_imageName -d -p $npm_package_config_
imagePort:$npm_package_config_internalContainerPort $npm_package_
config_imageRepo",
    ...
```

Note that the `run-s` and `run-p` commands ship with the `npm-run-all` package to synchronize or parallelize the execution of npm scripts.

- `npm run docker:run` will stop if the image is already running, and then run the newly built version of the image using the `docker run` command. Note that the `imagePort` property is used as the external port of the Docker image, which is mapped to the internal port of the image that the Node.js server listens to, port `3000`.
- The `publish` script is as follows:

```
package.json
    ...
    "predocker:publish": "echo Attention! Ensure `docker login` is
correct.",
    "docker:publish": "cross-conf-env docker image push $npm_
package_config_imageRepo:$npm_package_version",
    "postdocker:publish": "cross-conf-env docker image push $npm_
package_config_imageRepo:latest",
    ...
```

Note that `docker:tag` adds the latest version tag on the container. When we push the latest tags, both tags get pushed simultaneously.

- `npm run docker:publish` will publish a built image to the configured repository, in this case, Docker Hub, using the `docker image push` command.
- First, the versioned image is published, followed by one tagged with `latest` in `post`. The `taillogs` script is as follows:

```
package.json
    ...
    "docker:taillogs": "cross-conf-env docker logs -f $npm_package_
config_imageName",
    ...
```

- `npm run docker:taillogs` will display the internal console logs of a running Docker instance using the `docker log -f` command, a useful tool for debugging your Docker instance.
- The open script is as follows:

```
package.json
    ...
    "docker:open": "sleep 2 && cross-conf-env open-cli http://
localhost:$npm_package_config_imagePort",
    ...
```

- `npm run docker:open` will wait for 2 seconds, accounting for latency, and then launch the browser with the correct URL for your application using the `imagePort` property.

- The debug script is as follows:

```
package.json
    ...
    "predocker:debug": "run-s docker:build docker:run",
    "docker:debug": "run-s -cs docker:open:win docker:open:mac
docker:taillogs"
  },
...
```

- `npm run docker:debug` will build your image and run an instance of it in `pre`, open the browser, and then start displaying the internal logs of the container.

5. Customize the pre-build script to build your angular app in production mode and execute unit tests before building the image:

```
package.json
    "build": "ng build",
    "build:prod": "ng build --prod",
    "predocker:build": "npm run build:prod && npm test --
--watch=false",
```

Note that `ng build` is provided with the `--prod` argument, which achieves two things: the size of the app is optimized to be significantly smaller with **Ahead-of-Time (AOT)** compilation to increase runtime performance, and the configuration items defined in `src/environments/environment.prod.ts` are used.

6. Update `src/environments/environment.prod.ts` to look like you're using your own `appId` from `OpenWeather`:

```
export const environment = {
  production: true,
  appId: '01ff1xxxxxxxxxxxxxxxxxxxxx',
  username: 'localcast',
  baseUrl: 'https://',
  geonamesApi: 'secure',
}
```

We are modifying how `npm test` is executed, so the tests are run only once and the tool stops executing. The `--watch=false` option is provided to achieve this behavior, as opposed to the development-friendly default continuous execution behavior.

7. Create a new file named `Dockerfile` with no file extensions in the project root.
8. Implement or replace the contents of the `Dockerfile`, as shown here:

```
Dockerfile
FROM duluca/minimal-node-web-server:lts-alpine
WORKDIR /usr/src/app
COPY dist/local-weather-app public
```

Be sure to inspect the contents of your `dist` folder to ensure you're copying the correct folder, which contains the `index.html` file at its root.

9. Execute `npm run predocker:build` and see that it runs without errors in the Terminal to ensure that your application changes have been successful.
10. Execute `npm run docker:build` and see that it runs without errors in the Terminal to ensure that your image builds successfully.
    - While you can run any of the provided scripts individually, you really only need to remember two of them going forward:
    - `npm run docker:debug` will test, build, tag, run, tail, and launch your containerized app in a new browser window for testing.
    - `npm run docker:publish` will publish the image you just built and test to the online Docker repository.
11. Execute `docker:debug` in your Terminal:

```
$ npm run docker:debug
```

- A successful `docker:debug` run should result in a new in-focus browser window with your application and the server logs being tailed in the Terminal, as follows:

```
Current Environment: local.
Server listening on port 3000 inside the container
```

```
Attention: To access server, use http://localhost:EXTERNAL_PORT
EXTERNAL_PORT is specified with 'docker run -p EXTERNAL_PORT:3000'.
See 'package.json->imagePort' for the default port.
GET / 304 2.194 ms - -
GET /runtime-es2015.js 304 0.371 ms - -
GET /polyfills-es2015.js 304 0.359 ms - -
GET /styles-es2015.js 304 0.839 ms - -
GET /vendor-es2015.js 304 0.789 ms - -
GET /main-es2015.js 304 0.331 ms - -
```

You should always run `docker ps` to check whether your image is running, when it was last updated, and whether it clashes with any existing images claiming the same port.

12. Execute `docker:publish` in your Terminal:

```
$ npm run docker:publish
```

- You should observe a successful run in the Terminal window like this:

```
The push refers to a repository [docker.io/duluca/localcast-weather]
60f66aaaaa50: Pushed
...
latest: digest:
sha256:b680970d76769cf12cc48f37391d8a542fe226b66d9a6f8a7ac81ad77be4f58b size: 2827
```

Over time, your local Docker cache may grow significantly; for example, it's reached roughly 40 GB on my laptop over two years. You can use the `docker image prune` and `docker container prune` commands to reduce your cache size. For more detailed information, refer to the documentation at `https://docs.docker.com/config/pruning`.

By defining a `Dockerfile` and scripting our use of it, we created living documentation in our code base. We have achieved DevOps and closed the configuration gap.

Make sure to containerize **lemon-mart** like you've done with **local-weather-app** and verify your work by executing `npm run docker:debug`.

VS Code offers a visual way to interact with npm scripts. Let's take a look at VS Code's npm script support next.

npm scripts in VS Code

VS Code provides support for npm scripts out of the box. In order to enable npm Script Explorer, open the VS Code settings and ensure that the `"npm.enableScriptExplorer": true` property is present. Once you do, you will see an expandable title named **NPM SCRIPTS** in the **Explorer** pane, as highlighted with an arrow in the following screenshot:

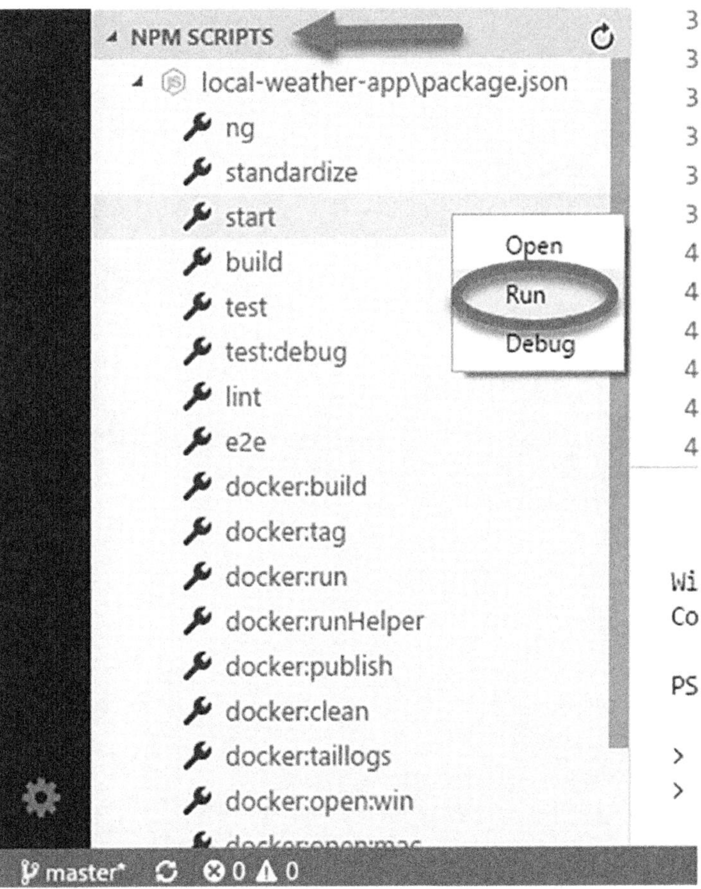

Figure 10.14: NPM SCRIPTS in VS Code

You can click on any script to launch the line that contains the script in `package.json` or right-click and select **Run** to execute the script.

Let's look at an easier way to interact with Docker next.

Docker extensions in VS Code

Another way to interact with Docker images and containers is through VS Code. If you have installed the `ms-azuretools.vscode-docker` Docker extension from Microsoft, as suggested in *Chapter 2, Forms, Observables, Signals, and Subjects*, you can identify the extension by the Docker logo on the left-hand navigation menu in VS Code, as circled in white in the following screenshot:

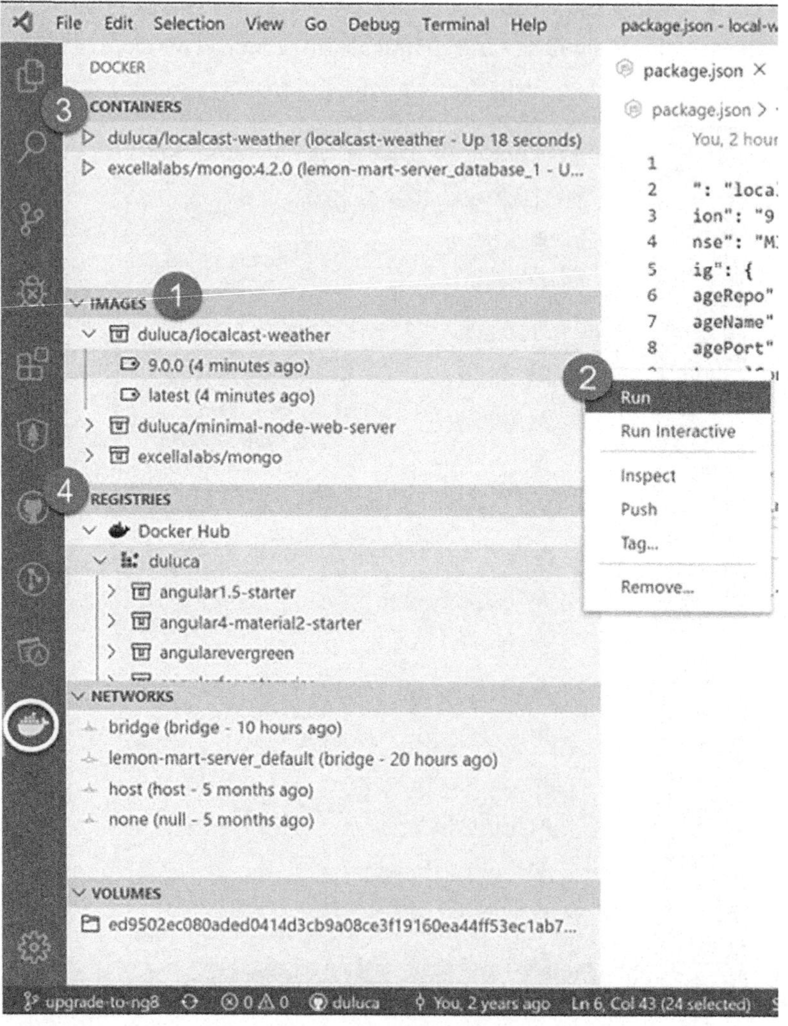

Figure 10.15: Docker extension in VS Code

Let's go through some of the functionality provided by the extension. Refer to the preceding screenshot and the numbered steps in the following list for a quick explanation:

1. **Images** contain a list of all the container snapshots on your system.
2. Right-clicking on a Docker image creates a context menu to run various operations like **Run**, **Push**, and **Tag**.
3. **Containers** list all executable Docker containers on your system, which you can start, stop, or attach to.
4. **Registries** display the registries that you're configured to connect to, such as Docker Hub or **AWS Elastic Container Registry** (**AWS ECR**).

While the extension makes it easier to interact with Docker, the **npm scripts for Docker** (which you configured using the `mrm` task) automate many of the chores related to building, tagging, and testing an image. They are both cross-platform and will work equally well in a CI environment.

The `npm run docker:debug` script automates a lot of chores to verify that you have a good image build!

Now let's learn about deploying our containers to the cloud and later achieve CD.

Working with containers in the cloud

One of the advantages of using Docker is that we can deploy it on any number of operating environments, from personal PCs to servers and cloud providers. In any case, we expect our container to function the same across the board.

Earlier in the chapter, I mentioned that working with full-fledged cloud providers like Azure, AWS, and Google Cloud is complicated. To deploy your containers in the cloud you will likely need to use one of these providers. Now and then, a provider that offers easy and seamless container hosting pops up, but over the years, these options have disappeared.

Cloud services offer a wide variety of methods for running containers ranging from managed to unmanaged solutions. The key difference between managed and unmanaged is the level of control and responsibility shared between the user and the cloud provider. This is referred to as the Shared Responsibility Model. In a managed configuration, you concede more control and responsibility of the underlying infrastructure to the cloud provider. This consequently results in increased security and usually a cheaper cloud bill.

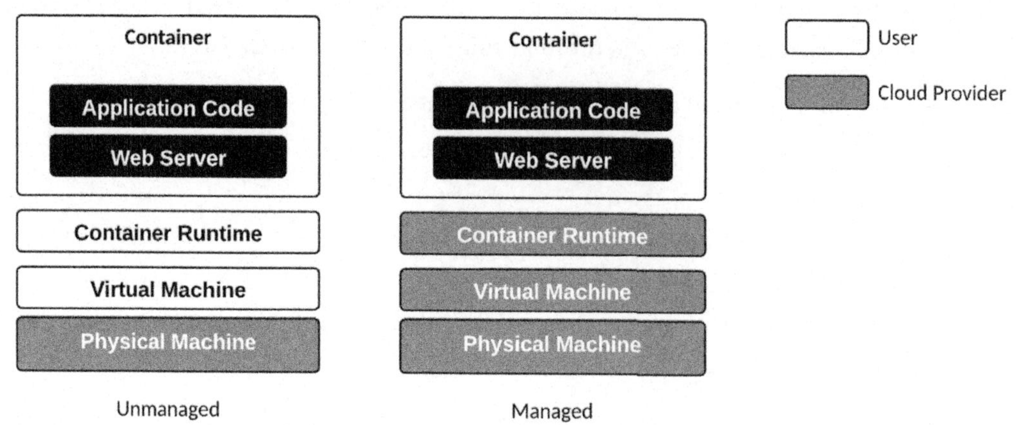

Figure 10.16: Shared Responsibility Model

The figure above demonstrates the shared responsibility model for running containers in the cloud. In the unmanaged model, the cloud provider gives you access to a virtual machine. The cloud provider manages and maintains the physical machine, which is totally abstracted away fro user. Now it's up to you to configure the **Operating System (OS)** and secure it. On top of the OS, you can set up a container runtime or a cluster that involves many virtual machines.

Read the excellent article by Kaizhe Huang on ECS Fargate Threat Modeling at `https://sysdig.com/blog/ecs-fargate-threat-modeling`.

A container cluster is a group of hosts set up to run containerized workloads. Container orchestration software like Kubernetes automates and manages the containers across the cluster infrastructure. This allows you to scale container instances to respond to changes in load. Clusters also provide rich features like service discovery. You can learn more about Kubernetes at `https://kubernetes.io`.

In the managed model, the cloud provider gives you access to a container runtime environment with cluster-like features, including Kubernetes support. The cloud provider secures the runtime, and the user is only responsible for the container. These offerings are **serverless**. In this space, each cloud provider offers a variety of services that significantly differ in capabilities.

Here is a list of some popular options:

- **AWS Fargate** is a serverless compute engine that runs containers without managing servers or clusters. Integrates with **Elastic Container Service (ECS)** and **Elastic Kubernetes Service (EKS)**.
- **Google Cloud Run** is a fully managed serverless platform for stateless containerized applications. Auto-scales and bills per request.
- **Azure Container Instances** can run individual containers without adopting higher-level orchestration services. Per-second billing.
- **Amazon ECS** offers highly scalable Docker container management across a cluster of **Elastic Compute Cloud (EC2)** instances. Tight integration with other AWS services. AWS EKS is the Kubernetes-flavored version of AWS ECS.
- **Google Kubernetes Engine (GKE)** is a managed Kubernetes environment running on Google Cloud. Easily deploy containers with native Google Cloud integrations.
- **Azure Kubernetes Service (AKS)** is a fully managed Kubernetes cluster service hosted on Azure. Streamlined deployments to containers with auto-scaling capabilities.

The main advantages of the serverless options (AWS Fargate, Google Cloud Run, Azure Container Instances) are that they are fully managed, automatically scale, and have payas-you-go pricing models. However, they offer limited customization compared to provisioned Kubernetes. The provisioned Kubernetes options (Amazon ECS, Google GKE, Azure AKS) offer more control, customization, and the ability to run stateful applications. However, they require manual scaling and managing of the infrastructure.

Overall, serverless options are easier to use but less flexible, while provisioned Kubernetes offers more customization but requires DevOps know-how to manage the infrastructure. Your choice depends on whether the workload fits the serverless constraints and how much control vs simplicity is preferred.

So far, you've deployed your code to the cloud, mastered the fundamentals of working with Docker containers, and understood the nuances of deploying containers in the cloud. **Continuous Deployment (CD)** is the manifestation of my motto, ship it, or it never happened. Next, we'll go over how you can integrate deployments as part of your CI pipeline to achieve CD.

The `npm run docker:debug` script automates a lot of chores to verify that you have a good image build!

Continuous deployment

CD is the idea that code changes that successfully pass through your pipeline can be automatically deployed to a target environment. Although examples of continuously deploying to production exist, most enterprises prefer to target a development environment. A gated approach is adopted to move the changes through the various stages of development environment, test, staging, and, ultimately, production. CircleCI can facilitate gated deployment with approval workflows, which is covered later in this section.

In CircleCI, you need to implement a deploy job to deploy your image. You can deploy to many targets in this job, such as Google Cloud Run, Docker Hub, Heroku, Azure, or AWS ECS. Integration with these targets will involve multiple steps. At a high level, these steps are as follows:

1. Configure an orb for your target environment, which provides the CLI tools required to deploy your software.
2. Store login credentials or access keys specific to the target environment as CircleCI environment variables.
3. Build a container in the CI pipeline if not using a platform-specific `build` command. Then use `docker push` to submit the resulting Docker image to the target platform's registry.
4. Execute a platform-specific `deploy` command to instruct the target to run the Docker image that was just pushed.

By using a Docker-based workflow, we achieve great amounts of flexibility in terms of systems and target environments we can use. The following diagram illustrates this point by highlighting the possible permutation of choices that are available to us:

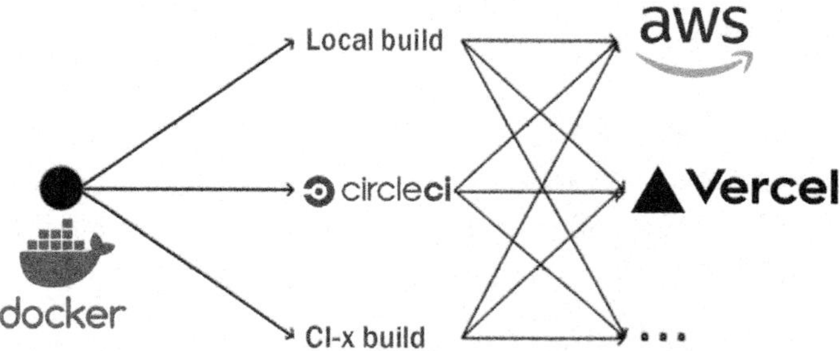

Figure 10.17: n-to-n deployment

As you can see, in a containerized world, the possibilities are limitless. We will use the deployment related npm scripts we added later in this chapter to implement the deploy job in our CI pipeline.

Outside of Docker-based workflows, you can use purpose-built CLI tools to quickly deploy your app. Next, let's see how you can deploy your app to Vercel using CircleCI.

Deploying to Vercel using CircleCI

Earlier, we configured the LocalCast Weather app to be built using CircleCI. We can enhance our CI pipeline to take the build output and optionally deploy it to Vercel.

This section uses the **local-weather-app** repository. The `config.yml` file for this section is named `.circleci/config.stage9.yml`.

Let's update the `config.yml` file to add a new job named `deploy`. In the upcoming *Workflows* section, we will use this job to deploy a pipeline when approved:

1. Create a token from your Vercel account.
2. Add an environment variable to your CircleCI project named `VERCEL_TOKEN` and store your Vercel token as the value.
3. In `config.yml`, update the `build` job with the new steps and add a new job named `deploy`:

```
.circleci/config.yml
...
jobs:
  build_and_test:
    ...
    - run:
        name: Move compiled app to workspace
        command: |
          set -exu
          mkdir -p /tmp/workspace/dist
          mv dist/local-weather-app /tmp/workspace/dist/
    - persist_to_workspace:
        root: /tmp/workspace
        paths:
          - dist/local-weather-app
  deploy:
    docker:
      - image: circleci/node:lts
```

```
    working_directory: ~/repo
    steps:
      - attach_workspace:
          at: /tmp/workspace
      - run: npx vercel deploy --token $VERCEL_TOKEN --prod /tmp/
            workspace/dist/<< parameters.project >> --yes
```

In the `build` job, after the build is complete, we add two new steps. First, we move the compiled app in the `dist` folder to a workspace and persist that workspace so we can use it later in another job. In a new job named `deploy`, we attach the workspace and use `npx` to run the `vercel` command to deploy the `dist` folder. This is a straightforward process.

Note that **$VERCEL_TOKEN** is the environment variable we stored in the CircleCI project.

4. Implement a simple CircleCI workflow to deploy the outcome of your `build` job continuously:

.circleci/config.yml

```
...
workflows:
  version: 2
  build-test-and-deploy:
    jobs:
      - build_and_test
      - deploy:
          requires:
            - build_and_test
```

Note that the `deploy` job waits for the `build` job to complete before it can execute.

5. Ensure that your CI pipeline executed successfully by inspecting the test results:

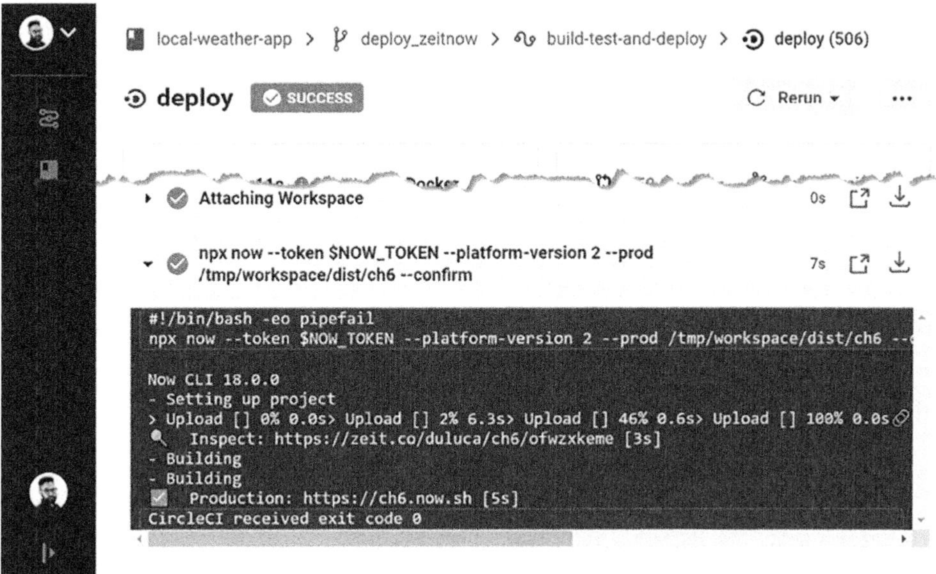

Figure 10.18: Successful Vercel deployment of local-weather-app

Most CLI commands for cloud providers need to be installed in your pipeline to function. Since Vercel has an npm package, this is easy to do. CLI tools for AWS, Google Cloud, or Microsoft Azure need to be installed using tools such as `brew` or `choco`. CircleCI offers orbs, reusable snippets of code that help automate repeated processes, speed up project setup, and make it easy to integrate with third-party tools.

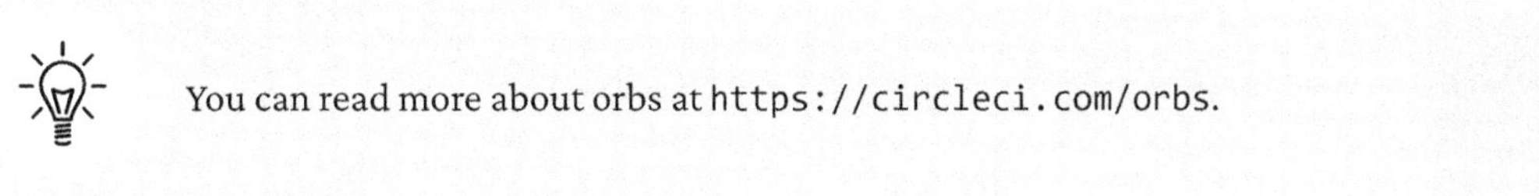
You can read more about orbs at `https://circleci.com/orbs`.

Check out the Orb registry for more information on how to use these orbs at `https://circleci.com/orbs/registry`.

CD works great for development and testing environments. However, it is usually desirable to have gated deployments, where a person must approve a deployment before it reaches a production environment. Next, let's see how you can implement this with CircleCI.

Gated CI workflows

In CircleCI, you can define a workflow to control how and when your jobs are executed. Consider the following configuration, given the jobs `build` and `deploy`:

```
.circleci/config.yml
workflows:
  version: 2
  build-and-deploy:
    jobs:
      - build
      - hold:
          type: approval
          requires:
            - build
      - deploy:
          requires:
            - hold
```

First, the `build` job gets executed. Then, we introduce a special job named `hold` with type `approval`, which requires the `build` job to be successfully completed. Once this happens, the pipeline is put on hold. If or when a decision-maker approves `hold`, then the `deploy` step can execute. Refer to the following screenshot to see what a **hold** looks like:

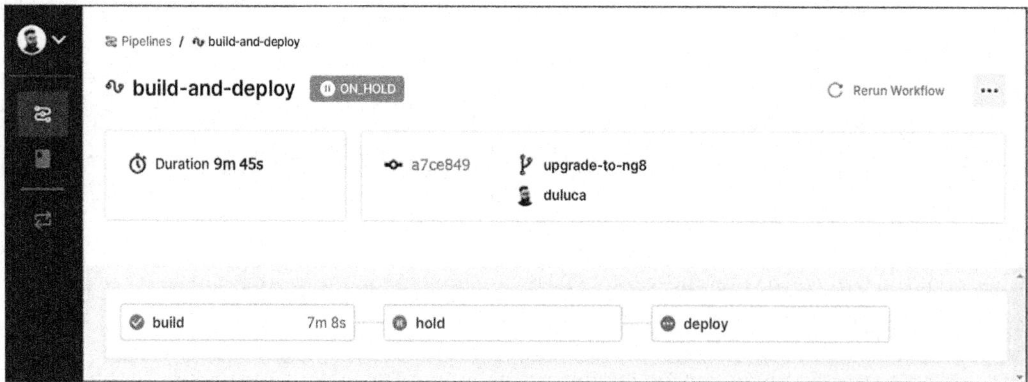

Figure 10.19: A hold in the pipeline

Consider a more sophisticated workflow, shown in the following code snippet, where the `build` and `test` steps are broken out into two separate jobs:

```
workflows:
  version: 2
    build-test-and-approval-deploy:
      jobs:
      - build
      - test
      - hold:
         type: approval
         requires:
           - build
           - test
         filters:
           branches:
             only: main
      - deploy:
        requires:
          - hold
```

In this case, the `build` and `test` jobs are executed in parallel. If we're on a branch, this is where the pipeline stops. Once the branch is merged with `main`, the pipeline is put on hold, and a decision-maker has the option to deploy the build or not. This type of branch filtering ensures that only code that's been merged to `main` can be deployed, which is in line with GitHub flow.

Next, we will go over how we can integrate code coverage reports with our CI runs to get better insight into our test coverage and optionally fail builds that don't meet a certain threshold.

Code coverage reports

A code coverage report is a good way to understand the amount and trends of unit test coverage for your Angular project.

To generate the report for your app, execute the following command from your `project` folder:

```
$ npx ng test --watch=false --code-coverage
```

The resulting report will be created as an HTML file under a folder named coverage; execute the following command to view it in your browser:

```
$ npx http-server -c-1 -o -p 9875 ./coverage
```

You may need to specify `--project` for the `ng test` command. Similarly, the coverage report may be generated in a sub-folder under **coverage**. You can select the folder to view it.

Here's the folder-level sample coverage report generated by `istanbul` for LemonMart:

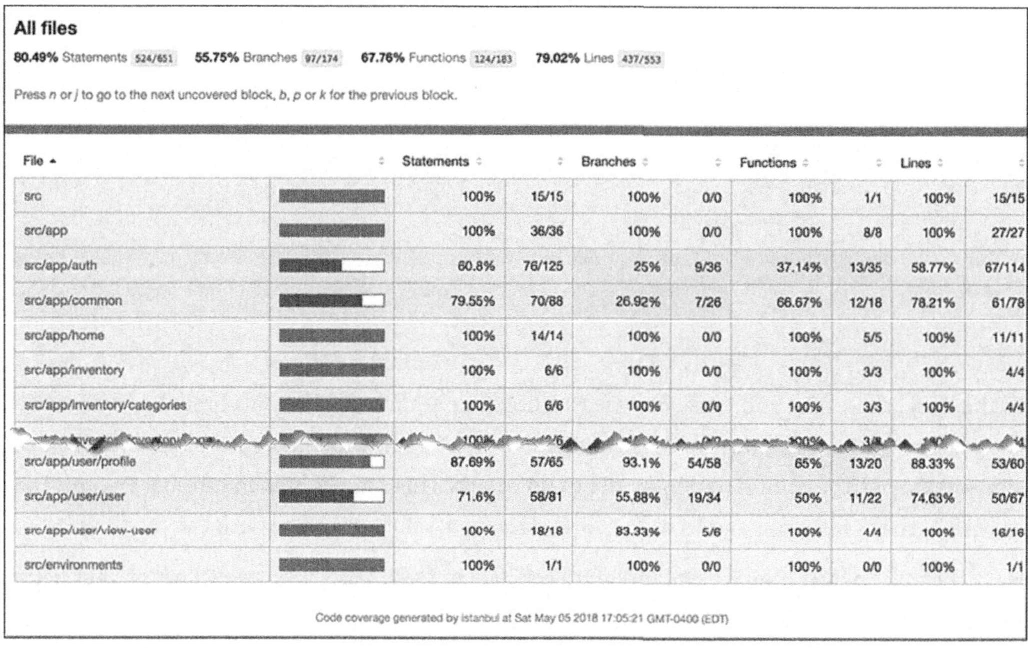

All files

80.49% Statements 524/651 **55.75%** Branches 97/174 **67.76%** Functions 124/183 **79.02%** Lines 437/553

Press *n* or *j* to go to the next uncovered block, *b*, *p* or *k* for the previous block.

File	Statements		Branches		Functions		Lines	
src	100%	15/15	100%	0/0	100%	1/1	100%	15/15
src/app	100%	36/36	100%	0/0	100%	8/8	100%	27/27
src/app/auth	60.8%	76/125	25%	9/36	37.14%	13/35	58.77%	67/114
src/app/common	79.55%	70/88	26.92%	7/26	66.67%	12/18	78.21%	61/78
src/app/home	100%	14/14	100%	0/0	100%	5/5	100%	11/11
src/app/inventory	100%	6/6	100%	0/0	100%	3/3	100%	4/4
src/app/inventory/categories	100%	6/6	100%	0/0	100%	3/3	100%	4/4
[illegible]	[illegible]	[illegible]	[illegible]	[illegible]	[illegible]	[illegible]	[illegible]	[illegible]
src/app/user/profile	87.69%	57/65	93.1%	54/58	65%	13/20	88.33%	53/60
src/app/user/user	71.6%	58/81	55.88%	19/34	50%	11/22	74.63%	50/67
src/app/user/view-user	100%	18/18	83.33%	5/6	100%	4/4	100%	16/16
src/environments	100%	1/1	100%	0/0	100%	0/0	100%	1/1

Code coverage generated by istanbul at Sat May 05 2018 17:05:21 GMT-0400 (EDT)

Figure 10.20: Istanbul code coverage report for LemonMart

You can drill down on a particular folder, such as `src/app/auth`, and get a file-level report, as shown here:

All files src/app/auth

61.6% Statements 77/125 **25%** Branches 9/36 **38.24%** Functions 13/34 **59.65%** Lines 68/114

Press n or *j* to go to the next uncovered block, *b*, *p* or *k* for the previous block.

File		Statements		Branches		Functions		Lines	
auth-guard.service.ts		48.72%	19/39	0%	0/14	33.33%	3/9	47.22%	17/36
auth.service.fake.ts		84.62%	11/13	100%	0/0	60%	3/5	81.82%	9/11
auth.service.ts		57.69%	30/52	28.57%	4/14	21.43%	3/14	55.32%	26/47
cache.service.ts		75%	12/16	50%	3/6	60%	3/5	73.33%	11/15
role.enum.ts		100%	5/5	100%	2/2	100%	1/1	100%	5/5

Code coverage generated by istanbul at Thu May 10 2018 02:50:40 GMT-0400 (Eastern Daylight Time)

Figure 10.21: Istanbul code coverage report for src/app/auth

You can drill down further to get line-level coverage for a given file, such as `cache.service.ts`, as shown here:

All files / src/app/auth cache.service.ts

75% Statements 12/16 **50%** Branches 3/6 **60%** Functions 3/5 **73.33%** Lines 11/15

Press *n* or *j* to go to the next uncovered block, *b*, *p* or *k* for the previous block.

```
export abstract class CacheService {
  protected getItem<T>(key: string): T {
    const data = localStorage.getItem(key)
    if (data && data !== 'undefined') {
      return JSON.parse(data)
    }
    return null
  }

  protected setItem(key: string, data: object | string) {
    if (typeof data === 'string') {
      localStorage.setItem(key, data)
    }
    localStorage.setItem(key, JSON.stringify(data))
  }

  protected removeItem(key: string) {
    localStorage.removeItem(key)
  }

  protected clear() {
    localStorage.clear()
  }
}
```

Code coverage generated by istanbul at Thu May 10 2018 02:50:40 GMT-0400 (Eastern Daylight Time)

Figure 10.22: Istanbul code coverage report for cache.service.ts

In the preceding screenshot, you can see lines **5**, **12**, **17**–**18**, and **21**–**22** are not covered by any test. The **I** icon denotes that the `if` path was not taken. We can increase our code coverage by implementing unit tests that exercise the functions that are contained within `CacheService`. As an exercise, you should attempt to at least cover one of these functions with a new unit test and observe the code coverage report change.

Code coverage in CI

Ideally, your CI server configuration should generate and host the code coverage report with every test run. You can then use code coverage as another code quality gate to prevent pull requests from being merged if the new code reduces the overall code coverage percentage. This is a great way to reinforce the **Test-Driven Development** (**TDD**) mindset.

You can use a service such as Coveralls, found at `https://coveralls.io`, to implement your code coverage checks, which can embed your code coverage levels directly on a GitHub pull request.

Let's configure Coveralls for LemonMart:

In the **lemon-mart** repo, the `config.yml` file for this section is named `.circleci/config.stage9.yml`.

1. In your CircleCI account settings, under the **Security** section, ensure that you allow the execution of uncertified/unsigned orbs.
2. Register your GitHub project at `https://coveralls.io/`.
3. Copy the repository token and store it as an environment variable in CircleCI named `COVERALLS_REPO_TOKEN`.
4. Create a new branch before making any code changes.
5. Update the `.circleci/config.yml` file with the Coveralls orb as shown:

```
.circleci/config.yml
version: 2.1
orbs:
  coveralls: coveralls/coveralls@2
```

6. Update the `build` job to store code coverage results and upload them to Coveralls:

```
.circleci/config.yml
jobs:
  build_and_test:
    ...
      - run: npm test -- --watch=false --code-coverage
      - store_test_results:
          path: ./test_results
      - store_artifacts:
          path: ./coverage
      - coveralls/upload
      - run:
          name: Tar & Gzip compiled app
          command: tar zcf dist.tar.gz dist/lemon-mart
      - store_artifacts:
          path: dist.tar.gz
```

`store_test_results` and `store_artifacts` will store test results and code coverage data to be analyzed in other jobs or orbs. CircleCI can display XML formatted coverage reports in its web UI. The `coveralls/upload` command uploads the code coverage data we just stored for analysis.

Note that the orb automatically configures Coveralls for your account, so the `coveralls/upload` command can upload your code coverage results.

7. Commit your changes to the branch and publish it.
8. Create a pull request on GitHub using the branch.

9. On the pull request, verify that you can see that Coveralls is reporting your project's code coverage, as shown:

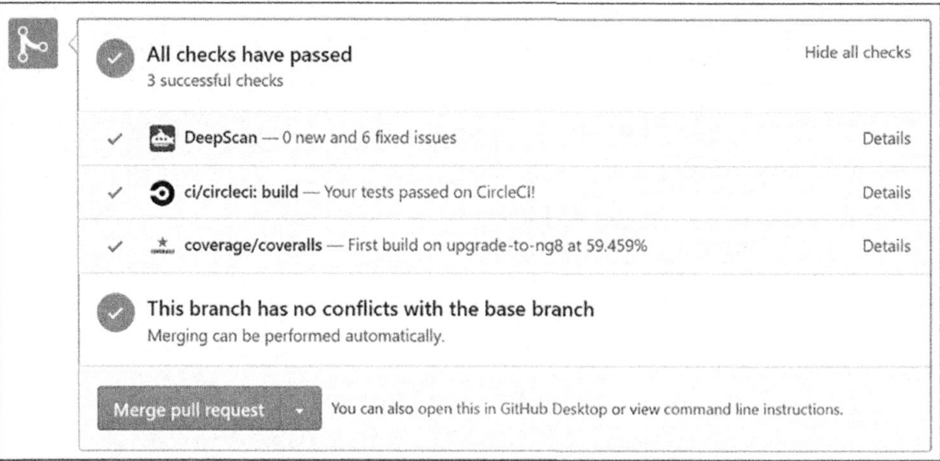

Figure 10.23: Coveralls reporting code coverage

10. Merge the pull request to your main branch.

Congratulations! Now, you can modify your branch protection rules to require that code coverage levels be above a certain percentage before a pull request can be merged into the main branch.

You can set coverage thresholds at `https://coveralls.io`.

The LemonMart project at `https://github.com/duluca/lemon-mart` implements a full-featured `config.yml` file. This file also implements `Cypress.io`, overriding Angular's default e2e tooling. The Cypress orb can record test results and allow you to view them from your CircleCI pipeline.

Leveraging what you have learned in this chapter, you can incorporate the `deploy` scripts from LocalCast Weather for LemonMart and implement a gated deployment workflow.

Good engineering practices and DevOps practices are key to delivering successful projects and building a satisfying career. Thanks for reading this book!

Summary

In this chapter, you learned about creating a value delivery stream using CI/CD pipelines. We covered the importance of automated unit testing to enable the delivery of quality code at speed in an enterprise context. You configured a CI pipeline using CircleCI. You learned about trunk-based development using GitHub flow and enforcing quality gates. You deployed a web application to Vercel and leveraged `ng deploy` for Firebase.

Next, we covered DevOps and IaC techniques using Docker and npm scripts. You containerized your web app, learned about working with containers in the cloud, and learned how to implement gated CI workflows. Also, you became familiar with orbs, workflows, and code coverage tools.

We leveraged CircleCI as a cloud-based CI service and highlighted that you can deploy the outcome of your builds to all major cloud hosting providers. You have seen how you can achieve CD. We covered an example deployment to Vercel via CircleCI demonstrating how you can implement continuous deployments.

With a robust CI/CD pipeline, you can share every app build with clients and team members and quickly deliver bug fixes or new features to your end users.

Congratulations! You have completed your *Angular for Enterprise Applications* journey. I hope you learned something new. The best way to learn and grow is by teaching and sharing, so I hope you keep this book around as a reference and share it with friends, family, and colleagues.

> *If you got this far, send me a picture of yourself with the (e-)book or a note on how the content impacted you, and I'll share an exclusive digital badge with you for your achievement.*
>
> *Continue your journey at* `https://AngularForEnterprise.com`.

Exercises

1. Add CircleCI and Coveralls badges to the `README.md` file on your code repository.
2. Implement Cypress for e2e testing and run it in your CircleCI pipeline using the `Cypress orb`.
3. Implement a Vercel deployment and a conditional workflow for the LemonMart app. The resulting `config.yml` file is in the `lemon-mart` repo, named `.circleci/config.stage9.yml`.

Further reading

- *Working Effectively with Legacy Code*, Michael Feathers, 2004
- *The Three Laws of TDD*, Robert "Uncle Bob" Martin, 2005, `http://butunclebob.com/ArticleS.UncleBob.TheThreeRulesOfTdd`
- *Succeeding with Agile: Software Development Using Scrum*, Mike Cohn, 2009
- *TestPyramid*, Martin Fowler, 2012, `https://martinfowler.com/bliki/TestPyramid.html`
- *Jasmine 2 Spy Cheat Sheet*, Dave Ceddia, 2015, `https://daveceddia.com/jasmine-2-spy-cheat-sheet`
- *The Practical Test Pyramid*, Ham Vocke, 2018, `https://martinfowler.com/articles/practical-test-pyramid.html`
- *SOLID Principles*, Wikipedia, 2019, `https://en.wikipedia.org/wiki/SOLID`
- *Dockerfile reference*, 2020, `https://docs.docker.com/engine/reference/builder/`
- *CircleCI orbs*, 2020, `https://circleci.com/orbs/`
- *Deploying container images*, 2020, `https://cloud.google.com/run/docs/deploying`
- *ECS Fargate Threat Modeling*, Kaizhe Huang, 2019, `https://sysdig.com/blog/ecs-fargate-threat-modeling/`

Questions

Answer the following questions as best as possible to ensure you've understood the key concepts from this chapter without googling anything. Do you know if you got all the answers right? Visit `https://angularforenterprise.com/self-assessment` for more:

1. What is the testing pyramid?
2. What are fixtures and matchers?
3. What are the differences between a mock, a spy, and a stub?
4. What is the benefit of building Angular in prod mode?
5. How does GitHub flow work?
6. Why should we protect the main branch?
7. Explain the difference between a Docker image and a Docker container.
8. Why do you prefer a managed container runtime over an unmanaged one in the cloud?
9. What is the purpose of a CD pipeline?
10. What is the benefit of CD?
11. How do we cover the configuration gap?

12. What does a CircleCI orb do?
13. What are the benefits of using a multi-stage Dockerfile?
14. How does a code coverage report help maintain the quality of your app?

Appendix A

Setting Up Your Development Environment

Sharing a consistent development environment between you and your team members is important. Consistency helps to avoid many IT-related issues, including ongoing maintenance, licensing, and upgrade costs. Further, you want to ensure the entire team has the same development experience. This way, if a team member runs into a configuration issue, other team members can help resolve the issue. Creating a frustration-free and efficient onboarding experience for a new team member is also essential.

Easy and well-documented onboarding procedures ensure that new team members can quickly become productive and be integrated into the team. On an ongoing basis, achieving a consistent and minimal development environment remains challenging for teams. Automation can help deliver and maintain a consistent environment across developer machines.

The recommended operating systems are Windows 10 or Windows 11 Pro with PowerShell v7+ and Developer Mode enabled or macOS Ventura or Sonoma with Terminal and XCode developer tools installed. It is recommended to use the Chromium-based Google Chrome or Microsoft Edge as a web browser because they offer almost identical developer experience.

Most of the suggested software in this book are cross-platform tools, so they also work on Linux systems. However, your experience may vary with these systems.

This appendix covers:

- Recommended web development tools
- CLI package managers
- Install automation for Windows and macOS
- Project setup with the Angular CLI
- Optimizing VS Code for Angular

Let's start by reviewing the recommended web development tools and how you can quickly install these tools via automation scripts. Later in the appendix, we will go over how you can create such scripts.

Recommended web development tools

This section covers the recommended for developing to develop a web application, as follows:

Tool	Description	URL
Git	Version control system	`https://git-scm.com`
GitHub Desktop	**Graphical User Interface** (**GUI**) to run Git commands and interact with GitHub	`https://desktop.github.com`
Node.js	Cross-platform JavaScript runtime environment	`https://nodejs.org`
Visual Studio Code	Cross-platform **Integrated Development Environment** (**IDE**)	`https://code.visualstudio.com`
Docker Desktop	Lightweight container virtualization platform	`https://www.docker.com/products/docker-desktop`

Table A.1: Tools needed for web development

To automatically install all the web development tools required for this book, execute the following commands for your OS to configure your environment.

On Windows PowerShell, execute:

```
PS> Install-Script -Name setup-windows-dev-env
PS> setup-windows-dev-env.ps1
```

On macOS Terminal, execute:

```
$> bash <(wget -O - https://git.io/JvHi1)
```

For more information, refer to `https://github.com/duluca/web-dev-environment-setup`.

The macOS script installs Node version 20, which is the **Long-term Support** (**LTS**) version at the time of publishing. To ensure you always have the latest LTS installed, the script installs `n`, a Node version manager. Using `n`, you can easily switch between different versions of Node.

Once you've installed your IDE, you're ready to start development. In the next section, you'll learn about CLI-based package managers. You'll see that using CLI tools is superior to dealing with individual installers. Automating CLI tools is much easier, making setup and maintenance tasks repeatable and fast.

CLI package managers

Installing software through a **Graphical User Interface** (GUI) is slow and challenging to automate. As a full-stack developer, whether a Windows or a Mac user, you must rely on **Command-Line Interface** (CLI) package managers to install and configure the software you depend on efficiently.

Anything that can be expressed as a CLI command can also be automated.

Installing Chocolatey for Windows

Chocolatey is a CLI-based package manager for Windows that can be used for automated software installation. To install Chocolatey on Windows, you need to run an elevated command shell:

1. Launch the **Start** menu.
2. Start typing in **PowerShell**.
3. You should see **Windows PowerShell Desktop App** as a search result.
4. Right-click on **Windows PowerShell** and select **Run as Administrator**.
5. This triggers a **User Account Control** (UAC) warning; select **Yes** to continue.
6. Execute the install command found at `https://chocolatey.org/install` in **PowerShell** to install the Chocolatey package manager:

```
PS> Set-ExecutionPolicy Bypass -Scope Process -Force; [System.Net.
ServicePointManager]::SecurityProtocol = [System.Net.ServicePointM
anager]::SecurityProtocol -bor 3072; iex ((New-Object System.Net.
WebClient).DownloadString('https://chocolatey.org/install.ps1'))
```

1. Verify your Chocolatey installation by executing `choco`.
2. You should see a similar output to the one shown in the following screenshot:

```
Administrator: PowerShell
PowerShell 7.4.1
Welcome back, Doguhan!
PS C:\Users\duluc> choco
Chocolatey v2.2.2
Please run 'choco -?' or 'choco <command> -?' for help menu.
PS C:\Users\duluc>
```

Figure A.1: Successful installation of Chocolatey

All subsequent Chocolatey commands must also be executed from an elevated command shell. Alternatively, it is possible to install Chocolatey in a non-administrator setting that doesn't require an elevated command shell. However, this results in a non-standard and less secure development environment, and certain applications installed through the tool may still require elevation.

WinGet is the Windows Package Manager that is provided by Microsoft. You can learn more about WinGet at `https://github.com/microsoft/winget-cli/` or from the Microsoft Store.

I prefer Chocolatey over WinGet, because it offers better resilience when the script encounters an unexpected configuration. For more information on Chocolatey, refer to `https://chocolatey.org/install`.

Installing Homebrew for macOS

Homebrew is a CLI-based package manager for macOS that can be used for automated software installation. To install Homebrew on macOS, you need to run a command shell:

1. Launch **Spotlight Search** with ⌘ + *Space*.
2. Type in `terminal`.
3. Execute the following command in Terminal to install the Homebrew package manager:

```
$ /bin/bash -c "$(curl -fsSL https://raw.githubusercontent.com/
Homebrew/install/HEAD/install.sh)"
```

4. Verify your Homebrew installation by executing `brew`.
5. You should see a similar output to the following:

```
du — du@dougi-mbp21 — ~ — -zsh — 74×27

~ via v20.11.0 on (us-east-1) on duluca@gmail.com took 30s › brew
Example usage:
  brew search TEXT|/REGEX/
  brew info [FORMULA|CASK...]
  brew install FORMULA|CASK...
  brew update
  brew upgrade [FORMULA|CASK...]
  brew uninstall FORMULA|CASK...
  brew list [FORMULA|CASK...]
```

Figure A.2: Successful installation of Homebrew

6. To enable access to additional software, execute the following command:

```
$ brew tap caskroom/cask
```

Homebrew Cask extends Homebrew and brings its elegance, simplicity, and speed to the installation and management of GUI macOS applications such as Visual Studio Code and Google Chrome. Read more about it at `https://github.com/Homebrew/homebrew-cask`. On macOS, if you run into permissions issues while installing brew packages related to chown'ing `/usr/local`, you need to execute the `sudo chown -R $(whoami)`

`$(brew --prefix)/*` command. This command reinstates user-level ownership to `brew` packages, which is more secure than broad superuser/`su`-level access.

For more information, check out `https://brew.sh/`.

Install automation for Windows and macOS

Remember, *anything that can be expressed as a CLI command can also be automated.* Throughout the setup process, we ensured that every tool being used was set up and its functionality was verifiable through a CLI command. This means we can easily create a PowerShell or Bash script to string these commands together and ease setting up and verifying new environments.

Let's implement rudimentary – but effective scripts – to help set up your development environment.

PowerShell script

For Windows-based development environments, you need to create a PowerShell script:

1. Create a file named `setup-windows-dev-env.ps1`.
2. Insert the following text, also available at `https://github.com/duluca/web-dev-environment-setup`, in the file:

```
setup-windows-dev-env.ps1
# This script is intentionally kept simple to demonstrate basic
automation techniques.
```

```
Write-Output "You must run this script in an elevated command shell,
using 'Run as Administator'"

$title = "Setup Web Development Environment"
$message = "Select the appropriate option to continue (Absolutely NO
WARRANTIES or GUARANTEES are provided):"

$yes = New-Object System.Management.Automation.Host.
ChoiceDescription "&Install Software using Chocolatey", `
  "Setup development environment."

$no = New-Object System.Management.Automation.Host.ChoiceDescription
"&Exit", `
  "Do not execute script."

$options = [System.Management.Automation.Host.ChoiceDescription[]]
($yes, $no)

$result = $host.ui.PromptForChoice($title, $message, $options, 1)

switch ($result) {
  0 {
    Write-Output "Installing chocolatey"
    Set-ExecutionPolicy Bypass -Scope Process -Force;
Invoke-Expression ((New-Object System.Net.WebClient).
DownloadString('https://chocolatey.org/install.ps1'))
    Write-Output "Refreshing environment variables. If rest of the
script fails, restart elevated shell and rerun script."
    $env:Path = [System.Environment]::GetEnvironmentVariable("Path",
"Machine") + ";" + [System.
Environment]::GetEnvironmentVariable("Path", "User")

    Write-Output "Assuming chocolatey is already installed"
    Write-Output "Installing Git & GitHub Desktop"
    choco.exe upgrade git github-desktop -y

    Write-Output "Installing NodeJS and NVS"
    choco.exe upgrade nodejs-lts nvs -y
```

```
    Write-Output "Installing Docker"
    choco.exe upgrade docker-cli docker-for-windows -y

    Write-Output "Installing AWS"
    choco.exe upgrade awscli -y

    Write-Output "Installing VS Code"
    choco.exe upgrade VisualStudioCode -y

    RefreshEnv.cmd
    Write-Output "Results:"
    Write-Output "Verify installation of GitHub Desktop and VS Code
manually."
    $awsVersion = aws.exe --version
    Write-Output "aws: $awsVersion"
    $dockerVersion = docker.exe --version
    Write-Output "docker: $dockerVersion"
    $gitVersion = git.exe --version
    Write-Output "git: $gitVersion"
    $nodeVersion = node.exe -v
    Write-Output "Node: $nodeVersion"
    $npmVersion = npm.cmd -v
    Write-Output "npm: $npmVersion"
  }
  1 { "Aborted." }
}
```

3. To execute the script, run:

```
PS> Set-ExecutionPolicy Unrestricted; .\setup-windows-dev-env.ps1
```

Alternatively, you can install and execute the script directly from the PowerShell Gallery, located at `https://www.powershellgallery.com`, by executing the following command:

```
PS> Install-Script -Name setup-windows-dev-env PS> setup-windows-dev-env.
ps1
```

By executing this script, you have successfully set up your development environment on Windows.

If you're interested in publishing your own scripts to the PowerShell Gallery or generally interested in advancing your PowerShell skills, I suggest you install PowerShell Core, a multi-platform version of PowerShell, from `https://github.com/PowerShell/PowerShell`.

Now, let's investigate how you can achieve a similar setup on Mac.

Bash script

For Mac-based development environments, you need to create a Bash script:

1. Create a file named `setup-mac-dev-env.sh`.
2. Run `chmod a+x setup-mac-dev-env.sh` to make the file executable.
3. Insert the following text, also available at `https://github.com/duluca/web-dev-environment-setup`, in the `setup-mac-dev-env.sh` file:

```
#!/bin/bash

# In order to be able to execute this script, run 'chmod a+x
setup-mac-dev-env.sh' to make the file executable

echo "Execute Installation Script"
read -r -p "Absolutely NO WARRANTIES or GUARANTEES are
provided. Are you sure you want to continue? [y/N] " response
if [[ "$response" =~ ^([yY][eE][sS]|[yY])+$ ]]
then
    echo "Installing brew"
    /bin/bash -c "$(curl -fsSL https://raw.githubusercontent.
com/Homebrew/install/HEAD/install.sh)"

    echo "Installing git"
    brew install git
    brew upgrade git

    echo "Installing GitHub Desktop"
    brew install github
    brew upgrade github

    echo "Installing NodeJS"
```

```
            brew install node@20
            brew upgrade node@20

            echo "Installing Docker"
            brew install docker
            brew upgrade docker

            echo "Installing AWS"
            brew install awscli
            brew upgrade awscli

            echo "Installing VS Code"
            brew install visual-studio-code
            brew upgrade visual-studio-code

            echo "Results:"
            echo "Verify installation of AWS, Docker, GitHub Desktop
and VS Code manually."
            gitVersion=$(git --version)
            echo "git: $gitVersion"
            nodeVersion=$(node -v)
            echo "Node: $nodeVersion"
            npmVersion=$(npm -v)
            echo "npm: $npmVersion"

            echo "Ensuring Node LTS is installed"
            npm i -g n@latest
            n lts
        else
            echo "Aborted."
        fi
```

4. To execute the script, run:

```
$ ./setup-mac-dev-env.sh
```

By executing this script, you have successfully set up your development environment on Mac. Here is an example of a more sophisticated install and verify routine, where you can check to see if a particular program, like `brew` or `node`, is already installed, before attempting to install them:

```
echo "Checking if brew is installed" which -s brew
if [[ $? != 0 ]] ; then echo "Installing brew"
/usr/bin/ruby -e "$(curl -fsSL https://raw.githubusercontent.com/
Homebrew/install/master/install)" < /dev/null
else
echo "Found brew"
fi

echo "Checking for Node version ${NODE_VERSION}" node -v | grep ${NODE_
VERSION}
if [[ $? != 0 ]] ; then
echo "Installing Node version ${NODE_VERSION}" brew install nodejs
else
echo "Found Node version ${NODE_VERSION}"
fi
```

By now, you should have a good idea of what automating the execution of your scripts looks like. However, the harsh reality is that these scripts do not represent a highly capable or resilient solution. They can't be executed or managed remotely, nor can they quickly recover from errors or survive machine boot cycles. Moreover, your IT requirements may exceed what is covered here.

If you're dealing with large teams and experiencing frequent staff turnover, an automation tool can be extremely beneficial. Conversely, if you're working alone or part of a smaller, more stable team, such a tool might be overkill. I encourage you to explore tools such as Puppet, Chef, Ansible, and Vagrant to help you decide which best fits your needs, or to determine if a simple script would suffice.

Project setup with the Angular CLI

The Angular CLI tool, ng, is an official Angular project to ensure that newly created Angular applications have a uniform architecture, following the best practices perfected by the community over time. This means that any Angular application you encounter going forward should have the same general shape.

Nx tools are popular in the Enterprise App Development space to scaffold, generate, and maintain Angular applications. You can learn more about Nx at `https://nx.dev`.

Setting up your development directory

Setting up a dedicated dev directory is a lifesaver. Since all the data under this directory is backed up using GitHub, you can safely configure your antivirus, cloud sync, or backup software to ignore it. This helps significantly reduce CPU, disk, and network utilization. As a full-stack developer, you're likely to be multitasking a lot, so avoiding unnecessary activity has a net positive impact on performance, power, and data consumption daily, especially if your development environment is a laptop that is resource-starved or you wish to squeeze as much battery life as possible when you're on the move.

Creating a `dev` folder directly in the `c:\` drive is very important on Windows. Earlier versions of Windows, or rather NTFS, can't handle file paths longer than 260 characters. This may seem adequate at first, but when you install `npm` packages in a folder structure that is already deep in the hierarchy, the `node_modules` folder structure can get deep enough to hit this limit very easily.

With `npm 3+`, a new, flatter package installation strategy was introduced, which helps with npm-related issues, but being as close to the root folder as possible helps tremendously with any tool.

Create your dev folder using the following commands. For Windows:

```
PS> mkdir c:\dev
PS> cd c:\dev
```

For macOS:

```
$ mkdir ~/dev
$ cd ~/dev
```

In Unix-based operating systems, ~ (pronounced tilde) is a shortcut to the current user's home directory, which resides under `/Users/ your-user-name`.

Now that your development directory is ready, let's start generating your Angular application.

Generating your Angular application

We will be using the npm create command to generate your Angular application, which uses the Angular CLI to generate the code. The Angular CLI goes beyond initial code generation; you'll use it frequently to create new components, directives, pipes, services, modules, and more. The Angular CLI also helps during development with live-reloading features so that you can quickly see the results of your changes. The Angular CLI can also test, lint, and build optimized versions of your code for a production release. Furthermore, as new Angular versions are released, the Angular CLI helps you upgrade your code by automatically rewriting portions to remain compatible with potential breaking changes.

Installing the Angular CLI

The documentation at `https://angular.dev/tools/cli` guides you on how to install `@angular/cli` as a global npm package. However, I advise against doing this. Over time, as the Angular CLI is upgraded, keeping the global and in-project versions in sync becomes a constant irritant. If they're not aligned, the tool tends to complain endlessly. Additionally, if you're working on multiple projects, you end up with varying versions of the Angular CLI over time. As a result, your commands may not return the results you expect, or the results that your team members are getting.

The strategy detailed in the next section introduces a bit more complexity to the initial configuration of your Angular project. However, you'll more than make up for this pain if you must return to a project a few months or even a year later. In that case, you could use the version of the tool that you last used on the project, instead of some future version that may require upgrades that you're not willing to perform. In the next section, you'll use this best practice to initialize your Angular app.

Initializing your Angular app

The main way to initialize your app is by using the Angular CLI. Let's initialize the application for development:

1. Under your `dev` folder, execute:

   ```
   npm create @angular
   ```

   Angular creates all new projects using the standalone project configuration.

2. Follow the on-screen instructions and name your app `my-test-app`; otherwise, accept the default option by pressing **Enter**.
3. On your terminal, you should see a success message.

Your project folder `my-test-app` has been initialized as a Git repository and scaffolded with an initial file and folder structure.

The alias for `@angular/cli` is `ng`. If you were to install the Angular CLI globally, you would execute `ng new my-test-app`, but we didn't do this. To use the Angular CLI, you would have to run it as `npx @angular/cli`. However, we just installed the Angular CLI under the `node_modules/.bin` directory of your app, i.e., the `my-test-app` directory. This means you can run `ng` commands as `npx ng` in the `apps` directory using the version attached to your project, such as `npx ng generate component my-new-component`, and continue working efficiently.

Optimizing VS Code for Angular

It's essential to optimize your **Integrated Development Environment** (**IDE**) to have a great development experience. If you leverage the automated tools I present in this section, you can quickly configure your IDE and Angular project with dozens of settings that work well together.

Configuring your project automatically

To quickly configure your Angular application and VS Code workspace, run the following commands:

1. Apply the Angular VS Code configuration:

```
npx mrm angular-vscode
```

2. Apply the `npm` scripts for Docker configuration:

```
npx mrm npm-docker
```

These settings are constantly tweaked to adapt to the ever-evolving landscape of extensions, plugins, Angular, and VS Code. Always make sure to install a fresh version of the task by rerunning the `install` command to get the latest version.

3. Execute `npm run style:fix`.
4. Execute `npm run lint:fix`.

For more information on the `mrm` tasks, refer to:

- `https://github.com/expertly-simple/mrm-task-angular-vscode`
- `https://github.com/expertly-simple/mrm-task-npm-docker`

You may verify your configuration against the sample projects on GitHub. However, note that the configuration pieces will be applied at the root of the repository and not under the `projects` folder.

Congratulations – you're done setting up your development environment!

Summary

In this appendix, you mastered using CLI-based package managers for both Windows and macOS to speed up and automate the setup of development environments for you and your colleagues. You also created your first Angular project and optimized its configuration for development using Visual Studio Code. You then implemented automated style checkers and fixers to enforce coding standards and styling across your team. The lint checker and fixer you implemented will automatically catch potential coding errors and maintainability issues.

The automated scripts you created codify your team norms and document them for new and existing members. By reducing variance from one developer's environment to the next, your team can overcome any individual configuration issue more efficiently and remain focused on executing the task at hand. With a collective understanding of a common environment, no single individual on the team carries the burden of having to help troubleshoot everyone else's issues. The same idea applies to the shape and style of your code files.

When a team member looks at another team member's code, it looks stylistically identical, which makes it easier to troubleshoot and debug an issue. As a result, your team is more productive. By leveraging more sophisticated and resilient tools, mid-to-large sized organizations can achieve considerable savings in their IT budgets.

Further reading

The article *Automating the Setup of the Local Developer Machine* by Vishwas Parameshwarappa is a great place to start for using Vagrant, found at `https://www.vagrantup.com`. You can find the article at `https://Red-gate.com/simple-talk/sysadmin/general/automating-setup-local-developer-machine`.

Other tools include Chef at `https://www.chef.io`, and Puppet at `https://puppet.com`. Some developers prefer to work within Docker containers during coding at `https://www.docker.com`. This is done to isolate different versions of SDKs from each other. Specific development tools cannot be scoped to a given folder and must be installed globally or OS-wide, making it difficult to work on multiple projects simultaneously. I recommend avoiding this type of setup if you can. I expect IDEs will automate such chores in the future, as CPU core counts increase and virtualization tech gains better hardware acceleration.

Questions

Answer the following questions as best as possible to ensure you've understood the key concepts from this chapter. Do you know if you've got all the answers right? Visit `https://angularforenterprise.com/self-assessment` for more:

1. What are the motivations for using a CLI tool as opposed to a GUI?
2. For your specific operating system, what is the suggested package manager to use?
3. What are some of the benefits of using a package manager?
4. What are the benefits of keeping the development environments of the members of your development team as similar to one another as possible?

Join our community on Discord

Join our community's Discord space for discussions with the authors and other readers:

`https://packt.link/AngularEnterpise3e`

packt.com

Subscribe to our online digital library for full access to over 7,000 books and videos, as well as industry leading tools to help you plan your personal development and advance your career. For more information, please visit our website.

Why subscribe?

- Spend less time learning and more time coding with practical eBooks and Videos from over 4,000 industry professionals
- Improve your learning with Skill Plans built especially for you
- Get a free eBook or video every month
- Fully searchable for easy access to vital information
- Copy and paste, print, and bookmark content

At www.packt.com, you can also read a collection of free technical articles, sign up for a range of free newsletters, and receive exclusive discounts and offers on Packt books and eBooks.

Other Books You May Enjoy

If you enjoyed this book, you may be interested in these other books by Packt:

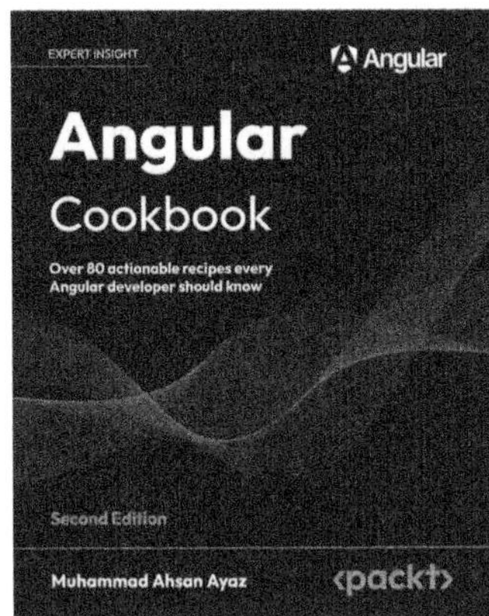

Angular Cookbook – Second Edition

Muhammad Ahsan Ayaz

ISBN: 9781803233444

- Gain a better understanding of how components, services, and directives work in Angular
- Get to grips with creating Progressive Web Apps using Angular from scratch
- Build rich animations and add them to your Angular apps
- Manage your app's data reactivity using RxJS
- Implement state management for your Angular apps with NgRx
- Optimize the performance of your new and existing web apps
- Write fail-safe unit tests and end-to-end tests for your web apps using Jest and Cypress
- Get familiar with Angular CDK components for designing effective Angular components

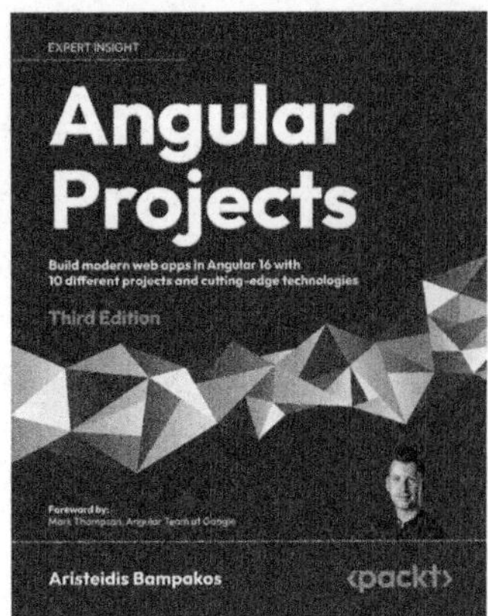

Angular Projects – Third Edition

Aristeidis Bampakos

ISBN: 9781803239118

- Set up Angular applications using Angular CLI and Nx Console
- Create a personal blog with Jamstack, Scully plugins, and SPA techniques
- Build an issue management system using typed reactive forms
- Use PWA techniques to enhance user experience
- Make SEO-friendly web pages with server-side rendering
- Create a monorepo application using Nx tools and NgRx for state management
- Focus on mobile application development using Ionic
- Develop custom schematics by extending Angular CLI

Learning Angular – Fourth Edition

Aristeidis Bampakos

Pablo Deeleman

ISBN: 9781803240602

- Use the Angular CLI to scaffold, build, and deploy a new Angular application
- Build components, the basic building blocks of an Angular application
- Discover new Angular Material components such as Google Maps, YouTube, and multi-select dropdowns
- Understand the different types of templates supported by Angular
- Create HTTP data services to access APIs and provide data to components
- Learn how to build Angular apps without modules in Angular 15.x with standalone APIs
- Improve your debugging and error handling skills during runtime and development

Packt is searching for authors like you

If you're interested in becoming an author for Packt, please visit authors.packtpub.com and apply today. We have worked with thousands of developers and tech professionals, just like you, to help them share their insight with the global tech community. You can make a general application, apply for a specific hot topic that we are recruiting an author for, or submit your own idea.

Share your thoughts

Now you've finished *Angular for Enterprise Applications, Third Edition*, we'd love to hear your thoughts! Scan the QR code below to go straight to the Amazon review page for this book and share your feedback or leave a review on the site that you purchased it from.

https://packt.link/r/1805127128

Your review is important to us and the tech community and will help us make sure we're delivering excellent quality content.

Index

Symbols

A

B

C

D

E

F

G

H

I

J

K

L

M

N

O

P

S

T

U

V

W

Download a free PDF copy of this book

Thanks for purchasing this book!

Do you like to read on the go but are unable to carry your print books everywhere?

Is your eBook purchase not compatible with the device of your choice?

Don't worry, now with every Packt book you get a DRM-free PDF version of that book at no cost.

Read anywhere, any place, on any device. Search, copy, and paste code from your favorite technical books directly into your application.

The perks don't stop there, you can get exclusive access to discounts, newsletters, and great free content in your inbox daily

Follow these simple steps to get the benefits:

1. Scan the QR code or visit the link below

`https://packt.link/free-ebook/9781805127123`

2. Submit your proof of purchase
3. That's it! We'll send your free PDF and other benefits to your email directly

Printed in Great Britain
by Amazon